Insurgency and Counterinsurgency

Insurgency and Counterinsurgency

A Global History

Jeremy Black

ROWMAN & LITTLEFIELD
Lanham • Boulder • New York • London

Published by Rowman & Littlefield
A wholly owned subsidiary of
The Rowman & Littlefield Publishing Group, Inc.
4501 Forbes Boulevard, Suite 200, Lanham, Maryland 20706
https://rowman.com

Unit A, Whitacre Mews, 26-34 Stannary Street, London SE11 4AB,
United Kingdom

British Library Cataloguing in Publication Information Available

Library of Congress Cataloging-in-Publication Data
Names: Black, Jeremy, 1955– author.
Title: Insurgency and counterinsurgency : a global history / Jeremy Black.
Description: Lanham, MD : Rowman & Littlefield, [2016] | Includes bibliographical
   references and index.
Identifiers: LCCN 2016014744 (print) | LCCN 2016014794 (ebook) | ISBN
   9781442256316 (hardback : alk. paper) | ISBN 9781442256323 (pbk. : alk. paper) |
   ISBN 9781442256330 (electronic)
Subjects: LCSH: Insurgency—History. | Counterinsurgency—History.
Classification: LCC U240 .B57 2016 (print) | LCC U240 (ebook) | DDC 355.02/1809—
   dc23
LC record available at http://lccn.loc.gov/2016014744

∞ ™ The paper used in this publication meets the minimum requirements of American
National Standard for Information Sciences Permanence of Paper for Printed Library
Materials, ANSI/NISO Z39.48-1992.

Printed in the United States of America

For Gary Meredith

Contents

Preface

This is an up-to-date study of insurgencies and of counterinsurgency warfare that also gives the necessary due weight to the subject on the global scale. Indeed, it is crucial to avoid grounding the contemporary experience in a narrative and analysis that is Western-centric. Such a grounding is the conventional approach, one that begins with the American and French Revolutions, in 1775 and 1789, respectively, and, moreover, takes an approach that offers an account of insurrections that emphasizes their modern and secular characters providing, in turn, support for a specific account of modernization. Nevertheless, this approach is not only limited, indeed teleological, in its treatment of modernization but also misleading in that this teleology has only limited meaning in much of the world.

Instead, the emphasis in this book will be on the need to adopt a longer timescale and an approach that makes more sense of the global dimension. Although the literal terms *insurgency* and its antonym, *counterinsurgency*, are modern constructs, the phenomena were present earlier even if the phraseology to allude to them or to invoke them was not or was not similar. Moreover, my coverage suggests both that the Western approach is not the norm and that understanding one insurgency does not go a long way toward understanding another one. Rather than focusing on the European and North American experience, it is important to counter the impact of repeatedly underrating the Chinese one. Indeed, China had the biggest insurgencies of the nineteenth and twentieth centuries, as well as significant insurgencies, probably the biggest in scale for each century, in the fourteenth, seventeenth, and eighteenth. In addition, Latin America is poorly covered in studies on the subject at the global level, and notably so after the Latin American wars of independence in the 1810s–1820s.

With the exception of an introduction and a conclusion, interwoven thematic and chronological approaches will infuse this book's narrative in order better to probe the linkage between beliefs, events, people, and time progression. This approach reflects the extent to which power politics, technology, and ideologies changed with time, creating, as they did, new parameters and paradigms. The chronological approach captures the role of particular conjunctures in framing governmental and public views. The significance of conflict within states and the differing forms it took will be key variables. These differences were both military and political, in the latter case, for example, the willingness to compromise.

The chronological approach also makes it possible to consider how and why lessons were "learned" or, as that phrase so often implied, rather asserted, and in both insurgency and counterinsurgency warfare. The "learning of lessons" about insurgencies is very much part of the story. At each stage, there will be a consideration of those "learned" by contemporaries, the manner in which norms were developed within militaries and societies, and their impact in terms of doctrine and policy. Frequently, the process of "learning" was limited and apparently affected by a determination to follow predetermined paths. This was a process seen to a degree with the American response to the Vietnam War, although one could argue that the army proved more adept at "learning."[1] At any rate, the "learning" was often politicized.

All books are researched, written, and assessed with reference to the particular perspectives they offer and also in terms of the earlier literature, of current assumptions, and of established views about probable future developments. Here, much arises from the importance of insurgency and counterinsurgency warfare over the past decade and a half, notably in Iraq and Afghanistan, but not by any means only there. These conflicts are indeed highly pertinent and have helped condition, if not determine, current attitudes. This is not least because the role of religion in insurgencies in recent years has made the predominantly secular account of the earlier literature appear overly limited and somewhat teleological. The best example of earlier work is *Modern Insurgencies and Counter-Insurgencies: Guerrillas and Their Opponents since 1750* (London and New York, 2001) by Ian Beckett, a major British military historian. This excellent work very much focuses on the twentieth century, more especially from the 1930s, and concentrates on revolutionary guerrilla warfare. The emphasis in Beckett's book is on the movement from a "purely military form of conflict" to a "wider comprehension of the potential of irregular modes of conflict."[2]

The focus in my book is very different. Insurgency is treated in broader terms—as a phenomenon with more varied means and ends. This is in line both with the diffuse, often inchoate, variety of activity that is in practice involved and with the dictionary definition, "rising in open resistance to established authority."[3] Practice and definition (what is a rising?) in this case may both appear to range too broadly, but that situation captures the variety of social circumstances and political contingencies, as well as goals. For example, does the suffragette militancy in Britain in 1912–13, as votes for women were pursued with violence, constitute an insurgency? Or the student activism in the West in the late 1960s? It can also be asked whether new religious figures, such as Jesus, were leading an insurgency, whether violent or nonviolent, and whether that process is continued by Christian "liberation theology."

The variety of circumstances helps ensure that there was no set context for military operations and no consistent means of operation. As a result, it is frequently a case of discussing what is not readily comparable but that is a truth of history that is too readily sacrificed to theory. Approaching the subject in a broad fashion helps us to gain a clearer understanding of what we are dealing with—over time, geographical spread, and type of insurgency. The more samples, the stronger and safer the conclusions. It is easier to grasp the subject in all its forms and thus to appreciate better that the next insurgency need not be like the last one. There is still a place for the detailed analysis of particulars, but the approach of this book helps us to understand better the character of insurgency and counterinsurgency and, indeed, the nature of war.

These issues lead to ones relating to practicality, especially whether to hold ground, remain mobile, or hide and use terror; and whether and when brutality or humane conduct (hearts and minds) works. The latter point relates both to the significance of the information dimension and also to that of the political realm. Insurgency and counterinsurgency clearly match Clausewitz's concept of a war where the political element is very prominent. He himself was involved in planning for a Prussian insurgency against Napoleon and in dealing with a Polish insurgency at the close of his life. The significance of politics, Clausewitz's point, is valid, but the nature of politics itself changes, as in the significance of influencing opinion via the media, notably opinion outside the theater of operations. As a related aspect of change, the extent to which norms become tested, stretched, ignored, or reset in insurgencies and counterinsurgencies helps make ideas such as necessity contentious.

The wide definition of insurgency and, thereby, of counterinsurgency warfare offered in this book may surprise and even irritate. There is clearly room to debate the approach taken. It is deliberately a wide one because the intention is to challenge the established account and to propose that a different one should be offered. The resulting debate will be more significant than any individual contribution, including this book. Nevertheless, in the late 2010s, it appears increasingly inappropriate in discussing insurgencies to follow an approach first advanced when there was a very different understanding of the supposed pattern of historical development. Instead, a more fractured and less clear-cut present situation requires a rereading of the past that does not adopt a teleological conspectus. That rereading has been attempted here.

I have benefited greatly from the opportunity to teach military history for over three and a half decades, at the universities of Durham and Exeter, and more generally. For this book, I particularly profited from opportunities to speak at COIN workshops in Exeter, and at the National Defense University, at North Texas, Oxford, and William Paterson universities, and to the Chalke Valley Literary Festival, as well as to visit Afghanistan, Brunei, China, Costa Rica, Cuba, Fiji, France, Hungary, India, Malaysia, Nicaragua, Pakistan, Panama, the Philippines, Serbia, Slovakia, Slovenia, Spain, Sri Lanka, Tunisia, and the United States.

The two anonymous reviewers who commented on the proposal and the three who commented on the draft were all most helpful. So also were the comments of Pete Brown, Mike Cailes, Guy Chet, Tony King, Spencer Mawby, Anthony Saunders, Mark Stevens, Don Stoker, and Heiko Whenning on earlier drafts of the book and of Theo Farrell on parts of the book. I much appreciate the time and effort this entails. I have also benefited from opportunities to discuss the subject with Kristofer Allerfeldt, Ong Wei Chong, and Gian Gentile. Their advice has been most helpful. The collaborative nature of the project is further exemplified by the important role of my editor, Susan McEachern. She has provided the necessary mix of enthusiasm, skill, and wisdom that makes for a great editor. The book is dedicated to Gary Meredith, a good friend to Sarah and myself, and a most agreeable companion as the wine is poured.

Abbreviations

BL	London, British Library, Department of Manuscripts
CAB	Cabinet Office papers
COIN	Counterinsurgency
FO	Foreign Office papers
JMH	*Journal of Military History*
NA	Kew, London, British National Archives
RUSI	*Royal United Services Institute Journal*
WO	War Office papers

Chapter One

Introduction

History is the events of the past and the accounts we provide of these accounts. The latter are very much affected by current concerns, as are the questions asked. As a consequence, it is scarcely surprising that insurgencies and counterinsurgency warfare have each risen in attention over the past quarter century. In particular, the lengthy Afghanistan and Iraq commitments of the United States from 2001 and 2003, respectively, encouraged much greater interest in COIN (counterinsurgency), and this, at once, entailed interest in the present, past, and future of such conflict.[1] America's opponents could not afford anything similar to the American military and therefore had to resort to asymmetrical means. Although the historical background was sometimes flimsy, there was a welcome reexamination of past episodes, notably, at first, British methods from the late nineteenth century on and those of the United States in the Philippines from 1899 but, subsequently, extending more widely.

This interest followed and built on Rupert Smith's idea of "war amongst the people," which he argued constituted a new military paradigm.[2] This was an idea advanced in the 1990s that was encouraged by the experience of conflict in Somalia and, even more, Rwanda and the former Yugoslavia in the 1990s. It was also fostered by the claim that American dominance and the capabilities of modern weaponry made great-power warfare obsolescent and that the United States would therefore have to prepare for other types of warfare, notably asymmetrical conflict. The idea of a "war between civilizations,"[3] more particularly Islam and the West, served as a bridge between the concept of asymmetrical warfare and the development of COIN as a nexus of doctrine and practice.

This thesis will be considered in chapters 10–12. Here it suffices as an introduction to note that the role of conflict within states, the resistance to

1

established authority referred to in the dictionary definition of *insurgency* given in the preface, has been crucial, both in terms of the histories of the latter and with reference to the history of war. However, conflict within states has been underrated on the whole in military history and indeed in most national historical narratives wherein, with the exception of Marxist and Marxist-influenced historical writing, conflict within states often has been regarded as irrelevant, even inconsequential, and certainly as contrary to themes of nation building and national integration.

This underrating is also the result of a widespread preference for considering war between states, notably after the discussion of an initial independence struggle whenever that is relevant. Indeed, such struggles are generally presented as wars between states because of the emphasis on the protonationalism or nationalism supposedly (or actually) present in the independence struggle. At the level of public culture, the unglamorous role of regular armies, which do not tend to be the underdog in insurgency struggles, also has an impact.

Linked to this process but also separate from it, conflict within states has been brought into the general narrative when it can be made readily comprehensible. In most cases, this is as part of an account of armed opposition to imperial rule. Indeed, this theme predominated in twentieth-century discussion of insurgencies. In addition, civil wars that approximated in military terms to conventional conflicts between states have attracted particular attention and have been studied in these terms rather than as the insurgencies they were. It was the rejection of established authority that was most significant. In contrast, studying these as conventional wars is the case, most obviously, with the English (1642–46) and American (1861–65) civil wars but also more generally, for example, with the Spanish Civil War (1936–39).

Although attracting less attention, there were early instances of a process that was very typical with successful insurgencies. For example, the Portuguese insurrection against Spain in 1640 rapidly became a conventional war between the two powers, with Spain fighting a border war rather than one within Portugal.[4] Although the Dutch retained positions within Belgium, the same was true of the successful Belgian insurgency against Dutch rule in 1830. The resistance in Brazil in the 1630s–50s to the Dutch occupation of the northeastern coast is an aspect of the same process, although the Brazilian forces did not make an extensive transition to new-style European infantry.[5]

Most insurgencies and civil wars, however, lack any easy characterization. In part, this situation captures the extent to which civil wars, insurgencies, insurrections, rebellions, revolutions, and mass opposition, while often similar, are not necessarily identical, indeed often far from it. As a different but related point, phenomena, such as geopolitics and strategy, predate descriptive words, while terms and their meanings change greatly across time and, moreover, do not adequately translate. In addition, the understanding and presentation of individual insurgencies are both contested and subject to change. As a result, it is, for example, possible to offer a localist view of conflicts that are habitually seen as nationalist. The habitual view emerges because they would in time become nationalist or because we are conditioned to view and analyze conflict with either a nationalist or a class framework.

A key element is that of goal. Clausewitz divides wars as being fought for the overthrow of the opposing regime or something less than this. Such a classification is very valuable for insurgencies and thus for counterinsurgency conflict.

Issues of definition are repeatedly significant for political as well as methodological reasons. For example, is it only outcome that earns the designation *war*? This is a question posed by the contrast between the American War of Independence (1775–83) and the unsuccessful Irish rebellion/revolution of 1798 against British rule. Similarly, there are major disagreements over whether events in India in 1857–59 should be referred to as a mutiny, a rebellion, or a war of independence against Britain. So also with smaller-scale instances of what has been defined as *rebellion*, such as the Ghost Dance campaign of 1890–91, in which the American government responded with overwhelming force to a messianic revival movement among the Sioux, crushing it.[6]

There have been attempts to classify insurgencies, for example, for Africa in the 1990s, to distinguish between "liberation insurgencies," "separatist insurgencies," "reform insurgencies," and "warlord insurgencies," as well as "bandit organizations."[7] This typology faces problems, not least due to omission, application, and significant overlaps, but it captures the range of insurgencies and the extent to which they have very different meanings and connotations. There are also issues of definition with related phenomena, such as warlords, brigandage, and death squads.[8] Aside from questions of definition, there are others of explanation. Assessing the Roman Empire, Susan Mattern suggests: "One way to view insurgency, resistance, and banditry is as attenuated areas or holes in the network of social relationships that linked the empire together and bound it to the senatorial aristocracy and to the emperor."[9]

The range, variety, divisions, and diffusion of insurgencies is an aspect of the inherent role of chaos and disorder in insurrectionary contexts and circumstances. More particularly, in opposition to the idea of a revolutionary party providing coherence and discipline in a radical process of transformation, there is frequently no coherent center and several different entities that do not necessarily cooperate because they do not have the same goals. The insurgencies in Syria in 2014–16 provide a key instance, as does the rivalry in Afghanistan in 2015–16 between the Taliban and ISIS. The structure of such insurgencies is not a matter simply of chaos. Instead, they can be dynamic and complex.

Linked to this, there is a danger in seeking to categorize insurgencies in that, by so doing, those who seek to understand and those who wish to crush them may be lured into (or trick themselves into) hidebound and simplistic views. Instead, a key point about modern insurgencies, especially in the Middle East, is that they defy categorization because there are so many different groups, with contrasting ideologies and objectives, opposed to each other as well as to the regime they oppose.

In the case of the United States, it is easy to see the War of Independence as an insurgency, and that argument is employed to defend the right to own arms. However, the extent to which other episodes in American history similarly merit such a description is a matter for debate, debate that can be highly controversial. In part, the issues are that of the intentions of those acting, the assumptions and/or rhetoric of their opponents, and the functional definition of the means used and/or considered. Episodes that repay attention include Mormon activities in 1856–58 that were judged by the government as rebellious, the Civil War (1861–65), the subsequent opposition to Reconstruction, the civil rights movement of the 1950s–1960s, and the black power movement of the 1960s.

Many of the issues of political definition can be highly controversial. The extent to which there was terrorism in Palestine by Jewish organizations in 1945–48, as part of an insurrection designed to overthrow British rule, became highly controversial when Israel itself faced terrorism, notably when Menachem Begin, a key figure in this terrorist campaign as head of the Irgun Tsva'i Lohem (Military Fighting Organization), became prime minister of Israel from 1977 to 1983. Another former member, who moved on to be prominent in the Lohamei Herut Yisrael (Fighters for the Freedom of Israel, often called the "Stern Gang"), Yitzhak Shamir, was prime minister in 1983–84 and 1986–92. In this and other cases, a hard-and-fast process of definition is contentious, both in the state in question and more generally.

So also with counterinsurgency struggles. Counterinsurgency is often marked not by the will to defeat and subjugate but by the will to impel subjects/citizens back into sincere and peaceful loyalty. Linked to this, the degree to which "hearts and minds" is not a modern invention is a point that is lost on many policymakers and analysts. Instead, the attempt to win via "hearts and minds" policies and strategies has a long history and a historical track record that may make these policymakers and analysts fairly skeptical about its efficacy. Moreover, in many countries, the absence of strong, or even any, police forces frequently ensured that troops were employed to maintain order and control, as is also the case for many countries today, for example, in Thailand. That again raises the definition of the use of force. Given that the military in many countries, for example, much of Latin America, was and is the arm of the state, with its prime opponents being internal, then civil violence, if not civil war, and the paramilitary policing involved become key aspects of military activity. The extent to which insurgencies are defined as criminal rather than as wars is significant in affecting military responses. Thus, in August 1942, the German High Command determined that all insurgencies were Communist-inspired criminal banditry, a decision that was wrong in fact and that permitted a criminally brutal response.[10]

There is also the question of insurgencies within the military. There is a literature on mutinies,[11] but it is far from comprehensive. Moreover, it is not always clear how far concern over conditions is the key element or whether, instead, mutinies and other disobedience arise from political issues. This question extends to individual but frequent acts of defiance, such as assaults on officers and noncommissioned officers by subordinates in the U.S. Army during the Vietnam War. These attacks reflected tensions and anger but not much antiwar activism.[12] Fragging, instead, was part of a broader aspect of indiscipline, especially among citizen soldiers who have not had to face the harsh punishments of regular forces, coupled with a lack of belief in the cause for which they were supposed to be fighting. Unpopular officers were also killed during the two world wars. At a different scale, the degree to which insurgencies in the military can be treated differently, depending on whether they included all ranks or involved an attack on the established system of control, is, more generally, instructive.

As another instance of the problems of definition, there is the extent to which insurgencies, as it were, can be directed against other insurgencies. In part, these can be seen as counterrevolutionary insurgencies, as happened in the Vendée (against the French Revolution) in the 1790s and with the Whites against the Russian Revolution in 1919–21. Both of these counterrevolutionary insurgencies failed. Given the politicized nature of the reading of insurgencies and, in particular, the emphasis on the popularity of radical insurgencies, there is frequently a tendency to question the viability, and certainly the popularity, of counterrevolutionary insurgencies. This approach reflects the inherent politicization of the issue by contemporary and subsequent commentators, notably the sense of progressivism imbuing many historians' accounts wherein counterrevolutions are seen as going against the grain of the "forward movement of history." At the same time, it is necessary to underline that in this type of insurgency, as in others, there is no consistency. Thus, although both were counterrevolutionary and unsuccessful, the Vendée rising was very different from the operations of the Whites. The differences were many, ranging from context to geography. The Whites operated in geographically extensive zones, thereby encompassing their opponents, unlike the geographically compressed Vendée. Moreover, the Whites had experienced armed forces and fairly cohesive command and control structures.

This type of insurgency, however, did not exhaust the issue. Thus, during the English Civil War (1642–46), as also later with the Russian Civil War, the pressure on the localities from the search for supplies and the erosion of local neutralism led to a violent response. In England, the response was in the shape of the Clubmen movement in 1644–45. Local people sought to keep troops out and, in particular, to limit the demands of garrisons. In the event, the Clubmen were dispersed by Parliamentary forces.

The range of insurgencies is not restricted to land because there is the question as to how far piracy can be seen as a form of insurgency and, indeed, how best to conceptualize the maritime dimension. Large-scale piracy was not simply a matter of the Western world, where the treatment of pirates could be glamorous, at least for historical figures. Such piracy was also very important in Asian coastal waters, notably in the East and South China Seas and in the Indian Ocean. The very flexibility of piracy ensured that it could be linked with smuggling and slaving or, indeed, overlap with (licensed) privateering and legal trade. In turn, prohibitions and regulations of trade helped encourage smuggling and thus conflict, as with China in the 1540s. This was an instance of the extent to which insurgency was, in part, a consequence of government policy rather than being designed to overthrow government.[13] The response to a perceived loss of legal fidelity in a society is an aspect of this situation.

As another instance of the overlap of criminality and insurgencies, the past few decades have seen drug cartel insurgencies in Latin America in which an alternative regime based on drugs is established and government is opposed by a paramilitary arm of the cartel. In turn, there is considerable variety. For example, in Colombia, FARC was/is a Marxist-Leninist revolutionary organization, with its own army, that ran/has been running a drug trade for decades. Different emphases can be placed on its revolutionary character or its criminality. Powerful drug syndicates, such as the Zetas and the Sinaloa cartel in Mexico and the leading Colombian drug cartels of the 1980s and 1990s, unlike FARC, do not have field armies, but they have/had squads of varying sizes that conducted terrorist operations of various dimensions, especially in the northern provinces of Mexico. In a way, these cartels are an insurgency, and the Mexican government's fitful struggles against them are a counterinsurgency, a process earlier seen in the United States on a smaller scale with Prohibition. Moreover, the cartels have penetrated the political parties and the military and police of Mexico and, as a result, can orchestrate to a degree the Mexican government's counterinsurgency moves against drug rivals. Thus, Mexico can be characterized within an insurgency and counterinsurgency framework. The narcotics production and trade from Andean and Central America to the United States might appear to be a transnational insurgency of sorts, with new types of warlords.[14]

More broadly, insurgency was not generally the opening response to grievances nor the first option as a means, and this remains the case. For example, across the world, negotiations between landlords and village communities or those between employers and employees over obligations and remuneration were, as a result of the autonomy of the latter, a constant feature, and in the event of disputes, the major response was not violence but litigation and appeal to the agents and institutions of government and justice. Thus, in eighteenth-century Russia, villages drew up petitions expressing their grievances and sent representatives with them to local and central authorities. Similarly with slavery. If circumstances were propitious, slaves could engage in social protest and labor bargaining. In Barbados during the eighteenth century, the insurrectionist attitudes that had led to plans for slave revolts in 1649, 1675, and 1692 were replaced by an emphasis on limited protest that was designed to secure the amelioration of circumstances.[15]

More generally, where grievances tipped into violence, it was not usually the case that a large-scale insurgency resulted. Instead, most peasants and employee violence was local, the response to specific grievances directed against particular landlords and employers who were felt to be abusing their position. This essentially specific nature of relations helped ensure a local pattern of grievance, disorder, and purposed action. Trade unions and other mass movements were to seek to superimpose a more widespread pattern, frequently, in the twentieth century, with some success, and the perception of revolutionary masses existing made this aspiration more threatening, but it was not the major trend for most of history.

There is also the problem created by the standard emphasis in the history of war on battle. As a result, much of the discussion fails to give sufficient weight to the alternative "little" or "small" war[16] of raids, skirmishes, and small-scale clashes that were far more frequent aspects of war. "Little" or "small" war was/is at once a technique, a product of asymmetric goals and capabilities,[17] and a political and ideological choice or necessity. Such warfare was true both of conflict between regular forces of specialized military units and of insurgencies involving rebellions against such forces, and this range of conflict reflects the variety of war and the difficulty of defining it.[18]

Counterinsurgency operations frequently focused on this "small" war, as was abundantly seen in the Scottish Highlands in 1746 alongside full-scale battle at Culloden, as loyal troops suppressed Jacobite action. The Scottish Highlanders who provided the core Jacobite support were regarded by their opponents as "barbarians" and, indeed, were compared unfavorably with the Gauls of the first century BCE by Thomas Ashe Lee, a British army officer who sought a historical comparison to the campaign by reading Julius Caesar, the Roman general who had overcome the Gauls. This represented an instance of learning from past authors or, at least, considering tasks in the perspective of readings of them, which is a common theme in both insurgency and counterinsurgency. Having conquered Gaul (France), Caesar faced a major insurgency, which he wrote about at length. His fame was such that he was a worthy exemplar.

William, Duke of Cumberland, the commander of the British army and the younger son of George II, allowed his soldiers to plunder Jacobite property on the march north in 1746, and his actions were criticized, notably in loyal Scottish circles. Thus, John Maule, MP, reported from London:

> There are many here who much disapprove of the plundering that has been but too much practised by the Duke's army, no good can result from it, and the rebels will certainly make reprisals a hundred fold, so that the whole country will be a scene of blood and rapine and many a man that has merit with the government undone. In the meantime, it is not lawful for any man to complain lest he be taxed with disaffection. [19]

The Duke, however, regarded such action as effective, writing:

> The orders which were sent to the Governor and Commandant of Fort William, before it was threatened with a siege, to seize all the cattle and demolish the habitations of those in Lochaber, who were actually out in rebellion, has had a very good effect, as all the rebels of that country have deserted, to go home to their own habitations . . . which will only discourage the men and add to their present distraction. [20]

At the same time, this repression was but the first stage of a political strategy that involved a reorganization of Highland society. This reorganization was followed by recruiting more Highlanders for the army. Indeed, many played a key role in the conquest of New France (Canada) from France in 1758–60 and, subsequently, in resisting the American Revolution.

The success of integrating Highland Scotland into the British imperial project was such that there was to be no other insurrection there, unlike in Ireland, where insurgencies in the sixteenth and seventeenth centuries were followed by others in 1798, 1916, and, successfully, 1919–21. These and other contrasts underline the extent to which, although context and practice have varied very greatly, the "military" can often not be differentiated from the "political," and certainly not in the case of insurgencies and civil wars. That argument emerges frequently in this book and should be understood throughout. Indeed, the points raised in this introduction need to be borne in mind at every stage of this book. They ensure that there is no clear analysis that can shape what is in practice a very varied narrative of both insurgencies and counterinsurgencies. It would be all too easy to shape this by a careful selection of material, and this practice is frequently followed by the use of case studies that, to no surprise, frequently support the analysis offered. In fact, the variety of insurgencies is such that it is highly questionable whether there was, as often claimed or implied, a paradigm insurgency in any particular period. Trends can be discerned, but, however tempting, they should be seen as just that and should not be reified into clear-cut analytical building blocks.

In many respects, the subject is too important for such a misleading approach, while the need to adopt a global perspective makes it far less viable than might have been the case when writing against the background of a more restricted range of apparent significance. It is important not to confuse correlation with causation. In particular, the idea of a cutting-edge tendency that is followed by other movements appears less viable than it did when many were writing with a conviction that, in some cases, possibly owed at least something to ideological commitment and teleological belief. At the very least, the methodology and conceptualization that were well established in the late twentieth century now appear less well established.

Chapter Two

Insurgency to 1500

This short chapter does not seek to cover all insurgencies across all time up to 1500. Instead, the intention is to show that insurgencies have happened across organized human history and are therefore far from being a characteristic of modernity. The latter is an implication of certain assumptions about the subject and approaches taken to it, but these are mistaken. In addition, insurgencies are not necessarily characterized by guerrilla warfare, which itself can be quite varied in character and intention. The same point is true about "small war."

Across history, the prevalence of empires, as well as the power of rulers, ensured that the nature of control, as well as the practice of politics, frequently entailed insurgencies and their suppression. In most cases, there was no alternative to the dissolution of political links other than through violence, especially because that dissolution entailed the renunciation of obedience in pursuit of a different identity for legitimacy. Whatever the limitations of control, consent, indeed obedience, to authority was generally assumed to be the political practice, even if, at the same time, the identity of authority was frequently contested. In a contest over legitimacy and legality, the denial of consent and obedience was resisted by those claiming authority and was punished with violence, frequently brutally so. This was a reflection of hierarchical norms and of the prevalence of social differentiation and deference as key elements in belief and behavior alongside religious, cultural, and political norms focused on obedience. These norms were reiterated in a number of media, including papal bulls and church decoration.[1]

TYPES OF INSURGENCY

The diverse nature of polities and societies, the range of circumstances, and the unpredictability of contingencies, however, ensured that the subsequent character of insurgencies, both military and nonmilitary, was quite varied, as were the outcomes. In particular, to adopt an approach focused on the viability of counterinsurgency action and thus the parameters of insurgency effectiveness, the state of international relations was crucial, a point that has continued to the present. Specifically, the questions of whether the ruler(s) confronting insurgencies had alternative commitments and whether foreign powers were willing to intervene on behalf of insurgents were vital, and each was often an aspect of the same conflict. Thus, the English barons who rebelled against King John, forcing him to accept the restrictions enshrined in Magna Carta (1215), benefited from his earlier defeats and those of his allies by Philip Augustus, king of France (r. 1179–1223), notably the major French victory at Bouvines over John's allies in 1214. These defeats created an impression of vulnerability. Perception is generally a key element in both insurgencies and counterinsurgencies. Moreover, French military intervention in England played a major, albeit unsuccessful, role in the subsequent crisis. Indeed, it became one in which Philip's son, Louis (later Louis VIII), invaded in pursuit of what became his unsuccessful claim on the English throne. This claim significantly changed the character of the insurgency and thereby underlined the extent to which there was variety within insurgencies as well as between them. This point helps explain the difficulty of adopting a convincing typology.

For much of human history, the definition of insurgencies and the application of this definition are made somewhat problematic because the "states" against which insurgencies were launched were frequently in practice undefined or inchoate. Moreover, these "states" were not generally seen, notably by leading landowners, as enjoying the right to monopolize warfare and alone to initiate and legitimate conflict, or, at least, that was not the practice. Similarly, today, albeit in a very different context as far as sovereignty is understood in international law, issues of legitimacy come into play, not least with the claim to the attributes of sovereignty, including waging war, by groups such as al-Qaeda and ISIS. Transnational movements, more generally, pose these challenges of, and to, legitimacy and definitions.

Functionally if not legally, in terms of what happened, conflicts launched by groups defying the relevant state's claims to sovereignty by rulers can, and could, amount to war. Thus, turning to the past, there was most obviously a distinction between wars begun by imperial powers such as classical Rome, Ottoman Turkey, Safavid Persia, Mughal India, Ming or, later, Manchu China, and Georgian and Victorian Britain with outside polities and, on the other hand, conflict within these and other empires. However, before this distinction is pushed too far, conflict within these empires could be large in scale, bitter, and sustained, more so, indeed, than external warfare, and could be regarded by contemporaries as war. The civil wars of the Roman Republic and Empire were frequently on a great scale and often lasted several years. Moreover, these conflicts affected Roman strategic culture, notably in terms of control over military units and their location. Similar points can be made about Chinese empires and those of Mughal India and Ottoman Turkey. Civil wars in the Roman world arose from a number of factors, including divisions within the elite, social tensions, and rebellions by subject peoples, notably Batavians, Iceni, and Jews.[2] These categories, furthermore, cannot necessarily be readily separated.

The Romans, moreover, faced rebellions from slaves. These created great alarm as they threatened the total overthrow of the social order rather than the renegotiation of terms. Slave insurgencies, most famously the Spartacus rising, tended to attract particular attention from twentieth-century writers concerned to establish a long-term provenance for what was presented as modern insurgency warfare. The Thracian-born Spartacus had been enslaved for desertion from the Roman army and became a gladiator before leading a major slave uprising in 73 BCE. He built up a large army, possibly ninety thousand strong, and, advancing along the length of the Italian peninsula and devastating the great agricultural estates, vanquished a number of Roman forces before being defeated and killed in 71 BCE by the praetor, Marcus Licinius Crassus. As an instance of the exemplary punishment the Romans sought and that has followed the suppression of many insurgencies, six thousand of Spartacus's followers were crucified and their bodies left hanging along a major road. Crassus himself was to be killed fighting a powerful foreign foe, the Parthian Empire, being routed at the Battle of Carrhae in 53 BCE.

Notably as a result of Stanley Kubrick's highly successful film *Spartacus* (1960), Spartacus became a key figure. Slave rebellions served the Communists as an example of the continuity of resistance to social oppression, a resistance that they claimed to exemplify in the modern world. Soviet writers frequently embellished slave and serf revolts. Slave rebellions also served Western writers and filmmakers seeking to make Rome dramatically accessible. The scriptwriter of *Spartacus*, Dalton Trumbo, had been a self-proclaimed member of the Communist Party of the USA, while the film was based on the novel *The Gladiators* (1939) by Howard Fast, another party member. From the perspective of many American viewers, this was opposition to a political system that had also crucified Christ a century later. Thus, Americans could be seen as the modern descendants of the linked opposition to slavery, imperialism, and paganism, and there was even a Cold War subtext in their minds, with Roman/Soviet oppression opposed to both Christianity and American democracy. The Romans could also be seen as anticipations of the Germans of the Third Reich. Similar assumptions and values were advanced in other American films, such as *Ben Hur* (1925 and 1959), *Demetrius and the Gladiators* (1954), and *Gladiator* (2000), while Spartacus returned in the 2010 American television series *Spartacus: Blood and Sand*. These films also contained a message of civil rights for African Americans.

Other slave revolts also challenged the Roman world. That led by Eunus the Syrian began in 135 BCE and involved about sixty thousand to seventy thousand slaves, mostly on Sicily but also on the Italian mainland. This revolt led to a fall in the grain shipments that kept the Roman population quiescent, and the anger of the Romans was shown in the slaughter of the last twenty thousand of the rebel slaves when they surrendered in 132 BCE. Nevertheless, there were other revolts on Sicily, notably in 104–100 BCE, that in turn were also crushed. Rebel slaves lacked weaponry, cohesion, and military organization, but guerrilla tactics offered opportunities.

More generally, the murder of masters by slaves helped lead to a fear of slaves, resulting in the controversial Roman law that, in such cases, all the household slaves should be executed as collective retribution. Such murders by slaves were seen as insurrections against the fundamentals of the social order.

In the twentieth century, an emphasis on modern insurgency warfare as arising from socioeconomic exploitation and alienation encouraged a search for earlier anticipations. In a similar pattern, nationalist writers in the nineteenth century sought similar earlier models for insurgencies, and their confessional counterparts in the sixteenth and seventeenth centuries did the same. This pattern has ensured that insurgencies are frequently portrayed in a highly ahistorical fashion and, indeed, more so than in the case of conflict between states. This problem has remained the case to the present and, in the case of antiquity, underplays the role of religious messianism in encouraging native and slave revolts.[3]

The socioeconomic analysis of power led both to a particular understanding of the politics and civil conflict of the late Roman Republic and to strong interest in slave insurgencies. Conversely, there was less interest in considering the pursuit of power by military figures who staged rebellions and engaged in civil war, such as Marius and Sulla in the 80s BCE under the late Roman Republic, in terms of insurgencies, although there is no reason why this should not be the case. A similar pattern of a varied nature of insurgencies to that seen in the case of insurgencies against empires could be found within smaller polities, although in the latter case it was less easy to establish a large insurgent force.

Insurgencies could reflect a difference over what was agreed to be a distinctive group. At the same time, the existence of a sense of separateness could also be significant in the politics of conflict. This sense was given biblical authority by the discussion in the Old Testament and the Apocrypha of the successful revolt in 166–158 BCE against the Syrians by the Jews of Israel under Judas Maccabeus, which was an insurgency against imperial rule by the Seleucids, a Hellenistic dynasty who ruled part of the empire created by Alexander the Great.

Turning to the Middle Ages, this sense of separateness was seen, for example, in the rebellions in Scotland against English control in the 1290s and 1300s, rebellions that succeeded in the 1310s, notably in the conventional warfare that led to the Scottish success in battle at Bannockburn in 1314. In their earlier response to the rebellions, King Edward I of England (r. 1272–1307) could gain major victories in battle, such as Dunbar in 1296 and Falkirk in 1298. However, as so often with counterinsurgency struggles, it proved impossible to translate victory into a permanent settlement. English success rested as much on divisions among the Scots, notably between the Bruces and the Balliols/Comyns, who were at the same time leading families and patronage groups, and exploiting these divisions required political skill. Edward II (r. 1307–27), crucially, lacked both this and the necessary military ability. The two were linked. Had the English been able to maintain and support a permanent military presence in lowland Scotland, the part of Scotland that was both wealthiest and most vulnerable to English power, the Scottish kingdom might have been so weakened and divided as to cease being a powerful challenge. Divisions among the Scottish nobility, which greatly helped the English, might have been exploited to spread the power of the king of England, who would have been able to mount a more effective claim to the crown of Scotland, either for himself or for a protégé. The less intense pace of English military pressure under Edward II helped Robert Bruce to consolidate this position in Scotland and, crucially, to defeat his Scottish rivals. He became Robert I in 1306 and thus an insurgent who had to maintain control.[4]

The French commitment was also significant for England. Hostilities between England and Scotland arose in 1296 largely because of the quarrel from 1293 between Edward I and Philip IV of France, in which the Scots became involved. Had there not been that additional complication, then Scotland might have been treated more cautiously by Edward I, while Edward III would have been able to follow up his success in battle and politics in the early 1330s. Instead, he came to focus on the Hundred Years' War with France.

Opposition in Italy, for example, by the Lombard League, to rule by German-based emperors in the twelfth and thirteenth centuries and in Flanders against French rule in the fourteenth also reflected a protonationalism that was a key element in encouraging and sustaining insurgencies. This was readily apparent in the case of the successful Swiss defiance of Habsburg rule in the fourteenth century.

At the same time, as in Scotland and Italy, such insurgencies against "foreign" rulers and rule were also, in part, civil wars, as with those in Wales in 1282–83, 1287, 1294–95, 1316, and 1400–1408. In the early conflicts, more Welshmen fought for Edward I (r. 1272–1307) than against him. The revolt of 1400–1408 by the heavily outnumbered Owain Glyn Dŵr (Owen Glendower) saw the extensive use of guerrilla tactics and devastation, but these could not challenge the English castle garrisons effectively. Glyn Dŵr was leading his followers toward a dead end: English power, including support in Wales, was such that it was possible only during periods of English civil conflict, such as the Percy rising of 1403, for Welsh opponents to make much headway. Thereafter, Welsh military action was part of civil conflicts within Britain, notably the Wars of the Roses and the civil wars of the 1640s.

Emphasis on protonationalism reflects a silent writing down of socioeconomic and religious insurgencies or, rather, insurgencies that can be thus categorized. In part, that analysis and process represents the strong interest in national origins seen during the nineteenth century and again after the Cold War. The success of religious insurgencies in medieval Europe was limited. The most prominent, the Cathar heresy in southern France in the early thirteenth century, led to a brutal counterinsurgency struggle in the shape of a crusade that provided regional political figures, notably Simon de Montfort (ca. 1160–1218), with opportunities to pursue their own territorial interests. The slaughter of those judged heretics contributed greatly to the brutality of the conflict.

Socioeconomic insurgencies could also be brutal, although at one level they could overlap with more peaceful attempts to enforce and oppose new tenurial or other economic relationships. So it is in the case of later European colonies with what are sometimes termed slave revolts. The success of such "renegotiation" owed something to economic conditions. Thus, a general fall of population in the late fourteenth and fifteenth centuries as a result of the Black Death (plague) of the 1340s made it easier for some peasants to negotiate improved working conditions.[5] This negotiation could take the form of forcing new arrangements on the landowners in a way that might be regarded as an insurgency. More generally, the nature of the social system was significant and, notably, whether the social system contained "vertical" links: those between different social strata. Such links made it easier to negotiate an end to demands and to episodes of violence. At the same time, notably, but not only, in the absence of such links, there could be a marked brutality in the response to peasant demands and violence, a brutality that reflected fear, contempt, and hatred. These elements could be seen in insurgencies in England in the fourteenth century. They reflected overlaps of political, social, and economic tensions and of action by different social groups. Thus, in 1326, amid a mounting political crisis, order in London collapsed, and Walter de Stapeldon, the treasurer who had been left in charge when Edward II fled the city, was killed in Cheapside, precipitating the fall of Edward's government. This was more effective than the Peasants' Revolt of 1381, but it is the latter that attracts far more scholarly and public attention, in part because it can be related to modern social tensions. Thus, the poll tax riots of 1990 in London against Mrs. Thatcher's government were discussed in terms of the role of a poll tax in contributing to the Peasants' Revolt. The latter was more wide ranging than is generally appreciated and drew on resistance to landlord demands in a volatile rural economy. Political reputation also played a role as the government was affected by failure in the Hundred Years' War with France. The rising in 1381 indicated a lack of social and ideological quiescence on the part of the bulk of the population. Alienation was readily apparent. Thus, in Norfolk, the insurgents took control of all the major towns, attacked, plundered, or killed prominent figures, especially JPs (justices of the peace), burned manorial court rolls that reflected gentry juris-diction, and attacked foreign settlers. The insurgency there, however, was crushed within a month by the warlike Bishop Despenser of Norwich, who brought leadership and determination to the gentry.

The crisis at the center of power, London, was instructive. With the help of dissatisfied Londoners, the rebels from rural areas occupied the city and murdered prominent figures, including Simon of Sudbury, archbishop of Canterbury and chancellor, who was responsible for the poll tax. The rebels, however, did not wish to create a new governmental system but, rather, to pressure the young king, Richard II, into changes of policy, thus fulfilling their concept of good kingship. Astutely, Richard averted further violence by promising to be the rebels' leader, but as soon as the rebels returned home, Richard revoked his promises and punished the leaders. Similarly, in 1450, a royal pardon destroyed the cohesion of Cade's Rebellion and enabled the government to regain control.

The resonance of these insurgencies continues. The Peasants' Revolt of 1381 is still cited by the British Left. In addition, the Maccabees, the Scottish War of Independence, the Lombard League, William Tell and the Swiss struggle against the Habsburgs, Owain Glyn Dŵr, and the Cathars all today play a significant role in nationalist, protonationalist, and regional narratives, indicating the great importance of the sacrifice and fight for liberty found and presented in such episodes. This is far from an exhaustive list of early insur-gencies that can still hold a resonance today. For example, Armenian nation-alists make reference to a revolt in 538–39 against Byzantine rule. As with other struggles, the emphasis is on independence, and as a result, the syncret-ic measures of conciliation frequently employed in the past are criticized today or, indeed, treated as in effect betraying the national cause and thus truly treasonable.[6] As a consequence, there can be a serious misreading of the past, as with the film *Braveheart* (1995), about William Wallace, who led Scottish opposition to Edward I of England in the late 1290s. This film reflected internal Hollywood dynamics, notably, as an answer to the need for an action film at that point as well as the ability to read the Scots as American colonists resisting the British.

EMPIRES

In China, despite clear and potent ideological norms against insurgencies, there were major ones, notably the Rebellion of the Feudatories in 154 BCE, the Yellow Turban Uprising of 184 BCE, and the An Lushan Rebellion in 755–63 CE. The last inflicted serious damage on the Tang Empire, which had to make major changes in foreign and domestic policy as a result. In addition, a key insurrection led to the end of Mongol rule, which, having been established by a long process of conquest in the thirteenth century, collapsed in the fourteenth century. Khubilai, the great khan of the Mongols, had moved his capital from the steppe to Beijing in 1264. However, the fourteenth century was an age of Mongol decline in China, in part because of conflict within the ruling elite, especially in the 1320s, but other factors also played a role. Corruption in the bureaucracy angered many subjects, as did animosity between the rulers and ruler, natural disasters, and less competent rulers. The Mongols were driven from China by rebellions that became acute from the early 1350s. The Red Turban army, a key insurgent force, was able to capture the major city of Nanjing in 1356 and from there to dominate the Yangtze valley. Other rebel armies initially posed the major challenge in the region, but they were defeated by the Red Turban in 1363 and 1367. The head of the Red Turban after 1355, Zhu Yuanzhang (1328–98), in 1368 moved north on Beijing. The Mongol emperor fled back to the steppe ahead of the approaching Chinese army, and Zhu Yuanzhang proclaimed himself emperor, founding the Ming dynasty. Subsequent warfare with the Mongols cannot be described as an insurgency but included the conquest of eastern Mongolia and southwestern China as well as major defeats of Mongol armies.[7]

Thus, the Ming, the most powerful dynasty in the world until shortly before its overthrow in 1644, owed its position to a successful insurgency and not, as with the Mongol, Mughal, Ottoman, and Safavid dynasties in China, India, Turkey, and Persia (Iran), to conquest from abroad. The result of this insurgency, however, had to be protected by subsequent conflict, through a series of wars with the Mongols beginning in 1410.

More generally, across much of Eurasia, the repeated political decay of essentially nomadically based empires, a decay brought about through frequent succession struggles, and the absence of a common ethnic base provided opportunities both for attacks by other powers and for insurgencies. The Turkic-Mongolian nomadic and seminomadic societies had sufficient legitimizing principles insofar as there had to be a consensus among ruling clans as to whom should be the leader and his willingness to heed the superior clans. This arrangement worked well enough from the late 300s (the Huns) until the eighteenth century (the Crimean Tatars). The degree of civil war among the Turkic-Mongolian societies of the period from the 400s to the 1110s was no more than it was in contemporary western and central European societies.[8] However, the empires based on nomadic and seminomadic peoples lacked legitimation as far as many of the conquered were concerned. For example, in Islamic India, the fissiparous character of the dominant Turko-Afghan military society, which was especially prominent in northern India, was compounded by a more general absence of cohesion in territories, such as the Sultanate of Delhi under the Lodi dynasty in the fifteenth century. These territories essentially rested on the military prowess of the ruler and his ability (and need) to win over support through continued success.

In turn, dynastic divisions frequently interacted lacking the lubricant of success. Thus, in Persia (Iran), the late 1570s and 1580s saw acute instability in the Safavid Empire as the Qizilbash tribal confederation, on which Safavid power rested, was affected by a civil war that was related by serious disputes in the ruling dynasty. French defeat at the hands of Spain was a background to the elite divisions that played a major role in the French Wars of Religion that began in the 1560s.

There were also, however, frequent instances of a different political context for insurgencies. A crucial one was provided via insurgencies by subject peoples and areas within multipolar political systems, some of which had a scale or grandeur that led to them being imperial and/or claiming imperial status. These insurgencies raise anew the issue of the definition of insurgencies, for the situation of being subject people could be redefined through conflict. Thus, toward their neighbors, the Chinese sought to employ a tribute system as a sign of what was intended to be a peaceful system of nominal dependence on the emperor, with this dependence, in theory, defining the real presence and ranking of foreigners. Confirming the succession of rulers in this fashion ensured, in Chinese eyes, their legitimation as well as their vassalage. However, this relationship could be rejected, as by the Jurchens to the northeast in modern Manchuria. In turn, this rejection led to large-scale military activities by the Chinese. Thus, the killing of Jurchen leaders was important to a major campaign in 1466–67 in which about fifty thousand Chinese and ten thousand auxiliary Korean troops advanced north. In response to this pressure, the Jurchen reestablished tributary relations with China. Thus, what to the Chinese was an insurgency had been brought to an end.

A similar contrast in the understanding of insurgencies could be seen elsewhere, again with tribute systems opening the possibility of seeing insurgencies where they were not readily apparent to all of those involved. In

1426, having been heavily defeated, King Janus of Cyprus agreed to pay an annual tribute to the Mamluk ruler of Egypt. This led to the Mamluks becoming involved in Cypriot politics when, in a dynastic civil war, the succession to King John II (r. 1432–58) was contested by his daughter Charlotte and his illegitimate son, Jacob, who claimed the throne on the basis of being a man. This claim was important to his winning Mamluk support. The Mamluks invaded on his behalf in 1460, and in 1464 he succeeded in conquering the entire island, becoming James II.

Acquiescence in control was a key element in defining the parameters for insurgencies and their suppression. Thus, in Dai Viet (North Vietnam), which was conquered by the Ming in 1407, serious resistance began in 1418. Helped by the Ming focus on the more threatening Mongols, this resistance led to the Ming expulsion in 1428, an episode that has been resonant in Vietnamese-Chinese relations to this day, notably after a Chinese invasion in 1979 was thwarted. The ability of Dai Viet to acquire a cannon capability to match that of the Chinese was valuable in this resistance, but the political situation was far more significant.

The moral dimension to insurgency and counterinsurgency presented in China was also seen elsewhere. Insurgencies were widely perceived as a rejection of the divinely decreed order, an order that was cosmological and moral, and thus that it was immoral and wicked to attack.[9] These beliefs did not prevent insurgencies. However, the strength of the beliefs helped ensure that insurgencies were frequently conceptualized in a certain form and notably as a restoration of true order, especially by means of replacing "evil" ministers and "unjust" monarchs who had allegedly broken a fundamental compact of good governance. Thus, in Hungary in 1704, those involved in the Rákóczi rising against rule by the Habsburg Leopold I addressed a proclamation to foreign observers, justifying their rebellion in terms of the inviolability of the contractual agreement between the ruler and his subjects and the related right of subjects to resist unjust rulers. In 1705, a rebel assembly at Szécsény formed a Confederation of Hungarian Estates for Liberty and called for the reestablishment of lost liberties. In 1707, the Habsburgs were formally dethroned. In the event, the rising was overcome in 1711.

INSURGENCIES AND IDENTITIES

That the Dai Viet insurgency maintained a lasting political division underlines the extent to which insurgencies prior to 1500 are part of the "deep history" of modern senses of identity, which is the long-term resonance of the insurgencies. This point can be seen in the case of Scotland and Switzerland. Scottish nationalists make frequent reference to the defeat of occupying English forces at the battles of Stirling (1296) and Bannockburn (1314).

Indeed, this element of insurgency warfare arguably had a more lasting consequence than the insurgencies of social discontent that attracted much scholarly and political attention in the twentieth century, especially on the left wing. This contrast underlines the extent to which history is not only what happened in the past but also how we provide accounts of it. That is particularly true, as this book indicates, with the history of insurgencies. The collapse of European Communist regimes, notably the Soviet Union, in 1989–91, has been followed by a modern general strengthening of interest in religious and ethnic dimensions to politics, or, at least, these dimensions have become far less marginal in discussion and political strife. As a result, these dimensions have become more prominent in the descriptions and analysis of insurgencies in the past.

To return, for example, to the case of China, underlining the significance of ethnic identities in the fifteenth century, the Ming also frequently used force against insurgencies by non-Han peoples within the area understood as China. For example, in the 1450s, there were frequent operations against non-Han peoples, especially the Yao and Miao. These operations were followed, in the 1460s and 1470s, by operations in southern Sichuan, as well as by the Yongyang insurgency in Hubei. As a separate episode, rivalries among the elite also led to rebellions in China. In 1399, Zhu Yuanzhang's fourth son, Yung-Lo, rebelled against Chien wen, his nephew, beginning a civil war that led to his seizing power in 1402. In 1457, imperial bodyguards were employed to replace Jingdi (r. 1449–57) as emperor by his predecessor and half-brother, Yingzong (r. 1435–49, 1457–64). Four years later, there was an attempted coup in the capital mounted by disaffected generals controlling the garrison, but it was suppressed by loyal troops.

Similar issues affected other empires, although there were also variations, often marked, in the importance of particular types of insurgency. Border areas were frequently a problem, not least as the nature of control was often tenuous. For example, the long-standing Egyptian-based Mamluk Empire, which included modern Israel, Palestine, Lebanon, Syria, and western Saudi Arabia, faced a rebellion on its northern borders in 1465–71, one that was made more serious, as with many such insurgencies, by the international context. In this case, Shah Suwār deposed his brother as emir of Dhu'l-Kadr (in southeastern Anatolia) and, with the secret backing of the neighboring Ottomans (the rulers of the Turkish Empire), renounced the emirate's ties of vassalage to Egypt, only to be defeated in 1471. On the other hand, there was often the possibility of delegated control over border areas, as with the Ottomans in Wallachia and Moldavia in modern Romania. Such control frequently assisted both conquest and retention and made resistance and insurgencies less likely. Delegated control could be regarded as a confession of the weakness of central control, since the janissaries, the elite infantry, of the army could not be everywhere. Having local authorities loyal to the sultan in

Constantinople but of the same ethnicity and religion as the subject population might have assisted in defusing incipient insurrectionist tendencies. As
long as the tax money came to the central fisc, the Ottoman Turks were
apparently not so concerned about whether their control was direct or delegated.

Insurgencies could also come from key elements within regimes, notably
the military and, whether linked to this or separate, figures in the ruling
dynasty. In the Songhai Empire in West Africa (in the area of the Niger River
Valley), the military challenged control, a process that was constrained, or at
least affected, in most empires by an emphasis on dynastic continuity. Askia
Muhammad (r. 1493–1528), a leading general under Sonni Ali (r. 1464–92),
launched a bid for the throne after Sonni Ali died and, in 1493, although
outnumbered, defeated the forces of Sonni Ali's son, Sonni Baru, at Anfao.
Such battles were crucial in insurgencies of this type. In turn, although frequently successful in wars of expansion, Askia Muhammad was challenged
by a rebellion headed by one of his generals, the Karta of Kabi (in northwestern Nigeria), and a campaign against the latter proved unsuccessful.

Quarrels between Askia Muhammad's children also became a problem,
and in 1528 Muhammad was deposed by one of his sons. This fate was
reminiscent of that of the Ottoman ruler Bayezid II in 1512 and prefigured
that of Muhammad Khudabanda of Persia in 1587. In 1591, the Songhai
emperor, Ishāq II, was heavily defeated by an invading Moroccan army at
Tondibi after it had crossed the Sahara. He was then deposed and replaced by
his brother, Muhammad-Gao. Polygamy/concubinage and an absence of
primogeniture (inheritance by the eldest male), notably but not only in Islamic societies, helped repeatedly to ensure that there were several claimants on
the succession, and their claims were often settled with violence. Not all such
rebellions were successful. In 1558, Süleyman the Magnificent's son, Bayezid, rebelled against his father. However, after defeat near Konya in 1559, he
fled to his father's enemy, Shah Tahmasp I of Persia, only for the latter, in
1562, to allow an Ottoman executioner to kill Tahmasp. Conversely, in 1549,
Süleyman's plan to profit from the revolt of Tahmasp's brother, Alqass Mir-
za, miscarried when the latter was captured. In 1581, Akbar, the Mughal
ruler of northern India, overcame a revolt by his half-brother, Muhammad
Hakim.

Such events do not tend to receive much attention in studies of insurgency
warfare, but that reflects a presentmindedness that leads to a misreading of
the significance of these challenges. Moreover, their importance helps explain the extent to which other forms of insurgency that today attract more
scholarly attention, notably peasant risings, could be regarded in the past as
more marginal in significance, and, in particular, of only local consequence.
Those that were not, for example, the Peasants' Revolt in England in 1381,

were unusual. As a result, peasant risings could generally be left to local agencies to deal with in a way that military risings could not be.

The significance of insurgencies focused on succession disputes was seen in Japan, where these disputes reached the state of open warfare in the fifteenth century. Notably, the Ōnin War of 1467–77 arose from a succession dispute within the Ashikaga house, that of the *shogun* or head of government. This conflict led into the local and regional struggles that characterized much of the age of Sengoku (the Country at War), from 1467 to 1568. This was insurgency warfare different from that of peasant revolts. Opportunism and betrayal were central to the politics of conflict, with treachery playing an important role in both battles and the seizure of fortresses, as well as in coups. Military operations were partly designed so as to display strength and thus induce surrender and deter treachery. The absence of political cohesion in Japan was a key factor in encouraging the turn to civil war. In contrast, Japan was not involved in foreign war during this period.

In England, the equivalent to the Sengoku was the Wars of the Roses, which arose from a crucial loss of royal prestige under the unimpressive Henry VI (r. 1421–61, 1470–71). As with so many rebellions, this loss of prestige reflected the crucial role of international developments. Total defeat by France in 1450–53, in the last stage of the Hundred Years' War, led not only to this loss but also to the presence in England of battle-hardened veterans and nobles accustomed to military life and decisions through force. Moreover, in part as a legacy of the Hundred Years' War, both France and Burgundy meddled in the subsequent civil wars in England, the rival foreign powers supporting different sides there. As with many rebellions, the Wars of the Roses also reflected the nature of armed force in that society. The willingness of powerful nobles to raise troops was crucial to the ability of rulers to field armies. The form of clientage described as "bastard feudalism," a system similar to that in Japan, was not necessarily a cause of civil conflict. However, in the event of a breakdown in relations between monarch and nobles, this clientage made it easier for the nobles to mobilize their strength and to direct it against the monarch.

The deliberate killing of leading opponents was a key element of the Wars of the Roses, and, linked to this, betrayal was an important aspect of the militarized politics of these and other magnate insurgencies. So also in Scotland. For example, James III (r. 1460–88) faced serious aristocratic opposition led by his brothers. In 1488, unable to muster sufficient support, he was killed shortly after his defeat at Sauchieburn at the hands of rebels who took over the government, only themselves to face rebellion in 1489. As elsewhere, it proved possible to bring particular insurgencies to an end but not to stop the situation that itself led to insurgencies, a situation that thereby was a latent state of insurgency.

The international context was frequently important to the course of insurgencies. For example, the death of the bellicose Duke Charles the "Bold" of Burgundy in battle at Nancy in 1477, at the hands of an army of Lorrainers, Germans, and Swiss, left his daughter and successor, Mary, both vulnerable in the face of rebellions and short of money and troops. Rebellion in Flanders (in modern Belgium) led Mary to concede the Grand Privilège of 1477, under which the ruler was obliged to seek the consent of the provincial estates (Parliament) in order to raise taxes and troops. In 1487, renewed rebellion saw the key city of Ghent negotiate a treaty with neighboring France and accept a French garrison, while in 1491 the French supported a rebellion in Gelderland (in the modern Netherlands) by Karel van Egmond, who contested the control of the duchy by Mary's husband, Maximilian. However, in 1492 the rebellion was overcome, and the following year, the privileges granted in 1477 were declared void.

Similarly, dynastic strife and related insurgencies within the Islamic khanate of Kazan, to the east of Muscovy, the farthest north Islamic territory, were exploited by the rulers of Muscovy in a series of conflicts in the sixteenth century. These conflicts ended with the conquest of Kazan by Ivan IV, "the Terrible," in 1552. Once the city had fallen, there were several serious insurgencies in the khanate against Russian rule—in 1553, 1554, and 1556. They were repressed with great brutality, a brutality that reflected both a long-standing fear and anger based on conflict and slave raiding by the khanate and religious hostility toward Muslims. Towns were destroyed, men slaughtered, women and children taken prisoner, and the countryside devastated. Only in 1556 did organized resistance cease. [10]

POLITICS AND INSURGENCY

The insurgencies of this period cannot readily be separated, directly or indirectly, from much of the politics in it. In large part, this situation was an integral aspect of the character of politics, notably the personal nature of rulership, the monarchical character of states, and the prevalent role of violence. As a consequence of these factors, attempts to change ruler could be the key element in politics. For example, following a revolt from 1452 to 1457, Uzum Hasan (r. 1457–78) took control of the Aqquyunlu, a tribal confederation that in the 1460s came to dominate Persia (Iran). In turn, conflict among his sons and grandsons in the 1470s and 1490s helped ease the conquest of Persia in the 1500s by one of his grandsons, Isma'il, the head of the Safavids, a militant Shi'a Muslim religious order.

It would be mistaken to assert that these conflicts are in some way less significant or modern than subsequent assumptions about insurgencies might suggest. Instead, these conflicts demonstrated the extent to which politics in this period entailed violence, with rebellion a key element in the process. Some of these insurgencies were large in scale and sustained, and they did not necessarily entail methods of conflict that contrasted with those of wars between polities (states). However, the political context and desired outcome of the insurgencies were generally different from those of the wars, although a degree of compromise was frequently involved in settling disputes, whether domestic or international. Linked to this, the military capability of central government was often a matter of disparate shifts and expedients. A politics of primacy, governmentally ascribed rank, and vassalage meant that the impression of power helped to ensure a degree of control, but there was an inherent instability to this system. Linked to this, conflict, both insurgencies and conflicts between rulers, could reflect a failure to manage the impression of power adequately.

Chapter Three

Contesting Religion and Power, 1500–1700

Religion as a dynamic, explaining both a willingness to sustain an insurgency and the difficulty of subjugating it, can be seen throughout history. Indeed, religion links the ancient world to the present, for example, Jewish insurgencies in what eventually became modern Israel against Hellenistic and, later, Roman rule to Sunni-Shi'a conflict in the Middle East in the 2010s and on many occasions earlier. Moreover, the rising number today of those who can be seen as religious fundamentalists or at least devout, a factor encouraged by their higher birth rates compared with those of the more secular, suggests that this situation will be even more the case in the future.

The role of religion in insurgencies can also be seen in Europe prior to the Protestant Reformation that began in 1517, a movement that greatly increased the contention already focused on religion. Thus, in 1420–31, the heretical Hussite movement in Bohemia (much of the modern Czech Republic) defeated a series of crusades authorized by the papacy. Despite the frequency of attributing results to providence (a precursor to more recent teleological explanations of inevitability) as well as to religious zeal and the related confidence and determination, neither, however, explains success nor failure. In the case of the Hussites, their victories benefited not only from a sense of conviction but also from the use of handgunners and field fortifications, from a mastery of terrain, notably the use of hills, and from superior command, especially by Jan Žižka, factors seen in victories such as Sudoměř (1420) and Vitkov (1420). It proved possible for Žižka (ca. 1360–1424) to create an effective infantry army, mostly composed of peasants and townsmen, and be able to see off heavy cavalry.

More generally, contemporaries were accustomed to seeing insurgencies staged for their edification and entertainment. The first and most serious for

Christians, and there were parallels in other religions, was the rebellion of the angels in heaven that led to their expulsion to hell. Led by the devil, this insurgency created a defined sphere for evil. In the human world, the equivalent was the sin that led Adam to "the fall," the expulsion from the Garden of Eden. Long depicted, these themes and images were given a new application when they were linked to the Reformation. Thus, religious difference in the present was provided with an existential character as part of the great dramas of divine and human history.

So also with more specific references and stories. Insurgencies were understood in terms of the defiance of norms of order. They were seen in the Bible, for example, Absalom's rebellion against David, and were also very much to the fore in the literature of the period. The most famous English playwright, William Shakespeare (1564–1616), depicted a range of insurrections. These included popular rioting, as with the Roman "mob" in *Coriolanus* (1607–8) and that in England, in the shape of Jack Cade's rising of 1450 in *Henry VI* (1591–92), as well as insurrections led by senior figures, such as the Thane of Fife in *Macbeth* (1606) and the Percies in *Henry IV* (parts 1 and 2, 1597–98), and the psychological grasping for an undeserved mastery, as in *Macbeth*.

The living nightmare inflicted on Macbeth and his wife as a result of their murderous seizure of the throne from Duncan, the rightful king, was an admonitory image of the evil of insurgency, an image that was counterpointed with the virtue depicted as surrounding the opposing force that eventually overcame them. So also with the force of Henry Tudor that overthrew Richard III in 1485 at the battle of Bosworth. The play of *Richard III* (1595–96) captured the moral dilemma of depicting insurrection, as the seizure of power by Henry, who became Henry VII (r. 1485–1509), the first of the Tudor dynasty, had to be justified, which was done by presenting Richard instead as a vile usurper whose removal was necessary in order to right the moral universe wronged by his overthrow and murder of his young nephew, Edward V (r. 1483). That was an approach attractive for a playwright and necessary in the political context. It was also an approach that confirmed religious and social assumptions. Unfortunately, historians, including myself, lack the ability to match the quality of Shakespeare's writing and, if some of the scholarly writing on insurgencies does indeed also offer a moralistic perspective (albeit one different to that of Shakespeare), that perspective maybe also suffers from a grasp of the subject that is less than complete.

The sixteenth and seventeenth centuries are frequently referred to as the age of religious warfare, thus inviting discussion of contrasts within the Western world between this period and that of the age of wars over political ideologies that supposedly began with the American (1775) and French (1789) revolutions. This approach, however, faces many problems, especially the attempt to categorize ideologies in terms of religious warfare and then wars over political ideologies. The application of the approach is also weakened by a tendency to concentrate on Western developments. In this chapter, instead, there will be a focus first on the Islamic world, then on China, and lastly on Christian Europe. This organization will serve to show that insurgencies in which religion played a key role were significant, but so also were those in which it was marginal.

This point is also readily apparent if the broader question of the consequences of insurgencies is considered. For example, the Ikkō-ikki, armies of followers of the Hongan-jī branch of the True Pure Land Buddhism, who fought in Japan in the 1570s to assure their rebirth, were a factor in the warfare of the period but were not crucial in the lengthy and bloody struggle over Japanese unification. So, also, in seventeenth-century Japan, when a rising by Christian converts was suppressed at Shimabara in 1638. This was less important than the success of Ieyasu in establishing the Tokugawa shogunate through civil warfare in 1600 and 1614–15, warfare in which religion did not play a role. The most significant political change in the period, the overthrow of Ming rule in China by Manchu invaders in the 1640s, was not one in which religious strife was the key element.

The organization in this chapter underlines the need to think of war without assuming that Western developments were necessarily the most significant or typical. In practice, a Western paradigm for the history of war and, indeed, for that of state development can be highly misleading. Moreover, such a paradigm may appear increasingly implausible in the future given the relative decline of Europe. As a separate issue, the West may well be detached from Europe in part due to a realignment of American assumptions and interests as well as those of Australia and Canada, in part due to the relative economic decline of Europe, and in part possibly as a result of the impact of demographic and cultural change within Europe, notably large-scale immigration as well as a rise in Muslim political consciousness.

OTTOMAN EMPIRE

Although other elements, notably power political, dynastic, and the struggle of the new against the established, played a role, religion was a key factor in the rivalry between the Shi'a Safavids and the Sunni Ottomans. The Safavids took over Persia (Iran) and Iraq in the 1500s from the Aqquyunlu as a result of campaigns that, in their decisiveness and impact, exceeded any campaigns in Europe during the century. Indeed, the closest was the Ottoman conquest of Hungary, which also entailed the destruction of an entire ruling order and the cultural devastation seen in the systematic ravaging of monuments and manuscripts in churches and libraries, and in Iraq in the destruction of Sunni sites. There was to be no large-scale insurgency against the Safavids or

Ottomans, in part because of this destruction, in the case of the Hungarians the death of the king, Louis II, and of much of the aristocracy at the battle of Mohács in 1526. There was to be an Ottoman-backed attempt by the Aq-quyunlu leader, Sultan Murād, to defeat the Safavids in 1514, but it failed and has not attracted much subsequent attention.

The Ottomans ruled what would subsequently be described as the Turkish Empire, which, in 1500, encompassed modern Turkey and the Balkans and, by 1550, in addition, modern Hungary, Iraq, Syria, Lebanon, Israel, Pales-tine, Egypt, Algeria, and western Saudi Arabia. The serious insurgencies linked to the long-standing Ottoman rivalry with the Safavids are worthy of consideration given the present situation in the region. In contrast, in the case of many of the insurrections that generally attract attention, notably the American Revolution of 1775–83, there are no modern equivalents in the same areas. Support among the peoples of eastern Anatolia (modern eastern Turkey) for the Safavids and for their millenarianism threatened Ottoman control of the region and, therefore, Ottoman security as well as the Ottoman sense of religious identity and purpose. In turn, Ottoman control was brutally enforced. Thus, in 1502, those known to have Safavid sympathies were branded on the face and deported.

A serious insurgency in the region in 1511 was led by Shah Kulu, a Safavid proselytizer. The rebels occupied the city of Antalya, defeating and killing the governor-general of Anatolia (and allegedly roasting his corpse), advanced toward the capital, Constantinople (Istanbul), and defeated and mortally wounded the grand vizier (chief minister), Khadim 'Ali Pasha, near Sivas in July. Contemporaneous with the Italian Wars (1494–1559) in Chris-tian Europe, which attract much scholarly attention, this is a battle that is generally ignored. As Kulu was killed in the battle, while the insurgents took heavy losses, the insurgency was gravely weakened: the institutional imma-turity of the insurgency exacerbated the factor of charismatic collapse. Nevertheless, the insurgency continued. This was a fundamental challenge to Ottoman power, and far more so than recent wars with foreign states, notably Venice, which had been defeated. Indeed, although foreign wars could create a political crisis if unsuccessful, it was dissension within the empire that was most serious for the Ottomans.

Insurgencies, if enjoying success, frequently lead to a crisis of authority, a crisis, whatever the form, that can be central to the eventual political out-come of the insurgency, whether success or failure. Thus, the seriousness of the Shah Kulu insurgency discredited both the sultan, Bayezid II (r. 1481–1512), and his sons Ahmed and Korkud, and provided an opportunity for another son, Selim, to advance into Constantinople in 1512 and to oblige his father to abdicate in his favor. He had his brothers killed, a means of settling the succession and also of lessening both the chances of insurgency and the related prospects of any insurgency acquiring legitimacy.

Then, in order to ensure that the Ottoman claim to defend orthodoxy was clear, Selim I (r. 1512–20) obtained a *fatwa* declaring his opponents heretics. Invading the Safavid dominions, Selim defeated the Safavids at Chaldiran near Tabriz in 1514, a victory that very much helped to strengthen his position. Selim consolidated his position in eastern Anatolia, especially by winning over the Kurdish chiefs who felt themselves distrusted by Isma'il, the Safavid ruler. Thus, Selim's ability to make his support appear more attractive and necessary than that of the Safavids and the success brought by victory were important, in this case, to a key means of establishing control and overcoming insurgencies—namely, success through alliance. Distrusting the Kurds, Isma'il had relied on his loyal Türkmen, who proved an unwelcome alternative to his subjects, thus prefiguring the unpopularity that was to affect Nadir Shah in the mid-1740s as a consequence of his favor for Afghans and Uzbeks. The role of the Kurds between the Ottoman and Safavid Empires anticipated, albeit in a very different context, their role between Turkey, Iraq, and Iran over the past half century, each seeking to control the Kurds and facing, in turn, opposition that was sustained, albeit different in character and intensity.

In the case of insurgencies in Anatolia in 1526–28 against rule by Selim's son, Süleyman I (the Magnificent, r. 1520–66), Safavid supporters again proved a major problem for the Ottomans. The 1527 insurgency was led by Kalenderoghlu, a millenarian dervish, and initially defeated the Ottoman army sent to suppress it. In a parallel to the problems that were to confront Christian rulers, notably Philip II of Spain (r. 1556–98) in the Low Countries (Netherlands) from the late 1560s, the rebellion involved both religious opponents and disaffected landowners. In the case of 1527, this was those landowners who had lost fiefs when the territory of Dhu'l-Kadr was annexed by Süleyman in 1522. This annexation reflected the movement of the frontier of Ottoman control as a result of the conquest of the Mamluk dominions in 1516–17, notably neighboring Syria in 1516. Once Dhu'l-Kadr was not a frontier region, it became less necessary for the Ottomans to accommodate local interests, and particularly on their terms. The political and military equations of any insurgency or counterinsurgency in the region had changed.

In turn, the 1527 insurgency altered the situation. However, in a standard response, one also seen with Philip II of Spain in the southern Netherlands in the 1580s, the landowners in Dhu'l-Kadr were won back, with their fiefs restored, and conflict then focused on the religious opponents. Having lost impetus, they were overcome, unlike in the Low Countries, where, in resisting Philip, the Protestants benefited from the number of towns that had to be taken by the Spanish forces, the impact of the watery environment on operations, and the consequences of Philip's other commitments, notably in France and against England.

In the case of both Dhu'l-Kadr and the Netherlands, division among the insurgents proved a serious weakness that could be worked on to help the counterinsurgent cause, providing it with both means and goal. This process also served the agenda of subsequent political analysis, notably with the sense of betrayal from within and, in particular, the theme of abandonment by the social elite. Thus, the argument that insurgents needed to be reliant on their own efforts and not on those who proved fair-weather friends was frequently repeated and indeed was a seductive one. It was an argument that was readily transferable from nationalist commentators in the nineteenth century to left-wing ones in the twentieth and to fundamentalist ones today and proved a way to link past, present, and future and to demonstrate apparent historical grounding for the analysis. There was clearly much weight to this analysis, but it may be asked how far it is also repeated as a pat account rather than resting on an informed grasp of the complexities of the situation. The theme of betrayal can be an overly glib way to describe the desire to preserve the social framework and/or to find some means of compromise. Moreover, it should not be assumed that the total overthrow of the existing situation was the natural and necessary goal and means of insurgencies and insurgent activity. In addition, those accused of betrayal and compromise were frequently accused because they disagreed with individuals claiming the leadership of change.

In 1517, Selim conquered Egypt, ending Mamluk rule. This conquest brought with it the acquisition of the Mamluk position in the Hijaz (western Arabia), which included the custodianship of the holy places of Mecca and Medina, following on from the recent capture of Jerusalem. Religious identity and purpose was thereby given an important additional strand for the Ottomans, notably the defense of the Sunni order. As caliph, the Ottoman sultan acted as spiritual leader. In 1522, divide and rule was the policy in newly conquered Egypt, where the governor, Mustafa Pasha, defeated a Mamluk insurgency, having bought off its allies among the Arab sheikhs with tax cuts. The rebel heads rolled around Cairo by Mustafa Pasha and the executions that Ibrahim Pasha, the grand vizier, ordered there in 1525 in response to a fresh crisis demonstrated the reliance of Ottoman rule, both in Egypt and more generally, on force and its use in an exemplary fashion. Repeatedly, this has been seen as a means to overawe opposition and to both end insurgency and prevent its renewal.

In the case of the Ottomans, it would be mistaken to put too much of an emphasis on religion as the basis for insurgencies in that it was not the key element in the insurgency against them in Egypt. Moreover, there was another large-scale insurgency in the important region of Anatolia from 1596, in part due to dissatisfied cavalrymen who lacked employment and favor, allegedly because they had not fought well against the Austrians in the battle that year at Mezőkeresztes, although that long battle had ended with Ottoman victory. The initial insurgency was not defeated until 1601, and it revived under a new leader in 1602 who was victorious until bought over by being appointed governor-general of Bosnia. This appointment also won over much of his clientage system, a crucial element in politics, including in the politics of insurgency and counterinsurgency.

Rebellion in Anatolia, however, continued, and in 1605 the leading rebel, Tall Halil, won a major battle at Bolvadin, which provoked the sultan, Ahmed I, to take the field, only for Tall Halil to avoid battle and be bought off with the governor-generalship of Baghdad. This rebellion was not the best basis for the successful pursuit of the war with Austria (1593–1606) by the Ottomans, but buying off rebels in this fashion was another instance of the porosity of allegiance, the role of betrayal, and the nature of compromise. At both the individual and the collective levels, buying off rebels was a key means in counterinsurgency conflict, underlining the political character of the latter. Buying off could, and can, take a variety of forms and faced, and faces, a number of challenges. Ideological commitment on the part of insurgents is a major challenge, but whatever the rhetoric or the reflection of commentators, it is not immune to the calculations of personal and sectional advantage. This situation remains the case as the treatment of insurgencies in Afghanistan and Colombia over the past decade indicate.

Kalenderoghlu Mehmed then became the new insurgent leader. An expedition against him in 1606 failed when the unpaid troops mutinied, and, in 1607, Kalenderoghlu defeated Ottoman forces near Nif and in Ladik, both in Anatolia. However, the customary weakness of rebel forces, their lack of a capability without the artillery and assured supplies, and the professional military and logistical support bound up in these, to mount sieges was shown with the failure to take the town of Ankara or the citadel (as opposed to the less well-defended town) of Bursa. An ability to take the citadel was crucial in order to ensure control of the town. The significance of towns as centers of government, economic activity, and communications, as the site of religious buildings and monuments, and as the location of wealth was such that control over them was regarded as of great practical and symbolic value.

Again, there are modern parallels, as in the importance for ISIS of seizing Mosul in Iraq in 2014, for Syrian insurgents of seeking control over Aleppo and Damascus, and for their Afghan counterparts of attempting to seize control over Kabul, Herat, Kandahar, Kunduz, and the other major cities. Moreover, there are parallels with the need in the current situation to gain possession of advanced weaponry, not least because of the concern to limit the counterinsurgency use of airpower. This matches the earlier drive by insurgents to acquire and use cannon.

Meanwhile, another rebellion against Ottoman rule broke out in Syria when the execution of the governor-general of Aleppo in 1605 led his son, Ali Janbulad, to rebel. The means of government and politics in the Ottoman world involved a high level of violence. In turn, Kuyuju Murad, who became grand vizier in 1606, showed himself a resourceful commander with the key counterinsurgency skills. Albeit facing a less difficult situation than those confronting Spain with the Dutch or Vasilii Shuiskii in Russia, he was able to match the military means of mounting campaigns and defeating rebels with the political skill necessary to divide his opponents. In 1607, Kuyuju Murad won over Kalenderoghlu by appointing him governor of Ankara before mounting a rapid-tempo campaign that led to the crushing of Ali Janbulad's forces, followed by the capture of Aleppo and the execution or submission of most of the rebels. In turn, in 1608, Kuyuju Murad turned against Kalenderoghlu and defeated him near Malataya. Victory and executions in 1609 further weakened the rebels in Anatolia. The rebellion ended in 1611.

These successes indicated the intensely political character of a counterinsurgency warfare in which opponents had to be divided and bought off. Yet the international context and the religious element, which was both international and domestic, also help explain why the Spaniards proved less successful against their Dutch rebels than the Ottomans against theirs in Anatolia. Environmental factors also played a role. The Dutch benefited from the maritime dimensions of their conflict with the Spaniards, whereas the Ottomans could more readily maneuver regarding the Austrians, Persians, and rebels within the empire because of the inland nature of these competitions and conflicts. In Anatolia, the Ottomans benefited greatly from the end of war with Austria in 1606, an end that did not bring humiliation, and from not being at war at this juncture with the Safavids of Persia (Iran), as they had been in 1578–90. Moreover, it was difficult to sustain rebellion in the impoverished Anatolian countryside, which was a recurrent point in the failure of insurgencies. Surplus agricultural production anyway was limited, but the destruction of crops by counterinsurgency forces, including crucially the possibility of seeding the harvest for the following year, crippled the prospect of resistance.

Ottoman history also indicated the continued importance of insurrections from within the elite designed to overthrow the ruler. Thus, weak sultans, Osman (r. 1618–22) and Mustafa (r. 1617–18, 1622–23), were deposed. In these reigns, there were also insurgencies in areas distant from the center of authority, notably eastern Anatolia, Lebanon, and Moldavia. The overthrow and murder of Osman was linked to a rebellion by Caspar Gratiani, the *voyvoda* (subordinate ruler) of Moldavia, who had been deposed by the Ottomans for hostile behavior. This rebellion led in 1620 to war with Poland, and a failed siege of the Polish fortress of Chotin in 1621 resulted in a mutiny in the army.

Regional insurgencies were a common feature of the regional equations of power—namely, its tendency to face challenges in distant areas where there was a tension between an unwillingness to respect the wishes of central government and its local agents and their desire to demonstrate control in frontier regions. Thus, Isma'il, the first Safavid ruler, captured the city of Herat in 1510 after defeating the Uzbeks. When he subsequently tried to introduce Shi'a rites, he faced much opposition, which even executions could not end. Isma'il had earlier used force in Arabistan in southwestern Persia against the Musha'sha, Shi'a sectarians who saw their leader, Sayyid Fayyāz, as the incarnation of God. After he was killed in battle, his brother was established by the Safavids. This was a frequent pattern when trying to bring a semblance of control over border areas, and, as such, a counterinsurgency method, but it was not without problems. For example, farther north, leaders of the Kurdish Mawsillu were made governors of Baghdad only for a rival Mawsillu leader to defeat the Safavid governor in 1526 and to declare his support of the Ottomans. In turn, in the 1620s, Murad IV (r. 1623–40), the Ottoman sultan, faced a major rebellion by the governor of Erzurum, Abhaz Mehmed Pasha, a rebellion made more serious by the conflict with Abbas I of Persia.

CHINA

In China, insurgency ultimately proved far more serious than in Anatolia, and the international context was again a key factor. In the case of China, the distinction, at least in functional terms, between insurgency and foreign war was made more problematic not only because of the complex nature of frontier areas but also due to the extent to which China, like many other states (including the Ottoman empire in, for example, the Tarsus Mountains in southeastern Anatolia), had numerous inner frontiers, to use a modern term. Their character varied, but such frontiers, both in China and elsewhere, often marked the division between sedentary, agrarian societies that were largely under the control of government and regions, often forested, arid or mountainous, where the agriculture was less intensive, population density lower, and the control far less. [1]

In China, these inner frontiers were particularly conspicuous in the case of the many areas occupied by non-Han peoples, those who were not part of the majority ethnic group, the group, moreover, from which the Ming dynasty came. For example, in the 1590s, tensions over Han intrusions and governmental authority interacted with internal rivalries in the Yang clan, which had hereditary overlordship over Bozhou, a mountainous region bordering the three provinces of Sichuan, Guizhou, and Huguang. This situation resulted in conflict with the government, a conflict in which the Miao people eventually supported Yang Yinglong, who was able to deploy about one hundred thousand men. Such numbers are never precise, but they capture the significance and severity of insurgency warfare and also the strain it posed for those areas supporting such an insurgency. This strain was the case whether insurgent forces advanced or whether they remained on the defensive, but more so in the latter case.

As with many insurgencies, for example, also in the Ottoman empire, the course of the conflict with Yang Yinglong reflected a contrast between an empire that needed to balance differing commitments over a wide area and, on the other hand, a local force that lacked such problems but, in this case, was unable to benefit from external support. While difficult conflict with Japanese invaders in Korea took precedence, Ming efforts were limited and, in 1599, the initial Chinese force sent against the Miao was destroyed as the result of an effective feint by Yang. However, in 1600, with Toyotomi Hideyoshi, who had led the invasions, dead and Japan no longer in a state to intervene in Korea, over two hundred thousand troops were deployed against Yang. Most were provincial and tribal forces but, crucially, there were also experienced units from the war in Korea that led each advancing column. Captured Japanese troops took part. In the face of converging columns, the mountains and ravines provided no refuge, Yang committed suicide, and the hereditary overlordship was ended.

It is instructive to consider parallels and contrasts with subsequent insurgencies in China, notably those of the Communists from the late 1920s. Such comparisons were actively discouraged as the Communists wished to present themselves as modern and thus actively contrasted themselves with or ignored what could be regarded as premodern. The value of this contrast, however, can be questioned, not least as the ethnic identity of such tribes can be regarded as a form of protonationalism, a limited, early form of nationalism. The ideological dimension was clearly very different from that of the Communist insurgency of the 1920s–1940s, but it is less obvious what should be drawn from the contrast than appeared the case during much of the discussion at the time of the Cold War.

Ming China succumbed to insurgency within half a century of the success over the Miao. Much of this was due to the Jurchens or Manchu who, organized by Nurhaci (1559–1626), came to dominate the lands north of the Great Wall and to renounce fealty to the Ming in 1616. Repeated and increasingly successful Manchu attacks put acute strain on China, which from 1582 suffered from weak emperors, increasingly arbitrary central government, oppressive taxation, and growing independence or autonomy by ambitious commanders and other figures. Out of this chaos, two regional warlords emerged within China and without any matching improvement in the quality of the emperor. In the early 1640s, Zhang Xianzhong dominated the Yangtze valley and the eastern plain, and from 1644, he established himself in the province of Sichuan. Li Zicheng, a former bandit, was more powerful in the north and benefited from the focus of Ming forces on the Manchu. The insurgencies grew in scale at the same time that the treasury was exhausted by war and there was little money to pay the troops. The "Little Ice Age," which lasted from the thirteenth to the late eighteenth centuries, hit average temperatures and caused serious environmental crises in China and elsewhere, affecting the ability to sustain struggles as well as encouraging a sense of disorder. The court could not cope with so many difficulties simultaneously and veered between devoting resources to suppressing the rebels and then backing off before someone could obtain political capital by succeeding against them. The political paralysis of the factionalized Ming was crucial to Li's success. With its garrison unequal to the task of protecting it, Beijing fell to Li in 1644, the incompetent Chongzhen emperor (r. 1627–44) committing suicide as the city fell.

Li proclaimed the Shun dynasty, but his army was poorly disciplined and he lacked the support of legitimacy, powerful allies, and an administrative apparatus. Wu Sangui, who commanded the largest Chinese army on the northern frontier, refused to submit to Li and, instead, turned to the Manchu. Having jointly defeated Li in the battle of Shanhaiguan that year, they conquered China, greatly helped by the support of other leading Ming generals who were attracted by the Manchu promise of "restoring" dynastic order.[2] China was conquered in the 1640s and 1650s.

In turn, Wu and other former Ming generals launched a major rebellion from 1673. They had been well rewarded by the Manchu, but the Kangxi emperor (r. 1662–1723), the most impressive ruler of the age, was determined to limit their military strength and maintain control and pressed for their retirement. This Rebellion of the Three Feudatories was particularly serious because it arose from within the structure of the Chinese state. In a conflict that spanned much of China, the feudatories overran most of the south and came close to overthrowing the Manchu, leading the emperor to campaign in person. However, as a result of their earlier policies, Wu and his allies could not readily win Ming support, which remained a factor after the fall of the dynasty and, like the Taiping in the nineteenth century, were unable to translate their success in the south into the conquest of the north. Initially successful, the feudatories were driven back to the southwest by 1677 thanks to the use of loyal Chinese forces, Wu died in 1678, and state control was restored in his former provinces by 1681.

The Chinese example indicates the extent to which, despite any label of religious warfare, conventional causes of insurgency continued to be important, notably both regional and political discontent. The failure of the Rebellion of the Three Feudatories prefigured that of the Taiping rebellion in China in the mid-nineteenth century and contrasted with eventual Communist success in the late 1940s. The scale of this rebellion brings into question the tendency to define "premodern" insurgencies in terms of peasant risings or obscurantist religious or dynastic struggles, a tendency that was, and is, part of a social and ideological analysis that instead looks favorably toward the later impact of industrialization and left-wing political consciousness and/or alternatively an anti-imperialist analysis based on opposition to Western colonial control. Such an analysis makes scant sense of the Rebellion of the Three Feudatories other than in terms of a failure of conception, notably a limited consciousness. Indeed, the rebellion did not lead to a radicalization comparable to that seen in England in the 1640s with its civil wars. However, this approach in terms of limited consciousness does not make sense of the political culture of the period. Instead, it says more about the left-wing idea of false consciousness.

INDIA

In India, another classic cause of insurrection, dynastic disputes, in the shape of conflict over the succession, remained crucial, with large-scale warfare accordingly in 1658–59. Aurangzeb (r. 1658–1707), one of the four sons of Shah Jahan, won battles against his brothers repeatedly and thus gained power. In turn, Aurangzeb faced a sustained insurgency that involved religion. This is an insurgency that is much employed in modern Hindu narratives of Indian history, notably the sectarian anti-Muslim ones linked to the powerful Bharatiya Janata Party. In the western Deccan, around Poona, Shivaji Bhonsla (1627–80), leader of the Marathas, a Hindu warrior caste, created a powerful force and, from 1669, repeatedly asserted his independence against the Mughal dynasty, which was Islamic. The Marathas were able to hold their own against Mughal heavy cavalry and field artillery thanks to their own cavalry's superior mobility. The Marathas relied on a tactic of harassing the Mughals, an operational preference for gaining logistical mastery by cutting the supply lines of opponents, and a related strategy of exhausting them by devastating territory rather than risking battle. This interacting range of policies matched those that were to be defined by later writers on insurgency warfare and indicated that no formal theory was necessary. However, Maratha strategy has not affected postindependence (post-1947) Indian military doctrine.

In 1689, Shivaji's heir, Shambhaji, was captured and killed, the capital, Raigarh, was captured, and the Maratha state was annexed by the Mughals. However, resistance continued under Shambhaji's brother, Rajaram. The Mughals repeatedly failed to get to grips with the Maratha fighting system of *bari-giri*: cutting supply links, launching devastating raids, and using hit-and-run tactics. The Mughals responded to the Marathas by fielding larger forces, which both exacerbated the problem of lesser mobility and drove up the already high cost of campaigning. The Marathas did not defeat the Mughals in decisive battle but rather denied the Mughals safe control of territory. This was a frequent feature in insurgency warfare and often a key factor.

Nevertheless, the Maratha advantage of mobility was lost when they defended forts, again a frequent feature of insurrectionary conflict as the insurgents sought to transform themselves into convincing state actors. These forts provided clear targets for the Mughals as well as for their effective siege equipment and their willingness to negotiate, not least to bribe commanders and notably in 1699, when many hill forts fell as a result.

Separately, in India, there were serious insurgencies when areas that were conquered by the Mughals rebelled. Thus, having obtained the submission of the region of Khandesh in 1577, the Mughal ruler, Akbar, faced insurgency there in 1599 and commanded in person to overcome it in 1600–1601. He had earlier done the same with the regions of Gujarat in 1573 and Bihar in 1574. Some areas proved particularly rebellious, notably the borderlands to the northwest, where the Pathans rebelled, for example, in the 1650s and 1660s. These were to be an area of insurgency in the late twentieth and early twenty-first centuries, demonstrating a significant theme, that of the continuance of insurrectionary traditions in some areas. This continuance reflected opportunity, notably in the shape of terrain and cover but also the dynamics of local social structures, cultural traditions and ideological drives, and the difficulties of overcoming these.

The Mughals also had their own counterinsurgency techniques. These reflected not a disinclination to use force but a tendency to see it as part of a wider range of policies in which violence was an aspect of a stance that attracted as well as deterred and sought consent as well as intimidation. Key elements included the sharing of benefits, notably in the form of subsidies and the granting of tax-raising privileges as well as by recruiting troops, which was another way to share benefits as well as lessen discontent. In addition, road building, the construction of forts and military outposts, and the establishment of *thanas*, or permanent police posts, all proved significant. Many of these techniques were also to be seen with later British rule, as in Baluchistan in the southwest of modern Pakistan. Thus, latent military power, which can be defined as military capability, as well as the actual use of force were both aspects of the politics of control.

CHRISTIAN EUROPE

In Christian Europe, religion became a more significant factor in insurrection from the 1520s as a consequence of the Protestant Reformation, which had begun in 1517. The resulting warfare was an element of a more sustained and fundamental religious conflict. Indeed, the maintenance of religious control became a key element of defending order. Thus, catechizing (instructing) the young, religious education, confirmation, confession, preaching, the nature of church services, and the building and decoration of churches were all central to insurgency and counterinsurgency. The practice, sustaining, and inculcation of particular religious activities were crucial to confessional distinctiveness. Other battlefields of religious activity included conversion, publications, censorship, marriage, the household, and poor relief. To use a modern distinction, the conflict was as much about soft power as hard power, an idea that was understood at the time.

It is no accident that the Society of Jesus, or Jesuits, was originally envisaged by Ignatius Loyola, a former solider, in 1534 as a quasimilitary Catholic order,[3] nor that it became very powerful. Iconoclasm, the destruction of religious imagery, played a key role in Protestant action and was important to the process of gaining control, as in the city of Utrecht in 1578. More generally, there was a deliberate assault on religious sites as part of a process of destroying the values of opponents, a process to be seen anew with French Revolutionary, Napoleonic, and Communist forces and in Yugoslavia in the 1990s. Thus, in Viviers in France, the cathedral was plundered by Huguenot (French Protestant) soldiers in 1562, and the roof of the nave was pulled down five years later. The use of military rhetoric was commonplace in the tasks both of defending the church and of pursuing proselytism in the face of adversity. Nor is it surprising that clerics were routinely slaughtered by both sides in the Wars of Religion. The latter sat in a tradition of the violent extirpation of heresy by Christians, a tradition seen, for example, in the crusade against the Albigenses or Cathars in southern France in the early thirteenth century and in the Hussite wars of the early fifteenth. Blood lust was an element, notably concerning victims (the clergy) who could not defend themselves effectively or at all, their helplessness serving to fuel even more the sense of lethal dominance held by the perpetrators.

There was a marked degree of popular engagement in religious violence. Direct popular action could play a prominent role, notably in the form of riots and massacres, for example, the St. Bartholomew Day massacres of Huguenots in France in 1572. Military forces were created by churches and aristocrats able to elicit popular support, as in France, Scotland, and the Low Countries. In 1562 at Vassy, the most prominent Catholic aristocrat in France, Francis, Duke of Guise, with his affinity (armed following), was involved in a dispute with a Huguenot congregation that led to the massacre of the latter. The Huguenots saw this as a sign of war. What the incident indicated was that a prominent aristocrat traveled through France in peacetime with numbers of supporters sufficient to start a conflict. Moreover, there was no effective deterrent against such action.

The massacre led to the first of the French Wars of Religion, a series of which occurred between 1562 and 1598. After what eventually was a series of civil wars there, it became clear that no side in a very divided country could dominate the other. Alongside religious division and political failure in France, there was military collapse. By the late 1580s, the small size of the armies there, about five thousand to seven thousand men on each side, indicated the breakdown of the political and governmental system, which led to a multiplicity of forces pursuing local struggles and to an absence of the institutional framework necessary to consolidate resources behind a large field army. Lack of finance was important to the steady decline in the effectiveness of the royal army, notably its artillery. Moreover, desertion was relatively easy in civil wars and was a regular occurrence as both leaders and men returned to their estates and their homes. The nadir of royal power was in 1589, when Henry III, a Catholic, was assassinated by a Catholic zealot while unsuccessfully besieging Paris, from which he had been driven in town fighting by the more radical urban elements of the Catholic League.

Foreign intervention on behalf of the combatants, particularly by Spain on behalf of the Catholics and by England on that of the rival Huguenots, complicated the situation, as was the case more generally during the Wars of Religion in Christian Europe. Foreign encouragement of domestic disaffection was not restricted to these periods, but it was especially strong then, both because restraints on intervention greatly lessened and because ideological factors subverted senses of dynastic or national loyalty. These were key aspects of what would later be discussed as transnationalism, a phenomenon that did not originate in the modern age. Foreign intervention as well as religion helped ensure that the French Wars of Religion represented a more lengthy as well as profound crisis than the War of the Public Weal in 1465–69, when Louis XI had been faced by rebellious aristocrats. He had used cannon in his successful suppression of opposition, but divisions between the aristocrats also played a major role.

In the event, compromise eventually ended the French Wars of Religion in 1598, with the Edict of Nantes granting the Huguenots privileges including the right to fortify towns, which was a reflection of the power they already wielded. The complexity of these conflicts was indicated by the fact that Henry IV (Henry of Navarre), who had converted to Catholicism in order to gain control of Paris, had to compromise with the Huguenots as well as with the Catholic League, led by the Guise family, and with Spain, which had intervened with great force in the 1590s.

The Dutch Revolt saw the highly unpopular religious and fiscal policies of the ruler, Philip II of Spain, and his neglect of the Dutch nobility lead, in 1566–67, to a breakdown of control. In 1566, the Calvinists seized churches and destroyed their Catholic images, a dramatic demonstration of a shift toward force. Concerned about his duty to the church and about the danger that the crisis, which was actually at the time easing, might benefit Protestantism and French goals, Philip, in turn, sent a large army under a veteran general, Ferdinand, 3rd Duke of Alba, to restore order. Arriving in 1567, Alba imposed unpopular new taxes and treated opponents harshly, which thereby helped justify rebellion, notably from 1572, on the grounds of preserving "ancient liberties." Cities that resisted Alba in the early 1570s were sacked with heavy casualties, including mass executions of the defenders. Two thousand Dutch troops had their throats cut after the surrender of Haarlem in 1573. The slaughter of civilians, for example, cutting the throats of the population of Zutphen, led many troops to surrender. However, Alba's policies were expensive and failed to overawe the Dutch. The value of citizens' militias was shown in the Dutch resistance, as with the successful defense of the town of Leiden against Spanish siege in 1574. Facing bankruptcy, the Spaniards turned to negotiation, although, in the event, religious issues proved insuperable in 1575.

In turn, major divisions between Catholics and Protestants among the rebels and the developing radicalism of the Protestant cities of Brabant, notably Bruges and Ghent, led to a collapse of the revolt's precarious unity, particularly from 1577. The Catholic nobles of the south proved willing to reconcile themselves with Philip and to restore social discipline. Able, partly as a result, to gain control of the dynamic of events as his predecessors had failed to do, Alessandro Farnese, later Duke of Parma, was an effective commander for Philip, capturing a large number of rebel cities from 1579 to 1587, notably Antwerp in 1585 after a long siege that captured the attention of Europe. This was counterinsurgency warfare as large-scale conventional operations. These operations, however, also highlighted the difficulty of translating military into political success. In military terms, the Spanish reliance on garrisons in order to control a distrusted population used up large numbers of troops, as did the sieges required to take Dutch positions. Nevertheless, Parma consolidated the political allegiance of the Walloon nobility in the south by establishing a zone of military control. His steady, remorseless, systematic advance and the prospect that it would continue had the potential to hit the Protestant resistance hard and also affected foreign powers.

At the same time, a state had developed in the north of the Low Countries, one that was capable of creating effective military and financial structures. Initially, military entrepreneurs there raised armies of their own accord in the 1560s and 1570s, but this worried the economically dominant urban oligarchs because they feared that mercenaries would leave them to their fate when their pay was in arrears or, even worse, betray their towns to the Spaniards. To try to ward off this danger, the oligarchs declared that supreme command over the troops lay with the provincial States (parliaments) and the States General, and the right to appoint officers was assigned to the former. Thus, the army served as the military expression of the insurgency, providing it with a coherence and continuity later to be seen with the organized Continental Army in the American Revolution.

In the event, the diversion of Spanish forces into France in the early 1590s in order to resist Henry IV played a key part in helping the Dutch regain the initiative and capture territory. Moreover, the need to support the loyal Cath-

olic population of the northeast of the Netherlands affected Spanish operations as it further ensured a relaxation of the focus on the core area of the
resistance. In turn, peace with France (1598) and England (1604) led Spain to
regain the initiative in the 1600s. However, under great financial pressure,
Philip III (r. 1598–1621) had to accept a twelve-year truce in 1609. The
Dutch Revolt had not been suppressed, and it was not to be when war between Spain and the Dutch resumed in 1621–48.

Philip II's forces had been more successful in suppressing the Moriscos
Revolt in Granada in southern Spain in 1568–70, a revolt that reflected the
attempt to suppress Islamic culture. Large numbers of Moriscos (former
Moors who had nominally converted to Christianity) were slaughtered as the
revolt was brutally repressed. The Moriscos unsuccessfully sought Ottoman
(Turkish) assistance, while the Spaniards benefited from importing large
quantities of firearms from Italy to equip the forces raised by the nobles.
However, continued Spanish concern about the Moriscos as a fifth column
led to the expulsion of the Moriscos from Spain in 1609, a brutal example of
"ethnic cleansing" and one that indicated it was not an invention of the
twentieth century. The Moriscos suffered because Granada was beyond the
effective range of Ottoman power, while being very much exposed to that of
the Spanish state. Indeed, despite a major effort, the Ottomans had failed to
capture Malta in the mid-Mediterranean in 1565. Instead, in 1570, they successfully invaded Venetian-ruled Cyprus, a more vulnerable target in the
eastern Mediterranean. Again, the issue of competing commitments came to
the fore, in this case with regard to possible support for the insurrectionary
cause, the Moriscos. Messianic thought played a role in Morisco rebellious-
ness.[4]

The crucial domestic political dimension in insurgencies was displayed in
the contrast between the Moriscos Revolt, in which there were no significant
political or social links between the opponents, and the situation in Sweden,
where Sigismund III of Poland (r. 1587–1632) was king from 1592 until
deposed in 1599. Like much military history, the conflict in Sweden was a
struggle in which the classic agenda took on a lot of its meaning in terms of a
politics in which violence was often more effective in the forms of conspira-
cies, coups, and rebellions. Thus, the movements of troops in the Swedish
civil war of 1597–98 were less consequential in explaining Sigismund's
failure to maintain his position in Sweden than were dynastic division within
the ruling Vasa family, related aristocratic factionalism, and religious suspi-
cions. In particular, Sigismund's keen support for Catholicism, a support
vital to his position in Poland, helped his uncle, Duke Charles of
Södermanland, to organize the successful opposition to him in Protestant
Sweden.

Many insurgencies lacked such an overt religious dimension, although it
became more significant with the Reformation, not least because this encour-

aged discussion of a right to rebel when a sovereign could be legitimately challenged. The Thirty Years' War initially began in 1618 as a rising against Habsburg (Austrian) authority in Bohemia (in the modern Czech Republic), a rising in which Protestant opposition played a major role. This was an insurgency that brought together Bohemian antipathy to the terms of Habsburg control, Protestant opposition to a Catholic zeal that was becoming more threatening as the Counter-Reformation gathered pace, and the strength of aristocratic politics. Similar factors had led to a Protestant insurgency against the Habsburgs in Transylvania in 1602–6 and were to lead to subsequent insurgencies there. Initially successful, the Bohemian rising was crushed by regular troops at the Battle of White Mountain in 1620, after which the Protestants in Bohemia were harried in a systematic program of Catholicization. This was accompanied by the expropriation of the estates of aristocrats who had rebelled and the creation of a new aristocracy from supporters of Ferdinand II, the victorious Habsburg emperor.

It is appropriate, as well as considering the role of religion in the case of Bohemia, to note the frequency of insurgencies in which social and political, not religious, dimensions were to the fore while allowing that those criteria covered a broad range of circumstances. In some cases, social divisions were clearly to the fore. Thus, in northeast Italy, there was a major peasant insurgency in the region of Friuli in 1511. The city of Udine was sacked and many aristocrats were murdered, but the insurgency was eventually suppressed.

At a larger scale, the German Peasants' War of 1524–25 was a major conflict motivated in large part by social tension and economic discontent encouraged by the volatile atmosphere in Reformation Europe, notably the questioning of authority. In the early stages of this insurgency, which embraced other social strata as well as peasants, the rulers were frequently forced to rely on fortified positions, such as the castles of Salzburg and Würzburg. However, in 1525, the forces of princely power and seigneurial authority restored control, benefiting in a series of battles from military experience and confidence, including the use of cannon and cavalry. The defeated peasants, who were short of weapons and of the necessary experience, were slaughtered in large numbers, a reflection both of the fear they had created and of the lack of restraint in insurgency and counterinsurgency warfare.

This war, which was the subject of a book by Friedrich Engels, the most prominent supporter of Karl Marx, was to be much mentioned by the Communist authorities in East Germany in 1945–89 as they sought to establish an effective pedigree for their analysis and prospectus of continual social revolution. Indeed, the discussion of the past in this fashion was a major aspect of the later politics of insurrections. Major peasant risings in Transylvania in 1596 and 1784, Lower Austria in 1597, and Bohemia in 1775 were also suppressed.

Rebellions in Spain, rebellions that reflected opposition to the beginning of Habsburg rule but without a religious dimension, also failed. The rising of the Comuneros in Castile (1520–21) and of the socially more radical Germanías (brotherhoods) in Valencia (1519–22) and Majorca (1522–23) were suppressed, notably with the victory at Villalar over the Comuneros, whose failure to retain aristocratic support was crucial. At Villalar, their army was largely bereft of the valuable leadership and fighting force of the Castilian nobility, which had been alienated by the growing social radicalism of the movement. Similarly, radical goals alienated elite support from the insurgency in Naples in 1647–48, an insurgency that saw a high level of popular participation and social division.

The control of towns was a military and governmental process within states, one driven by rulers' determination to extend their authority. This was seen most clearly when town walls were breached and when town militias were subordinated to royal garrisons. Insurgencies could encourage this drive, as when ones in Ghent in Belgium were overcome in 1492 and 1540, with the latter followed by the construction by Charles V of a citadel in order to overawe the city. Urban opposition, however, raises the question of how best to define insurgency and insurrection. In particular, the relationship with showing a degree of independence was unclear. Thus, in 1650, when the States (parliament) of the province of Holland sought to save money by reducing the size of the Dutch army after the Peace of Westphalia that ended the Thirty Years' War, William II of Orange imprisoned eight of its members and sent his cousin, William Frederick of Nassau-Dietz, with a ten-thousand-strong army, to seize Amsterdam, the leading city in Holland. The city was warned in time to fortify and bad weather foiled the campaign, but having seen the seriousness of William II, Amsterdam changed policy. The Bicker faction had been dominant in the city, but their opponents manipulated the situation to their advantage, arranging a compromise with William.

War was generally a crucial feature in state development, both encouraging and inhibiting it.[5] However, the relationship between war and state development was most acute in the case of insurgencies and civil warfare. These frequently reflected key issues of political legitimacy and related divisions over the nature of political consent, as in the Russian Time of Troubles, the Thirty Years' War, and the English Civil War of 1642–46. Separatism within composite states was also an issue, notably in the Bishops' Wars in Scotland in 1639–40, the Catalan, Portuguese, Neapolitan, and Sicilian rebellions against Spanish Habsburg rule in the 1640s, and that in Sicily in the 1670s. Repeatedly, the major dimensions of war, first as conflict between armed units and, second, as an attempt to impose a political solution, were brought together. The interaction, however, was difficult and far from fixed, as repeated English attempts to impose and maintain control in Ireland indicated.

In the resulting conflicts there in the sixteenth and seventeenth centuries, religious divisions and aristocratic factionalism interacted.

Insurgencies faced important political and military disadvantages. Political ambiguity about the notion of rebellion ensured that there was often a fatal confusion of purpose. Militarily, untrained amateur rebel forces were rarely a match for professional troops who benefited not only from discipline and training but also from cavalry, firearms, and cannon. This was the case in 1549 in England when Kett's Rebellion (directed against landlord exploitation) was defeated in East Anglia, as was a Catholic revolt in the Southwest against the Protestant changes being introduced by the government. Local uprisings in England were also suppressed in Kent in 1553 and in the Northeast in 1569: the former was directed against a Catholic ruler, Mary, the latter against her Protestant successor, Elizabeth I. Insurgent forces lacked leadership, cohesion, training, and weaponry. More generally, lack of weapons and skill on the battlefield bedeviled insurgent armies everywhere. The insurgencies of England and their failure revealed the differing types of legitimacy at play and also the role of circumstance, notably leadership, in the playing out of the subsequent crises. Thus, the tension between differing concepts or accounts of the succession and of religion came into play.

In Italy, Spanish troops helped suppress a Corsican rebellion against Genoese rule in the 1560s as well as resistance in the region of Casale Monferrato to the Duke of Mantua's attempt to limit tax and judicial exemptions. In Japan, in 1588, Toyotomi Hideyoshi, the dominant figure, demanded the surrender of all weapons held by farmers. He also destroyed the fortifications of defeated rivals. This helped prevent insurgency, a point possibly pertinent to the gun ownership rates of the modern United States, although the context is totally different. In the early-modern period, most insurgencies could not challenge the government effectively if it had firm leadership and enjoyed the support of an important portion of the social elite.

The backing of major landowners was particularly necessary in the case of action against peasant insurgencies, as the peasants often operated across a considerable area. Thus, in 1514, the Crown and the nobility cooperated to suppress a large-scale peasant insurgency in Hungary. The rebel army lost impetus when it focused on the siege of Temesvár, the major city in eastern Hungary, and was then easily defeated by a force led by the *vajda* (prince) of Transylvania, Ferenc Rákóczi. Most of the Spanish army that suppressed the 1591 revolt in Aragon was scarcely professional, instead being recruited by the Castilian nobility from their estates, but it was successful. Moreover, the tension between nobles and peasants could create contradictions within insurgencies. Thus, in Hungary in 1703–11, Rákóczi's willingness to promise freedom to the serfs in arms and their descendants was unacceptable to the lords.

The pressures of war finance exacerbated social and political tensions, encouraging insurgencies, as in France in the 1630s and the Spanish Empire in the 1640s. The financial demands of the French government led to major peasant revolts: by the *croquants* in Gascony in 1636–37 and the *va-nu-pieds* in Normandy in 1639. The *croquants* appeared a particular threat because they had muskets and gunpowder and were led by some local gentry. These insurgencies had to be suppressed by large organized forces. Thus, three thousand troops under the Duke of La Valette defeated the *croquants* at La Sauvetat in 1637, while ten thousand royal troops were deployed against the *va-nu-pieds*, thereby affecting operations against Spain.

The extent to which these insurgencies involved groups other than the peasantry was to be controversial in the twentieth century as Marxist historians charted out what to them was an acceptable pedigree of peasant activism, class consciousness, and social division. In particular, there was dissension as to whether the alignments (and thereby dynamics) in society were primarily horizontal—based on those of similar socioeconomic position—or vertical. The latter, by encompassing people of different positions, was an analysis that was unwelcome to Marxists as it implied that the key elements were very different, notably those of locality and religion rather than the class issues on which the Marxists focused. Marxist historians had to ignore the presence of nonpeasants, such as disgruntled clergy and nobles, in early-modern insurgencies lest that compromise the Marxist theodicy of progressive forces moving ahead in a linear fashion from slavery to feudalism, merchant capitalism, industrial capitalism, socialism, and finally Communism, with no seemingly "progressive" intrusion of "reactionary" social elements permitted whatsoever. In practice, in Russia, serfs were the most prominent category among those involved in the Khlopko rebellion of 1603, the Bolotnikov rebellion of 1604–6, the Vasilii Ils' rebellion of 1669 and its larger sequel, the Stepan Razin uprising of 1670–71, but townsmen and disaffected members of the lower military service caste and of the priesthood were also involved.[6]

As peasant, like urban, risings were local or regional rather than national in scope and directed against the local or regional agents of authority, and especially, agents of the central government rather than seeking the overthrow of the state itself, it was possible for governments to temper their response. However, the prevalent elite emphasis on order and social subordination encouraged a forceful suppression of disorder, one reliant on elite backing for the government. Moreover, in some cases, there was a marked political and/or religious character to the disorder, and this certainly led to a violent response. Thus, Austrian and Bavarian troops were used to suppress the major peasant insurgency in Upper Austria around the city of Linz in 1626. The linkage of this insurgency to Protestantism and during a period of large-scale war within the empire (the Thirty Years' War) helped make it appear particularly threatening.

The ferocity of such risings and/or of their suppression could be very pronounced. In Russia, the increase in governmental pressure on the southern borderlands resulted, in 1670, in a major rebellion in the Volga valley under the leadership of Stepan Razin, a Don Cossack, against the social politics of the tsarist regime. The rebellion was mounted by disaffected Cossacks and peasants, many of whom had run away from conscription, but also involved townsmen, priests, and lower strata of the service nobility. Other nobles were slaughtered alongside officials.[7] The peasant-Cossack army was finally destroyed by regular Russian forces in 1671.

Insurrection in the more central part of Russia had been seen in the 1600s and 1610s. Boris Godunov, tsar from 1598 to 1605, faced serious problems, in part as a consequence of poor weather and rising crop failures from 1601. In 1604, he was challenged by a man, probably a runaway Moscow monk, claiming to be Dmitrii, the younger son of Ivan IV, the Terrible (r. 1533–84), a son who had probably been murdered at Godunov's command in 1591. The False Dmitrii's claims both showed the significance of legitimacy and of dynasticism as its key form (alongside religious orthodoxy) and provided the cover for opposition to Godunov to reject him as a usurper. In 1604, supported by some Polish nobles, the False Dmitrii invaded Russia and raised support among the Cossacks. He was defeated at Dobrynichi in January 1605, a serious defeat followed by the mass execution of prisoners. However, this battle did not mean the end of the conflict, because it did not lead the False Dmitrii and his supporters to surrender.

Instead, the rebellion continued. Godunov died in April 1605, and his weak young son, Fedor II, deserted by many of the nobles, was overthrown and murdered in Moscow in a riot that June. The False Dmitrii was then proclaimed tsar, but his Polish connections, who were Catholic (the Russians were Orthodox) as well as foreign, helped make him unpopular. He was overthrown and killed in May 1606 by a mob as part of a conspiracy organized by Prince Vasilii Shuiskii, who was proclaimed tsar. However, like Li Zicheng in China in 1644, Shuiskii lacked support and legitimacy; the serious social crisis and linked rebellion continued. Rebel forces were headed by Ivan Bolotnikov, who claimed to be acting for Dmitrii (although he could no longer produce him), and by the False Peter, another claimant to the throne. In 1607, a second False Dmitrii invaded, again with Polish support. The war became a matter of trying to win the support of the service nobility, of raids designed to hit opponents' supplies and thus force them to retreat, and of a quest for foreign intervention: Polish for the False Dmitrii and Swedish for Shuiskii. Poland and Sweden were bitter rivals, both political and religious, and thus the war within Russia became part of a wider struggle, with Sweden agreeing in 1609 to provide Shuiskii with mercenaries in return for the abandonment of claims to the Swedish-ruled province of Livonia. This entailed opposition to Poland's interest in the province. This pattern of intervention was very common with insurgencies that had elite leadership, for example, the Patriots in the American Revolution.

In the event, the Swedish mercenaries, their pay in arrears, switched sides at the Battle of Klushino in 1610, and this threw open the road to Moscow for the Poles. Shuiskii was overthrown in July in a conspiracy involving noble leadership and mob action. Polish troops entered Moscow that September, and the nobles there swore allegiance to the son of the Polish king, while the second False Dmitrii was murdered in December. However, hostility to the prospect of Polish control and to Catholicism led to rising opposition and in 1613 to a new tsar, Mikhail Romanov (r. 1613–45), the great-nephew of Ivan IV, gaining power and restoring order with the backing of the landowning class. This element was crucial. In contrast, the false claimants, like their counterparts in England under Henry VII (r. 1485–1509), failed because of their lack of legitimacy, which compromised popular and military backing.[8]

Peasant insurgencies could frequently be directed against invading and occupying forces. The harsh exaction of supplies by these forces, combined sometimes with scorched-earth policies, led to a reaction. For example, the Japanese invaders of Korea in 1592–99 were hindered by guerrilla opposition. The Swedes who overran Courland (modern western Latvia) in 1658 met serious guerrilla warfare, with peasant units mounting a number of counterattacks, one of which, in 1659, temporarily overran the western suburbs of Riga, the major city in Latvia.[9] Earlier, the peasants of the Sundgau region in Germany had risen against occupying Swedish forces in 1633. Although the scale varied, regular troops were harassed by guerrillas in Piedmont, Dauphiné, and Spain in the 1690s. In turn, in 1690, peasant retaliation against French executions in Piedmont led to a systematic sacking of the area by the occupying forces.[10]

The contrast between the overcoming of insurgent peasant forces, as in Brittany in 1675, and the greater success of new armies created in civil wars by the opponents of the sovereign (Netherlands from the 1570s, Scotland and England in the mid-seventeenth century) suggests the value of fighting like a regular force, a point that was to be reinforced by the American Revolution of 1775–83. That value was a matter of fighting techniques but also of experience, leadership, and unit cohesion, in part because of the new requirements for drill and synchronization created by the combination of pike and shot in the sixteenth and seventeenth centuries. In a gunpowder environment, the only successful method was synchronized drill because muskets were ineffective in battle when not used en masse, and that usage required training and drill. This made it more difficult for untrained popular forces to succeed. Moreover, cavalry remained very important, and insurgent forces tended to lack cavalry as well as artillery.

The insurgency that led to the English Civil War (1642–46) very much indicated the diversity of insurgencies and the variety of factors that led to success. The crisis initially began with another insurgency, one in Scotland, where religious factors were to the fore, in the shape of Presbyterian opposition to the attempt to impose a strong episcopal structure and welcome a revival of older ritual. This insurgency resulted in the total overthrow of the power and authority of Charles I (r. 1625–49), who was also king of England. He responded by turning to the force offered by his larger realm, England, but a range of factors ensured failure, not least the degree to which the Scottish rebels were, as a result of their success, in charge, in effect, of a state. Charles made a poor choice of commanders, while inadequate finance wrecked his logistics. The English army was badly prepared and deployed, and it collapsed when attacked in 1640 by the large and professionally officered Scottish army, much of which had gained experience in Dutch and Swedish service, notably in the Thirty Years' War.

Charles's failure against the Scots led him to turn for support in England to Parliament. There, "insurgency" took a different form initially, as opponents in Parliament chipped away at royal powers in 1640–41, in an atmosphere of mounting crisis. As so often in insurgency situations, control over the army proved the key element, and in this case the issue was brought forward by the problems of imperial control. The need to raise an army to deal with a major and successful Catholic rising in Ireland in November 1641 polarized the situation, already tense over church government, around the issue of army control. Charles, who faced problems arising from the self-interest of every side involved and his inability to negotiate, responded with a failed counterinsurgency attempt, one launched with insufficient preparation. On January 4, 1642, Charles tried to seize six senior hostile Parliamentarians, but he mishandled the attempt, and the six fled to the City of London. The local geography of insurrection and legitimacy proved crucial. Then, the members of the House of Commons left Parliament, which was located in Westminster (which was very close to the royal court) for the more distant City of London, sitting there in the Guildhall. Governments operating from national capitals, such as London, Madrid, Paris, and Moscow, were repeatedly to prove highly effective.

Meanwhile, the City of London's Common Council, on which Puritans (radical Protestants) had strengthened their position in elections in December 1641, elected a Committee of Safety charged with defending the City and bypassing the Court of Aldermen, among whom Charles still had supporters. There was no chance of Charles seizing his opponents in the City and when, on January 5, he appeared at the Guildhall to ask the corporation for help in bringing his six opponents to trial, he found scant support. As he left, the crowd made its hostility clear while Sir Richard Gurney, the lord mayor, was assaulted. Rumors that evening of a Royalist attack, which did not in fact come, led, despite Gurney's opposition, to the mobilization of the trained bands and much of the population in defense of the City. As so often, rumor played a major role.

The revolutionary atmosphere in London very much affected the general political and military situation. Charles left London on January 10, 1642, in order to raise funds and out of fear for his safety and, especially, that of his wife in the face of ugly and threatening demonstrations in Whitehall near the palace. Charles's departure, however, gravely weakened the Royalists in London. The Committee of Safety took over control of the trained bands from the Royalist lord mayor, and in March 1642, the Common Council established its ability to make decisions without the support of the aldermen and the lord mayor; the latter was imprisoned and replaced.[11]

In the eventual war, the insurgent side, that of Parliament, benefited from the support of the capital, the wealthiest parts of the country, the major ports, and the navy. Although this support did not make the result of the war inevitable, it helped finance and sustain the war effort. As with many insurrections, foreign intervention played a key role. In this case, the Scots entered northern England on the side of Parliament in 1644. Both were united by opposition to Charles and suspicion of his religious leanings, and their forces defeated the Royalists at Marston Moor near York on July 2, 1644, leading to the Royalist loss of the north of England. Charles obtained troops from Ireland, but the continental monarchies were unable to help, being busy fighting each other in the Thirty Years' War.

Aside from resources, ideology, and the international context, the social practice and institutional form of the respective forces were important, again a factor seen in some other major insurrections, notably the French and Russian Revolutions. The Royalists essentially relied on traditional notions of honor, obligation, and loyalty to raise troops. Charles headed the social hierarchy, and his armies reflected this. Royalists were concerned mostly to defend the established order in church, state, and society: the peers and gentry thought their position bound up with that of the king. Leadership for the Royalists was, in large part, a function of social position, although an increasing number of Royalist officers came from outside the social elite. Prominent landowners, such as Henry, 5th Earl of Worcester, a Catholic, provided Charles with much support. In turn, aristocrats, such as Robert, 3rd Earl of Essex; Edward, 2nd Earl of Manchester; and the 2nd Lord Fairfax, played a major role in the Parliamentarian leadership in the early stages but far less subsequently. The contrast between Oliver Cromwell and the Royalist cavalry commander, Prince Rupert, was one of different attitudes toward responsibility, position, quality, merit, and, it has been claimed, technological innovations.[12]

In the New Model Army, which became the war-winning Parliamentarian force, promotion was by merit, and Cromwell, initially the commander of its cavalry, favored officers and men imbued with religious fervor equal to his own. The New Model's equipment and tactics were essentially similar to those of its opponents, but it was supported by a more effective infrastructure and supply system, was better disciplined, and had a distinctive interaction of command style and ideological commitment. In this respect, the New Model prefigured the Continental Army of the American War of Independence, the Republican Army of the French Revolution, and the Red Army in the Russian Civil War. In each case, the army served as the expression of the political thrust of the revolution as well as providing its force. [13]

Yet other factors also played a role, not least the part of chance in battle, while it is seriously mistaken to assume that the principles of good military leadership were incompatible with aristocratic culture. As far as the New Model was concerned, its combat experience and resource base were important in securing success. Moreover, the war was not only a matter of battles but also a series of local struggles. This is more generally true of protracted insurrectionary conflicts and was the case whether it is the early modern period or more recent centuries that is under consideration. About half the soldiers killed in the English Civil War died in small-scale engagements. The role of local garrisons and their search for supplies was crucial to the struggle in the regions. For example, the failure of the Royalists to capture Lyme Regis in 1644, although a small-scale siege of no great significance in itself, undermined the Royalist position in the West Country. Nevertheless, the fate of local struggles could be influenced and, at times, determined, indeed increasingly so, by the campaigns of the main field armies.

The English Civil War (1642–46) was to be placed in a trajectory that included later revolutions and notably by twentieth-century Marxist scholars of the period, most prominently Christopher Hill. This served their purpose of locating their subject and asserting the significance of their work. The presentation they offered is interesting as the Marxists downplayed the part and notably the autonomous role of religion as a divisive force and an activating ideology and instead emphasized the part of socioeconomic considerations. This was not a unique position. For example, in discussing the American Revolution of 1775–83, there was a tendency among liberal commentators to downplay the role of religious considerations. Readers will have their own views of the motivation involved, and it is fair to point out that scholarship remains divided on these points. It is pertinent, moreover, at this juncture to highlight the danger of running insurgencies together and of reading from one to another. In particular, however, downplaying religious considerations is repeatedly questionable. In both the English Civil War and the American Revolution, there was also a tendency to minimize the extent to which leadership owed much to members of the social elite, which greatly qualified the democratic potential of the movements.

Such leadership also played a major role in other insurgencies in the mid-seventeenth century. Unlike in the British Isles, religion played little role in most of the insurgencies. Instead, these crises reflected the general atmosphere of strain derived from the demographic and economic crises of the period, which included falling agricultural production, famine, and disease. Other significant factors included regional particularism, especially in the Spanish monarchy, the burdens arising from the war, and unease over the political complexion of regimes, notably the Mazarin ministry in France. Domestic tensions channeled and exacerbated the role of war in creating policy disputes and financial pressures that both weakened crown-elite ties and challenged stages of the British rebellions; the particularist rebellions in Catalonia and Portugal in 1640 were essentially reactive calls that responded to governmental actions or problems. In the Spanish Empire, the financial burdens of war with France and the Dutch interacted with strong regional antipathy to rule from Madrid and to its attempts to share the cost of the conflict, although there was no rising in the Milanese (Lombardy). In France, the crisis led to civil war in 1648–52, the Fronde, which owed its origin to urban and aristocratic insurgencies as well as to attempts at constitutional change.

In sixteenth- and seventeenth-century Europe, there was a significant political dimension to insurgencies as religious difference might focus and accentuate domestic disaffection, which was an important issue that rulers had to consider when recruiting and employing troops. Indeed, the possibility of disaffection affected attitudes to the development of armed forces and to force structure. An emphasis on fortified positions away from external frontiers was one major consequence of concern about disaffection. The period of the Wars of Religion challenged reliance on national levies where there were important heterodox religious movements, as in the (Austrian) Habsburg hereditary lands, and instead encouraged a use of units, sometimes mercenaries and/or foreign units. Reliability was a key factor in fostering this use.

Changes in the political context worked against insurgencies in the second half of the seventeenth century. A reconciliation of rulers and elites after the civil wars of midcentury provided the basis for a process of domestic consolidation, creating what is sometimes termed the *ancien régime*. In Britain, after Oliver Cromwell's death in 1657, the army was unable to unite in order to resist a return to Stuart rule, in the person of Charles II (r. 1660–85) in 1660, albeit a return that itself greatly depended on the initiative of part of the army.[14]

The end of the Thirty Years' War (1618–48) and the Franco-Spanish conflict of 1635–59 was also significant as each had been associated with powers supporting insurgencies against their opponents. Thus, France had backed rebellions in Catalonia, Portugal, and southern Italy. The same pattern could be seen at a more minor level. For example, the international context was crucial when Ferdinand of Bavaria, Prince-Bishop of Liège (r. 1612–50), clashed with the city of Liège (in modern Belgium) over his attempt to control it. This struggle over urban independence was a long-standing form of struggle and one that had led to a series of insurgencies across the Middle Ages. During the Thirty Years' War, Ferdinand turned to Austria and Spain for military assistance against the city, only for their opponents, France and the Dutch, to provide counterpressure. It was not until 1649 that Ferdinand was able to deploy about three thousand troops in order to enforce his will. The Dutch had negotiated peace with Spain the previous year, France was convulsed by the Fronde, and the Wittelsbachs, the ruling house of Bavaria, now enjoyed peace in the empire. Control of Liège was more widely significant because of its role as a bridging point over the River Meuse.

Many mid-seventeenth-century insurgencies focused on the control of cities, including Amsterdam, Barcelona, Beijing, Constantinople, Lisbon, London, Moscow, Naples, and Paris. The concentration of people posed issues, not least of food supply and control, but so did traditions of urban independence and the case of advancing new ideas in these contexts. However, this control was not central to the large-scale Ukrainian revolt of 1648–54 by Cossacks against Polish rule.

More generally in the late seventeenth century, military service entailed the nobility accepting obedience and subordination, while the monarchy was able to co-opt the resources of the aristocracy to support the army and the state. Linked to this, there was a decline in the number of rebellions in Europe, including peasant insurgencies, after 1680. The reduced fear of insurgency after the mid-seventeenth century encouraged a reliance on indigenous troops, whether raised by limited conscription or as volunteers, although this was far less the case where governmental control was limited. In addition, the limited regard of soldiers for civilians in general, and peasants in particular, made it easier to resort to force. French troops suppressed revolts in the Boulogne region in 1662, the Vivarais in 1670, and Bordeaux and Brittany in 1675 more effectively than the forces used against the *cro-quants* in 1636 and the *va-nu-pieds* in 1639. The potentially harsh treatment of civilians has always been a key aspect of counterinsurgency culture and practice.

In 1685, in England, the Catholic James II succeeded his brother Charles II only to be rapidly challenged in a rebellion by Charles's charismatic (and Protestant) bastard, James, Duke of Monmouth, who claimed to be his legitimate son. Thus, religion and dynastic factors were linked in the challenge to James. Landing in western England, Monmouth readily recruited support. However, on July 6, he was defeated when he attempted a night attack on the recently advanced royal army on Sedgemoor: the last significant battle on English soil. The advantage of surprise was lost, and the poorly organized rebel army was defeated by its experienced opponents' superior firepower. In contrast, the militia had earlier been unsuccessful against Monmouth, which demonstrated the greater effectiveness of professional troops.

As a result, dissension and conspiracy among the officers was very important in explaining why James's army collapsed in 1688 in the face of foreign invasion (by William III of Orange) and linked rebellion. The latter, the Glorious Revolution, was an insurrection of a type that was to be contrasted a century later with the French Revolution. In 1688, a major role was taken by disaffected English aristocrats, who invited William of Orange to invade England. That he was the nephew and son-in-law of James II ensured that there was a dynastic dimension to the crisis as well as a possible dynastic outcome in the succession of William and his wife, Mary II. This is a dimension to insurgencies that tends not to receive sufficient attention. There was also a popular dimension to the insurgency, and that helped ensure the grounding of the eventual invasion and coup without the need to face a civil war (or counterinsurgency) comparable to those in Ireland and Scotland. For John Locke, the leading Whig theorist of the period, it is the errant sovereign who puts himself in a state of rebellion against the people; the people then have a right to resist.

The role of foreign intervention was readily seen in the contrast between the 1685 and 1688 invasions. No foreign power came to the support of Monmouth. In contrast, William III played a crucial role in 1688. His principal international opponent, Louis XIV, was thereby encouraged to back James, notably by sending a large force to Ireland and by challenging the Anglo-Dutch position in the Channel in 1690 and, even more, 1692, when an invasion attempt fell victim to the defeat of the French fleet at Barfleur. Later French invasion attempts on behalf of the Jacobites also failed in 1696, 1708, 1744, and 1759. These occasions underline the problematic definitional relationship between insurrections and interventions, as did the Jacobite rising of 1745–46 and the major French invasion preparations to which it gave rise but which were thwarted by the British navy. Again, this is far from the usual way in which insurgencies are considered, but, as suggested throughout this book, there is room for a wider definition. The Jacobite cause and its French support involved Catholic activism, but that was far from the sole issue at stake.

CONCLUSIONS

Religion was a significant cause and focus of political drives, including insurgencies and their suppression. Ambitions related to confessional success encouraged bold plans, including mass risings by coreligionists, for example, Shi'a in Anatolia and Christians in the Balkans.[15] An emphasis on religion as a factor causing and activating insurgencies and counterinsurgency and, in particular, removing the possibility of compromise does not mean that other drives and factors did not play a major role. In particular, economic strains, in part due to climate cooling, were highly significant,[16] especially in affecting the food supply. Political, economic, and/or regional discontent was frequently, although far from invariably, a primary reason for conflict and with religion in part used as a means to an end, notably in order to galvanize support and to demonize the enemy. A desire for power and dominion was crucial. The continued use of mercenaries, even of a different religious belief, was instructive as they could switch sides according to pay or its lack (as at Klushino) and thus change outcomes. Their use underlined the role of the pursuit of power rather than a focus on attempts to destroy heresy and also contributed to the fiscal and economic strains of war. The interaction of these factors contributed to causing crisis and thus encouraging insurgency, but it did not ensure any particular outcome.

The range of insurgencies emerges clearly from any consideration of the situation in this period. From large-scale banditry[17] to rebellions at the center, from political drives to religious division, insurgencies and the response to them captured the very variety and dynamics of history in this period. For example, the fiscal dimension played a role. The problem of arrears that was rife in military pay helped lead to uprisings, for example, by the Ottoman janissaries. This remained a factor. Thus, in 1759, during a panic about a potential French invasion, Sir Richard Bampfylde, MP, a militia officer, reported from Plymouth: "The uncertainty of our pay since we arrived at this place, has been the occasion of those disorders amongst the private men [ordinary troops]. . . . I am under great apprehensions of a future insurrection on that account."[18] Linked to the problem of arrears, the immaturity of banking systems was a major problem for governments in financing warfare. A different dynamic is suggested by the role of witchcraft trials as a response to a sense of crisis.[19] Most insurgencies did not generate theoretical works, but theory may be inferred from pamphleteering, other polemical devices, instructions, memoirs, and contemporaries' observations of leading insurgents.

The range and variety of the phenomenon underlines the folly of assuming that there is any clear trajectory of development however described or explained. That remained the case in the centuries to come.

Chapter Four

Entering the Modern?
The Eighteenth Century

From the perspective both of accounts of modernity and, more specifically, of insurgencies, this century is dominated by the American (1775–83) and French (1789–99) Revolutions. These, indeed, can be treated in terms of insurgency and counterinsurgency warfare, although that is less convincing for the French Revolution. These revolutions also benefit from being set in the comparative context of insurgency elsewhere in the world during the century. In this perspective, some insurgencies have been fitted into narratives of modernity, notably that of serfs in Russia in the 1770s (as earlier in rebellions in the seventeenth century) and that of the slaves and free blacks in the French colony of Saint-Domingue (Haiti) in the 1790s, but others do not readily conform to this analysis, for example, insurgencies in Scotland, China, and Peru. Indeed, this chapter demonstrates the mistake of beginning an account of eighteenth-century insurrections with the American Revolution.

In large part because military technologies and tactics did not change, there were no real developments in the nature of fighting, either in favor of or against insurgency, during the century. Instead, the key element affecting the course and prospects of insurgency remained that of international rivalry and, thus, the prospect of foreign intervention. These factors varied greatly. For example, they did not affect China and Japan in this period, with the major exception of China in Mongolia and Tibet. China was challenged in the first half of the century by the expansion of the Zunghars of Xinjiang, notably into Tibet in 1717.

The information and scholarship available on insurgencies in the eighteenth century concentrates on Western states, accentuating the tendency to focus military history on them. Moreover, the work on other states is frequently in area studies literature rather than in military history, let alone global military history. This, however, can lead to a neglect of the number, range, and character of insurgencies at the global scale and notably in East Asia and the Islamic world.

JAPAN

Japan offers a good example as it is not generally seen in terms of insurgencies for this period, although there was a significant earlier tradition of elite rebellions as well as of resistance in what to the Japanese state and elite were marginal areas, such as the mountains of central Honshu and among the indigenous Ainu people on Hokkaido.[1] However, in the eighteenth century, a rapidly rising population in Japan put considerable pressure on limited resources of food and land. This pressure led to an increase in social tension and in peasant risings. By the 1980s, 724 had been recorded by scholars for 1716–50, with a further increase in, and from, the 1750s, so that there were more than fifty annually on average in the 1780s. Moreover, their scale and the level of violence shown increased, while, with a degree of social radicalism, the focus shifted from village communities pressing their feudal overlords to cut taxes or provide more rice to attacks on the more prosperous members of the village communities. These uprisings also spread to the towns, with violent riots in Edo (Tokyo), Osaka, and other major cities in 1787. In 1788, there were 117 separate revolts.

In response, the Japanese government relied on the forces of the *daimyos* (regional lords). This was a local form of counterinsurgency to match that of the insurgencies, each of which reflected the decentralized nature of the country. In 1738, large protests near the silver mines at Ikuno were suppressed only as a result of action by troops from thirteen *daimyos'* domains, while, in 1769, all *daimyos* were instructed to stamp out protests irrespective of the merits of the grievances. The long-standing concentration of weaponry helped the *daimyos*, as the number and type of guns and ammunition held by peasants were regulated and registered.[2] In what was a frequent pattern, the peasants might not have seen themselves as opposed to the state, but its control had certainly been challenged. Moreover, the challenge to the established order was highly unwelcome.

CHINA

The situation was more complex in the case of empires, as resistance then could be regarded both as opposition on the part of lower-level polities to imperial incorporation and as insurgencies against governmental policies or control. This control was religious, ethnic, and political, with these concepts overlapping far more than they could be separated. This process can be seen in Tibet. Once established there as conquerors, finally as a result of conquest in 1720, the Manchu dynasty faced a number of insurgencies in Tibet, notably in 1727 and 1747–50. In dealing with them, contrasting policies were followed, particularly whether to rely on local authorities or to use Manchu agents. The degree of reliance on force also varied. The insurgency in 1727 led to a civil war in which the pro-Chinese faction, crucially supported in 1728 by Chinese forces advancing from three directions, triumphed. At the end of 1728, the Dalai Lama was made to leave Lhasa in order to stop his presence in the capital from being a motive for rebellions. The Chinese chose to rely on the Panchen Lama and on Pholhane, a noble they referred to as prince of Tibet.[3] In mid-century, however, having sent an army that suppressed an insurgency that had led to the death of the local agents of Chinese control, the Qianlong emperor (r. 1736–96) left Tibet with an autonomous government under the Dalai Lama, although with a reinforced Chinese garrison. This compromise proved reasonably stable.

The Chinese also faced insurgency in Xinjiang once they had conquered it in 1755. Amursana, a Khoit prince, who had lost out in the contest for power within Xinjiang and, as a result, had helped the Chinese in this conquest, rebelled later in 1755 as he felt that the new arrangements left him little scope. Pan-ti, the Manchu marshal who had commanded the invasion, was surrounded by Amursana's forces and committed suicide. In 1756, moreover, some of the Khalka Mongols launched a supporting rebellion. In 1757, however, the advance of Chinese forces transformed the situation, as did devastating smallpox among the Zunghars, many of whom were slaughtered by the Chinese, while subordinate tribes switched to the invaders. This switch reflected the fissiparous structure of the Zunghar confederation, a factor that frequently helped the imposition of control. As a reminder of long-term trends in opposition, the region is currently one with a resistance movement to Chinese control.

The contesting of control was also seen in China's southwest, where the vast area covered by the provinces of Sichuan, Yunnan, Guizhou, and Gaungxi posed serious problems for the government as these provinces were regarded as especially prone to disorder. In particular, the struggle to suppress the Tibetan minority of western Sichuan, who were known as the Gyalrong or Golden Stream tribes and who have also been called Jinchuan, was long lasting. The First Jinchuan War broke out in 1747 as the emperor sought to bring an essentially autonomous people under administrative control, a long-standing practice. Religious animosity played a role, as the Golden Stream followed the indigenous, animist, Tibetan Bon religion and Tibetan Buddhism's Red Hat sect, resisting the Yellow Hat sect, which the emperor supported. In part, the conflict involved a struggle between different types of prestige, magic, and providential support, a struggle which helped make conflict more intractable and also locates it in terms of persistent themes. Yellow Hat lamas were used to resist the Jinchuan employment of curse charms, "demon traps," and rain spells. The weather was a key area for action and conflict, one in which earthly and heavenly magic interacted.[4]

Success in the remote, difficult, mountainous terrain of Sichuan, where the Golden Stream had strong, well-sited, stone fortresses, proved limited for the Chinese. It was costly and time consuming to take the towers, but bypassing them led to a vulnerability to attacks on Chinese supply lines, a pattern already seen in India with Mughal attacks on the Marathas. In 1747, Andreas Ly, a Chinese Catholic priest in Sichuan, noted the report that the war was "being fought with tremendous difficulty because of the mountainous terrain of that region," while on February 2, 1748, he wrote:

> I heard of a terrible massacre of many in the Chinese army sent against the barbarians, in which very many officers and men were killed by the barbarians. While the campaign lasted, some were cut to pieces by the barbarians, or maimed by cold and hunger; others dashed themselves to pieces off the cliffs, unable to bear the onslaught of the enemy; a great many officers of the ravaged army hanged themselves because of the destruction of the army. Troops have been summoned from various provinces and new soldiers enrolled that they might take the place of the dead; the Chinese people openly groan over the increased burden.[5]

His record is unusual and underlines the difficulty of finding sources for many risings outside Europe.

The Andreas Ly quotation reflects the degree to which insurgents, when fighting in mountains, had a force multiplier working in their favor due to the nature of the terrain. It was easy for insurgents to create straight-line or semicircular fortified redoubts at higher elevations and easy for them, therefore, to control the commanding heights, funnel their fire downward, and turn the pathways of the counterinsurgents into shot-traps. Conversely, it was difficult for the counterinsurgents to move up as gravity and limited pathway access and breadth handicapped them, difficult for the counterinsurgents to fight back as they were exposed to enemy fire, and difficult for them to shoot upward as they would be lifting their sights into the sky and thereby often be handicapped, if not blinded, by the sun.

The failure of the first major campaign in the First Jinchuan War, the expensive one of 1748, resulted in the disgrace of Necin, the chief grand councillor since 1737. He was put on trial and sentenced to death. Necin's replacement, Fuheng, was ordered to bring the costly war to a close. Over two hundred thousand troops were deployed, a figure larger than that in comparable struggles in the century, and over seven million taels of silver were spent, mostly on hiring laborers to transport supplies. This was a constant issue in China, notably with the need to move supplies, particularly food, from resource-rich eastern China to poorer areas in the West. Alongside this strategic dimension to war, whether "foreign" or counterinsurgent in character, there were important operational and tactical dimensions to the movement of supplies. The political sphere was also significant in ending the war. Yue Zhongqi, a general with local knowledge, was able to persuade the Golden Stream leader, a former subordinate, to settle the conflict, which ended inconclusively in 1749. At this stage, China had no foreign foes, which permitted a focus on this opponent. Relations with the Zunghars did not deteriorate anew until the 1750s, and with Myanmar (Burma) until the 1760s.

Serious disputes between the local chieftains in western Sichuan, however, continued, and they interacted with issues relating to the form and character of Chinese authority. This was a frequent element across the world in turning local political divisions into what were, as far as the neighboring major powers claiming overlordship were concerned, insurgencies. Kurdistan and the Caucasus provided examples of this process. In the case of western Sichuan, the crisis led to the outbreak of the Second Jinchuan War in 1770. Demonstrating the relationship between confronting insurgencies and facing foreign foes, this war led to the abandonment of preparations for a new war with Myanmar in an effort to compensate for the earlier serious failure of Chinese operations there.

As in the First Jurchen War, the Chinese were hindered by the numerous stone towers of their opponents, which were now strengthened against Chinese cannon by the use of logs and packed earth. The use of earth was a common defense against the effects of artillery, from round shot to explosive shells, almost from the beginning of the gun, and remains so today because earth absorbs energy. The logs helped stabilize the structure, while wood is a composite material also capable of dissipating energy. Capturing the towers took major efforts, and the Chinese armies found themselves bogged down, while their supply lines were threatened. In 1773, Wenfu, the grand secretary as well as a general, was defeated and killed in a surprise attack at Muguomu. From late 1774, the situation changed as over two hundred thousand Chinese troops, drawing on an effective military infrastructure, were committed, while natives were also used by the Chinese government. Meanwhile, Chinese operational and tactical effectiveness improved with a switch to mobile columns, permitting the harassing of opposing supply lines. In addition, there was a methodical attack on the towers that benefited from improved cannon. Mobility and systematic effort were repeatedly to emerge as crucial when success in warfare was concerned.

Lasting until 1776, the difficult and expensive war led to the subjugation of the area, with the Chinese proving more effective than the British in North America. As increasing numbers of Jinchuan commanders surrendered, so opposition fractured. The opportunity was also taken to enforce the authority of Yellow Hat Buddhism at the expense of the traditional Bon belief. Moreover, supplementing the effective system of relay stations for troops, military colonies staffed with Chinese troops were established in order to consolidate control. However, the sixty-two million taels of silver spent on the war caused the emperor considerable concern.[6] Alongside the example of the British and the American War of Independence, this sum showed the cost of major counterinsurgency struggles, one that required the resources and organization of an empire to sustain.

As earlier in the seventeenth century, the Chinese army repeatedly acted in counterinsurgency warfare, both in borderlands and against risings in the interior. There was an overlap in the style of combat but also differences, as the conflict on the borderlands more commonly involved warfare with cavalry forces, which was not the case with most risings in the interior. These risings were both by Han Chinese, for example, the large-scale White Lotus insurgency of 1796–1805, and by non-Chinese subjects. A repeated and long-familiar theme was that of tribal risings as a response to the state's pressure for the integration and control of minorities. This pressure continued the long-standing use of force in Chinese expansion. For example, in 1726, the Miao people of the Guiyang prefecture in the province of Guizhou in southwest China were "pacified," with native chiefs forcibly removed and replaced by Chinese civil administrators. This process, forcibly ending shared power, indicated the potentially unstable nature of such sharing, particularly in the face of the pretensions of imperial authority, and aroused opposition. In 1731, this process led to an insurgency by the indigenous tribes in Taiwan that was put down in 1732. Resistance by the tribal population of southwest China in the mid-1730s, notably the Guizhou insurgency, was met by large-scale slaughter. Nevertheless, opposition continued. In 1740, there was a major insurgency by Miao people in eastern Guizhou and western Hunan.

Millenarian fantasies about a new order, similar to those that were to be seen among Native Americans, notably in the 1800s, played a role in the 1740 Miao insurgency, but it was suppressed. Such fantasies used to be regarded by scholars as a premodern characteristic and not one of the modern age, but that secular teleology and its marginalization of religious enthusiasm now appears less well grounded. In particular, the role of Islamic fundamentalism in certain current insurgencies is notable.

In the eighteenth century, confronting large-scale local uprisings continued to be a central part of the pattern of Chinese military activity. The seriousness varied, as did the need to deploy extensive resources from a great distance. On the island of Hainan, the Li people of the highlands used force from 1766 in what was to be a long-standing attempt to drive out settlers. This, however, was less serious than the 1774 Wang Lun sectarian insurgency in Shandong in eastern China as that was in a more central province. The latter insurgency was swiftly suppressed.[7] The scale and combination of insurgencies in the closing years of the century were formidable. Non-Chinese subjects again posed problems, with the Lin Shuangwen insurgency on Taiwan in 1787–88, the Yao insurgency in eastern Guangxi in 1791, and the Miao insurgency in Guizhou and western Hunan in 1795–97. These insurgencies followed the established pattern of opposition to the attempt to increase governmental power and to the spread of Han settlement. Thus, in the case of the Miao revolt, Miao marauders left the hills in order to attack lowland settlements. In turn, the army responded by brutal repression, creating more garrisons, and introducing military-agricultural colonists. A large number of fortified hamlets were built, while towns were fortified.[8] The long-term consequence was one of demographic change which, indeed, proved a vital element in counterinsurgency policy in China, one that brought it together with geopolitics. The same remains the case to this day, notably in Tibet. There, it is accompanied by another characteristic feature, the extension of communication systems. Traditionally this involved roads, but, from the nineteenth century, in much of the world, this process included rail, which is now also the case with Tibet.

The largest insurgency was the White Lotus movement of 1796–1805, one by Han Chinese subjects, especially in western Hubei, southern Shaanxi, and northern Sichuan. The insurgency indicated the importance of religious commitment as a source of opposition, in this case millenarian sectarian Buddhism, a belief that it was possible and necessary through violence to usher in a better world. At the same time, the pressures of unprecedented population growth were significant, notably in leading to land shortage. The rebels made extensive use of guerrilla tactics and benefited from the hilly character of their core area. The insurgency was put down only with brutal repression and after a formidable military effort. More than 117,000 regular troops were deployed, as well as hundreds of thousands of militiamen. The failure of the Jiaqing emperor (r. 1796–1820) to control his generals and governors, who profited greatly from the war, was a major factor in the protraction of the conflict which, in total, cost 120 million taels of silver, helping to weaken Manchu China. Indeed, the regime never really recovered and was left more vulnerable to British pressure at the time of the Opium Wars.

Nevertheless, the key point was that the insurgency was suppressed. The main insurgent force in Hubei was destroyed in 1798. The focus then moved to eastern Sichuan, where, however, the insurgents were unable to gain the initiative. In 1799, there was an important shift in Chinese policy. In place of the Qianlong emperor's opposition to civilian fortification, his son encouraged support for local initiatives that had started in 1796 in the shape of the organization of community militias protected by walled stockades. This defensive system protected the population and deprived the rebels of the ready supplies and easy success they required and gained by capturing settlements. By 1800, the insurgency was weak. The dates generally given for it,

1796–1805, are therefore misleading but capture well the difficulty of ending insurgencies. This point is more generally true of the dating of insurgencies,[9] for example, the Pugachev rising in Russia.

Comparison with insurgency in Europe in this period is not obvious, which indicates the problems posed by running together insurgencies in the same period. The major Chinese insurgencies involved greater numbers of people, which entailed particular issues of food supply. The 1790s includes not only the rising in the Vendée, as well as others in France, and the Haitian revolution (also in the French world), but also the White Lotus rebellion, the Whiskey rebellion in Pennsylvania, and the Irish Rebellion of 1798, and that is not an exhaustive list. These insurgencies were very different. It is possible to find some comparisons between them, not least if the theme pursued is that of a global crisis, but in practice, the contrasts are more notable.

ISLAMIC WORLD

The Islamic world also witnessed numerous insurgencies. Indeed, in 1791, William Lindsay, British secretary of legation at St. Petersburg, then capital of Russia, predicting the fall of the Turkish (Ottoman) Empire to Russian expansion which, in a war that had started in 1787, was then effective, remarked, "Half the Turkish Empire is either in open rebellion or, at least, independent."[10] As in a more general pattern, some insurgencies were by the Turkish military itself, generally in response to problems linked to unsuccessful war, notably pay arrears. In 1703 and 1730, these insurgencies led to the overthrow of successive sultans. As so often, defeat in war helped lead to political crisis. Sultan Mustafa II (r. 1695–1703) was seen as compromising Muslim honor by accepting the Peace of Carlowitz of 1699, a peace, entailing recognition of Christian Europe and major territorial cessions, including most of Hungary to the Habsburgs, rather than merely a truce. These terms contributed to the crisis of authority in 1703, when there was a mutiny in Constantinople by troops, already facing pay arrears and now ordered to suppress an insurgency in far-off west Georgia, a troublesome frontier region and one where scant glory or profit was likely to be found. The range of factors involved in the crisis underlines the danger of citing only one as the key element, which is a repeated point in insurgency and counterinsurgency warfare. In the resulting crisis, a rebel army was formed, and, at Havas, it defeated the far smaller army of Mustafa, who was then replaced by his brother Ahmed. The effectiveness of Turkish forces in such conflict attracts far less attention than that shown against Western forces, but that underplays the range of capability required.

In turn, Ahmed III was overthrown in 1730 in a janissary (elite infantry) insurgency. In part, this insurgency arose from discontent with Ahmed's mismanagement of the war with Persia. It had proved far harder for the Turks to intervene there successfully than had been anticipated when the Safavid dynasty was overthrown by Afghan invaders in 1722, a mistake that was also made by Peter the Great of Russia, although with far less serious political consequences for Russia. Moreover, there was anger among the artisans and guilds of Constantinople about the cost of supporting the war. This was a large-scale insurgency, one in which merchants and members of the *ulema* (clergy) took part. However, that very scale and diversity helped ensure divisions among the insurgents, and these came to the fore with time, which helped in the eventual restoration of order.

Within the Turkish Empire, there was also opposition in provinces that was treated as insurgencies, for example, that by Kara Mahmud, governor of Scutari, in the 1780s and 1790s, and by Pasvanoğlu Osman, governor of Vidin, in the 1790s. Large forces were deployed against these governors. Their activity reflected decentralization and autonomous developments in administration and army recruitment, as well as the long-standing cycle of inclusion with reward and exclusion with punishment, that affected and often characterized relations between sultans and provincial potentates. Insurgencies and amnesties were aspects of this cycle.[11]

The Turks, moreover, faced insurgencies, often serious, in frontier areas, for example, by Arab and Kurdish tribes in Iraq in the 1730s and 1740s. In 1741, these tribes threatened Basra, the major Turkish base in southern Iraq. Confrontation and war with Persia to the east of Iraq made these insurgencies far more challenging.

In Persia, religion was a key element in helping account for insurgencies. The Safavid attempt in the 1700s and 1710s to impose Shi'ite orthodoxy on Sunni Muslims in their dominions led to widespread opposition, for example, in Kurdistan and, in particular, in the eastern, Afghan regions of the empire, where Sunnis were the majority. Given more recent counterinsurgency warfare in Afghanistan from the 1980s and the extent to which the long memories of deep history are very important to the culture there and notably to tribal identities, this response is highly instructive. This opposition was especially pronounced among the Ghalzai tribe, which rebelled in 1704 and, more successfully, in 1709, in response to a harsh governor of Kandahar, the major city of the region. The Safavid army sent to suppress the insurgency mounted an unsuccessful siege of Kandahar in 1711 and was heavily defeated as it retreated. This defeat was followed by an insurgency by the Abdalis of western Afghanistan, a powerful confederation of tribes, in an area closer to Persia.

The Safavid failure to suppress them testified to a shortage of infantry, funds, fighting spirit, readiness, and experience, but, more particularly, the political skill vital to containing and responding to crises. Shah Husain (r. 1694–1722) proved a poor leader, indolent, mild, and, most seriously, unable to exploit divisions among the Afghans. Moreover, the Afghan success encouraged Sunni insurgencies elsewhere in the Safavid dominions, for example, from the Turkmen to the east of the Caspian Sea and the Lezhis from Daghestan in the eastern Caucasus mountains. The insurgencies became individually and cumulatively more serious. In 1716, the Abdalis captured Herat, the major city in western Afghanistan. In 1719, the Ghalzai leader, Mahmud, advanced west to Kirman in eastern Persia, taking the city, whose defenders had fled, and looting it savagely. In 1721, in contrast, Mahmud's advance became more than a raid. He besieged Kirman, failing to take the citadel but accepting money to leave. The Ghalzais then advanced to the center of Persia, defeating the far larger but poorly commanded Safavid army at Gulnabad on March 8, 1722, in part due to superior fighting quality. This was one of the major battles in history that tends to be ignored in compendia on the subject as they remain resolutely Westerncentric. The Afghans followed up by blockading Isfahan, the capital, defeating attempts at relief but lacking the numbers to storm the city and the artillery to breach its walls. In the end, famine caused by the lengthy blockade led to the surrender of the city on October 23, 1722, and to the abdication of Husain in favor of the Afghan leader. Control over capitals was important both in the West and elsewhere.

This was the most successful insurgency of the century, one in which rebellion had been followed by conventional campaigning, and battle by a decisive military outcome. However, violent Afghan disunity as well as unpopularity in Persia enabled Nadir Kuli, then a general for a relative of Husain, to defeat and overthrow the Afghans in 1729. Initially the power behind the throne but then shah from 1736 to 1747, Nadir's continual wars, from Iraq to India and Central Asia to Oman, and the heavy taxation necessary to pay for them placed a terrible burden on his subjects and encouraged repeated opposition. His brutal repression of successive insurgencies, notably by mass executions, as in 1744, did not end the opposition. Moreover, not all insurgencies were suppressed. Thus, in 1741, Nadir campaigned against the rebellious Lezhis in Daghestan in the eastern Caucasus but with little success.

Nadir was assassinated in 1747 by officers both concerned by his favor toward Afghans and Uzbeks and linked to his rebellious nephew, Ali Qoli. The latter seized power as Adel Shah, only to be swiftly deposed by his brother, Ebrahim, who in turn lost control of most of Persia as regional warlords took power.

AFRICA

These insurgencies underline the mistake of beginning an account of insurgency warfare, both in the eighteenth century and more generally with the

American War of Independence. So also with Africa and the longest-lasting state there, Abyssinia (Ethiopia). Insurgencies were a long-standing and repeated aspect of its politics, with provincial potentates frequently rebelling against the emperor. These insurgencies reflected the nature of politics, the diversity of regions in the farflung state, and the sensitivity of religious issues in a region of marked tension between Christianity and Islam. The international context was also an element. Thus, Mika'el Suhul (d. 1780), *ras* (ruler) of Tigrai (Tigré), an area of modern northern Ethiopia and southern Eritrea, benefited from proximity to a supply of Turkish muskets from the Red Sea. In 1746, he was brought to order by an invasion by his overlord, the negus (emperor), Iyasu II (r. 1730–55), but in the 1760s, Mika'el built up a large army and posed as a Christian and national champion against Muslim influences at the court of Iyoas I (r. 1755–69). Iyoas failed to have Mika'el assassinated and, at a battle at Azezo, Mika'el's musketeers wrecked the opposing cavalry, after which Iyoas was publicly hanged. A puppet negus was put on the throne by Mika'el. Thus, this was a successful insurgency, albeit one that, as in Persia, did not lead to political stability. Instead, as in Persia, provincial potentates became yet more powerful, looking toward the divided and violent politics of Abyssinia in the nineteenth century.

EUROPE UNTIL 1788

In Europe, the largest-scale (although not longest) insurgency of the century was the Pugachev rising in Russia in 1773–75. Launched by Cossacks under Yemelyan Pugachev, who claimed to be the dead tsar, Peter III (r. 1762), its numbers were swelled with peasant runaways, especially from the harsh working conditions of the mines and metallurgical plants of the Ural Mountains region. Regular farming serfs also played a major role. Some disgruntled priests, some townspeople, and some unhappy members of the lower service echelons of the nobility joined in. Cossacks and Bashkirs were promised their traditional way of life, including the freedom of land and water. The fortress of Orenburg on the River Ural was besieged, Russian relief forces beaten off, and the insurgency spread, especially into the Urals. However, despite Pugachev's establishing a College of War that was modeled on the Russian War Ministry and dividing his troops into regiments, there was no real coordination of the insurgent bands, and also a shortage of cannon and ammunition. The important Urals armaments industry was not organized to the benefit of the insurgents, many of whom were armed only with spears, axes, and sticks, weapons similar to those of Chinese insurgents. While Pugachev remained unable to take Orenburg and Yaitsk, whose fortifications defied attack, Russian troops advanced from a number of directions in the winter of 1773–74, and on March 22, 1774, Pugachev was defeated at Tatishchevo. He fielded 9,000 troops against the 6,500 of General Golitsyn. On March 23–24, a separate insurgent force of seven thousand to ten thousand men under Zarubin Chika was defeated near Ufa. Insurgent morale collapsed, the garrisons of Orenburg and Yaitsk were relieved, and a new insurgent force under Pugachev was dispersed.

Nevertheless, Pugachev raised another army, captured the fort of Osa in June 1774, and, on July 10, defeated a force of armed citizens outside the major city of Kazan on the Volga River east of Moscow. Kazan was captured on July 12 and those in Western dress killed, although the citadel held out. Pugachev won fresh support by promising freedom to the serfs of the Volga valley, which demonstrated the social radicalism he represented. The response was a widespread slaughter of the nobility in the Volga region. There was also a religious element in the rising—namely, support for the Old Believers and a strong cultural antipathy to the Westernization of Russia. A mutiny by the garrison of Saratov, a major city on the Volga, led to its fall to Pugachev, but the insurgent movement still lacked effective organizational structure. Moreover, Pugachev's appeals were increasingly unsuccessful as his arrival brought chaos and fighting and as the resilience of the government became more apparent.

Meanwhile, underlining the crucial international element, Russian troops withdrawn from the Balkans in the war with the Turks (with whom peace terms were finally agreed in July 1774) ensured that the insurgents' military position deteriorated while Russian success in that conflict afforded the Russians a new operational axis from which to assault the rebels. Defeated in late August, Pugachev was betrayed by disillusioned supporters in September and executed with great cruelty the following January, which reflected the fear to which his insurgency had given rise. Residual disturbances, set in motion through his uprising, albeit of lesser magnitude, continued after his death but were suppressed in 1775.[12]

A very different type of insurgency was provided by that in the Cévennes of southern France in 1702–11. This was an insurgency by persecuted Huguenots (Protestants) against government oppression, notably against forcible conversion with violence, and one in which both sides responded to religious antagonism with great barbarity, including the killing of prisoners. There was brutal repression by royal troops. This rising occurred during the War of the Spanish Succession (1701–14), but France's opponents were unable to send effective help to this inland region, although Britain, with its naval presence in the Mediterranean, tried to do so.[13]

Religious division was also a factor in western Ukraine, but as part of a complex situation: Ukrainian peasants following the Uniate Christian rite reacted violently to attempts by Polish landlords to impose harsh labor services and to support forcible conversion to Catholicism. The revolt of Semen Palej at the turn of the century was followed by serious uprisings in 1734–37,

1750, and 1768. Peasant insurgencies were in part due to, and in turn made more serious by, breakdowns in political and judicial order, as in the Polish civil wars associated with the Great Northern War (1700–1721), the War of the Polish Succession (1733–55), and the formation of the Confederation of Bar in 1768. The situation in western Ukraine was made more difficult not only by the weakness of the Polish army but also by the willingness of Russia to extend its role in Polish politics, a role which contributed to the successive failures of these insurgencies. The savagery of the 1768 insurgency was genocidal. The "Golden Charter" ordered the killing of Poles and Jews, a task carried out in a number of massacres.[14]

In a pattern seen across history, other frontier areas also saw serious peasant unrest, for example, the Carpathian foothills in Poland, the Lower Volga valley, Transylvania, and eastern Anatolia. Such areas were both those in which differing value systems and practices of power clashed and ones where the situation was inherently more volatile and violence a more normal means to achieve ends. Ethnic and religious divides were frequently part of the equation. Thus, in Transylvania in 1784, where peasants slaughtered landowners, priests, townsmen, and officials and advanced radical demands, including the abolition of a nobility and the distribution of their land to the peasantry, the rising pitted Greek Orthodox Romanian peasants against Hungarian Calvinists.

The Transylvanian insurgency also involved two other common features of major peasant insurgencies: heightened excitement created by an anticipation of major reforms and a linked belief that the insurgency really served the interests of the monarch. Joseph II's redefinition of landlord-peasant relations elsewhere in his dominions had made these relations appear precarious and dependent on monarchical wishes in Transylvania, and, at the beginning, the insurgents claimed to act in Joseph's name. Similarly, in Bohemia in 1775, the government attitude to peasant conditions had made them a volatile issue of more than local significance, and the insurgents claimed that an imperial decree, suppressed by the nobility, had freed them from their obligations. Such beliefs were a frequent element in insurgencies.

By the standards of twentieth-century revolutionaries, these were cases of false consciousness and of insurgencies that were flawed by only limited radicalism. These linked assessments, however, suffer from a misleading presentism and political bias. Indeed, those who supported twentieth-century insurgencies frequently found themselves totally misled. Moreover, it is far from clear that limited radicalism, in means and goals, was a cause or symptom of failure, either in terms of the course of events or with reference to the formulation of viable goals.

In the eighteenth century, there was also opposition to foreign rule, whether within imperial contexts or in terms of resisting the operations of occupying forces. In the first case, Ivan Mazepa, hetman of Ukraine, unsuccessfully rebelled against Peter the Great of Russia in the 1700s and allied with Charles XII of Sweden,[15] while, when Prince Cantemir of Moldavia rebelled against the Turks in 1711, he called the entire adult population to military service, and when the insurgency was suppressed, many fled to Russia. So also in the 1700s with Hungarian opposition to Habsburg rule.[16] The last can be seen as nationalist, but that "nationalism" included an important religious dimension, notably Protestant discontent at Leopold I's attempt to limit their rights. This was part of a pattern of Protestant insurgencies against the Habsburgs in the early eighteenth century, a pattern that looked back to a similar series of insurgencies, also unsuccessful, in the early seventeenth century.

The difficulty of classifying insurgencies, in this and other contexts, was fully shown by the Jacobite risings in Scotland in 1715 and 1745. In part, these insurgencies reflected Scottish opposition to being part of Britain. More particularly, they reflected, in part, Episcopalian and Catholic opposition in Scotland to dominance by Scottish Presbyterians after the 1707 union of the English and Scottish parliaments, and, in part, the attempt by supporters of the exiled Stuarts to regain control of both Scotland and England. Jacobite comes from *Jacobus*, the Latin for James, the name of the Stuart pretender. In 1745, the Jacobite uprising in Scotland saw major advantages for the Jacobites in taking the initiative, and at the tactical, operational, and strategic levels. At the first battle, at Prestonpans on September 21, 1745, a Highland charge overcame defensive firepower; the tactic also reflected a degree of Jacobite indiscipline and lack of organization that hindered more formalized tactics. This rapid victory consolidated the Jacobite position in central Scotland.

The Jacobites then invaded England, outmaneuvering defensive forces. They were helped by the unfortified nature of most of the British Isles, as the major British fortified positions were naval dockyards, such as Chatham, or overseas bases, notably Gibraltar. In contrast, there was no system of citadels protecting major domestic centers of government. This situation ensured that the Jacobites did not have to fight their way through a series of positions, losing time and manpower as they did so, and also meant that the regular army lacked a network of bases that could provide shelter and replenish supplies. After the Jacobites under Charles Edward Stuart (Bonnie Prince Charlie), the son of the Jacobite claimant, captured poorly fortified Carlisle, they faced no fortified positions on their chosen route to London.

The Jacobites turned back at Derby that December only due to disappointment about receiving limited English support, which contrasted with what the Scottish troops had been promised. The need to make promises reflected the extent to which the insurgent army was less under control than was the case for many of those in the twentieth century. Ideological drive may have been a key difference, but the willingness in the twentieth century to use terror to achieve control, as with the armies of the Russian and Chinese revolutions, was probably more significant. The Jacobite army was a newly created volunteer force, with nonbureaucratic supply and recruitment systems, and this necessarily affected its methods of operation, not least in matters of control and command, and logistics. Due to limited control, the troops were kept going with promises. At the same time, this process was more significant in the twentieth century than is often appreciated, and that helps explain not only the importance of success but also that of loot. Retreat to the barren Scottish Highlands gave the Jacobites less flexibility and room to maneuver as they were pursued by the regular forces, who had a good logistical support system.

In the final battle, at Culloden on April 16, 1746, the circumstances were not suitable for a Highland charge because the numbers enabled the Duke of Cumberland to rely on defense in depth, and this helped make the defensive firepower of the regular forces more effective. The Highland charge penetrated the lines of Cumberland's well-disciplined troops, but the Highlanders had already been greatly weakened by artillery and musket fire. As discussed in chapter 1, punitive expeditions were then used by the British to punish Jacobite support in the Scottish Highlands. Some of these expeditions were especially cruel and were characterized by killings, rapes, and systematic devastation that did not exempt loyal Highlanders. The situation was probably exacerbated by the extent to which much of the army disliked having to operate in Scotland. Even if Highlanders could flee the approach of troops and warships, the destruction of their homes and farm implements and the seizure of their cattle were for many, especially the weak, equivalent to sentences of death or at least severe hardship and malnutrition. Again in a pattern commonly seen with counterinsurgency struggles, reports of Jacobite atrocities had lessened whatever reluctance there might have been to punish the Highlanders, who were commonly presented as subhuman, although the cruelty that was inflicted varied in its intensity, and some honorable men applied their instructions in a favorable manner. The serious loss of Jacobite manpower at Culloden, combined with the punitive expeditions and the departure for France of the Jacobite leader, Charles Edward Stuart, ensured that guerrilla activity was not a viable option.

In contrast, guerrilla warfare was a marked feature of the Balkans, where the Turks were the dominant imperial power. The Balkans were far larger and more mountainous than Scotland, and the Turkish military presence was patchy. However, the attempt by the Russians to instigate Greek risings during their 1768–74 war with Turkey, and the risings that occurred as in the Morea in 1770, led to Turkish atrocities as part of a repression made easier by a lack of sufficient Russian support. Much of Greece, especially the Aegean islands, was more vulnerable to Turkish action than the more mountainous areas in the western Balkans.

Occupying regular troops were also harassed by popular opposition. At the time of the Great Northern War (1700–1721), there was intensive Polish guerrilla warfare against the Swedish invaders in 1703–4, while, in 1707, Swedish demands for food in Poland led to guerrilla warfare. Tyrolean peasant resistance to a Bavarian invasion in 1703 was followed by a Bavarian peasant rising against Austrian occupiers. Marshal Berwick, who led the Franco-Spanish invasion of Portugal in 1704, was surprised by the weakness of organized resistance but equally amazed by the vigor of the peasants in attacks on his communications and in fighting back in the villages. Their success in exacerbating his supply problems played a major role in inducing Berwick to retreat from Portugal.

In addition, guerrillas were used by both sides during the Spanish civil war that was important to the Spanish dimension of the War of the Spanish Succession (1701–14). The response from regular forces was generally harsh. For example, the French killed the survivors when the town of Xativa fell in 1707 and left no building standing except the church. Such activity produced a lasting legacy and looked forward to hostile attitudes during the French occupation of Spain in 1808–14.

Within North America, "small war," "petite guerre," and insurgency struggles were all seen, not only with conflict between European powers and Native Americans but also with regard to conflict between these powers. This conflict could extend to insurgent methods on the part of European settlers. Thus, having conquered Nova Scotia, the British sought to drive out the French settlers, the Acadians, only to face guerrilla opposition, notably frequent ambushes. [17]

Developments in the United Provinces (Netherlands) further indicated the variety of forms insurgencies could take as well as their potential overlap with conventional politics. Municipal autonomy, federal republicanism, and hostility to the House of Orange were powerful political and constitutional traditions and notably in the important province of Holland. Municipal coups, urban disorder, and the creation of unofficial citizen militias were customary means of procedure in periods of instability. In the 1780s, opposition to William V of Orange combined with traditional republican sentiment to produce the Patriot movement. Bourgeois free corps were formed to lend force to the overthrowing of Orangist municipal and provincial government. William's constitutional rights in numerous municipalities and provinces were abolished, and William had to leave The Hague in 1785. Two years later, a rapidly successful Prussian invasion reimposed Orangist predominance, bringing the insurgency to a close.

The coverage so far suggests that insurgencies of some type or other were frequent. However, aside from the use of legal action to pursue differences, for example, in the case of French, German, and Polish peasants, it is striking that peasant insurgencies, like their urban counterparts, were less common in

1720–80 than a century or two centuries earlier. Furthermore, violent unrest was generally small scale, for example, the killing or maiming of the land-lords' animals, the wholesale slaughter of game, arson, and the destruction of fences and hedges.

LATIN AMERICA

The failure of the major insurgency in Latin America, the Great Rebellion in Peru in 1780–81, was also instructive. As a reminder of the range of factors involved in insurgencies, this owed something to the rigorous collection of taxes, but also to millenarian beliefs. Like the White Lotus insurgency in China in the 1790s, the Great Rebellion showed the importance of popular religious convictions in encouraging a defiance of the conventional equations of military strength. The insurgency was headed by José Gabriel Túpac Ama-ru, a descendant of the last Inca rulers whom the Spaniards had overthrown in the sixteenth century.

More than one hundred thousand people died in the Great Rebellion, but the uprising was suppressed. As ever, a range of factors was involved. Mili-tary technology was one: at Arequipa in 1780, superior Spanish firepower helped ensure the defeat of local rebels armed with lances, sticks, and the traditional Andean weapon, the sling. Resources and determination were significant: assisted by a profitable surge of sugar production in Mexico and by the reforming initiatives of Charles III (r. 1759–88), Spain proved a dy-namic power. Moreover, the sociology of local politics, especially the exten-sive native cooperation with Spanish rule, was important. This factor ensured that insurgencies in Latin America, as often elsewhere, took on the character of full-fledged civil wars, which increased the bitterness involved as well as the antisocietal nature of much of the violence.

On the whole, unlike in St. Domingue (Haiti) against the French, slaves were not part of the equation. The 1798 "Revolt of the Tailors" in Salvador, Brazil, called for the abolition of slavery and was supported by some mulat-toes and whites as well as slaves, but the insurgency was small scale and was overcome in the context of white fear. Slave risings elsewhere were also suppressed, for example, in Mexico in the Córdoba and Orizaba region alone in 1725, 1735, 1741, 1749, and 1768.

The Spaniards also faced opposition in their northern borderlands from the Native Americans who did not accept Spanish control and influence. As a result, the Native Americans did not see themselves as insurgents, although Spanish views were frequently very different. The northern part of Mexico was not brought under Spanish control until the later eighteenth century. The terrain, the desert, the heat, and the Native American opposition were too great. The Spaniards sought to persuade Native Americans to live near Spanish *presidios* (fortified bases) and gave them benefits accordingly. Those who refused to accept this were fought and, if captured, deported in chain gangs to Mexico City. [18] There was also opposition in Central America, for example, the Tzeltal Revolt in 1712 against exactions and taxes. [19]

The range of insurgency in Latin America included that of New Orleans against Spanish rule in 1768–69: opposition to newly established Spanish rule, after trade outside the Spanish imperial system or in non-Spanish ships was banned, encouraged rebellion and an attempt to return to rule by France. The latter, however, rejected this attempt, a key development but an unsurprising one as the two powers were allies. Spanish forces reimposed control and the rebellion's ringleaders were executed. There was no comparison to the subsequent course of what became the American Revolution. The Spanish authorities were helped by the limited scale of the rising.

AMERICAN REVOLUTION

The extent to which insurgencies could take on the character of civil wars was to be seen in the American Revolution. This revolution was important due to the subsequent significance of the United States. As an insurgency itself, the American Revolution was not particularly unique, as the Spanish American wars of liberation over the following half century were to show. Nor was it novel: indeed, the similarities between many factors in the sixteenth-century Dutch Revolt and the American Revolution are apparent. This is even more the case if the role of religion in the latter is emphasized, notably opposition to the position and assumptions of George III (r. 1760–1820) as head of the Church of England. The Bible was used by preachers to help instill a military patriotism aimed against George. [20] Moreover, at the local level, there were a number of rebellions in the North American colonies before and after independence from Britain. [21]

A key similarity with the Dutch Revolt and with the later Polish insurgencies against Russia was the role of the international context. Here it is pertinent to focus not on the initial successful stage of the revolution, when, in 1775 and early 1776, the revolutionaries were able to take the initiative against the British, who had not anticipated events. Canada was invaded in 1775, while the British were driven from the thirteen colonies by the end of March 1776. Instead, it is appropriate to focus on the extent to which the British were willing and able not to settle politically but to mount a major effort in 1776 to reestablish their position. The ability of imperial powers like Britain to draw on wider resources in responding to insurgencies was, repeatedly, a key factor in helping explain the difficulties insurgents encountered.

This factor was seen, for example, in the Mediterranean island of Corsica in 1768, when it was sold by Genoa to France. Corsican resolve, knowledge of the terrain, and fighting qualities, combined with French overconfidence and poor planning, resulted in Corsican successes in 1768. In contrast, in 1769–70, the proximity of Corsica to France, larger French forces, better tactics, and the use of devastation, terror, and road construction produced success. Corsicans found carrying arms were killed. The French campaign indicated the potential of coordinated independent forces operating against irregulars, as well as the strength of major states. France was able to sustain a considerable force where provisions were in short supply, to overcome defeat, and to return to the attack, proceeding systematically to obtain a planned military outcome. The French benefited from the absence of foreign military support for the Corsicans. Pressure in Britain to help the Corsicans did not result in government action. Nor did governmental unease in the kingdom of Sardinia about French expansion.

Why, then, did the British fail in North America? Unlike the French in Corsica, they benefited from the colonists being subjects of the Crown, and many, indeed, were Loyalists and willing to fight accordingly. Moreover, the British were not at war with anyone else until the summer of 1778, which created a crucial window of opportunity for counterinsurgency efforts. As a result of this situation, Britain hit back with much force in 1776. An amphibious force relieved the garrison at Québec from American siege, while the major effort defeated the Americans at the battle of Long Island and captured New York. In 1777, the main British army was victorious at Brandywine and captured Philadelphia, the capital of the revolution, although a secondary British army was defeated at Saratoga and surrendered, while the subsequent British strategic reassessment was flawed.[22]

A military account, however, brings up the question of whether the British could have prevailed with better generalship or luck; whether, indeed, instead, as John Adams later suggested, the very act of revolution led to its success. This is a key element in insurgency/counterinsurgency struggles, but it did not lead to success for the Corsicans. If the defeat of an opponent is perceived as in part requiring their acceptance that they have been defeated, then the degree of will shown in rejecting that conclusion is crucial. In the case of the American Revolution, this is especially important because the British government did not want and could not afford a large occupation force, and even more so because its army was relatively small. Instead, like most powers, its rule largely depended on compliance, if not consent.

In the case of North America, this was a civil war, the solution to which was seen by contemporaries as political as much as military. The politicization of much of the American public and the motivation of many of their troops were significant aspects of what was conventionally regarded as "modernity" when this situation was understood in terms of mass mobilization and citizens' armies. In the current position, in contrast, "modernity" may be more readily understood in terms of often only partly engaged publics and relatively small, volunteer professional armies. Ironically, this description was truer for the American Revolution of the British than of the American Patriots. Such descriptions and comparisons can be misleadingly ahistorical, but they demonstrate the questionable nature of the tendency automatically to ascribe victory to a popular fight for independence.

Underestimating the resolve and military ability of their opponents, the British government wanted the American Patriots to return to their loyalty. The British did not wish to win and then to have to face continued opposition. The understanding of this may make British war making appear modern, involving as it did what would later be termed "hearts and minds." However, in practice, this technique was common to counterinsurgency warfare when the insurgency, far from being restricted to marginal groups in society, included the socially prominent.

As with Philip II of Spain when responding to the Dutch Revolt, the availability of a linked political-military strategy did not guarantee success. So also with the American Revolution. The Continental Congress rejected negotiations in 1776 and 1778. There was a social dimension to this rejection. The role of Patriots not in the elite, and many were not, helps modern scholars to explain the American Revolution as an insurgency.[23] Moreover, as a related but separate issue, the British found it difficult to build up the strength of their supporters. As a result of the political situation, Loyalist supporters were weak other than in the South, a situation that encouraged a British focus there from late 1778. Loyalist activity at times represented an insurgency against Patriot dominance, as with the unsuccessful Clow's Rebellion in Delaware in 1778.[24]

The revolutionaries also found the war an increasingly difficult conflict, and by 1781, their war effort was close to collapse, with much of the Continental Army mutinous and the government desperately short of money. Moreover, the American effort was heavily dependent on the changing international context. In 1778, France had come into the war against Britain, but by 1781, it was clear that the French government, concerned about the cost and also about Russian expansionism in eastern Europe, was looking for a way out. This episode serves to underline the extent to which the fate of insurgency warfare was often highly uncertain: contemporaries, such as Tom Paine, were repeatedly unsure whether success or failure would be the outcome. Linked to this comes the danger today of presenting the result as inevitable and then of analyzing it accordingly.

In the event, Franco-American cooperation against the second-largest British army in North America in 1781 led to the surrender of the latter at Yorktown, thus repeating the 1777 American success at Saratoga. The Yorktown campaign indicated the key element of the international dimension. The Americans were dependent not only on French troops and, crucially, artillery on land, but also on the ability of the French navy, in the Battle of the

Virginia Capes, to block the entrance to Chesapeake Bay to British warships and, thus, to prevent the relief of the British force at Yorktown. Conversely, British troops had been able to withdraw safely by sea from the New Jersey shore in 1778, while George Washington's plan to capture New York in 1782 could not be implemented, not least due to a lack of French support.

These contrasts underline the danger of thinking of this war and, indeed, of insurgency warfare in general in teleological terms, in this case, of the inevitable defeat of an *ancien régime* army by a revolutionary new force. In practice, the French military scarcely conformed to this model, while, indeed, the American Continental Army owed its tactics and structure to the general Western model and, more particularly, to the British example. George Washington did not wish to rely on militias but instead wanted a regular army that could provide America with legitimacy. Washington also stressed drill and discipline and was a believer in position warfare. Partly as a result, guerrilla warfare tended to occur only when American regular forces were very weak, as in the South in 1780–81. Then Nathanael Greene, the American commander in the South, found it in his "power to carry on nothing but a kind of fugitive war," while Daniel Morgan was ordered to "spirit up the people" in upper South Carolina and hinder British moves.[25] Moreover, the use of partisan bands appeared an obvious response to the defeat of American regular forces in the battle at Camden in 1781, the uncontrollable vastness of the South, and the need to counter Loyalist activity. The result was a civil war in which neither side was in control but British commanders were left frustrated.

Guerrilla warfare should not be taken as typical of the American war effort, although that approach proved very popular in American public myth, with its emphasis on citizen soldiers attuned to the natural environment, and notably with Hollywood, as in the film *The Patriot*. It also proved significant in later American discussion of insurgency and counterinsurgency warfare, particularly during the Vietnam War and over the past fifteen years.[26] In practice, American warfare was a hybrid type, an adaptation of European warfare to North American circumstances, not least to wars of conquest against Native Americans.[27] British warfare in North America was similarly a hybrid type, although that did not mean that the solutions were identical to those of the American Patriots.

The political dimension was to the fore in explaining why defeat at Yorktown in 1781 was so significant. Yorktown still left the British in control of New York, Charleston, and Savannah, and in 1782, they won a crushing victory at the Saintes over the French fleet in the West Indies, the fleet from which warships were sent to North American waters. This British naval victory lessened the chance of success for any American attack on New York or Charleston.

However, a key element, prefiguring to a degree the impact of the French defeat at Dien Bien Phu in 1954 and the shock of the Tet Offensive in 1968 for the Americans, was that Yorktown produced a crisis of confidence in the ministry of Lord North in Britain. A loss of political will was the key element. As a result, a new government under Charles, Marquess of Rockingham, came to power in 1782. Pledged to settle with the revolutionaries, his government and its successor, the Shelburne ministry, negotiated peace. This course of events brought out a central aspect of insurgency conflicts: as the revolutionaries were not in a position to invade Britain, the war could only come to an end when the British decided to cease making an effort, and this decision was very much a political one. In addition, the Americans did not support or help to initiate similar "revolutions" in other countries during its founding years.

NORTH AMERICA AND THE WEST INDIES

The success of the Patriots in overthrowing British power contrasted totally with the failure of slave revolts in North America in the eighteenth century, for example, the Stono rising of 1739 in South Carolina. This failure reflected the slaves' lack of power. Access to firearms was controlled, and major efforts were made to ensure that slaves were unable to coordinate action. Savage punishments maintained control. A Frenchman in Louisiana recorded the burning to death of three black slaves who had been conspiring with Native Americans to overthrow French rule.[28] Flight was a more common form of resistance to slavery there and elsewhere, for example, in Jamaica, where the escaped slaves then mounted what in effect was a permanent insurgency, notably from the Blue Mountains in North America, the West Indies, and South America.

Racism played a major role in the brutality with which slave insurgencies were suppressed. In Guadeloupe in 1802, thanks in part to amphibious capability, French authority was rapidly reasserted against the resistance of former slaves. The French also killed about a tenth of the population, approximately ten thousand blacks, including all the black soldiers captured. Although effective on Guadeloupe, a relatively small island, this policy made it impossible to reach a compromise with the rebels in Haiti. The British mistreatment of blacks, for example, on St. Lucia, also made it difficult to ensure control there. On St. Lucia, notably in 1796–97, the British tortured and shot prisoners of war and attacked the subsistence fields that supported the guerrillas.[29]

On Haiti, the army Napoleon sent in 1802 compromised any chance of success by terrible brutality. However, the army was also weakened, as so often with counterinsurgency conflicts, by its own deficiencies as well as the strengths of the opposition. The French suffered from poor leadership and planning, from the distance from France, from a lack of troops, money, and supplies, and from the British attitude. The last was important as the resumption of war between Britain and France in 1803 left the French vulnerable to British naval superiority. In turn, the Haitians benefited from their ability to work with the environment, from their use of irregular operations, and from the impact of yellow fever on the French.[30]

The ultimately successful Haitian revolution was a more important precedent for twentieth-century insurgencies than the American Revolution, particularly given the salience of racial issues. Most Americans did (and do) not appreciate this point, and the consequence was a sharply divergent ideological reading of the significance of respective revolutions.

Insurgencies often face insurrectionary challenges themselves, both during the process of gaining control and subsequently. In part, this degree of challenge reflects the extent to which insurgencies are themselves civil wars, but there is also the degree to which the overthrow of authority itself creates a new norm. This situation was very much seen in the aftermath of the American Revolution, but the lessons that might be read from that to the military dimensions of the revolution itself have not been adequately probed. Shays's Rebellion in Massachusetts in 1786–87, followed by the Whiskey Rebellion of 1794 in Pennsylvania, were the most prominent instances of a widespread unrest, also notable, for instance, in New Jersey, Virginia, Maryland, and South Carolina. The causes of the unrest were varied, not least economic problems and a strong localism, but the focus was a conviction, especially but not only in the western frontier areas, that political elites were using taxation for their own interests. This conviction looked back to agitation in the colonial period, including insurgencies then in Virginia and North Carolina. These taxes, which were largely motivated by the need to pay the debts left by the war, exacerbated the liquidity crisis (lack of money) in frontier areas. The resulting debt collection and repossessions gave a violent character to the dispute over taxation.

As with Britain in 1641, there was a resulting crisis over control over the military, in this case the militia. In 1794, rebel success in taking over Pennsylvania's militia exacerbated the situation and represented a major challenge to established power. As a result, four state militias were federalized, and an army of 12,950 men was assembled. It suppressed the rebellion without any real resistance: insurgent leaders fled or were arrested.[31] The army's march involved logistical rather than fighting problems. Thus, the "rebellion" itself did not prove a formidable challenge, and its suppression helped to increase the power of the federal government and to create a new norm.

EUROPE FROM 1789

Like the American Revolution, the French Revolution is a key episode in the teleology of modernization, but it provided a very different instance of insurgency warfare. This was not a revolution in part of an empire or of a state but, instead, one at its heart. Despite considering doing so in 1789, the French government did not use the army to suppress disaffection and opposition in Paris. Indeed, violent insurrectionary episodes, notably the seizure of the Bastille fortress-prison, helped set the tone and dynamic of politics. The troops lived and worked among the population, pursuing civilian trades when not on duty, and were thus subject to the economic and ideological pressures affecting the people. The political crisis of the revolution transformed the army. The majority of officers fled France, while there were serious mutinies, notably at Nancy in 1790, as well as the breakdown of discipline.[32] Long-established links and hierarchies were broken. Thus, in 1791, the names traditionally used for regiments were replaced by numbers. Once the revolutionaries had taken over the state, an international counterrevolutionary coalition was then repeatedly defeated from 1792 (when Prussian invaders retreated after being checked at Valmy), as were domestic opponents.

At the same time, it is important to note the extent to which the 1790s indicated that insurgents could be defeated by regular forces. This point prefigures the danger of arguing in the twentieth century from specific cases to a general situation and also of assuming that revolutionaries are necessarily more successful. Like the Genoese rising against Austrian occupiers in 1746, the Polish rising in the spring of 1794 resulted in the driving out of Russian garrisons, with the townspeople of Warsaw expelling the Russian garrison during bitter street fighting. An act of confederation called all citizens to arms. Local authorities required all men between eighteen and forty to drill every Sunday. Local militias played a major role, notably in hampering Russian communications, and thus led to the relief of the first Russian siege of Warsaw. A Polish munitions industry was rapidly improvised, although many had to fight with scythes or pikes. In the first battle, at Racławice on April 4, 1794, the Russians were defeated by a charge of peasant scythe-carrying men supported by line infantry. However, Russian and Prussian forces were soon able to defeat the heavily outnumbered Poles at Szczekociny (June 6) and Maciejowice (October 10) and to capture all the cities. Polish failure, which was more rapid than at the hands of Russia in 1733–35 and 1768–72, reflected the superior military resources of the partitioning powers, as well as the geographical vulnerability of Poland to attack from a number of directions, a situation also seen with the German attack in 1939. The Russians used considerable brutality, notably in storming the Warsaw suburb of Praga on November 4, killing nine thousand soldiers and seven thousand civilians, after which the city surrendered.

Each war, therefore, is specific to its circumstances. The same point can be made about the total British defeat of a French-backed Irish rebellion in 1798. Both the rebellion and the French invasion force were totally defeated. The nature of this insurgency remains a significant issue in Irish public culture, and its contentious character ensures that the situation requires careful consideration. Ireland was governed with scant role for the views and interests of the bulk of the population, but, although there was much popular protest in the shape of mobs defending livelihoods and customary practices,[33] the level of revolutionary resistance that this encouraged was low. In part, this was because of economic growth. As Ireland was drawn more fully into the market economy, its agricultural sector experienced growing diversification and commercialization. Textile production also developed markedly. Moreover, far from the Catholic majority being an amorphous mass of downtrodden victims, they were a flexible group that came to play a more central role in politics and a more active role in society.

A combination of social stresses and agrarian discontents led to outbreaks of organized violence in parts of Ireland, especially by the Houghers of 1711–12, the Whiteboys of 1761–65 and 1769–76, the Oakboys of 1763, the Steelboys of 1769–72, and the Rightboys of 1785–88. However, these outbreaks were sporadic, although troops were used against them. In addition, arson, cattle maiming, and attacks on agents, while very unsettling to local landowners, were not a serious military threat to the state. They were not part of a guerrilla resistance determined to seize control of the countryside. It was therefore possible for the government in London to regard such violence as a minor military priority.[34]

In contrast, the French Revolution radicalized Irish discontent, weakened patterns of social control, and provided the possibility of foreign support for a large-scale rebellion. Government concessions on Catholic rights failed to prevent the rise of radicalism, as did the loyalty of the Irish Catholic Church, which was concerned about the anti-Christian posture of the French revolutionaries. The United Irishmen, founded in 1791, largely as a Presbyterian movement pressing for political reform, was banned in 1794, but it reformed as a secret society that was openly republican and increasingly Catholic and began to plot revolution. In 1796, a supporting French invasion attempt was thwarted by a violent storm.

That year, growing British concern led to the adoption of a proactive policy toward possible internal discontent, including an Insurrection Act that decreed harsh penalties for administering and taking illegal oaths and also authorized curfews and searches for concealed weapons. Habeas corpus (detention without trial) was suspended, and a largely Protestant Irish Yeomanry, an armed constabulary nearly twenty thousand strong by the end of 1796, was established. This essentially sectarian policy alienated Catholic support. Calling on the army to disarm potential opponents helped to militarize the situation. The army violently disarmed the United Irishmen's Ulster network in 1797, while, as the United Irishmen movement sought to win Catholic backing, they alienated Protestant support.

Rising sectarian violence and harsh repression by the British army culminated in rebellion in 1798. However, the arrest of the Leinster provincial committee of the United Irishmen in March and of the organizers of a projected uprising in Dublin gravely handicapped the rebels. Lord Edward Fitzgerald had planned an insurrection in Dublin to be followed by coordinated risings elsewhere, but the scheme was nipped in the bud. Fitzgerald was seized on May 19, four days before the projected rising, the Yeomanry occupied key positions in the city, and there was no rising in Dublin. Controlling the major towns, the government dominated the communication foci, and this helped it retain the initiative.

The rebels were able to mount a serious military challenge only in County Wexford, where the local garrison was weak. The rising began on the evening of May 26, the blazing heather highlighting the meeting points. Having successfully ambushed a detachment of overconfident militiamen next day at Oulart Hill, the United Irishmen overran most of the county, establishing the Wexford Republic. However, attempts to exploit the situation by advancing further afield, notably on Dublin, were checked in early June. At the same time, a badly prepared and led rising in Ulster failed. In Wexford, in turn, the poorly led rebels concentrated at Vinegar Hill, losing the operational and strategic initiatives. The army was able to concentrate a force of twenty thousand men and a large artillery train and attacked the nine thousand rebels on June 21. The rebels fought for two hours, suffering heavy casualties, and finally retreated when their ammunition ran out. Their cohesion lost and many returning home, the rebels suffered heavy losses in government punitive operations over the following weeks. A French supporting force did not land until August 22 and was eventually defeated. The insurgents had suffered from military factors, notably a shortage of muskets, ammunition, provisions, discipline, training, and, particularly, cannon. The degree to which Irish political opinion was divided, and many Catholics unwilling to support the insurgents, was also highly significant. This element tends to be underplayed in the national historical account.

Organized and effective resistance to British authority was now at an end, but in County Wicklow, a band under Michael Dwyer continued to defy the government, successfully employing guerrilla tactics, until Dwyer surrendered in 1803 in the aftermath of the failure of Robert Emmet's rising in Dublin. A United Irishman, Emmet launched his small-scale rising by marching on Dublin Castle, but his poorly organized men were dispersed by the garrison, and the rising collapsed.

The very differing outcomes of the insurgencies in the 1790s help contextualize the successes of the French Revolution, underlining the significance of particular political alignments and developments in affecting the fate of insurrections. This point is readily apparent when considering the suppression of the insurgencies in France and elsewhere against the revolutionary regime. A large-scale royalist rising in the Vendée region of western France in 1793 was triggered by government attempts to enforce conscription. Initial royalist success, which benefited from the advantages of fighting in wooded terrain, led to brutal repression, including widespread atrocities against noncombatants as well as the destruction of crops. More generally, the army served as a coercive agency of de-Christianization, enforcing the revolutionaries' ban on Christian practice. In contrast, underlining the ideological dimension, strong piety was linked to more explicitly antirevolutionary violence and to support for royalism. The rebels called themselves the Royal and Catholic Army. This was a conflict of ambushes and massacres, but also of battles. The weakness of the government forces in 1792–93, a reflection of their commitment to war with Austria and Prussia, allowed the peasant insurgency to develop and spread, but, in turn, sixteen thousand troops were sent to the region later in 1793. They helped account for the major governmental victories at Cholet (October 15) and Le Mans (December 12), victories that played the key role in defeating the insurgency, notably by hitting its morale and ending its sense of impetus and purpose. The rebels also faced difficulties in capturing cities, especially Nantes, again a persistent problem for insurgencies: cities tended to be fortified and better defended. The atrocities by the government forces spurred the rebels to activity, but the switch by the government to a more conciliatory stance led some of the rebels to agree to terms in 1794.

Provincial opposition was mounted not only by royalists. The division among the revolutionaries that resulted in 1793 in the bloody purge of the Girondins by the rival and more radical Jacobins led, that year, to a series of revolts, especially in southern France, revolts termed "federalist" by the revolutionaries. Those in Bordeaux and Marseille were swiftly repressed, but the opposition in Lyon and Toulon was fierce, although overcome. These revolts overlapped with counterrevolutionary activity, and much of western and southern France was in a state at least close to insurrection from 1792. Particular disturbances arose from a background of widespread instability. Radical governmental policies encouraged popular opposition.

However, in 1794, with the Thermidor coup overthrowing the Jacobin government, there was a reaction at the center against radicalism. Instead, the government became the force of propertied order, a key step on the way to stability or, at least, to the lessening of opposition. By the end of the decade, France was under much greater central control, and Napoleon's seizure of power in 1799 was not followed by the regional risings seen in 1793.

The French revolutionaries also suppressed popular opposition and revolts in regions they conquered. Napoleon did so in Pavia, Italy, in 1796, using summary executions and the burning of villages, although his methods were largely ignored by later Italian commentators who praised him as a force for the modernization of Italy. These techniques were to be far less successful in Spain in 1808–14, where France faced an insurrection of a far greater scale, across a broader area, and receiving foreign support. These techniques also show that insofar as "total war" involved ideological conflict and great brutality, it did not have to wait for the twentieth century. Indeed, Clausewitz drew from the Spanish case his conviction that "People's War" could be of great value.[35] The insurrection was an anticipation of partisan warfare in the Second World War.

Brutality was not the sole issue in suppressing insurgencies. In addition, there was a continuation for the counterinsurgency side from the establishment of larger armies from the second half of the seventeenth century, not least with the development of conscription in the eighteenth. Scale was readily apparent, as well as the overcoming of organizational, operational, and logistical problems. The military effectiveness, in the widest sense, of Western states increased as formidable resources were devoted to warfare and as the practice of the mobilization of a large proportion of national manpower for warfare became more insistent. This greater effectiveness posed a serious problem for insurgencies.

Such insurgencies were not new, but they became more important in 1792–1815, in part because the French revolutionaries and Napoleon destroyed or took over existing power structures and also because they accelerated processes of change that much of the population already found inimical. In particular, attacks on the church and Christian practices, let alone full-scale atheistical de-Christianization, were far from popular. So also with the pressure of meeting onerous French demands for supplies and conscripts for their army, and with seizures of goods and money. The net effect was a widespread opposition, with insurgencies of various types seen across larger areas of Europe as French forces advanced, for example, into Naples. The French responded with troops, which were referred to as flying columns, by the use of the gendarmerie (mobile armed police), and by recruiting local allies.[36]

CONCLUSIONS

The international dimension repeatedly underlines the role of contingency. In the 1780s and 1790s, radical movements in the Austrian Netherlands (Belgium), the United Provinces (modern Netherlands), Geneva, and Liège, and a reforming patriotic movement in Poland were all suppressed by external force, in most cases rapidly, as the Irish rising of 1798 also was by the British. That this course failed in North America, France, Haiti, and, later,

Latin America was due not to any special characteristics of these revolutions—a unique social structure or a particular ideology—but, rather, to specific political circumstances, both domestic and international, and, ultimately, to the course of conflict and the related politics. The distance offered by the Atlantic played a major role in the cases of North America, Haiti, and Latin America. The presence of colonial militias was also significant in providing a basis for insurgent movements. Environmental factors were also significant, notably in Haiti.

The great variety of goals sought by insurgents and the strength of loyalist movements also repeatedly emerge. Where insurgency occurred, moreover, it was frequently reactionary insofar as the term is helpful: not, in other words, as a result of a demand for change, but, rather, a violent response to governments and rulers seeking change and believed to be desirous of more. This was the case with the Thirteen Colonies in 1775, with Hungary and the Austrian Netherlands in the late 1780s, and with Sweden in 1792. This element remained a factor during the nineteenth century, as with the American Civil War and subsequently in Japan. It is an element that tends to be downplayed in work on insurgencies as this work usually emphasizes their radical character.

Chapter Five

Insurgencies in an Age of Imperialism: The Nineteenth Century

This is essentially a military government. The regular army is too strong for the unarmed millions, who would otherwise not allow the government to stand for six months; and while the government has the direction of the army, the latter will continue to be paid, and the former supported by the bayonets in its authority.

—Richard Rush

The situation in Britain in 1820 was in fact far more complex than Richard Rush, the markedly hostile American envoy, argued.[1] Not least, he did not capture the range of social, political, and ideological factors making for stability and cohesion. Nevertheless, Rush appreciated the role of force in ensuring control.

The Westerncentric character of most military history and the preference for studying conventional warfare between the armies of states are both repeatedly shown in the established treatment of insurgency and counterinsurgency warfare in the nineteenth century. First, the importance of the topic outside the West and notably in China is underplayed. Second, within the West, the amount of attention devoted to the Latin American Wars of Independence, wars that had a lasting impact, is generally inadequate. In contrast, much more attention is devoted to Napoleon, who, ultimately, was a military and political failure. In the case of Europe, those insurrections that played a key role in leading to independence or that can be otherwise seen as modern attract much attention, not least due to a focus on nationalism as a leading narrative for the century. In contrast, insurgencies that do not have this theme, for example, the Carlist ones in Spain, are neglected. Last, the American Civil War is generally approached by military historians as a conflict between regular militaries rather than as an ultimately unsuccessful insurrection.

This background helps to explain why this chapter adopts a distinctive approach. As elsewhere in the book, there is due attention to China. There is then a discussion of the Islamic world, before consideration of the Latin American Wars of Independence and then the situation in the United States. Lastly, Europe is considered.

Organization by geographical area captures the significance of spatial area for context as opposed to that of chronology, which, in practice, was less significant. As with the earlier discussion of the 1790s, it is helpful to appreciate that the Taiping rebellion in China partly coincided with the Risorgimento in Italy, the American and Mexican civil wars, and the 1863 Polish rebellion, but, nevertheless, there is little in the way of common themes. Nor would talk of an overlapping putative mid-century crisis, focused on the European risings in 1848–49 or an earlier one of 1815–30 encompassing Europe and Latin America, be of much assistance to considering the issue on the global scale.

CHINA

The Taiping rebellion began in 1850 as a reaction against Manchu rule that included an attempt to create a new Han Chinese dynasty that would unite Christianity and Confucianism. Unlike the American Civil War, this was not a separatist struggle. Their ideological conviction helped make the Taipings formidable in battle, although the leadership was flawed and divided. The rebellion led to a lengthy and debilitating civil war which lessened any chance that the Chinese would be able to resist Western pressure successfully, let alone to project power. The Taiping forces relied heavily on spears, halberds, and matchlock muskets, although they also acquired several thousand modern firearms.

However, Taiping numbers were considerable. About three-quarters of a million troops took Nanjing in 1853: mines created breaches in the wall, through which the outer city was stormed, and human wave attacks carried the inner city's walls. That winter, a Taiping expedition advanced to within seventy miles of Beijing, but it was insufficiently supported, retreated in 1854, and was destroyed the following year. Their westward advance was also stopped after bitter fighting in 1854–55, while the Taipings were affected by civil war in 1856, by regime resilience, and by the shift of foreign support to the Manchu in 1860: Taiping attempts to take Shanghai were blocked by Anglo-French firepower then and in 1862. The ability of the regime to rely on domestic support against the Taipings was highly significant because there were relatively few fortresses in the interior. The regime permitted key officials with potent regional links to raise their own armies and helped maintain coherence by providing some of their funds.[2] In 1860, the imperial siege of Nanjing was broken by the Taipings, but in 1864, the city was captured, and in 1866 the last Taiping force was defeated.

After the chaos of the Taiping years, there was a Chinese reaffirmation of control over border areas that had also rebelled. Muslim rebellions in southwest China (1856) and northwest China (1863), the Panthay and Shaan-Gan uprisings, respectively, were defeated after considerable effort. The Panthay revolt in Yunnan in southwest China came to a close in 1873 with the death of its leader and the fall of its capital, Tali. The expansion of the road system across Yunnan helped the Chinese. In turn, the insurgency in Chinese Turkestan in northwest China was defeated in 1876–78. As with the Chinese conquest of the region in the 1750s, this was a formidable organizational achievement, as the logistical task of supporting troops at this distance and across arid lands was difficult. The Chinese were helped by divisions among their opponents and by the suicide of the latter's ablest leader, Ya'qub Beg of Khokand, in 1877, following the capture of his capital at Turfan. It is all too typical of priorities among military historians that Tao Tsung-t'ang, the victorious Chinese general and a veteran of the suppression of the Taiping rebellion, is largely unknown.

JAPAN

Modernization in Japan led to civil war and insurgency in the 1860s and 1870s. The civil warfare of 1866–68 demonstrated the superiority of Western weaponry, and the privileged, caste nature of military service was replaced by conscription, which was introduced in 1869. The two systems, one traditional, one European and modern, were brought into conflict in 1877 with a samurai insurgency in the southwestern domain of Satsuma. This brought a substantial samurai force armed with swords and matchlock muskets into combat with a new mass army of conscripted peasants. Individual military prowess and bravery succumbed to the organized, disciplined force of an army that, on an individual basis, was less proficient.

Conscription, both in Japan and more generally in the nineteenth century and subsequently, was a key aid to counterinsurgency. In Persia (Iran) in the twentieth century, for example, conscription broke down the division between a small, and sometimes Westernized, regular army and very differently armed levies that were often tribal in character. Moreover, even if intended primarily for helping engage in conventional, state-to-state warfare, conscription created a vital numerical resource, for counterinsurgency required large numbers of troops.

ISLAMIC WORLD

Confronted by a range of domestic and international problems, the Turkish empire faced insurgencies from the Christian Balkans to Muslim Arabia. There were also rebellions in the center. In Constantinople, in 1807, the attempt by Sultan Selim III (r. 1789–1807) to introduce control over the janissaries led to a major rebellion. This was in part a struggle within the complex military system of the empire as Selim was supported by provincial forces whom he brought to Constantinople. The janissaries survived the crisis, which ended Selim's reign, only to be brutally suppressed by Sultan Mahmud II (r. 1808–39) in 1826.

As an instructive precursor to current issues in tackling Muslim insurgencies, the Turks confronted a major challenge on what therefore became a frontier of power in Arabia. The authority that the sultan claimed in Arabia and, more generally, Ottoman Muslim legitimacy as a whole were challenged by the fundamentalist Wahhabis in the early nineteenth century, continuing an opposition already serious in the eighteenth century. In accordance with orders from Mahmud II, Mehmet Ali, the viceroy of Egypt (r. 1805–48), successfully defeated them in the 1810s, recapturing the sacred cities of Mecca and Medina in 1812–13. With the Saudi ruler Abdallah I (r. 1814–18) executed in 1818 and his capital seized, the Wahhabis were relegated to the harsh terrain of the desert. There, they remained a long-standing nuisance rather than a threat. Internecine conflict among the tribal leaders helped the Egyptian forces against the Wahhabis, but the difficulty of securing stability is a lesson still relevant today.

Mehmet Ali also provided help to suppress the Greek insurgency against Turkish rule that broke out in 1821. Mehmet's forces crushed the rising on Crete in 1824 and had an initial success when they landed in southern Greece in 1825. The Greeks were reliant on irregulars, many of whom were brigands. The Egyptian intervention was crucial because of weaknesses and division in the Turkish army. In turn, the destruction of the Turkish-Egyptian fleet at the battle of Navarino Bay in 1827 by an Anglo-French-Russian fleet helped to sway the struggle in Greece in favor of independence, not least because naval support provided opportunities for action against Turkish garrisons such as that at Nauplion. Greece gained independence in 1830. Thus, the international context had proved a vital element, as it also had with the Spanish opposition to French rule. In the 1830s, Mehmet Ali, already autonomous, successfully rebelled against Turkish rule over Egypt, which was never reimposed. He then advanced north into Syria, but Western pressure helped stop his advance. He benefited in this and other conflicts from the strength of his well-organized military system, which included conscription.

The Turks faced a series of insurgencies in their Balkan territories. Again, the international context was crucial. The Serbian insurgency of 1804–13 began as a reaction to harsh control by semi-independent Turkish troops and became a fight for independence. The Serbs plundered and destroyed Muslim settlements and drove the Muslims out. However, the Serbs were defeated by Turkish forces, who in turn burned down Serbian villages. Crucially, Austria and Russia then preferred to focus on war with Napoleon and did not provide the Serbs with assistance. As a result of this nonintervention, the Turkish abandonment of Serbia proved to be a longer process.

In an insurgency launched in 1876, the Bulgarians lacked adequate weaponry, organization, and leadership, but harsh Turkish reprisals, notably by Muslim irregulars, rallied crucial international support. Russian intervention in 1877 led to Bulgarian independence. At the same time, in contrast to Bulgaria, control of the marginal areas in the Balkans was only of so much significance militarily and politically. Thus, in 1852–62, insurrection on the Herzegovinian-Montenegrin border and, in 1885, irregular rebellious bands in Macedonia made scant impact on the Turks. The overlap between insurgency, brigandage, and unconventional warfare made it difficult to suppress opposition.

The same was true in the Asian borderlands of the empire. Opposition there attracted and continues to attract less attention than in the European section of the empire, but this opposition could be significant, for example, in Iraq and Jordan.[3] This significance was underlined when, as in Lebanon, this opposition attracted international intervention, by France in that case. The Ottoman recognition of the freedom of religion in 1856 did not prevent sectarianism and strife in Lebanon.[4] Elsewhere, tribal chiefs, for example, in Jordan, reacted violently to attempts to adapt long-established military-fiscal relationships, notably the emphasis on a regular army supported by taxation. This policy also led to a tribal uprising in Afghanistan in 1841 against the British and their attempt to create a new system to support their client as ruler.

There were also insurgencies in Persia, including, in the late 1840s, unsuccessful revolts by the Babi movement, a radical Shia tendency. Islamic revivalism caused serious problems in Sudan, leading, in one of the most successful insurgencies of the period, to the overthrow of Egyptian rule there in the early 1880s. At Sahykan in 1883, an Egyptian army was heavily defeated by that of Muhammad Ahmad Abdallah, a revivalist who persuaded many Sudanese that he was al-Mahdi, the Messiah. He had declared a *jihad* in 1881. The Mahdists were finally defeated by a large-scale British invasion, notably at the battle of Omdurman, outside Khartoum, in 1898.

LATIN AMERICA

The Latin American Wars of Independence revealed many of the characteristics of more recent insurgency struggles, including the interrelationships with international developments and supporters, the role of political determination, and the extent to which the supporters of the opposing side were terrorized. Ethnic tensions also played a major role in the wars. They are in a pattern beginning with the War of American Independence and continuing with the slave revolution on the French colony of Saint-Domingue, which led in 1804 to the establishment of the independent state of Haiti. The international dimension was also important in Saint-Domingue, as, in 1803, a British blockade was a significant element in wrecking the French attempt to recapture the colony. The French had been able to begin this attempt only because Britain and France were temporarily at peace in 1802–3. As an instance of how interpretations change, reflecting in large part political as well as academic fashions, the international dimension to this struggle has been downplayed for decades, with the emphasis instead being on the strength of the local resistance, an element far more conducive to accounts linked to the "empowerment" of insurgents.

This is not the sole instance of a significant international dimension. In explaining the Latin American Wars of Independence, there was also the key element of Napoleon's invasion of Spain in 1808. The invasion provoked the seizure of power across the empire by *juntas* supporting the imprisoned king. This seizure accustomed the colonies to self-government, and when, from 1814, the restored royal family attempted to reimpose control across Spanish America, it was resisted. In Santo Domingo (modern Dominican Republic), the French occupation was overthrown in 1808 with its army defeated at Palo Hincado.

Taking place over a far larger area (Mexico to Chile) than the War of American Independence and lacking the military and political coherence of the latter (for there was no equivalent to the Continental Congress or the Continental Army), any description of the Latin American Wars of Independence risks becoming a confused account with rapid changes of fortune. Major mountain chains and the problems posed by disease, such as yellow fever on the eastern coast of Mexico, accentuated the problems of operating. As in the War of American Independence, there was no automatic success for the revolutionary forces, and they were not inherently better at combat than their opponents. Instead, both sides adapted to the issues and problems of conflict across a vast area in which it was difficult to fix success or, indeed, to arrange logistical support. These problems helped ensure the significance of local and regional dimensions. The result, as in Mexico, could be the fragmentation of the insurgency.[5] The same was true of the army whose units engaged in counterinsurgency operations with little central supervision, while their commanders tried to build up local power bases. Logistical needs helped compromise the popularity of both sides, while the expropriation and looting involved in obtaining supplies inflicted much damage on society. Meanwhile, the royalists were also badly hit by shifts in policy within Spain, shifts which alienated support in Latin America and indeed culminated in a civil war in Spain in 1823. At the same time, fighting ability and command skills, especially those of José de San Martin in Chile in 1817–18 and of Simón Bolívar in the more intractable struggle in northern South America and the Andean chain in 1813–25, were important in wearing down the resistance of the increasingly isolated royalist forces.

The international dimension was crucial. Indeed, rather than treating these independence struggles simply as a failure of European power, it is more accurate to regard them as an aspect of a shift in power within the West— namely, the major expansion of British informal empire. There had long been British interest in the commercial penetration of Latin America and in supporting its independence from Spain. British volunteers and diplomatic and naval support were important in the Wars of Independence, not least in dissuading possible French intervention on behalf of Spain. Once independent, the Latin American powers, which, while colonies, had been excluded by the colonial powers from direct trade with Britain, developed close trading relations and became prime areas for British investment.

The ethnic dimension helped complicate the Latin American Wars of Independence. Largely supported by *mestizos* ("half-European, half Indian" people), the insurgencies were seen as a threat to *criollos*, who feared a race war, and this perception encouraged the *criollo* elites of Cuba, Mexico, and Peru to side with Spain. As a result, the royalists were able to use local militias against the rebels. In turn, Bolívar executed prominent *mestizo* leaders, allegedly for advocating race war but also to retain control of the struggle.

The royalists could win repeated successes, not least from using light cavalry columns. A new generation of active royalist officers from Spain, who had gained experience in insurgency conflict against the French, arrived in Latin America in the mid-1810s and helped the royalists devise new counterinsurgency techniques. In the Papantla region, near Veracruz in Mexico, which had rebelled in 1812, the royal reconquest of the towns by 1818 did not end the insurgency. Instead, it developed into a guerrilla war, with royalist garrisons in the towns unable to control rural hinterlands. In the summer of 1820, a change of approach under a new royalist commander, José Rincón, altered the tempo of the war. Whereas previously the rainy season had served as a break in campaigning, providing the rebels with an opportunity to recover, Rincón planned no such break. In a campaign against the rebel stronghold of Coyusquihui, he circled the area with forts and kept campaigning, which hit the rebels. However, the royalists were badly affected by disease. Both sides agreed to a settlement that year.[6]

Despite royalist successes, notably in Venezuela in 1806, 1812, 1816, and 1818, in Bolivia in 1811 and 1815, in Chile in 1814, and in Mexico in 1815, it proved most difficult to bring the struggle to a close. Insurgents withdrew to more isolated regions from which resistance continued.[7] The royalists failed to devise an effective strategy for reconciliation,[8] and their emphasis on repression, including, in Venezuela, the forcible relocation of civilians into camps, proved counterproductive. Such relocation was also to be seen in Cuba in the 1890s, in the Boer War (1899–1902), in British policy in Malaya in the 1950s, and in American policy in South Vietnam. In Latin America, the ability of revolutionary commanders to exploit the failure of reconciliation and to persist in the face of adversity was crucial. Ultimately, the royalists were defeated in battle in Peru, a bastion of royalism, in 1824, that of Ayacucho on December 9 proving decisive. Antonio José de Sucre, with 5,780 troops, defeated the viceroy, José de la Serna, and his 9,300 troops by repelling attacks before using his reserves of infantry and cavalry to break through and encircle part of the opposing force. The loss of many of the senior royalist commanders, including the captured viceroy, in this battle left the royalists leaderless.

The situation was different in Mexico, where an insurrection in 1810 had been hit hard in 1811–12 and 1815, while the guerrilla war had nearly ended by 1820. The royalist effort, however, was weakened by the liberal constitutional revolution in Spain in 1820, rather as the British effort in North America was undermined by the change in the government in 1782. Viewed as an unwelcome development by *criollo* conservatives and by those who wielded power in Mexico, this revolution led to a declaration of independence. In 1821, Augustín de Iturbide, the leading general, searching for a solution based on consensus, agreed with the rebels on a declaration of independence that proved widely acceptable. Under great pressure elsewhere, Spain accepted the situation that year,[9] again as with the British in the American Revolutionary War.

After the Wars of Independence, Latin America tends to disappear from military history. This is particularly mistaken for any account of insurgencies because they were important in leading to a series of civil wars. Some were large scale, for example, that in Argentina in 1852–62, in which foreign intervention played a crucial role, as in 1852, when Juan Manuel de Rosas was defeated at Caseros by domestic opponents (provincial federalists) supported by troops from Brazil and Uruguay. Federalists and *unitarios* had earlier waged a civil war in Argentina in 1828–29. Moreover, across Latin America, states splintered or held together as a result of rebellions and their fate. Successful rebellions by Venezuela, Texas, and Bolivia, in 1829–30, 1835–36, and 1840–41, respectively, led to their independence from Grán

Colombia, Mexico, and Peru. For Paraguay, which declared independence in 1811, the war of independence was largely fought in order to win freedom from Buenos Aires.

Texas had been troublesome after Mexico declared independence from Spain. In 1826, there was an attempt to create a Republic of Fredonia near Nacogdoches that was rapidly put down in early 1827. Significantly, militias composed of local American settlers joined Mexican troops from San Antonio in suppressing this attempt, as the rebels angered important American settler interests as well as the Mexican government. However, Texas's population grew rapidly in the 1820s and early 1830s as a result of immigration from America, which owed much to the Southern land hunger also seen in movement into Arkansas and Mississippi. This immigration led to Mexican concern about the degree of central governmental control in Texas, and, as a result, American immigration was stopped from 1830. In 1832 and 1833, Texan conventions called for separate statehood within Mexico, as well as the freedoms and liberties they regarded as their due. Slavers in Texas were hostile to Mexico's opposition to slavery, and, when Texas won independence, slavery again became legal.

Fighting between Mexicans and Texans began in October 1835, when troops sought to take back a cannon they had provided to help settlers deter attack by Native Americans, part of the equation of threat and force. The following month, a convention, known as the Consultation of All Texans, created a provisional state government that was designed to negotiate with Mexico. However, the Mexican strongman, an authoritarian centralist, General Antonio López de Santa Anna, characteristically tried to deal with the situation by force. The abrogation in 1835 of the 1824 constitution, under which the Americans had settled in Texas, and the claim that their failure to convert to Catholicism meant that their land grants were void, were unacceptable to the Texans. The centralist policy was resisted in Texas not only by most of the Anglo colonists but also by many Texans of Hispanic origin, which was an aspect of the fluidity of loyalties and identities in the region, a fluidity also seen in the Latin American Wars of Independence.

On February 23, 1836, Santa Anna and his army reached the town of San Antonio, where the outnumbered Texan defenders of the poorly fortified Alamo mission were defeated in a storming on March 6. Meanwhile, on March 2, the Texans had declared independence. Santa Anna pressed on farther east. However, he had divided his forces and was operating without reliable information. Santa Anna was surprised, outfought, and rapidly beaten at San Jacinto on April 21 by a smaller army under Sam Houston that successfully took the initiative, launching a surprise attack.

On May 14, 1836, the captured Santa Anna signed agreements bringing peace, withdrawing the Mexican army, and recognizing Texan independence. The remaining Mexican forces in Texas far outnumbered the Texan army and, indeed, the force defeated at San Jacinto. However, the Mexican commanders obeyed Santa Anna's order to retreat, and Texas was evacuated. The inability of Mexico to sustain the struggle in part arose from the limited number of Mexican settlers in the northern provinces. The uninviting topographic layout of northern Mexico and an inability to progress much beyond subsistence agriculture reflected itself in the motley population of that area and accordingly in an inability to build up and sustain a meaningful population base. In contrast, Santa Anna was more successful in suppressed federalist revolts in Tampico and Mexico City in 1839 and 1840, respectively, although he failed at Acapulco and in Michoacán in 1854 and 1855, respectively. The latter failure led to his fall.

In Brazil, where a rebellion in 1822 by the regent, the eldest son of the king, followed by a civil war ultimately ended in 1825 had led to independence from Portugal, regional insurgencies in 1832–45, for example, the Sabinada in Bahia in 1837–38, did not lead to a fragmentation similar to that in former Spanish America. In part, this was because of the rebels' failure to cooperate, a failure that owes something to the environmental characteristics of Brazil, including the dispersed nature of population and the divisive consequences of the large numbers of rivers. Social tension played a major role in these risings, with popular opposition to social and economic dominance by the elite, especially by large landowners. Government forces were hindered by the size of the areas of operations, poor communications, and a lack of adequate training, pay, and food leading to desertion, and the situation was exacerbated by the disruption caused by the conflict. In the case of the rebellion of the Cabanos in the region of Pernambuco in 1832–35, guerrilla operations created grave difficulties for the government forces until, at the close of 1834, more active measures were put into place, especially maintaining the initiative, destroying Cabano crops in the forest regions, and harrying those suspected of being Cabanos. The use of *corpos de batedores* in this fashion was both arbitrary and effective. The population suspected of sympathy for the rebels was removed, and the Cabanos were isolated and increasingly short of food. Desertion by the Cabanos was encouraged, not least by the active use of the church, and the rebellion was overcome.[10]

Similarly, insurrection against Mexican rule in the Yucatán, an insurgency mainly sustained by the Maya-speaking poor and fired by more wide-ranging peasant resentment, broke out in 1847. The main focus was not independence but rather disputes over social conditions, for example, access to agricultural land and taxation. These disputes played a major role in the so-called Caste War. Like many civil wars, this was brutal. Raiding and the seizure of goods were crucial to rebel logistics, while government troops destroyed rebel settlements and fields and killed prisoners. The rebels also killed civilians, including pregnant women. Religion was significant, with the Cult of the Speaking Cross developing from 1850 and providing cohesion for the rebels, prefiguring the cult of "Santa Muerta" in Mexico today. Nevertheless, the insurrection had largely been suppressed in 1848. Forced to retreat to the more isolated southeast of the Yucatán, a jungle area with few roads, some of the rebels submitted in 1853, but others continued their resistance for several decades.[11] This looked toward twentieth-century opposition there.

Insurgencies against what was seen as foreign rule became less common in Latin America after the Wars of Independence, but Spain's continued colonial presence in Cuba was marked by two large-scale insurgencies, each of which was to be extensively memorialized by the Communist regime that took power in Cuba in 1959. As with the original Latin American Wars of Liberation, there was a link between political division in Spain and in its colonies. The first insurgency, in 1868, was linked to a successful army rebellion in Spain. In Cuba, the rebels concentrated on taking advantage of the terrain through ambushes and by harrying Spanish forces with rifle fire, especially if, as at Palo Seco in 1873, the Spaniards formed infantry squares and thus offered concentrated targets. In turn, the Spaniards benefited greatly from ethnic, geographical, and social divisions among the Cubans and from the willingness of many Cubans, in part as a result, to support Spain. In particular, from 1870, the Spaniards were helped by ethnic tensions, as Cuban whites increasingly rejected what they now saw as a black-run revolution focused on opposition to slavery, while conservative loyalists provided powerful support for Spain. Spanish forces also employed harsh measures, including the killing of rebel families and the forced relocation of the rural population so as to create free-fire zones and to prevent the rebels from gaining access to civilian aid. Once civil war in Spain ended in 1876, twenty-five thousand troops were sent to Cuba, and a combination of military action and conciliatory promises led to a settlement there in 1878 that restored Spanish control. These equations of strength, effectiveness, and success were very common in counterinsurgency warfare. The area in dispute was smaller than that in the United States during the Civil War (1861–65), but the terrain and ecosystem were more difficult. Mountains were prominent in Cuba, and there was thick overgrowth as well as many short rivers that flowed into the Caribbean.

The insurgency, however, was to resume and to lead to a large-scale conflict in the mid-1890s that highlighted the problems of both guerrilla and counterinsurgency warfare. The insurgents hit the economy, destroying the sugar and tobacco crops, in an attempt to create mass unemployment and to force refugees to become a burden on the Spaniards. The insurgents were initially successful in evading attempts to engage them in battle, in part because the Spanish forces attempted to cover the entire country. The insurgency indicated both the difficulties of counterinsurgency operations for regular forces and the nature of low-level conflict. This was a war in which raids and ambushes played a major role and in which control over supplies was important to both the regulars and the insurgents. Preventing opponents' access to supplies was the goal of many operations. Thus, in December 1895, the insurgents ambushed a Spanish column at Mal Tiempo, capturing two hundred rifles and replenishing supplies of ammunition. The use of machetes in this attack underlined the extent to which insurgency warfare still involved hand-to-hand conflict. In this ambush, the Spaniards were not able to bring their Mauser rifles effectively to bear.

In turn, the Spaniards sought to fix their opponents so that they could use their firepower as at Manacal earlier that month, when Spanish artillery helped drive the insurgents from a defensive position. The new Spanish captain-general, Valeriano Weyler (1838–1930), had extensive experience of the range of counterinsurgency operations. He had served already in Cuba (1868–72), had fought the Carlist rebels in Spain (1874–75) as well as rebels in the Philippines (1888–92), had maintained order in the Basque provinces and Navarre (1892–93), and had been used against striking miners in Catalonia. In Cuba, Weyler combined defensive lines with effective field offensives. He also had a social strategy based on the enforced movement of people to the towns, where, surrounded by barbed wire in what the Spaniards called concentration camps, they were hard hit by disease and food shortages. Due in particular to yellow fever, 150,000–170,000 Cubans died in the camps. The insurgents were driven from western Cuba in 1896. Successful American intervention in 1898, which led to the end of Spanish rule, prevents us from knowing how long Weyler's policies would have achieved results.[12]

Opposition to Spanish rule had provided a structural reason for insurgencies in Cuba. Elsewhere, structural reasons in large part reflected the interplay of state weakness and political division. The wars of independence had seen the disruption of the colonial state with its emphasis on bureaucracy and the rise, instead, of the *caudillos*, regional chieftains who used control over land and armed clients to seek a form of power that was personal rather than institutional. Similarly, guerrilla bandits rose to prominence.[13]

Meanwhile, there was also a widespread pattern of insurrection in independent countries, with force being used to contest power as well as to resist government. Thus, in Mexico in 1858–61, the War of Reform pitched Conservative opponents against the Liberal government of Benito Juárez. The difficulty of achieving a lasting settlement in Mexico reflected the complex interplay of sectional advantage and regional power bases. French military intervention encouraged the Conservatives in 1863 to offer the throne of Mexico to Archduke Maximilian of Austria. In response, there was a long guerrilla war led by Juárez, one that saw frequent atrocities on both sides, notably the killing of prisoners. French and Austrian support was significant. However, the French, forty thousand troops at the peak, were unable to progress from seizing positions to stabilizing the situation. Due to guerrilla conflict, which compensated the Republicans for failures in battle, as at San Luis Potosi in 1863, the French found it difficult to consolidate control. Putting aside his pronounced social bias, Peter Scarlett, the British envoy in Mexico, reporting in February 1865, captured a key element:

> Fresh bands of guerrillas seem to start up everywhere like the heads of the hydra as often as others are put down, and partly from the natural and habitual love of a plundering life on the part of a lawless and ruffianly population, and partly from the inadequate and insufficient number of foreign troops, especially cavalry, to deal with this evil, the eradication of it is indeed a labour of Hercules.[14]

However, conventional warfare was also important, as in 1866, when the Republicans successfully besieged Oaxaca, repulsing a relief column. French withdrawal from Mexico in 1867, a withdrawal that reflected developments in Europe, notably the troubling rise of Prussia, victorious over Austria in 1866, was followed by Maximilian's defeat in battle and execution, securing victory for the Republicans.[15]

In turn, in Mexico, Porfirio Díaz, a prominent figure in the war against Maximilian, rebelled in 1871 when he lost the presidential election to Juárez. He failed, was given amnesty in 1872, and then, in the Revolution of Tuxtepec in 1875–76, rebelled successfully against Juárez's successor, Sebastián Lerdo de Tejada (having lost the election to him in 1875). Díaz then held power until he himself was displaced in 1911 by another rebellion arising from a contested presidential election.

In Latin America, notions of rightful authority were frequently contested, and the normal processes of politics often involved force, as in the seizures of power in Argentina and Colombia in 1861, in Guatemala in 1871, in El Salvador in 1876, in Venezuela in 1899, and on many other occasions. Due to force-space ratios and the difficulty of sustaining armies, much of the fighting was a matter of rapid advances and short battles. Towns were usually stormed rather than besieged. The killing of prisoners was frequent, both because the facilities and food for holding and supporting them were limited and in order to hit opponents' morale and to intimidate others from backing them, which were key elements in the politics of war. The willingness of troops to resist was a major factor in the fighting. There was, moreover, the slaughter of civilians and the destruction of property by regulars and irregulars alike. The wars also showed the extent to which ideology, in the shape of struggles between Conservatives and Liberals, played a major role in conflict before the revolutionary warfare touched off by the Russian Revolution.

Foreign intervention was frequently significant, with Conservatives and Liberals both looking for support from foreign colleagues. Thus, in 1836, Peru backed a failed attempt to overthrow the Conservative government in

Chile, and in 1863, the forces of El Salvador unsuccessfully intervened in Nicaragua in order to support a Liberal insurgency, but, in 1864–65, Brazilian forces successfully intervened in Uruguay on behalf of the Liberals. In 1871, Honduras helped a rebel in El Salvador gain power. The military played a key role in insurgencies, as in Brazil in 1889, when the monarchy was overthrown in a coup that led to army officers benefiting from salary increases. In 1891, a military revolt there brought the vice president, Floriano Peixoto, to power.

THE AMERICAN CIVIL WARS AND AFTER

The warfare in Latin America provides a context within which to assess the American Civil War of 1861–65 initially as a successful insurgency but eventually as a complete failure. The American Civil War was not particularly long, as civil warfare in mid-century Argentina and Mexico indicated, but the scale, in terms of the manpower and resources used, was larger. This reflected the greater wealth of America and the ability of both sides to mobilize resources for what was very much a novel struggle. On the other hand, as a percentage of the available manpower and material resources, the contrast may not have been so great.

As a prelude to the American Civil War of 1861–65, it is instructive to consider the Mormon (Latter Day Saints) attempt to create an independent nation, the so-called Kingdom of God on Earth, or at least Utah, where the Mormons moved in 1850. There were tensions over Mormon hopes for an extensive state (Deseret) in the American West and Southwest and over the attempt to prevent non-Mormons from arriving. In addition, Mormon claims, both political and other, notably the public endorsement of polygamy in 1856, proved incompatible with federal pretensions, leading federal officials to decide that the Mormons were in a state of rebellion.[16] In 1857, President James Buchanan determined that the Mormons were in rebellion. This decision led to the appointment of a non-Mormon to succeed the Mormon leader, Brigham Young, as governor of the Utah Territory and to the dispatch of 2,500 troops to provide necessary support. This represented much of the army that could be used for an expedition once the numbers linked to garrisoning fortified positions were taken into account.

Young represented these troops as "a hostile force who are evidently assailing us to accomplish our overthrow and destruction," and prepared a response including a withdrawal from northern Utah into the Wasatch Mountains. Mormon militias burned three of the army's supply trains in early October 1857, although they were instructed not to take life. This move helped to delay the army force, which had at any rate been dispatched too late in the year. Captain Stewart Van Vliet, who was sent to Salt Lake City in

September, in order to demand supplies for the army, reported that the Mormons would not help and that they would fight to stop the army entering Utah, if necessary responding with a scorched-earth policy and taking refuge in the mountains, where they had stored food and could destroy American forces.

War, however, was avoided as the result of an agreement in 1858 in which Young lost the governorship, the Mormons were pardoned, and the army stayed outside Salt Lake City. Instead, it established Camp Floyd nearby, and this position helped support emigrant trains on the Oregon Trail, which the Mormons had earlier attacked. In 1861, as a result of the decision of the federal authorities, Utah lost territory to Colorado and Nevada, although conflict was avoided and plans to partition Utah were abandoned.

The South launched a far more formidable and widespread insurgency than the Mormons. This was an insurgency both by secession, beginning with South Carolina, on December 20, 1860, and by forming the Confederate States of America. In turn, responding to Confederate forces opening fire on the federal island position of Fort Sumter in Charleston Harbor on April 12, 1861, President Abraham Lincoln went to war to maintain the Union. Lincoln's clear intention to invade the Lower South played a major role in leading much of the Upper South, notably Virginia, North Carolina, and Tennessee, to join the Confederacy, which gave the insurgency strategic depth and far more resources. Alongside the insurgency at this level, the Civil War was a conflict within the states that seceded, most clearly in Appalachia and Missouri. In these states, there was internal conflict between Confederate supporters and Unionists.

Each side faced formidable problems in the Civil War. Unprepared for the difficulty of the struggle both militarily and politically, Union forces had to try to shift the political balance within the South in order to lead to its surrender. Conversely, the Confederates had to hope that their military success would lead the Union to change policy and/or encourage Britain and France to enter the war.

The factor of scale was certainly very different to that in Switzerland, another federal state, in 1847. A secessionist league of Catholic cantons, the Sonderbund, fought the Protestant-dominated Swiss Confederacy. The war lasted only twenty-five days, and the Confederate forces, ably led by Guillaume Dufour, won the key engagement, at Gislikon. The secessionists lacked determination and military resources, and only ninety-three people were killed in the war.[17] In contrast, and on a totally different scale, the Taiping rebellion in China, which was not a secessionist struggle, lasted for over a decade.

The eventual defeat of the Confederate insurgency can be differently explained. In April 1865, in his farewell address to his soldiers, Robert E. Lee, the commander of the main Confederate field army from 1862 to 1865, the Army of Northern Virginia, argued that they had been "compelled to yield to overwhelming power," a theme that was to be taken up often, as by Jubal Early, a Confederate general, in an 1872 address at Washington and Lee University. Indeed, the Union had a formidable advantage, notably in manpower, manufacturing plant, railway track, agricultural production, trade, money, and bullion, but also in other factors. The disparity was greatly accentuated by the economic and financial dislocation stemming from the Union naval blockade of the Confederacy, although the blockade was not airtight: blockade runners got through, the Confederacy acquiring Enfield rifled muskets by this means.

Yet resources no more explain the course and outcome of insurgencies than of other conflicts. A host of factors affect the use and effectiveness of resources, notably their coordination and deployment. For example, the creation of the US Military Railroad as a branch of the War Department and the introduction of income tax and paper currency all were important to Northern effectiveness. Unlike the Confederacy, the Union could raise substantial loans without causing damaging inflation. Moreover, more than resources are involved in war. The respective goals were also significant. In the case of the Southern insurgency in 1861–65, there was an asymmetry of grand strategic aims. The Confederacy, ultimately, had only to fend off the Union, a goal which did not require its conquest. In contrast, the Union had at least to crush Confederate military power and probably to occupy considerable swaths of the Confederacy in order to force it back into the Union. Thus, as is often the case, the weaker power was helped by having the more modest goal, although it had to persuade the strong power to stop attacking.

At the same time, the counterinsurgency goals changed. For the Union, the failure of conciliation as a means to end the conflict was eventually linked to the definition of more radical war goals by Lincoln. Reflecting the lack of any prospect of compromise, these goals, however, put even greater premium on military victory, while, in turn, this premium made the issue of warlike ardor and political determination in the North of more importance. As so often, shifting goals were important to the viability of both insurgencies and the attempt to suppress them. Frustration on the home front with the intractability of the struggle affected Union goals, and George B. McClellan, the commander of the Army of the Potomac, the main Union army, who had advocated a conciliatory strategy to undermine Southern support for the insurgency, was replaced by Lincoln in late 1862 after he failed to deliver. [18]

The emphasis shifted to how best to win a long conflict, while the Union became committed to the emancipation of the slaves in those parts of the South still in rebellion. This was seen as a way to weaken the Southern economy and thus war effort, as well as providing a clear purpose to maintain Northern morale and a means to assuage the sin that was leading a wrathful God to punish America. Counterinsurgency warfare thus, as so often, extended to include heaven. A strong sense of religious mission helped empower many of the Union soldiers. Having denied God's support by supporting sectional interests, America was to be made new, an affirmation of faith that reflected broad chords in American culture. From 1862, in what was seen as applying the "hard hand of war," Union commanders attacked Southern private property and inflicted collective punishments as well as deporting Confederate supporters, although casualties among noncombatants were very few. Equally, the Confederates were convinced of divine support, a conviction that helped sustain them as the war went badly. Contempt for their opponents also played a major role.[19]

As so often, counterinsurgency involved a process of national mobilization. Claims of necessity were employed to justify the extension of governmental power. This process was eased by the absence of Southern representatives in Congress and the relatively weak position of the Northern Democrats, the opposition to Lincoln's Republicans, who were unable to exploit Republican losses in the November 1862 congressional elections. The power of the federal government was enhanced at the expense of the states, and a host of measures, including conscription (agreed by the Senate in February 1863) and the establishment of a national banking system, were important in themselves and for what they signified. Conscription led to popular resistance that had to be suppressed by force, notably the New York City draft riots in 1863. In practice, conscription did not amount to the *levée en masse* of the French revolutionaries of the 1790s.[20] The critical Democratic presidential platform, agreed by the Democrats in August 1864, declared that "under the pretense of a military necessity or war power higher than the Constitution, the Constitution itself has been disregarded in every part."

In the event, Lincoln, in 1864, won the election and the Republicans, a substantial majority in Congress. Northern morale thus affirmed Lincoln's position, just as his leadership helped ensure the resilience of this morale. The reelection provided the background for the pursuit of a strategy designed to stop Southern support for the war by crippling morale and destroying infrastructure, a goal shared by his troops. This policy began with the destructive shelling of Atlanta during the siege and the subsequent burning down of government buildings and civilian property there. Having captured Atlanta, General William T. Sherman had the civilian population moved out and destroyed much of the city.[21] Although Sherman's devastation of the Confederate hinterland in Georgia and South Carolina in 1864–65 increased the resolve of some Southern soldiers, the Union's ability to spread devastation unhindered exacerbated the already serious tendency to desertion, helped destroy civilian faith in the war, and made the penalty for, and limitation of, guerrilla warfare apparent. Moreover, the slave basis of Southern society collapsed as Union forces advanced, with thousands of slaves using the opportunity to escape. The Confederacy had made the singular error of not utilizing slave soldiers, which contrasted with many slave societies in history.

By making territory his objective, Sherman moved beyond the unproductive nature that that goal and method frequently entailed. Instead, he used the occupation of territory to fulfill his aim of focusing on the psychological mastery of Southern society. This mastery matched the desire (on both sides) to inflict humiliation and vengeance. Sherman sought to wreck Confederate morale.

Confederate attacks had not matched Sherman's operations. Confederate invasions of the North under Lee in 1862 and 1863 had led to Northern panics, as had Jubal Early's raid toward Washington in 1864. However, none of these invasions could be sustained in the face of undefeated Union forces, and each, anyway, lacked the depth of penetration seen with Union advances from the outset, let alone by Sherman in 1864–65.

In their different ways, Sherman and Grant, both of whom were convinced that victory could be won, ensured that the uncertainty of war undermined the Confederacy, for they managed risk and uncertainty. In contrast, their opponents came, in 1864–65, to experience risk in a highly damaging fashion. The tempo of Union operations exploited the uncertainty of conflict and directed it against the Confederacy's military as well as its sociopolitical underpinning. As the war progressed, the nature of the tactics, moreover, moved against the Confederates, with their preference for the charge affected by Union trench positions and by the use by Union defenders of the Minié rifle with its range and speed of reloading.

The Confederate insurgency did not turn to large-scale guerrilla warfare despite the declaration by Jefferson Davis, the Confederate president, in July 1864, in response to Lincoln's emancipation proclamation: "We are fighting for independence—and that, or extermination, we will have. . . . You may emancipate every Negro in the Confederacy, but we will be free. We will govern ourselves . . . if we have to see every Southern plantation sacked, and every Southern city in flames."[22]

This was not an isolated theme. In a reaction to Sherman's advance, Davis pressed for a turn to partisan warfare, while, after the fall of Richmond, the Confederate capital in 1865, Davis suggested a turn to guerrilla warfare, with the army no longer obliged to guard cities. Indeed, this was not an alien concept, as guerrilla warfare had already been seen, for example, in 1862, in areas, notably southern Appalachia, where terrain was difficult and the number of regulars limited.[23] Moreover, in 1848, the last stages of the Mexican-American War had shown the problems the American occupying forces confronted due to continued opposition, and these problems made it valuable to bring the war to an end.

However, the Confederate political and military leadership had proved largely unwilling to encourage guerrilla warfare that, while alongside conventional operations was particularly important in Appalachia and in the Missouri-Kansas region, was not so in the crucial war zones. What is now termed guerrilla warfare, with the misleading implication that it was not waged by regulars, can better be described as irregular warfare by regulars, especially those engaged in raiding activities. The Union forces were able to counter these methods, both by defensive means, especially blockhouses and patrols, and by action designed to fulfill the exemplary threat of retribution and/or to find and engage those directly involved.[24] Indeed, General Orders No. 100, the codification of the laws of war written to guide the army, was a response to the Union's experience in Missouri with guerrilla opposition and civilian resistance. Major General Henry Halleck, the commander of the Department of the Missouri at the outset of the war and later general in chief of the army (1862–64) and chief of staff (1864–65), commissioned the General Orders No. 100, which argued that uniformed military personnel may not be punished for lawful acts in warfare, such as killing and wounding the enemy, but also, in article 14, that the army should only take "those measures that are indispensable for the securing the ends of war." Other articles gave commanders powers to dissolve property rights over slaves.[25] Hostility in occupied areas had led the frustrated Union forces to act in a harsh way, and this harshness gradually exhausted Confederate civilian energy and enthusiasm.[26]

Alongside irregular warfare by regulars, there was what would since be more conventionally referred to as guerrilla warfare. In part, this warfare was an outcome of the attempt by those opposed to secession to protect themselves from the secessionists. The latter could be extremely brutal, as in northeast Texas, where they hunted down those who opposed them. Control over food proved a key tool. Those who were captured were frequently executed.[27]

In 1865, Lee and his fellow generals ignored Davis's call. Such a policy was antipathetic to their understanding of military and social order and unacceptable under both heads. As a result, the most bitter episode in American history came to a more abrupt end than might have been anticipated.

Instead, with the Civil War coming to a rapid end with the successive surrenders of the Confederate armies in 1865, opposition switched to widespread resistance to Reconstruction, the attempt to push through radical Union goals, notably rights for African Americans. There was the possibility that, as a result of the resistance, the army would become a long-term occupation force in the South, with a task focused on controlling civilians and, possibly, even low-level counterinsurgency work. Indeed, the violent response of the Ku Klux Klan, a Confederate veterans' movement, and of the White League, "rifle clubs," and Red Shirts, represented a form of insurgency, notably insofar as violent and large-scale intimidation of African Americans was concerned. That Southern whites were armed ensured that the new state governments were in a vulnerable position. In 1866, the army intervened to prevent a pogrom, if not massacre, of the black population of New Orleans. However, violence continued, notably between Southern whites and African American militias supporting Reconstruction. In Louisiana, about 2,500 people were killed between 1865 and 1876.[28]

Demobilization and the drive for political reconciliation greatly affected options. The army, just over one million strong at the start of 1865, was only 38,540 strong by September 1866,[29] and half then were in garrisons in the West. Eventually, due to political expediency, the remaining troops in the South were withdrawn in 1877 by President Rutherford B. Hayes. The Southern whites, who had lost the war, found themselves politically dominant in a South now firmly within the United States. This political dominance was attributable to the one-party system in the South with no opposition to the Southern Democrats. This factor was felt especially in the Senate, where Southerners disproportionally controlled the Senate committee chairmen.

The American political and economic leadership preferred, instead, to focus on different domestic challenges. In 1877, Hayes used the army to overcome a major railway strike. Federal troops were deployed in Illinois, Maryland, Missouri, and Pennsylvania, and state militias were also employed.[30] Moreover, there was large-scale conflict with Native Americans from the late 1860s.

EUROPE

Compared with China and the Americas, Christian Europe did not see many large-scale or sustained insurgencies during the nineteenth century once the Napoleonic Empire had collapsed in 1813–15. Prior to this collapse, the extent of French control and the resulting policies and exactions led to a number of rebellions which were helped by the extent to which Napoleon's international opponents provided the rebels with help. Thus, the rising in Calabria in southern Italy benefited from British help in 1806, as well as from the distance of Calabria from centers of French power and the logistical problems facing the French which led to their seeking food in a region where it was sparse. It took a considerable effort and much time, including the use of flying columns, for the French to suppress the rebellion. However, a lack of effective rebel leadership, combined with the French ability to exploit local vendettas, both helped in the eventual outcome.[31]

British intervention was more sustained in the case of Spain, where Napoleon's attempt to seize the throne for one of his brothers led to a popular uprising in 1808 that achieved some success until Napoleon and a large force advanced into Spain. Moreover, Napoleon's subsequent operational victory that year did not lead to strategic success because, encouraged by French exactions and other aspects of French policy, resistance continued. In addition, French logistical demands placed a great strain on the Spanish economy and greatly exacerbated opposition, encouraging resistance.[32] Opportunistic banditry played a role in resistance, but the efforts of Spanish troops were more significant. Poorly armed, poorly supplied, and poorly trained, Spanish armies and irregulars were repeatedly defeated by the French, who, helped by improvements in counterinsurgency operations, conquered the regions of Andalusia (except for the besieged city of Cadiz) in 1810, Estremadura in 1811, and Lower Catalonia and Valencia in 1811–12.

Nevertheless, the Spanish army was able to maintain its structure and to continue fighting. The burden, in terms of garrisons and casualties, on the French of operating against Spanish forces was considerable. The Spaniards were generally unsuccessful in formal conflict, and British generals could be highly critical of their organization. However, their regular and guerrilla operations denied the French control over the Spanish countryside and, in particular, greatly harmed their communications and logistics. Moreover, due to the need to confront the Spaniards, the French were unable to concentrate their larger forces against the British, who were based in Portugal, from which they advanced into Spain. Thus, in 1813, the main French field army, which was heavily defeated by the British at the Battle of Vitoria, was weakened by the detachment of substantial forces to deal with guerrillas in Navarre and the Basque country.

As with other states, the subsequent analysis of the struggle against Napoleon was affected by patriotic and nationalist interpretations, as well as by assumptions about the most effective nature of insurrectionary warfare. Because the struggle was seen as Spain's "Guerra de Independencia," it had a particular resonance. As with America in 1775–83, the subsequent emphasis was on guerrilla campaigns rather than on the regular Spanish army, which was largely ignored, but the latter in practice was important, notably in its ability to keep operating. Moreover, in Spain, there is not much stress on British support, but it also was highly significant.[33] French observers commented on the guerrilla tactics of the Spaniards, which helped provide them with an explanation of failure. Thus, Jean-Frédéric Lemière de Corvey, who had also served in the Vendée, emphasized in his *Des partisans et des corps irréguliers* (Paris, 1823) the ability of guerrillas to isolate regular troops, denying them mobility and defeating them without battle.

In large part, the situation in Europe, after Napoleon was finally driven from power as a result of defeat at Waterloo in 1815, reflected the relative density of states and, thus, the proximity of armies that could be employed to suppress insurrections. Foreign interventions played a major role, as when Austrian forces suppressed insurgencies in Piedmont and Naples in 1821, French forces put down an insurgency in Spain in 1823,[34] and Russian forces helped the Austrians defeat another in Hungary in 1849. The last was a large-scale war, the largest (though not longest) of the counterinsurgency struggles in Europe during the century, with the Russians deploying about 200,000 troops and the Austrians 175,000. The outnumbered Hungarians deployed 170,000 troops and were also outgunned. Defeated, many of the Hungarians returned home while the remaining forces surrendered. Some of the commanders were executed. Earlier, the rising in 1848 had seen the creation of a new, national Hungarian army based on a special force of Honvéd (Defenders of the Fatherland), originally formed from within the National Guard. Looking toward later ethnic conflict in the Balkans, notably in the 1910s, 1940s, and 1990s, the crisis led to the slaughter of peasants by others of different ethnic and religious background, notably in the Banat (Vojvodina): thousands were killed in 1848. This was an element of the military and political history of the century that is largely forgotten outside the region.

Austrian action in Italy reflected a classic feature in counterinsurgency at the international level, a concern to ensure an acceptable situation in nearby states. Aside from a general commitment to conservatism, the Austrians were fearful that radicalism in individual Italian principalities would affect the situation in Austrian-ruled Lombardy and Venetia. In crushing the insurgency in Naples and restoring the previous conservative royalist system of government, the Austrians benefited because their opponents played to the strengths of Austrian military capability. At Rieti, on March 7, 1821, the trained Austrian regulars rapidly broke the untrained and poorly disciplined Neapolitan Carbonari (an anti-royalist movement) under Guglielmo Pepe. The decision to fight a battle had exposed the Carbonari to unsuitable circumstances, as they were best prepared for guerrilla operations. This victory proved decisive and, sixteen days later, Austrian forces entered the city of Naples. As so often, however, when assessing counterinsurgency warfare, it is necessary to assess the role of military operations within a broader political dimension. In this case, this consideration raises issues of political relevance today, notably the extent to which the liberal movement in Italy was based on wide popular support. While that argument was necessary as part of the public myth of Italy once it became a united state in 1861, the earlier reality was of considerable popular support for conservatism and an only limited purchase for liberalism.[35] As a result of this situation, insurgent forces had to achieve military success in order to dictate and drive a political dynamic, as was to happen in Sicily and Naples in 1860–61.

So also in 1848 in France. An uprising by Parisian workers in February forced out King Louis-Philippe and the Orléanist monarchy, not least because the elderly king did not wish to use regular troops to try to destroy the revolution. That June, however, when the Parisian workers took to the barricades against the abolition of the national workshops, a form of publicly funded work, they were crushed by the Second Republic's Minister of War, General Louis-Eugène Cavaignac. There was a clear geographical-social edge to the counterinsurgency struggle, an edge readily apparent to contemporaries. Cavaignac used peasant regular troops and one hundred thousand National Guardsmen (who had refused to defend the king in February) to fight his way through the city's barricades against the insurgents' "Army of Despair." Sixteen hundred troops and over ten thousand insurgents were killed and, despite a poorly coordinated response by the armed forces, radicalism was crushed. This division among the working class was more apparent than Karl Marx's claim that the fighting in Paris was "the first great battle . . . between the two classes that split modern society."[36] There was no foreign intervention.

On behalf of Napoleon III (Napoleon I's nephew, formerly Louis Napoleon, the president), who consolidated his hold on power by the use of force in 1851, Baron Haussmann later redesigned parts of Paris to give the artillery a clearer field of fire, along straight boulevards, against insurgents. In turn, Napoleon III's total defeat by Prussia in 1870 led to his abdication and the creation of a republican government, which in 1871 suppressed the more radical Paris Commune. After extensive street fighting, in which about ten thousand Parisians were killed, about the same number who had been captured were promptly shot. Thus, a sociopolitical insurgency was totally defeated.

In the German states in early 1848, insurgents were successful against regulars in urban fighting. The barricade, a position from which they could fire on advancing regulars, was important at the tactical level. The organizational context was also highly significant. The reliance of most states on draftees who spent much of their time not on military duty ensured that discipline was limited. Indeed, opposition to officers was an aspect of the revolution. However, not all German states were affected, and regular troops subsequently defeated insurgent forces, in part because of the extent to which most were poorly led and lacked persistence.

In addition to suppressing insurrections in other states, imperial control within empires was maintained by force, notably in Poland in 1830–31, 1848, and 1863–64, with Russian armies suppressing independence insurrections. The Poles suffered from the difficulties of creating a war-winning government, from the resulting divisions, and, even more seriously, from the absence of any important diversion of the overwhelming Russian strength.[37] Imperial extension could also involve suppressing insurrections, as the Austrians experienced in Bosnia in 1878. Insurgents, focusing on the ambush of Austrian supply convoys, angered Austrian commanders, which led to brutal reprisals, including the large-scale slaughter of men, women, and children. In turn, this slaughter produced further resistance. All Muslims were treated as opponents and over one hundred thousand troops were added to the seventy-nine thousand initially sent.[38] Having suppressed opposition in Bosnia in 1878, the Austrians were to be faced by later risings there, but these also failed. The Austrians benefited from having no other opponents to fight at this juncture.

Troops were deployed in Britain in opposition to popular unrest. Popular hostility to economic transformation was a cause of a challenge to order that, depending very much on the perspective adopted, constituted insurrection, as with the Crofters' War against landlords in the Scottish Highlands in the 1870s. The Luddite riots of 1812 against new industrial technology led to the deployment of over twelve thousand troops to deal with popular unrest, and troops continued thereafter to be used against economic and other discontent. The Plug Plot Riots of 1842 in Scotland, Yorkshire, and elsewhere brought soldiers into conflict with demonstrators protesting about wage cuts and unemployment. Their name came from the removal of plugs from boilers to depressurize them and prevent machinery from being driven. Troops were also used in Britain against political radicalism. In 1839, a rising of over five thousand men, many of them coal miners, who sought to seize the town of Newport, South Wales, as part of a revolutionary uprising was stopped when a small group of soldiers opened fire and the rioters dispersed.

Alongside the swift suppression of insurgencies, they could be rapidly successful in overthrowing control, as in France and Belgium in 1830. The weakness of regulars in street fighting emerged in both Paris and Brussels. The Paris rising came first, which was significant to the international dynamics of what became a more general crisis. The French government was highly unpopular, not least due to its attempts to reverse the verdict of recent elections. Much of the army was disaffected, many of the loyal units were in Algeria, and there were only twelve thousand troops, many unreliable, near Paris. Many deserted, while Charles X failed to provide clear leadership, and Marshal Marmont, a Napoleonic veteran, was not up to the task. The troops were short of food and ammunition, while the lack of training, equipment, and discipline on the part of the insurgents did not lead to failure.[39] In contrast, albeit against less serious resistance, the new government successfully suppressed riots in Paris and Lyon in 1834.

Insurgency in Paris in July 1830 became an example elsewhere, although in each case there were also specific factors that were crucial to the causes, course, and consequences of the conflict. In August, an insurgency broke out in Brussels against the Dutch rule established in the post-Napoleonic peace settlement by the Congress of Vienna. Brussels's garrison of only just over two thousand troops was taken by surprise and, initially, the Dutch forces in Belgium failed to respond effectively. In September 1830, however, a stronger attempt was made to suppress the rising, which had become more radical. Ten thousand Dutch troops entered Brussels on September 23, but street fighting proved difficult in the face of determined opponents who employed the cover of barricades and fired from windows and housetops. The troops withdrew on September 26, and the Belgians declared independence the following month. In 1831, the Dutch invaded in greater force, meeting poorly organized defenders whom they drove back. However, Anglo-French intervention on the Belgian side led the Dutch to stop and then to pull back. Large-scale French military intervention played a key role. In the end, Belgium was recognized as independent and neutral.

British acceptance and notably the lack of hostile naval intervention also played a part in the success by the irregulars of Giuseppi Garibaldi in overthrowing Bourbon rule in Sicily and Naples in 1860. After the end of the war between France, Piedmont, and their opponent, Austria, in 1859, Victor Emmanuel II of Piedmont had forbidden Garibaldi to advance the cause of Italian unification by invading the Papal States. In response, Garibaldi resigned his generalship in the Piedmontese army and, with one thousand redshirted volunteers, sailed from Genoa in Piedmont to Sicily to help a revolt there against the Kingdom of the Two Sicilies (Sicily and southern Italy) of the Neapolitan Bourbons. This was a rapid campaign, with battles (at Calatafimi and Milazzo) and street fighting (at Palermo), which led to victory. Garibaldi and Victor Emmanuel then separately invaded southern Italy, helped by a revolution by part of the Neapolitan population: this was not a straightforward conquest. However, French regulars totally defeated Garibaldi's 1867 effort to overthrow the temporal power of the papacy in central Italy.

The most sustained insurgencies occurred in Spain, both against French rule, in 1808–13 and in the two Carlist Wars (1832–40; 1873–76). The latter were a result again, but in a very different context to the 1808–13 war, of sociopolitical rejection of liberal political tendencies linked to a contested royal succession. The three cases underline the significance of foreign intervention or its absence, as, indeed, do the Spanish civil wars in 1640–52, 1701–14, 1823, and 1936–39. Each case was unique, but the common elements, alongside foreign intervention, are instructive. The difficulty of imposing control in Spain, a state with a relatively low density of population and with strong and different regional political cultures, was significant. The commonplace use of force to settle political issues in Spain was very important in establishing norms. So also was a frequent determination to go on waging irregular warfare whatever the fate of conventional operations. In turn, counterinsurgency warfare entailed reprisals and other antisocietal methods that exacerbated the situation. This warfare was made more difficult by the mountainous terrain. Yet the determination to win political control meant that insurgents turned to conventional operations as frequently as possible. When these failed, opposition dissipated or became inconsequential other than in a local or, at most, regional context.

The ideology at stake in nineteenth-century insurgencies is usually discussed in terms of nationalism. This tendency furthered the political purposes of politicians and commentators then and subsequently drew on a powerful

cultural strain in nineteenth-century Europe. Moreover, an emphasis on nationalism served the purposes of later left-wing commentators keen to argue
that insurrectionary failures in the nineteenth century reflected a focus on
middle-class politics linked to nationalism rather than the broader-based insurgencies supposedly represented by twentieth-century Communism and/or
wars of national liberation. The latter argument, sometimes accompanied by
an attempt to draw a distinction between nineteenth-century insurrections
and twentieth-century insurgencies, is questionable, but so also is the easy
characterization of nineteenth-century insurgencies in terms of nationalism.
That approach does not, for example, describe the Carlist Wars, which were
in some respects a prelude to the civil war of 1936–39. This complexity,
moreover, was to remain the case in the twentieth century and very much
continues in the twenty-first century.

In the First Carlist War of 1833–40, Don Carlos, "Carlos V," resisted the
bequest of the Spanish throne to his niece, Isabel II, by her father, Ferdinand
VII. Opposition to a female monarch was combined with hostility to the
constitutional reform promoted by Isabel's supporters and, more generally, to
liberalism. Dynasticism was impacted in specific social and regional circumstances, with Carlism a conservative movement that drew on peasant anger
against liberal government. As the government and army stayed loyal to
Isabel, Carlos had to create his own forces. Initial success owed much to
Tomás Zumalacárregui, who became commander of the Carlist forces in the
Basque-Navarre region. As a reminder that, as in the twentieth century and
more recently, insurgencies were linked, not least through personal example,
he was a Basque veteran of the struggle against Napoleon, and this successful
struggle indeed served as an important model for the Carlists.
Zumalacárregui brought coherence to Carlist operations—always a necessity
in effective insurgencies—and created a successful guerrilla army that made
full use of the difficult terrain in order to seize the initiative. The army
overran much of the mountainous north—the center of Carlist support—
where regular troops were few; but it was less successful when it left the
mountains and sought to capture cities, which were dominated by the liberals.

Isabel also benefited from the international context—another key element
in insurrectionary struggles, although one that tends to be underrated by
those convinced of the value and inherent significance of guerrilla strategy
and tactics. The support of Britain, France, and, eventually, after the similar
Miguelists were defeated in 1834, Portugal for Isabel proved important.
Moreover, as so often with insurgencies, the weakness of the Carlists when
they sought to embark on conventional warfare led to their eventual defeat.
Zumalacárregui died in an unsuccessful siege of the city of Bilbao in 1835,
and the advance of the Carlists on the capital, Madrid, in 1837 failed to
topple the regime. The battles of the war are scarcely known, which distorts

the general account of warfare in nineteenth-century Europe. In practice, these and the related military operations throw light on factors that were crucial to success in this period as well as in others. Morale, experience, surprise, terrain, and numbers were crucial in battle. All were as important as effective tactics, if not more so. The campaigns of the war did not leave much room for complicated operational planning or for sophisticated tactics by complex formations. Surprise was important to a number of battles, notably the Carlist victories at Laveaga Pass (1835) and Descarga (1835), as well as the defeat at Aranzueque (1837), which ended Carlist operations in central Spain. In contrast, Mendigorría (1835) was a pitched battle that arose from the Carlist determination to inflict a decisive defeat on the government forces. The choice of a poor position as well as being unused to resting on the defensive ensured that the Carlists were defeated, being forced to retreat with heavy losses.

Yet government forces also faced serious problems, not least a shortage of pay and supplies. As with other civil wars, strategy, morale, and generalship were shot through with political considerations. In particular, Carlist divisions weakened the movement. In 1839, the Carlist commander in chief arrested and shot five generals from a rival faction before negotiating an agreement with the government. Those Carlists who rejected this agreement and fought on in Aragon and Catalonia under Ramón Cabrera were defeated and fled to France in 1840, although Cabrera returned to lead Carlist guerrillas in Catalonia in 1846–49.

The First Carlist War helped further the earlier politicization of the Spanish army and the militarization of Spanish politics. Generals, such as Ramón Narváez and Juan Prim, who seized power in 1843 and 1868, respectively, came to play a major role in government, while political support was necessary in order to obtain backing both within the army and in operations against the Carlists.[40]

The Second Carlist War (1873–76) was less serious because, although the government was divided, indeed, overthrown in a military coup in 1874 that restored the Bourbon dynasty, support for the Carlists was largely restricted to the north, especially Navarre and upland Catalonia. The Carlists were also affected by disunity, by the opposition of the major towns, by the lack of an adequate supply base of administration, and by an absence of international support. These factors looked toward success and failure for insurgencies over the following century, both in Spain and elsewhere.

IMPERIAL INSURGENCIES

Opposition to imperial rule was a key element in the insurgencies of the nineteenth century. The most successful were those in Latin America, but they were not the only ones. A key one was the Indian Mutiny of 1857–59. Victory in this was seen as crucial to British prestige and power in India. Many factors contributed to discontent among the Indian troops, and more generally in India. The military was the central element in the rebellion. A major cause of tension was the reluctance of many Indian soldiers to serve abroad for caste reasons and the newfound determination of the authorities to ensure that they were able to do so. The trigger for the rising was the British demand that their Indian soldiers use a new cartridge for their new Pattern 1853 Enfield rifle-muskets, a cartridge greased (to keep the powder dry) in animal fat. This was a measure that was unacceptable to Muslims and Hindus for religious reasons.

However, there was a concerted plan for mutiny, with communications between the rebels long before the issue of cartridges, a point overlooked in most popular histories. This plan was significant because of the low level of confidence between British officers and Indian subordinates: the army in India in 1857 contained about 232,000 Indian and 45,000 British troops. Discontent in the army was not new. Sir Gilbert Elliot, the governor-general of India, reported in 1807 on a mutiny in Vellore, attributing it to false reports of the British having "systematic designs . . . hostile to their religion and customs," that were based on orders about uniform and appearance. Elliot claimed that opponents of British rule had exploited this discontent. The mutiny was suppressed.[41]

In May 1857, most of the Indian troops in this army's largest section, the Bengal army (which comprised 135,000 Indian and 24,000 British troops), mutinied, while there was also a large-scale civilian rising in north-central India. As with many insurgencies, it was the character of the "mutiny" as a civil war that provided major possibilities for the counterinsurgency forces: the Madras and Bombay armies, about thirty thousand Indian troops of the Bengal army, and the rulers of Hyderabad, Kashmir, and Nepal all provided assistance. This assistance helped ensure that the British outnumbered the rebels in many of the battles in 1858. More generally, counterinsurgency policies and operations relied heavily on cooperation with local political figures.[42] Moreover, no major prince joined the rebellion, and it also had no foreign support. Crucially, neighboring Afghanistan provided no support for the rebellion. The religious dimension of the mutiny did not extend to such intervention.

In addition, the international context, in terms of the ability to move troops, was very much favorable for the counterinsurgency side, as has so often been the case: insurrections classically have lacked naval power projection and, more recently, their air equivalents. Alongside the movement of British troops into the region, for example, from Singapore, then a British position, the inability of the badly led rebels who, indeed, lacked effective coordination or a clear program to spread the rebellion helped the British regain the initiative. The British benefited from the willingness of the rebels to engage in battle, which gave the British the opportunity to use their force effectively.[43] The fighting could be very difficult. Illustrating the danger of selective quotation, Lieutenant Hugh Pearson of the Eighty-Fourth Foot wrote in July 1857 to his parents that the rebels did not dare "charge our little squares with their clouds of cavalry," a description apparently clear on the superiority of the counterinsurgency's regulars, but continued, "They had most magnificent gunners." Pearson noted the following month that the British forces had taken very heavy casualties, adding: "village fighting . . . desperate . . . we took two sepoy prisoners the other day and they were blown away from the guns: the stink of fresh flesh was sickening in the extreme, but I have seen so many disgusting sights and so much bloodshed that I have grown quite callous."[44]

Although peace was officially declared by the governor-general on July 8, 1858, the last battle was in May 1859. The interaction of the flow of campaigning with the balance of political sympathies was more significant as a factor than the environment. Lieutenant-Colonel Lister had written of an expedition to East Bengal in 1850 about the problems caused by "the facilities which their jungles afford, both materials and position, for throwing obstacles in the way of an advance or retreat."[45] In practice, these obstacles had not stopped British success.

Not only did imperial expansion ensure that insurgencies broke out against newly imposed control, but also the manner in which it proceeded affected the response of the imperial powers. This was particularly so if there was competition between the powers, as between Britain and France in West Africa.[46]

Although it did not regard itself as an imperial state, the United States also acted as one. It faced insurgencies, notably from Native Americans but also, in 1846–47, from the newly conquered Mexican inhabitants of southern California and New Mexico. In overcoming these, the Americans benefited from the strength of their forces, from supporting resources, and from divisions among their opponents.[47] Alongside military pressure, there was a disregard for any previous peace agreements. Although the Native Americans were blamed for insurgencies, it was the urge of the white Americans to push even farther into "Indian Territory" that lay behind most of them. Deadly force was applied by the Americans, not least with the killing of Native American women and children, for example, with the 1864 Sand Creek Massacre of Cheyenne and Arapaho.[48] In 1851–52, in operations against the Apaches, their crops were destroyed and Apaches, including women, children, and friendlies, slaughtered.[49] However, the Americans still faced defeats, as in 1837 at the Battle of Lake Okeechobee in Florida, where a large force of Americans was defeated by Seminole and African American allies who had prepared the battleground. Many Native Americans were skilled and proficient warriors, for example, the Comanches, who were espe-cially active in the Texas panhandle.

After the Civil War, the army also faced renewed opposition as it sought to impose American control over the Native Americans. The pressure of superior resources, not least the army's adoption in 1867 of the Springfield 45-70 carbine, a breech-loading, drop-block, single-shot rifle, was important to American control, as was a harsh war-making style and the impact of divisions among the Native Americans, divisions that provided the army with allies, for example, against the Sioux. Similarly, the fragmentation of the Chiricahua Apache offered Geronimo an opportunity to build up strength in the 1870s but also ensured that the Americans could find local supporters. Crucially, Apache scouts provided valuable information about water holes and mountain sanctuaries. Geronimo surrendered in 1886.[50] Other imperial powers, both Western and non-Western, also treated indigenous peoples in a harsh fashion.[51]

CONCLUSIONS

In the nineteenth century, insurgency and counterinsurgency warfare was as much an essential part of warfare as traditional, conventional warfare. Never-theless, despite the significance of insurgencies in many states, they contin-ued to feature little in the training and doctrine of the militaries of major powers. In the case of the United States, there was, for the military, a wel-come shift to war with Spain in 1898, such that the claim in *The Military Policy of the United States* (1904), a posthumous publication by the American officer and military commentator Emory Upton (1839–81) that "the military policy of a republic should look more to the dangers of a civil commotion than to the possibility of a foreign invasion" appeared outdated.[52] China and Japan also focused on conflict with each other in the 1890s, and the major European powers prepared for such warfare and armed according-ly.

Partly as a consequence, there was a tendency to underplay the lessons learned through counterinsurgency warfare. In part, this tendency reflected the relative limitation of processes for learning lessons compared to the fol-lowing century, in part assumptions about what war ought to be, and in part the difficulty of transmitting lessons from forces involved in colonial war-fare, for example, the British in India, to forces at home and the military training there. There were, however, examples of such transmission, includ-ing of learning from foreign armies. For example, Philip Kearny studied at the French cavalry school at Saumur in 1839 before serving in Algeria with the French cavalry and then returning to the United States. There, having introduced French counterinsurgency-based cavalry tactics, he became a general, only to be killed by Confederate forces in 1862.

Separately, the *francs-tireurs* (irregulars) that Prussian invading forces faced in France in 1870–71 affected subsequent planning to a degree. The 1906 Schlieffen Plan, for the German invasion of France via Belgium, envisaged the large-scale use of troops to end popular resistance in areas already occupied.

The nineteenth century saw the last large-scale insurgencies in the domestic history of a number of states, notably the United States and Japan: the urban riots in the United States, notably in the 1960s, did not match the scale of the Civil War. However, the United States and Japan were unsuccessfully to face major insurgencies in the twentieth century as a result of opposition to their forces operating abroad, while other states, especially China and Russia, confronted major domestic insurgencies in the twentieth century.

Chapter Six

The Ideology of People's War Refracted, 1900–1940

"Institutions will curl up like burnt paper" was the closing phrase in the poem "Escape" (1929) by the innovative British writer D. H. Lawrence (1885–1930). The early decades of the twentieth century were important not simply for the insurrections that occurred but also for the development of an ideology of insurrectionary warfare, one very much linked to the political Left, and for a sense that there would be a more general dissolution of authority. Although seizures of power were also mounted from the Right, there was not generally in their presentation a comparable theme of social transformation, although in practice, such a transformation was indeed sometimes intended. In terms of change, nationalism on the Left was given a particular direction toward people's wars or, at least, what could be presented as such. Moreover, as with the French Revolution, this led, at least for a while, to an accompanying rejection of conventional military structures and doctrine, first with the Russian Revolution of 1917 and then with Maoist thought and practice in the 1930s and again in the 1960s.

The emphasis on people's wars cut across the attempt in the years prior to the First World War, which began in 1914, to develop legal restrictions on warfare by defining, and thus separating, combatants and noncombatants. This was a process that directly related to the alleged legality of irregular warfare.[1] So also with the clash between people's wars and subsequent discussion of such legal regulation and restrictions. Regulatory attempts were treated by critics as a bourgeois affectation. Instead, there was a call and pressure by radicals for a total social mobilization for war that was, theoretically, different in kind from "the bosses' wars" of industrial society. More generally, by opting out of "traditional" combat, most likely because of clear disadvantages, the insurgent can fly in the face of attempts to regulate war and to make it more humane. Such attempts to develop cultural and legal restrictions on warfare are certainly not accepted as feasible by all (be they pacifist or realist), but they have had great traction, including from compliance to the Geneva Conventions.

Aside from the theoretical development of the idea of people's war, the pattern of insurgencies was also different because of the pronounced ideological division involved in many insurgencies and, certainly, as compared to the late nineteenth century. As a result, the insurgency that attracted and still attracts greatest attention is the Russian Revolution of 1917. This will continue to be the case due to the centennial in 2017. At the same time, however, the collapse of both the Soviet Union and Soviet Communism in 1991 and the end of the Cold War raise the question of the long-term significance and success of that revolution, a point that earlier could have been made about the French Revolution.

Indeed, the more general issue of relative importance comes to the fore, as repeatedly is the case during this book. Looking solely at the 1910s, it may be asked whether the overthrow of Chinese monarchy in the 1911–12 revolution did not have as lasting an impact as the Russian Revolution. The Portuguese republican coup of 1910 was of importance for what was still a very extensive and far-flung empire, while the Mexican revolution of 1911 is also of consequence. The Portuguese coup was rapidly achieved by part of the military, but it proved difficult to ensure stability. The Mexican revolution led to protracted conflict, although no body of revolutionary theory. Whichever approach to relative importance is adopted, the possibility is that these other conflicts will emerge into greater prominence, displacing some of the attention classically concentrated on the First World War (1914–18). The 1900s had seen the 1905 Russian Revolution, a revolution linked to the strains of an unsuccessful war with Japan. This revolution witnessed the experience of urban insurgency and a doctrine of "all power to the Soviets" or workers' councils but was crushed.

The First World War can be assessed in part in terms of insurgency warfare, although that was of far less consequence than during the Napoleonic Wars or the Second World War. The Arab overthrow of Turkish control of the Hijaz in western Arabia, an overthrow linked to the help of T. E. Lawrence, and the failed Easter Rising in Ireland in 1916 attract most attention in consideration of insurgency conflict during the First World War. However, it is also pertinent to see the disturbances of late 1918 that successfully challenged Austrian and German authority and policy as crucial to the political crisis that led each power to abandon the military effort and to a related overthrow of their imperial monarchies. Moreover, during the war, there was the occupation of large areas. Brutality toward conquered areas, such as by the Germans in Belgium and France, the Austrians in Serbia, and the Austrians and Russians in Galicia (southern Poland), was part both of a determination to use force in order to ensure control and of a wider intense social dislocation.

It was not only during war that armies acted to prevent the risk of insurgencies. In a very different context, they also did so in peacetime. The army played a key role in the insurgency in China in 1911–12, but not only there. Thus, in 1932, King Prajadhipok (Rama VII) of Siam (later Thailand) was overthrown in a bloodless coup by a military junta that imposed a constitution. The military was to play a major part in insurgencies in many states. There is a tendency to separate coups from insurgencies, but this typology does not work in many cases, and not least because both frequently involved a small group of activists. Moreover, the military could be the basis both for radical and for conservative changes in power, but also for the suppression of unrest.

There is no clear prioritization in this period, and a chronological approach can fail to capture the significance of particular types of insurgency. At the same time, the latter can overlap. The approach here is first to consider insurgencies against imperial control and then to look at insurgencies within particular states. For each category, there is an essentially chronological approach but a focus on particular struggles. Due attention is devoted to insurgencies in China and the Islamic world.

OPPOSING EMPIRES: 1900–1918

Insurgencies against imperial control coincided and often overlapped with resistance to the spread of this control. Indeed, the two were frequently part of the same process, as the nature and extent of imperial control was understood. This was also an aspect of the way in which imperialism and "deimperialism" occurred at the same time. Linked to this, the tendency to emphasize "wars of national liberation" after 1945 can lead to a downplaying of frequently extensive resistance in earlier stages.[2]

The suppression of insurgencies by imperial powers reflected their belief that their control was natural and necessary, moral as well as pragmatic, a belief that was widely diffused across society and within political systems. The process of overcoming insurgency can be seen clearly with the Americans in the Philippines. Indeed, because of American involvement and the recent need to discern a tradition of American COIN doctrine and operations, this has been one of the counterinsurgency operations that have attracted attention over recent decades.[3] Having totally destroyed the Spanish fleet in Manila Bay on May 1, 1898, the Americans chose to demand the Philippines from Spain. This was despite the fact that the victory was not followed by an invasion by American forces: they were not initially in place but instead concentrated on the Spanish colony of Cuba, a much closer target but one that became independent after Spain was defeated by the Americans. Instead of American invasion, there was a revival of the nationalist Filipino revolution that had broken out in 1896, only to be defeated by the better-armed and better-trained Spaniards the following year. In 1898, Filipino forces defeated most of the Spaniards on the major island, Luzon, and declared independence. The arrival of American forces led to inconclusive talks with the Filipinos and to the outbreak of war on February 4, 1899. That year, the Americans did well in a conventional war with the Filipino army in Luzon, capturing the revolutionary capital, Malolos, in March, but from November, the Filipino forces shifted to guerrilla operations.

For the Americans, this shift led to grave difficulties that were seriously exacerbated by a hostile environment in which disease was a particular problem. The counterinsurgency war continued to be large scale until 1902, when Miguel Malvar, the commander of the guerrillas in Batangas Province, surrendered on April 16, and the end of the war was officially declared on July 4. Nevertheless, the war continued to be significant thereafter. Like the Spaniards from the 1560s, the Americans benefited greatly from the lack of geographical, ethnic, religious, and political unity in the Philippines. However, although this lack gravely weakened the nationalists' appeal, it also ensured that there was no central target for the Americans to defeat or conquer. This situation helped lead to frustration and also encouraged harsh policies toward civilians, for example, on the island of Samar, where Brigadier General Jacob Hurd Smith declared that he would make "a howling wilderness." Many prisoners were killed, as were a large number of those who lived in hostile villages or, rather, villages considered hostile. Prison camps were created in which eleven thousand people died, which was ironic as the Americans had complained about the Spaniards in Cuba on that basis in the 1890s. In the Philippines, the mass population movements associated with the war speeded up the spread of cholera.[4]

In operational terms, the Americans, who deployed over one hundred thousand troops, found it hard both to understand local situations and to fix their opponents. For example, on the major island of Mindanao, it proved difficult to defeat Datu Ali, the leader of Muslim Moro resistance. When attacked at his fortress at Kudarangan in March 1904 by American forces enjoying a major advantage in artillery, he and his force escaped under the cover of night. Thanks to the American capacity for amphibious operations and the particular value of this capability in the Philippines, force projection was less of a problem than controlling terrain. Datu Ali was finally cornered and killed on the Malala River. Naval power also enabled the Americans to limit the insurgents' ability to resupply and to coordinate operations. The presence of the pro-American Filipino Federal Party was a help. The difficulties encountered on Mindanao looked toward the succession of Philippine insurgent forces, including against the Japanese occupation in the Second

World War, the postwar Huk insurgency, the insurgency against the Marcos regime, and recent Islamicist movements.

The Americans also deployed troops against insurrections elsewhere. In 1912, marines were sent into Cuba, now an independent republic, in order to protect extensive American property interests in the face of a large-scale (mostly black) peasant uprising which looked back to patterns of insurgency during the period of Spanish rule. This uprising was motivated by the savage strains of economic change, social pressure, and political discrimination. Slaves had been freed but remained in dire circumstances. The uprising focused on the plunder and destruction of property but was brutally suppressed by the Cuban army. It forcibly removed peasants from the countryside and summarily killed large numbers of black men, possibly up to thirty-five thousand.[5]

Even more extreme brutality was used by the Germans in 1905 to crush rebellions in German East Africa and German South-West Africa, now Tanzania and Namibia, respectively. The Germans practiced extermination, killing their opponents in large numbers. In South-West Africa, the Hereros, who had rebelled in 1904, were driven into a waterless desert (as many Armenians were to be by Turks in 1915), while prisoners were sent to labor camps such as Swakopmund, where they were treated with such great cruelty that over half of the inmates died there. In East Africa, the Germans used a scorched-earth policy against guerrilla warfare, and about 250,000 Africans died of famine. German policies reflected the determination to achieve absolute victory and to do so through conflict dictated by German operations leading to the annihilation of hostile forces, a determination that owed much to racism. There was also a denial of any idea of negotiations with opponents and a focus placed on combat rather than on the issues raised by civilians and prisoners of war.[6]

In contrast, Turkey's European empire collapsed. That was essentially due to external attack by Bulgaria, Greece, Montenegro, Romania, and Serbia in the First Balkan War of 1912–13 rather than to rebellions. Nevertheless, rebellions played a role in the gathering crisis of Turkish power in the Balkans and, notably, in encouraging hostile foreign intervention. Thus, in Albania, there was a separatist insurgency against Turkish rule in 1910–11. As a result of massacres and expulsions in the Balkans linked to the wars and to related conflicts, the relationship between Muslims and Christians was strained at all levels: from political elites to the ordinary people, polarization sharpened.[7]

Turkey exemplified the extent to which it was not only Western empires that faced insurgencies. In addition, in the late 1890s, the Japanese suppressed a popular resistance movement in newly conquered Taiwan, although in the mountainous forces of the interior, tribesmen continued guerrilla resistance for over three decades. In Kham, part of eastern Tibet that had been an autonomous section of China since the eighteenth-century expansion of the latter, attempts to increase control, notably by appointing Chinese officials, led to a rising in 1905. This was crushed when troops were sent from the neighboring province of Sichuan, and as a result, the pace of establishing Chinese administration (and language education) was stepped up. The rising was part of a pattern seen for centuries when China sought to increase central governmental power in hitherto largely autonomous regions inhabited by non-Han peoples.

In Siam (Thailand), modern weaponry helped Rama V (r. 1868–1910) suppress revolts that owed much to opposition to policies of modernization and centralization. These revolts included the Raja of Pattani's rising in the south in 1902 and the Holy Man's rebellion of the same year, the latter a messianic insurrection that reflected opposition in the northeast. As with the Turks encountering opposition in Jordan, this opposition indicated the extent to which insurrection was in large part a response to a shifting pattern of government. This entailed the imposition of a new type of control focusing on the levying of taxation and the establishment of military posts.

Alongside force, confidence was a key element in power. In 1904, the director of military operations in the British War Office warned:

> The fact cannot be too plainly stated that throughout Egypt and the Sudan, and throughout the great protectorates of Uganda and British East Africa [Kenya], our whole position depends entirely on prestige. We are governing with a mere handful of white officials vast populations alien to us in race, language and religion, and for the most part but little superior in civilisation to savages. Except for the small, and from a military point of view inadequate, British force in Egypt, the authority of these officials is supported only by troops recruited from the subject races, whose obedience to their officers rests on no other basis than a belief in the invincibility of the British government and confidence in its promises. If that belief and confidence be once shaken the foundations of all British authority between Cairo and Mombasa [on the Kenyan coast] will be undermined, and at any moment a storm of mutiny and insurrection will sweep us into the sea. [8]

This view captured a sense of precariousness in the face of insurgency and also the reliance of empire on a confidence in power. These factors came to play a role during the First World War. Indeed, in a display of strategic speculation, the Germans planned to exploit pan-Islamism to destroy much of the British Empire by supporting Muslim insurgencies in Egypt and India, and also to hit the French and Russian Empires. However, support for the German scheme was limited. In part, this was because the policy was compromised by Germany's alliance with the Ottoman (Turkish) Empire, which was unpopular in the Arab world. Moreover, Islam was no more a cohesive force than Christianity was.

Instead of being a weakness, empire proved a fundamental strength for Britain and France during World War I. The most prominent opposition, the Easter Rising in Dublin in 1916, enjoyed little support in Ireland, let alone elsewhere, and was rapidly crushed. About 1,200 men rose on April 24, seized a number of sites, and proclaimed an independent Irish republic, but the rebels suffered from bad planning, poor tactics, and the lack of German help, as well as the strength of the British reaction, which included an un-compromising use of artillery to shell targets in Dublin. Under heavy pres-sure, the insurgents unconditionally surrendered on April 29. The firm Brit-ish response was to play a major role in Irish public memory, notably in encouraging opposition to Britain. However, given the fact that Britain (in-cluding Ireland) was at war and indeed not doing well, the declaration of martial law, the series of trials, the execution of fifteen rebels, and the intern-ment of many were scarcely surprising.[9]

In contrast, the British were able, from 1916, to encourage Sharif Husse-in's successful insurgency against Turkish rule in the Hijaz, a conflict made famous by Lawrence of Arabia. In place of a hitherto unsuccessful campaign against the Turkish garrison in Medina, Lawrence encouraged a greater de-gree of mobility in 1917, and this wrong-footed the Turks, destroying their confidence and their ability to use the Hijaz railway safely. After the war, Lawrence's memoirs, *The Seven Pillars of Wisdom* (1926) and *Revolt in the Desert* (1927), were seen by many as significant guides to the principles and practice of guerrilla warfare.

In 1916, there was a major insurgency in Russian Central Asia as a result of an attempt to conscript large numbers of Muslims for war work, especially digging trenches. The brutal suppression of the insurgency led to heavy casualties, in part due to flight in harsh conditions and to large-scale deporta-tions. There was no international support for the insurgency.

France suppressed an insurgency in Tunisia in 1915–16 but in those years confronted the Volta-Bani War in modern Burkina Faso, then part of French West Africa. This insurgency began in opposition to conscription. Lacking comparable firepower, with consequences seen in battles such as Boho (1916), the rebels sought to develop tactics in order to weaken the French columns (most of whom were West African troops), to reduce local support for the French, and to limit the impact of their firepower. The French them-selves employed brutal antisocietal warfare: targeting their opponents' farms, herds, wells, and families in order to destroy the environment among which they operated. Once the rebels' centers had been subjugated, organized oppo-sition to French rule ceased. About thirty thousand of the local population had been killed.

OPPOSING EMPIRES: 1919–39

The First World War led to a series of postwar imperial struggles as the territorial situation in its aftermath was challenged in a series of insurgencies. These focused on the Muslim world, where control had been greatly changed as a result of the demise of the Turkish Empire and its reallocation. Opposition had varied causes and consequences. It included hostility to British hegemony in Egypt, Iraq, Iran, and Palestine; a rising in 1925–26 against French rule in Syria; the continuation of resistance in Libya to the rule Italy had unsuccessfully sought to impose since 1911; an upsurge from 1921 in action against Spanish attempts to dominate the part of Morocco allocated to it (an opposition that spread into French Morocco)[10]; and the Turkish refusal to accept a peace settlement that included Greek rule over the Aegean coast and British troops in Constantinople.

The situation varied greatly, depending both on the determination, resources, and goals of the imperial power and on the same for its opponents. Organization was also a key element for the latter. Thus, in Turkey, there was the basis for a concerted response. When in 1915 an Anglo-French expeditionary force had threatened to capture Constantinople (only to be blocked at Gallipoli), preparations had been made by the Turks to wage guerrilla warfare in Anatolia. Arms were dispatched and the necessary organizational infrastructure established.

After the armistice ending the war in 1918, these bands and local defense organizations rapidly emerged, especially after Greek forces landed at Smyrna/Izmir as part of the peace settlement imposed by the Allies, a settlement that also established British, French, and Italian zones of control. Mustafa Kemal (later Atatürk) was able to form the defense organizations into a nationalist political movement and an army with a unified command. This helped provide a basis for subsequent, successful resistance to Greece. Reporting in March 1920, the British general staff had been pessimistic about the prospect of overcoming the nationalists. Without any need to refer to theories of insurgency, guerrilla tactics were feared, and their interaction with the political situation in the Allied home countries was pointed out. Guerrilla tactics were seen as restricting Allied mobility while

> any serious retaliatory advances by the Allies into the mountains would require highly organized and costly operations necessitating road-making, and would be a very slow business . . . make the financial burden of policing and defending their new acquisitions intolerable to the Allies. . . . The position is one which can be dealt with politically more effectively than by military measures on the part of the Allies. If it is to be dealt with militarily, protracted operations by fully equipped armies must be prepared for . . . such numbers as would be necessary for the lines of communication . . . would have to be considerable in view of the guerrilla warfare which would certainly attend

operations in a country which is predominantly Turkish . . . guerrilla warfare, which is a method of fighting above all things to be avoided. The whole spirit of the art of conducting small wars is to strive for the attainment of decisive methods, the very essence of partisan warfare from the point of view of the enemy being to avoid definite engagements. Consequently, it usually happens that many more men are required than were originally estimated, and that warfare of this nature continues, as was the case in the operations of the Dutch in Achin, of the French against Abd el Kadir in Algeria, and the Spaniards in Cuba and Morocco. [11]

Thus, there was a "collective memory," at least in the sense of references in the last sentence to other states' counterinsurgency operations over the previous eighty years. In the event, the Greeks were totally defeated by the Turks in conventional warfare in 1921–22 while the British avoided war with the Turks by abandoning their presence in Turkey.

In Ireland, fighting against British control resumed after the war, but in a different form from the 1916 rising. Instead, relying on terrorism and guerrilla warfare, the Irish Republican Army (IRA) organized its active service units into flying columns that staged raids and ambushes in order to undermine the stability of British rule. Assassinations and sabotage were also employed so as to dominate the intelligence field and to suggest control. The British use of auxiliary police, especially the Black and Tans recruited from ex-soldiers, became associated with contentious reprisals against IRA terrorism, and the use of civilian clothes by the IRA helped encourage a lack of care in the targeting of reprisals. [12] The IRA was short of arms (many of which were gained by raids on the British) and explosives and was outnumbered by the army and the police, who, moreover, had many successes, notably in the counties of Cavan and Leitrim. There were also significant improvements in the methods used to fight the IRA, including the protection of vehicles against booby traps (improvised explosive devices), the use of wireless telegraphy, airpower, the active deployment of fighting patrols, and internment (detention without trial). Far from being a rigid force constrained by conventional operations, the British army was able to respond flexibly. [13]

However, the IRA was able to take the initiative, notably in the south and southwest, and to benefit from the limited options available to those trying to restore control. Furthermore, political and public opinion in Britain lacked enthusiasm for a long, tough struggle. The Liberal prime minister, David Lloyd George, who had long had a sympathy for nationalist causes, initially used bellicose rhetoric against the IRA but later changed his attitude. Committed to the Unionist cause, some of his Conservative ministerial colleagues in the coalition government supported tougher action in Ireland, but the cabinet did not split over the issue. The belief by Lloyd George and Winston Churchill, the secretary of state for war, that government policy was not working led to a change of policy in July 1921 toward effective independence. Unwilling to persist, the British government abandoned control over most of the island, although the majority Protestant Northern Ireland remained part of the United Kingdom.

As so often with counterinsurgency struggles, there were claims that, had the struggle persisted, victory could have been obtained. In July 1921, Lieutenant-General Sir Philip Chetwode, the deputy chief of the imperial general staff, claimed that victory was possible, but only if the army was given more power, including control of the police and the full support of British public opinion:

> The full incidence of Martial Law will demand very severe measures and to begin with many executions. In the present state of ignorance of the population in England, I doubt very much that it would not result in a protest which would not only ruin our efforts, but would be most dangerous to the army. The latter have behaved magnificently throughout, but they feel from top to bottom that they are not supported by their countrymen, and should there be a strong protest against severe action it would be extremely difficult to hold them. [14]

However, whatever the truth of this, public opinion would not have stood for a tough policy, while the government, confronting the need to increase the number of troops sent to Ireland,[15] was also faced by a range of difficult imperial commitments. The IRA thus benefited from such issues as the Russian Civil War and from new British commitments in the Middle East. In a wider, strategic sense, this is frequently the case for insurgencies: the need to hold on until the international situation leads their opponents to change policy.

Once the British had withdrawn from the bulk of Ireland, the IRA split, with a faction, the Irregulars, rejecting the peace settlement with Britain which had led to the partition of Ireland, with Northern Ireland remaining with Britain. This rejection led, in 1922–23, to a fresh insurgency struggle, but in this, the forces of the new Irish state successfully overcame opposition. In part, in a manner generally neglected in the Irish public myth, this success was a matter of more brutal conduct than that of the British, notably the execution of 77 insurgents and the internment or sentencing of 8,338. In addition, the "anti-treaty" rebels lacked a psychological drive comparable to what they had experienced against the British. Later Irish governments continued to use large-scale internment against the IRA.[16]

More generally, the British empire confronted serious problems in a number of colonies. In part, this was an aspect of the way in which (throughout its course) empire was not a pacified or finished product, so that the imperial project and decolonization were concurrent or, at least, greatly overlapped. In a volatile political situation in 1919, British-commanded Indian troops fired on demonstrators at Amritsar in northwest India, causing heavy casualties. This episode led to a major clash between the assumptions of the commander, Brigadier General Reginald Dyer, and his supporters and, on the other hand, critics of what was seen as undue force. Dyer's report made it clear that he regarded this force as a key constituent of control: "I fired and continued to fire till the crowd dispersed, and I considered that this is the least amount of firing which would produce the necessary moral and widespread effect it was my duty to produce if I was to justify my action."[17]

Dyer, however, was recalled. His methods no longer appeared appropriate and have indeed been much criticized since.[18] British leaders visiting India frequently go to Amritsar in order to express regret.

In 1920, a major revolt in the mid-Euphrates valley in Iraq was crushed by the deployment of a substantial force from Britain's Indian army as well as of aircraft from the newly formed Royal Air Force. The exploitation of new technology, in the shape of policing from the air, was to be important in counterinsurgency operations during the century and was presented as such from the outset.[19] More generally, problems were accentuated when the focus was on effective, rather than solely formal, control. The strengthening of empire could also cause a reaction. Thus, the deployment of a large British garrison in Waziristan in the 1920s helped provoke a major rising there in 1936. In addition, the combination of opposition in the colonies and financial problems in the metropole (homeland) ensured that, despite improved communications and the availability of airpower, colonies could become harder to administer and control. For example, drawing on religious and political antipathy, the Saya San rebellion challenged the British position in Myanmar in 1930–32. Opposition to British rule was exacerbated by the effects of the economic depression, helping to create a rebellion in the Irrawaddy Delta region. Religious identity and anger played a role in Myanmar.

More generally, the growth of anti-imperial feeling was related to indigenous notions of identity and practices of resistance, many of them central to a peasant culture of noncompliance with ruling groups. New organizations, such as the All-India Muslim League, founded in 1906, the National Congress of British West Africa (1920), the Young Kikuyu Association in Kenya (1921), and the African National Congress in South Africa (1923), fostered demands for change. They drew heavily on the activism of individuals educated in new institutions established by colonial governments, in part in order to provide officials.

In turn, the imperial authorities sought to improve their ability to cope with opposition, whatever its form. For example, concern with subversive ideas encouraged British intelligence organizations and operations that relied heavily on the cooperation of supportive imperial subjects, without whom these operations were in a very weak position. These organizations and operations reflected the fear that colonial populations were readily manipulated, as well as the range, ambiguities, and nuances involved in the term *cooperation* and the related concerns the latter gave rise to.[20] In colonies such as

India and Jamaica, administrators and officers had for a long time been concerned as to how best to control populous territories with very small forces. The military strength available was regarded as the crucial support of a moral authority on which rule and control rested. This was an attitude that helped lead some in Britain and among the British in India to support General Dyer's harsh and bloody resort to disturbances at Amritsar in 1919. The extent to which this authority was accepted, indeed even supported, by the colonized in the nineteenth century should not be exaggerated, but there is little doubt that it was under far more challenge by the interwar years. In part, this was because World War I had encouraged not only imperial consciousness but also a separate awareness in individual colonies. Amritsar indeed remains an important issue in Indian public history, being deployed to support the claim that British authority had an inherently repressive character, an argument that is only partially true. [21]

The style and content of imperial control varied. Italy, ruled from 1922 by Fascist dictator Benito Mussolini, was no longer prepared to accept the Libyan self-government recognized in 1919 and employed great brutality in subduing Libya in 1928–32 and defeating the opposition led by Omar Mukhtar. The tactics included the use of columns of armored cars and motorized infantry and the dropping of gas bombs. To destroy the backing for resistance, the population was ruthlessly suppressed. Wells were blocked and flocks slaughtered, both brutally effective means of economic warfare, and the population was disarmed and forcibly resettled in camps in which many died. A largely pastoral society, much of it nomadic, was thereby brought under control. The Italians benefited from the extent to which no neighboring power supported the Libyans. [22]

In turn, having conquered Ethiopia in 1936, the racist Italians proved harsh rulers, which led, from 1937, to a resistance movement. This was a resistance of ambushes and surprise attacks on precarious Italian supply routes, which the Italians countered by savage repression, building forts, and recruiting local troops. Ethiopia was harder to control than Libya, as the population was less concentrated, the terrain and cover less suitable for aerial surveillance, and the tradition of independence far stronger. The international dimension was important. From their neighboring colony of French Somaliland (Djibouti), the French, concerned about Italian expansionism, provided some help to the rebels; and from 1940, Britain, at war with Italy and in control of neighboring Sudan and Kenya, played a key role in eventually overthrowing Italian rule in 1941.

France had used great brutality in suppressing a Druze rising in Syria in 1925–26. Aircraft and artillery were employed to terrorize the civilian population, and the French brought in significant forces from elsewhere in their empire, notably North Africa. The rebellion was overcome in hard fighting, village by village. In Morocco in 1925–26, Spain dropped mustard gas on its

Moroccan opponents, but typhus and a lack of food did more to end the Riff rebellion than airpower.

The use of aircraft in maintaining imperial control looked ahead to more modern patterns, notably with the role of airpower in COIN operations. Anticipating arguments made by American advocates of airpower in the 1990s and 2000s, air attack was seen as a rapid response combining firepower and mobility; it did not entail the deployment of large forces and was therefore presented both as cost efficient and as appropriate for the much-reduced military establishments arising from postwar demobilization and expenditure slashing. Airpower, however, had only limited value in overcoming dispersed "light" insurgent forces and in securing territory.

In 1937–39, in contrast to the French in Syria in 1925–26, the British used less brutal methods in response to the Arab Rising in Palestine, an insurgency motivated by hostility to the British willingness to accept Jewish immigration but one that essentially reflected the failure of the idea that Arabs and Jews would cooperate peacefully and thus that Britain could govern Palestine without using force. Troubled by Zionist formulas, Arab nationalists appreciated that European Jewish immigration differed from the settled presence for many centuries of Arab Jews. Initially, the Arab Rising posed a serious problem for the British, not least as, in response to sniping and sabotage and short of information about the rebels, they were unable to maintain control of much of the countryside.

However, the opposition lacked overall leadership and was divided, in particular between clans. The British benefited from their influence, if not control, in neighboring areas. In Transjordan (modern Jordan), the army, the Arab Legion, was paid for entirely by the British and was commanded by British officers. The British even more controlled the Transjordan Frontier Force.[23] Moreover, in Palestine, recruiting Jewish auxiliaries, the British also developed an irregular capacity of their own, notably Orde Wingate's Special Night Squads. Faced with a firm opposition from about three thousand guerrillas, the British used collective punishments and fines, the destruction of the property of suspected opponents, and detention without trial to weaken Palestinian support for the guerrillas. There was also a brutal mistreating of some of the detainees. British practices, notably collective punishments, were to be inherited by Israel.

The British also changed their military response, notably with the introduction of active patrolling. In September 1938, faced by the prospect of war with Germany, the chiefs of staff warned of a danger that "the infection of lawlessness may spread to neighboring Muslim countries."[24] In the winter of 1938–39, significant reinforcements were sent, so that about fifty thousand troops were deployed, a response that would not have been possible had Britain been at war with Germany. A more energetic stance led to the reoccupation of rebel strongholds. Reconnaissance was the prime use of airpower, although there was also bombing and strafing. Villagers were pinned down by the threat of bombing by patrolling aircraft until the army could reach the scene, a technique known as the "air pin." At the same time, military means were combined with political shifts. In particular, the policy of partition between an Arab and a Jewish state was abandoned.[25]

In coping at the same time with rebellion in Waziristan on India's north-west frontier, a rebellion that drew on tribal opposition as well as Muslim *jihadi* sentiment, the British benefited not only from superior numbers and firepower but also from tribal rivalries and financial inducements. At the same time, the control imposed in Waziristan was essentially that of a stale-mate. Looked at differently, the "small wars" appeared acceptable because politicians were able to continue the nineteenth-century practice of leaving the implementation of policy and definition of victory largely to the men on the spot.[26]

CHINA, 1900–1920

The most successful insurrection of the 1910s was the republican revolution of 1911 in China. It was, however, not to be one that attracted much attention from commentators on revolutions, certainly in comparison with the Russian Revolution of 1917 and the Chinese Communist struggle to take over from 1927 to 1949. This contrast reveals much about the degree to which political and related preferences and assumptions play a major role in assessment, especially when the winning protagonists advocated revolutionary social transformations. Moreover, foreign intervention ensures that the Boxer Rebellion of 1900 attracts greater attention. An uprising aimed against the humiliation and pressure of foreign imperialism, this antiforeign movement began in 1897 and became nationally significant in 1900. The murder of Christian converts was followed by the siege of the foreign legations in Beijing and their eventually successful relief by an international force. The swords and lances of the Boxers provided no protection against firearms. Aside from the significance of Japanese and Western intervention, the Boxers were opposed by the powerful provincial governors in the Yangtze area and in the south.

In contrast to the Boxer movement, the origins of the 1911 revolution in China were fundamentally military. Long-standing regionalism was signifi-cant for the nature of military power. The Taiping rebellion in the mid-nineteenth century had further helped ensure that regional military units had gained considerable autonomy, while also needing to control their regions in order to provide for themselves. Defeat by Japan in 1894–95 had led to a second phase in military modernization, which gathered pace after the failure of the Boxer Rebellion, in the reform program adopted by the government in the 1900s. A key feature of these new forces was a strong nationalist commitment. As with the Young Turks movement in the Ottoman Empire in 1908, a modernizing, nationalist military proved a basis for a successful insurrection.

Rather as the Wei dynasty of the Toba in China had fallen to mutinies beginning in 524, the 1911 revolution began with a military uprising in Wuhan on October 10. With the news rapidly transmitted and action coordinated by telegraph, the revolt spread across most of China, and the fate of the Manchu dynasty was sealed when Yuan Shikai, commander of the Beiyang (Northern Ocean) army, after some hesitation, decided to back it. This backing provided a key element of force and also a means to legitimation. Yuan became president on February 12, 1912, when the emperor abdicated. However, as also when some other insurgencies proved successful, fighting continued as it proved difficult to create a stable new order. In 1913, Yuan's forces stormed Nanjing, but he died in 1916 soon after the failure, as a result of regional rebellion and military discontent, of his attempt to become emperor.[27]

The ascent of the military in Chinese politics after the revolution was made more problematic by rivalries between the generals. The extent to which these can be seen in terms of insurgencies is highly problematic. For example, in a war in 1920, the forces of key generals Wu Peifu and Zhang Zuolin converged on Beijing, resulting in the overthrow of a third, Duan Qirui, who was also the prime minister. He lacked enough troops to prevail as well as close links with sufficient other generals/warlords. At this stage, the internal conflict in China contained, with these powerful, regionally based generals, elements similar to that in Russia, but there was no equivalent to the Communist Party. The 1911 revolution had assisted in the shift of power from the center to the periphery.

CHINA 1921–39

Civil war in the 1920s led to the dominance of most of China by the Guomindang (Nationalists) under, from 1926, Jiang Jieshi (Chiang Kai-shek), a successful warlord with concrete national and nationalist assumptions. Initially, the Guomindang cooperated with the Soviet Union and the Chinese Communist movement, but in 1927, suspicious of its intentions, Jiang suppressed the movement. This violent suppression led the Communists, influenced by the Soviet Union, to begin a series of risings. There were, however, serious divisions over strategy among the Communists, while these divisions, in turn, were influenced by military developments. Leading Communists, such as Li Lisan, secretary general from 1928 to 1931, followed the traditional interpretation of Marxism-Leninism, seeking to exploit the revolutionary potential of urban workers. In contrast, a number of leaders, including Mao

Zedong, more correctly perceived that the real potential in China, very differently from the Soviet Union, rested with farm laborers. However, in considering Mao, it is necessary to appreciate the degree to which his achievements were exaggerated and his reputation was subsequently greatly enhanced, and not only by Chinese commentators.

Initially, the Red Army suffered from a policy of trying to capture and hold towns. However, this only provided the Guomindang with easy targets. In 1927, in particular, the Communists in the province of Hunan were defeated when they attacked Changsha, the provincial capital. They captured Changsha in 1930, only to be rapidly driven from it with heavy losses. The dismal failure of the urban rebellions forced the emergence of a new, rural-centered guerrilla movement.

The Red Army proved far more successful in resisting attack in rural areas, especially if in the traditional hideouts of social bandits—namely, remote and mountainous areas, such as the Jinggang highlands on the Hunan-Jiangxi border. There, Mao managed to build up a force from defeated Communist units and local opponents of exploitative landlords. Mao regarded the rural base as an essential part of his revolutionary strategy. Without a base, he argued, it was impossible to develop a fighting force or to implement the revolutionary program to obtain the support of the rural population. Drawing on his own ideas, on the traditions of the rural outlaw world, and on the experience of Guomindang brutality, Mao used violence for political ends from the outset in order to terrorize others and to destroy potential rival leaders of the rural population. Under Guomindang attack and short of arms, Mao relocated into southern Jiangxi in 1929, where he was able again to build up his local strength. He also pressed hard for the politicization of the Red Army, emphasizing the need for political officers. In Jiangxi, the well-motivated Red Army could mount a mobile defense, trade space for time, and harry its slower-moving opponent, especially as the urban-based Guomindang lacked much support from the peasantry in this region.

This lack was a key weakness in Jiang's successive "bandit extermination campaigns," which were the most sustained large-scale counterinsurgency campaigns of the century. In the first, launched, in late 1930 and mounted with about forty-five thousand troops, Mao benefited from fighting on territory that favored the defensive, and this factor helped in mounting ambushes that caused heavy casualties among the attackers. Mao also staged a ruthless purge of the Communist Party in Jiangxi, alleging that his opponents were Guomindang infiltrators. In February and May 1931, other Guomindang campaigns were launched against the Fourth Red Army, led by Zhang Guotao, in the mountains of southern Hubei. Again, terrain and local knowledge helped thwart the attacks. As with Mao, there was also a brutal purge by Zhang of rival Communists. In April 1931, there was yet another drive on Mao's Jiangxi position, this time with over one hundred thousand troops deployed under He Yingqin, the minister of military administration and chief of staff. Initial failure was followed in July by direct intervention by Jiang, who also brought reinforcements to the campaign. The Communists were driven back with numerous casualties but escaped destruction, in part because of the Guomindang need to respond to the Japanese invasion of Manchuria. The outcome of this campaign served to underline the extent to which counterinsurgency operations repeatedly depended, at least in part, on the range of commitments. Thus, the British had been handicapped in opposing the American War of Independence by French intervention.

In turn, in 1932, after the battle for Shanghai with Japanese forces was over, Jiang attacked the Communists anew, deploying about four hundred thousand troops and benefiting from the advice of Hans von Seeckt, who had earlier been commander in chief of the German army in 1920–26. Attacking Zhang Guotao's Fourth Red Army, Jiang used a scorched-earth and blockade strategy that destroyed the economic basis of the opposition. Having exposed themselves to defeat through positional battles, the Fourth Red Army staged a breakout from August 1932, leaving a guerrilla force that maintained opposition in the mountains. Zhang's Fourth Red Army retreated to Sichuan, losing many men on their long march. Jiang also attacked Mao in Jiangxi in 1932. The Communists were put under heavy pressure but again escaped destruction, not least because of a lack of determination on the part of many Guomindang units as well as the problems they encountered with the coordination of independently advancing columns. It was the ability to survive, regardless of losses, that was to play such an important part in the later success of the Red Army and indeed of guerrilla forces in other conflicts. However, withdrawing units to avoid attack left local areas undefended.

For the 1933 campaign, launched in October with possibly about 750,000 troops, the Guomindang, learning from previous campaigns, forcibly moved peasants in order to deprive the Communists of local support, especially of food and information, and also sought to control the countryside through the establishment of large numbers of blockhouses, with new ones built to accompany the advance. By 1934, fourteen thousand blockhouses had been built. Moreover, roads and landing strips for aircraft were constructed. Serious pressure was brought to bear. The Communists tried and failed to thwart this strategy by conventional warfare rather than resting on the defensive and mounting ambushes. Their forces were increasingly affected by desertion,[28] which was a reflection of the coercion used to ensure recruitment. This coercion was a central aspect of the nature of Communist control, one that saw repeated purges throughout the early 1930s as the fanaticism of the party was directed against whatever could be held suspect.

Jiang, however, failed to focus on the campaign, in part because of his concern about deteriorating relations with Japan. In accordance with instructions from Joseph Stalin, the Soviet dictator, Mao's army meanwhile launched a breakout from Jiangxi in October 1934, beginning the so-called Long March across several thousand miles of difficult terrain to Shaanxi, in which most of those who set out fell by the wayside due to disease, privation, fighting, and desertion. During the march, Mao regained influence and then power from Moscow-backed leaders who favored more conventional warfare. Mao's return led to the revival of a coherent guerrilla strategy. Guomindang blockhouses were bypassed while its air attacks proved unable to stop the Communists. In October 1935, Mao reached the bare mountains of northern Shaanxi, a new rural base remote from the urban centers of Guomindang power. The attack Jiang ordered on the Communists in Shaanxi in late 1935 was unsuccessful, in part because Zhang Xueliang, to whom it was entrusted, was unenthusiastic (preferring to fight Japan), while the forces sent were weak. Indeed, Jiang refused to release his key divisions for the campaign. In 1936, however, Mao's attempt to invade Shaanxi in order to create a supply line to Soviet-run Mongolia failed. Funded and provided with arms by Stalin, Mao became a factor in the complicated negotiations of power in China, while the Red Army, capitalizing on its survival, became larger. However, there was no comparison with the urban and central geographical position of the Communists during the Russian Civil War.

In 1937, Mao published *Guerrilla Warfare*, a pamphlet in which he argued that unlimited guerrilla warfare offered a new prospect that was more effective than what was presented as more primitive guerrilla warfare:

> In a war of revolutionary character, guerrilla operations are a necessary part. This is particularly true in a war waged for the emancipation of a people who inhabit a vast nation . . . the development of the type of guerrilla warfare characterized by the quality of mass is both necessary and natural. . . . We consider guerrilla operations as but one aspect of our total or mass war. . . . All the People of both sexes from the ages of sixteen to forty-five must be organized into anti-Japanese self-defense units.[29]

Operationally, the emphasis included words and phrases used to describe conventional warfare in the period, such as "mobility, and attack . . . deliver a lightning blow, seek a lightning decision."[30] Yet general revolutionary wars were presented by Mao as very different from conventional warfare, being defined in terms of

> the whole people of a nation, without regard to class or part, carry on a guerrilla struggle that is an instrument of the national policy. . . . All these struggles have been carried on in the interests of the whole people or the greater part of them; all had a broad basis in the national manpower, and all have been in accord with the laws of historical development.[31]

With particular reference to Japan, Mao argued that Japanese brutality helped the guerrillas greatly and thus that the latter would benefit if their operations made the Japanese more oppressive, an approach very much taken by anarchists and terrorists.

Mao's arguments about guerrilla war were to be very influential, or at least much cited, in the second half of the century, notably in the 1960s and 1970s. In particular, although there were also different and distinctive national traditions, the expectation of a long-term conflict and the theory of "people's war" proved significant, for example, for the Palestinian Fatah movement.[32] Looking to Mao's example as well as their own circumstances in the late 1950s and early 1960s, the North Vietnamese Politburo anticipated many years of struggle. Mao's texts were also to be studied by writers on counterinsurgency, such as the French officer David Galula, author of *Counterinsurgency Warfare* (1964), and to contribute to the counterinsurgency doctrine that insurgencies developed in phases. In the long term, even given Mao's mistaken lack of interest in the actual and potential roles of religion, his emphasis on the significance of the people as a key element, and therefore of social revolution, continues to be relevant, albeit in a different context.[33] In the short term, however, the Communists had failed by 1937 to overthrow their opponents or even hold Jiangxi, and the Guomindang were in a dominant position. That changed, from 1937, due to the breaking out of the Sino-Japanese War and the tremendous pressure repeated Japanese success placed on the Guomindang, rather than to Communist successes.

The Chinese term *Nei Zhan*, translated as "internal war," originated in the 1920s in order to describe the civil war between the Guomindang and the Communists. When China was ruled by imperial dynasties, COIN efforts against insurgencies by ethnic minorities were described as "war against the barbarians." This approach stemmed from the Chinese worldview of China as the "middle kingdom" around which everything else revolved. China's introduction to modernity and the concept of the nation-state in the 1910s had changed the situation.

LATIN AMERICA

In the Caribbean and Central America, the United States presented itself as the supporter of liberty but, to its critics, acted as a quasi-imperial power, as indeed was the case. Interventions in Haiti from 1915 (with appreciable combat involved in 1915–16 and 1918–20) and in the Dominican Republic from 1916, in order to protect American interests, led to nationalist resistance. Popular guerrilla movements proved able to limit the degree of control enjoyed by occupying American forces, who found that rebel ambushes restricted their freedom of maneuver. American bombing was no substitute, particularly in the face of guerrilla dominance of rural areas at night. However, the Americans were not defeated in pitched battles. In 1922, the guerrillas in the Dominican Republic conditionally surrendered, while the American forces left in 1924. The Guardia Nacional (National Guard), created by the American occupiers as a way to help maintain both order and their interests, became a key force.

In Nicaragua, the Americans sent in the marines in 1926 in order to end the civil war and to stop the risk of Soviet-backed Mexican intervention. In 1927, the Americans, who had significant commercial interests to protect, imposed a settlement, including elections in 1928, which enabled the head of the army to become president. However, this agreement was resisted by a rebel peasant army under César Augusto Sandino that took refuge in the mountains and turned to guerrilla warfare. The campaigning revealed the vulnerability of regular troops to ambushes and the serious problems of fixing opponents and forcing battle. *The Times* of January 3, 1928, noted of the ambush of a marine unit in a mountain pass:

> The insurgents opened fire from a mountain battery and with automatic rifles and grenades made of glass and scraps of metal attached to sticks of dynamite. . . . Finding it useless to fire at the hidden enemy he hurried his men forward through the pass . . . to the outskirts of Quilali where he deployed and engaged the enemy in the open. The insurgents then retired.

The paper also reported that the discipline and training of Sandino's forces had improved. Unable to suppress the rising or capture Sandino, and with opposition to the war growing in Congress, the Americans trained a Guardia Nacional and withdrew their troops in 1933. The conflicts in the Caribbean and Central America led to the development of American counterinsurgency doctrine and its focus by the marines, not the army. The marines produced a *Small Wars Manual* in 1940.[34]

Much conflict in Latin America was insurrectionary in character. Serious political instability reflected ideological rivalry, economic pressures, and social divisions, as well as the limited practice of democracy and the frequent use of force to maintain power. There was still a great variety in the type, character, and consequences of insurgencies. For example, in Venezuela in 1902, a revolution led by General Manuel Antonio Matos against the Liberal president Cipriano Castro was initially successful, only to be heavily defeated at La Victoria (1902) and Ciudad Volivar (1903). Castro himself had seized power by force in 1899 as a result of victory at Tocuyito. In 1920, a civilian revolt in Bolivia led to the overthrow of the Liberals by the more left-wing Republicans.

The overlapping complexity of factionalism, coups, and rebellions was amply demonstrated in Mexico. Economic and social strains during modernization created political pressures, not least because the benefits of growth and power were very unfairly spread during the modernizing dictatorship of Porfirio Díaz (1877–1911). Most farmers were landless, while much of the middle class was uneasy. Rivalry within the elite came to a head in 1910–11 as Francisco Madero, who pressed for economic and political liberalization, stood for the presidency, only to be jailed and to lose. In turn, Madero called for the overthrow of Díaz, leading to the 1911 Mexican Revolution. Madero was elected president in the election that year but could not control the disorder he had helped provoke. Landless peasants took part in regional rebellions. In 1913, a military coup by General Félix Díaz against Madero was successful when Madero was abandoned and killed by the commander of the government forces, General Victoriano Huerta, who became president. In return, this led to a revolt by Venustiano Carranza, a provincial governor, who forced the resignation of Huerta, won support by promising land reform, and defeated the forces of Francisco "Pancho" Villa, a revolutionary who had earlier been his ally. In 1920, Carranza was overthrown by his army commander, Álvaro Obregón, who, in turn, became president and suppressed opposition. The frequent use of the term *general* in part reflected the extent to which those in control of armed bands called themselves generals in an effort to legitimize themselves and also was a throwback to the Latin American Wars of Independence, wherein the major figures were typically military men.

Much of the fighting in Mexico was of the character frequently seen in civil wars. Thanks to low force-space ratios as well as the difficulties of sustaining forces, much of the fighting was a matter of rapid advances and short battles, while towns were usually stormed rather than besieged. The killing of prisoners was frequent because the facilities for holding them were limited, in order to hit opponents' morale, and so as to intimidate others. Indeed, the willingness of troops to resist was a key factor in the fighting and one that had to be overcome by opponents.

As so often, the nature of military force and its relationship to social trends was a key element in the dynamics of insurgency and counterinsurgency warfare. In Mexico, there was a long-established practice of seeking and contesting power by force, as well as tension between the central state and the regions. Those who were able to assemble force inserted themselves into the situation, creating regional power bases that could, depending on politics, play a key role both in insurgency and in counterinsurgency violence.[35] Brigandage was also significant and looked toward more modern "organized crime."

Far from being a meaningless list of conflicts, the risings in Latin America indicated the widespread normative use of force, in part because of the extent to which authority and, therefore, opposition were militarized, as well as the role of ideology, generally in the case of opposition between Liberals and Conservatives. Some struggles were long-standing. For example, in Mexico in 1926–27, the army, with air support, suppressed the Yaqui Indians in the troublesome province of Sonora. In such cases, airpower brought an impression of greater strength to long-established practices of asserting control over recalcitrant people and regions. This impression had substance as far as mobility, range, and firepower were concerned.

Ideology was more to the fore in the case of violence over religion, a cause of conflict also with the French and Russian revolutionaries. In Mexico, in 1927–29, the War of the Cristeros was a major Catholic rising against the revolutionary state with its agrarian reform and its attack on the church. The rising led to intractable guerrilla warfare, with the army, which was on the side of the state, able to control the towns and railways but not the countryside. In 1929, a compromise between church and state ended a bitter war that had cost seventy thousand lives.[36]

More generally, the military across Latin America acted against insurgents and thus enforced the conservative social order. The frequent inability of rebels to confront the army directly encouraged a brutal military policing that often relied on acts of terror. This was seen in Bolivia in the 1920s, where peasants and striking miners were killed by the army. In 1930, this army overthrew the civilian government and put in a new one. The labor movement itself was suppressed in 1932. The army was also used to overcome peasant opposition in Honduras in 1932 and 1937. In El Salvador, General Martínez, who had seized control of the country in 1931, suppressed peasant opposition in 1932 with a series of massacres.[37] In turn, in Bolivia, as in Mexico and frequently more generally, an ethnic dimension played a role in regional opposition, with the indigenous peoples being central to peasant opposition. In addition, an awareness of the example of past insurrections was seen in 1932–35 when, referring back to 1780–81, the Grupo Tupac Amaru in Bolivia called for people's ownership and revolution and fomented insubordination among the Bolivian army.[38]

The growing economic strains arising from the acute global economic depression that began in 1929 had led to an increase in domestic as well as international tensions. This was seen in Brazil, where the military revolts in 1922 and 1924 were small scale and suppressed by the loyal majority of the army. In 1930, in contrast, the government was overthrown when the army proved unwilling to resist a rebel army advancing on the major city of São Paulo and, instead, seized power before handing it to Getúlio Vargas, the leader of the revolt. In turn, in 1932, federal forces suppressed a three-month-long "constitutionalist" revolt against Vargas. The scale of this struggle, as of many insurgencies, was considerable: the federal forces, seventy-five thousand strong and supported by air attacks on São Paulo, were opposed by forty thousand men, largely from the São Paulo militia. In Bolivia, a bloodless revolution in 1936 led to the introduction of "military socialism" that lasted until 1939, when the army changed direction.[39]

EUROPE

European insurgencies are far better known, in large part due to the important role of the Soviet Union for world history. The Russian Revolution was the product of an insurrectionary seizure of power by Bolsheviks in 1917. Supported by Germany, this was a key step in what became a broader seizure of power, notably with the Bolsheviks successfully seeking in 1918 to remove competing socialist parties. In turn, a variety of opponents sought to overthrow the Bolsheviks, which led to the Russian Civil War in 1918–21.

The failure of the anti-Bolshevik forces owed much to their serious internal divisions as well as to their political and strategic mismanagement. The Bolsheviks' central position was crucial. They had control of Moscow and Petrograd (St. Petersburg), the vital populous and industrial areas, as well as of key arms factories around Moscow and rail links. The industrial centers, where Bolshevik support was greatest, were also the hubs of the transport system. As a result, the Bolsheviks fought on interior lines, which the British general staff report saw as a major advantage enabling the Bolsheviks in a very changeable conflict "to concentrate at will" against individual opposing armies.[40]

Moreover, the Bolsheviks ruthlessly mobilized all the resources they could for the war effort, although that also harmed their support. Conscription was pushed hard, businesses were nationalized, grain seized, and a firm dictatorship imposed with opposition brutally suppressed. The size of the Red Army rose to five million men by the end of 1920. Such a large force of the people under arms corresponded with Bolshevik ideas about mass mobilization and also provided troops for the number of challenges that the Bolsheviks had to confront.

Like the French revolutionaries from 1792, the Bolsheviks overcame their oppositional tendencies and created a new state and military system reliant on force and centralized control in order to direct resources ruthlessly. The Red Army gave force to this internal transformation and also represented it.[41] A brutal secret service, arbitrary imprisonment, concentration camps, large-scale torture, and the mass killings of those suspected were all integral parts of the Bolshevik system. Bolshevik violence, indeed, contributed to a general social and political fragmentation. This, alongside famine and exhaustion, helped the Bolsheviks suppress resistance.

The Bolsheviks were assisted by the extent to which the rival Whites (or conservatives) proved unable to win and sustain peasant backing. Lacking a broad social base and largely failing to see the need to create one, their governments were selfish, greedy, factious, and incompetent. The British general staff was pessimistic about the prospect for a leading ally, Anton Denikin, the White commander in the south:

> Unless he can offer to the wretched inhabitants of the liberated districts . . . conditions of existence better than those which they suffered under the Bolshevik [Communist] regime, he will in the course of time be faced with revolt and hostility in his rear just at the time when the Bolsheviks will be concentrating large numbers of troops for a counter-offensive. [42]

Foreign intervention on behalf of the Whites suffered from a lack of agreed aims and of resolve. The financial burdens left by the First World War placed further limits on an interventionism that was far from popular in the countries intervening. Thus, Britain and France in particular each had a range of onerous commitments, while Canada, Japan, and the United States were also under pressure.

Opposition to the Bolsheviks in Russia was also encountered from the Left, indicating the range of insurrection, the fissiparous character of revolutionary movements, the radical disruption caused by violent changes in authority, and the way it made renewed uses of violence seem normative. In February 1921, the sailors and workers on the Kronstadt island naval base to the west of Petrograd, the leading naval base, rose against the government and in favor of Soviet democracy. After an initial attack on the island had failed, fifty thousand troops, covered by heavy artillery and supported by aircraft, advanced across the ice and restored state control. Those who surrendered were shot without trial or sent to concentration camps. The Finns complained about the number of corpses of the executed that washed up on their shore.

The Bolsheviks also faced peasant opposition, which reflected the burden of the civil war, the exactions of the new regime, and opposition to its determination to control rural life. Much of this opposition, especially in the Volga valley, was large scale, although poorly organized and lacking foreign support. Its repression involved a significant deployment of government forces. Over one hundred thousand troops, supported by aircraft and using poison gas, were deployed in June 1921 to overcome the Antonov revolt in Tambov Province. In this case, as in others, there were mass internments, shootings, and deportations to concentration camps. [43]

Islamic opposition was also crushed in the Soviet Union. The Red Army employed the brutal techniques already developed in the civil war, including mass deportations and executions, in anti-insurgency campaigns in Central Asia and the Caucasus. [44] Overwhelming force, the use of artillery against mountain villages, and the ability to call on some local support all played a role, as when the Soviets suppressed uprisings in the Caucasus areas of

Daghestan and Chechnya in 1920–21, 1924, 1928, 1929, 1936, and 1940.[45] These areas saw insurgencies anew from the 1990s.

During the Soviet period, insurgency and counterinsurgency, or, more mundanely, force and opposition, were linked to government social policy. This included not only social transformation seen elsewhere in the Soviet Union, notably the collectivization of agriculture, but also attempts at cultural revolution. Muslim courts were suppressed in Central Asia in 1926, followed in 1927 by Muslim schools and colleges, as well as an attempt to end the veil. In response, Muslims attacked women who unveiled, and the campaign to end the veil was called off in 1929.[46] The closure of churches and monasteries led to an insurgency in Georgia in 1921–22. Another in 1924 was brutally repressed, with about seven thousand to ten thousand people killed, followed by large-scale emigration.

Outside the Soviet Union, other insurgencies in the 1920s and 1930s also adopted what could be seen as a conservative perspective to challenge authority. Thus, in Albania, an area with a practice of violent autonomy, including a high rate of clan vendetta murders, there were unsuccessful uprisings in 1926 and 1937 against Ahmet Zogu, who had seized power in 1924, and made himself King Zog in 1928. He relied not on the small army but on his clan retainers and loyal clans, the leaders of which he made colonels and paid what in Albania was called "peace money." Zogu's limitation on the right to carry weapons was not extended to tribes on which he depended.[47]

In contrast to the Russian Civil War, foreign intervention was to prove more significant during the Spanish Civil War (1936–39). Prior to that there had already been counterinsurgency fighting in Spain in 1934 when the army suppressed a coal miners' uprising in the Asturias region. The ability of the miners to unite, seize weapons from depots and arms factories, and defeat the local police led to the deployment of twenty-six thousand troops against about ten thousand to twelve thousand rebel fighters who fought hard and used machine guns and artillery as well as rifles, albeit being very short of cartridges. The deployment of the Spanish Foreign Legion from Spanish Morocco ensured that the rebels faced good, well-trained troops with high morale. The latter were supported by naval fire and by the Spanish air force, which bombed and strafed rebel-held towns and positions, demoralizing the defenders, who lacked anti-aircraft defenses. The defeat of the insurgency was followed by the widespread killing of prisoners and civilians.[48]

In 1936, the Spanish Civil War was launched by a group of senior army officers who called themselves the Nationalists. They were opposed to the modernizing policies of the left-leaning Republican government and concerned about the possibility of a Communist seizure of power after the narrow left-wing electoral victory in the hard-fought elections that February. The officers' attempt to seize power that July, an attempt that matched nineteenth-century practices in Spain, was only partially successful, in part because the Nationalists had failed to carry the whole of the military, and that failure led to a bitter civil war. To add a further element of complexity in determining what precisely in this context was an insurgency, the Nationalists, legally traitors, can be seen as in revolt against a prerevolution posed by large-scale and violent worker strikes and assaults on the clergy under the government against which the Nationalists rebelled.

Moreover, once the Nationalists rose, there was also a form of revolution in the Republican zone that led to the alienation of centrists as well as conservatives. This revolution matched that in the Nationalist zone. A key feature was the consolidation of areas of control on both sides as flying columns suppressed local opposition. This consolidation involved large-scale violence, with those judged unacceptable murdered. G. H. Thompson, the British first secretary in Spain, reported in October 1937 after his visit first to the Republican zone in Valencia (its capital after the Nationalists approached Madrid in 1936) and then to the Nationalists' zone at Hendaye:

> When I first went to Valencia . . . rare was the night that passed without shots. Sometimes the remains of the previous night's "bumping-off" party would still be lying in the dust by the river . . . the not unfamiliar spectacle of five or six men sneaking along the darkened streets to some unhappy doorway. During the late spring and early summer the position improved as the government . . . fought the anarchists and shot them down in hundreds, chiefly in Barcelona. Recently, Valencia's deteriorating fortunes and the increasing miseries of the population have led to a revival of repression and a renewal of the offensive against the so-called "Fifth Column" of supposed Nationalist sympathisers . . . [in turn, in the Nationalist zone] the spy, the *agent provocateur*, the secret police, the denunciation as a suspected "Red" . . . the firing-party. [49]

The confiscation of property was another way to enforce control.

In the war, foreign intervention by Italy and Germany played a major role in helping the Nationalists win, although their logistics and generalship also proved more effective than those of the Republicans, who could not support the army or the civil population adequately. The Nationalists benefited from the extent to which their commanders and officers had fought in Morocco in the 1920s against colonial insurgents, whereas most of their opponents lacked this experience. The comments of a British military attaché in April 1938 after visiting Nationalist Spain are instructive for they indicate the difficulties of determining whether there was a particular style in insurgency warfare,

> a war in which the majority of the participants are almost entirely untrained, a war in which comparatively small forces are strung out on a vast length of front, a war in which modern weapons are used but not in the modern scale, and, finally, a war in which there have been more assassinations than deaths in battle. . . . In view of these singularities, it will be obvious that the greatest

caution must be used in deducing general lessons from this war: a little adroit-ness and it will be possible to use it to prove any preconceived theory.[50]

CONCLUSIONS

Accepting the caveat at the end of the previous quotation, a caveat that is valid for the subject as a whole, there were nevertheless marked trends in insurgency and counterinsurgency warfare in this period. Revolutionary left-wing insurgencies were encouraged by the Russian example, while anti-imperial insurgencies became more frequent and notably as Western imperial power in the Islamic world became more widespread. At the same time, not all insurgencies could be fitted into either category. At the tactical, operation-al, and strategic levels, there was a major change in the technology on offer for counterinsurgency forces, notably airpower, petrol-powered vehicles, and radio. The last allowed both sides to communicate but gave an advantage to the controller of the relevant infrastructure.

This technological change was seen not only with empires but also with other states, both Western and non-Western. For example, drawing on the energy and determination of the fundamentalist Islamic Wahhabi movement, Ibn Saud, the creator of Saudi Arabia, whose chasing out of the Hashemites from the Arabian Peninsula was itself a successful insurgency, in turn faced insurgencies, notably the Ikhwan (Brethren) revolt from 1928 to 1930. Brit-ish arms supplies were vital in helping crush the insurgency. At the battle of Sabilla on March 29, 1929, Ibn Saud won by using trucks with mounted machine guns against the Ikhwan when they were in the open. Such trucks were important in Libya and Syria in the 2010s. However, this technology was not the sole factor. Later in 1929, a surprise night attack defeated the Ikhwan at the battle of Hafr Al-Batin.

International rivalries and links were also significant. In 1932, a rebellion in the Hijaz, armed by the emir of Transjordan, an opponent of Ibn Saud, was crushed by the latter as a result of better intelligence and the use of armored cars as well as mounted troops. In 1929, King Amanullah of Afghanistan was overthrown by tribal opponents drawing on a widespread hostility to his state building. A lack of British support for the king was important.[51] Conversely, in the late 1930s, British-supplied light bombers were used to help the Af-ghan army suppress insurrections.

In Persia (Iran), major tribal insurgencies that owed something to opposi-tion to conscription were defeated in 1929 and 1932. These insurgencies came in the aftermath of Reza Shah's reunification of the country in the early to mid-1920s (following his coup in 1921), after central power had effective-ly been dissolved during the First World War. In some respects, outbreaks of order were the aberration for Iran in the first three decades of the century. The tribesmen suffered greatly from the capabilities brought to government forces by armored cars, trucks, new roads, automatic weapons, and observation aircraft. Combined with expenditure, organization, and political skill, these helped shift the historic balance between the tribes and regular forces, with the tribes also suffering, especially in the mid-1920s and 1929, from the lack of support from their former British patron.[52] Indeed, the next successful insurgency in Persia, the Islamic Revolution of 1977–78, was to be not a tribal rising but a mass insurgency in the urban centers of the country. The chronology and analysis of insurgencies in these states are as significant as those in Europe and European colonies that generally have attracted attention. In particular, it is apparent that anticolonial insurgencies, while important, were not the prime type of insurgency outside Europe.

Chapter Seven

Insurrections at a Height, 1940–60

Insurgency warfare in the mid-century decades took place in a number of quite different contexts. In particular, as a basic distinction, there was such warfare both during the Second World War and after it. First, there was opposition during the war to conquest by new imperial powers in the shape, in particular, of Germany, Japan, and the Soviet Union. Second, there was the resistance to longer-established imperial powers, particularly France, Britain, and the Dutch. Third, there was the case of insurrectionary civil wars in independent states, notably China, Greece, the Philippines, and Vietnam.

THE SECOND WORLD WAR

The Japanese and German treatment of occupied areas testified to the character of total war and, in turn, affected the course of the conflict and greatly encouraged opposition. Much of the civilian population was treated harshly by the Germans and Japanese, and large numbers with great cruelty. Brutalized, many of the defeated were not prepared to accept the verdict of battle, notably so as the war continued. As a result, in areas of China occupied by Japan from 1937, Japanese control outside the cities was largely limited and episodic. The British chiefs of staff noted in December 1939 that "Japanese authority in China is limited to certain main centers and to lines of communication, and Chinese guerrilla forces continue to take a considerable toll of Japanese garrison posts. . . . The Japanese army is heavily committed in China, where 30 out of a total of 48 divisions are engaged . . . little, if any, economic return is being obtained from the territories overrun. . . . Japan is living on her capital,"[1] the last a point that some Japanese commentators appreciated. As was typical in foreign assessments, the chiefs of staff saw the international dimension as crucial. Indeed, they agreed that Chinese success depended "on the maintenance of morale and the availability of military equipment . . . [and] depends greatly on the support offered by the more powerful democracies,"[2] by which Britain, France, and the United States were meant. With Burma (Myanmar), Indochina (Vietnam), and the Philippines, respectively, each had colonies in the region.

In rural parts of China, the ratio of strength and space told against the Japanese, especially when their opponents, most notably (but not only) the Communists, employing guerrilla tactics, moved into the rural areas of northern China, the part of China where the Japanese were present in greatest force, and hit Japanese communications. Thanks to their hard-learned experience of resisting the Guomindang government, the Communists were prepared for guerrilla opposition, and their radical social policies also attracted at least some peasants.[3]

However, a rigorous study of their effectiveness and popularity has not been encouraged by subsequent mythmaking. Far from being concerned only about the Communists, Japanese military leaders were surprised and frustrated by their failure, despite committing much of the army and air force, to achieve victory in China over the Guomindang. But Japanese failure helped fuel their determination to cut off foreign support for China, notably via Burma (Myanmar) and Indochina (Vietnam).

Also reflecting both policy failures and the strength of opposition, the Japanese consistently failed to win over sufficient Chinese support. The Japanese established the "Provisional Republic of China" in north China in 1937 and the "Reorganized National Government of the Republic of China" based in central China in 1938. These various bodies created their own forces, but the Japanese found these armies of limited value and treated them with suspicion while the governments were rapidly discredited in Chinese eyes. Across China, there was, in practice, both collaboration, especially from peripheral members of local elites, and resistance, as well as the full range of each.

Japanese policy in China, which included the large-scale slaughter of civilians, as in Nanjing in 1937 and the "kill all, burn all, loot all" offensive in 1942, also showed that brutality did not work, a lesson that their racialism and rigidity prevented the Japanese from learning. This brutality did not break Chinese morale but testified to the Japanese failure to provide any answer to the quagmire of their own making. Brutality was intimidating where the Chinese population was exposed to the Japanese military, but where their situation was protected by Chinese forces, the situation was different.

Resistance to Japanese occupation broadened as Japan launched a wider war of conquest from December 1941. The Western colonial powers had enjoyed only limited popular support in Southeast Asia, and resistance to Japanese occupation was far higher in China than in their colonies. Nevertheless, despite Japanese attempts to win support by creating puppet regimes and appealing to anti-Western nationalism, the harshness of their rule, as well as Japanese racism and contempt for other races, greatly compromised support. Thus, there was large-scale famine in Java because, once it was conquered from the Dutch in 1942, food was taken thence to Japan. This harshness was exacerbated as the Japanese military situation deteriorated, while this deterioration, in turn, compromised support. In the Philippines, resistance by American and Filipino troops who had not been captured when the Japanese conquered the country in 1942 was supported by civilians alienated by Japanese occupation practices.

Allied efforts to stir up resistance in Japanese-occupied territory were more difficult than in German-occupied Europe, in part because of the distances involved and the resulting logistical problems, but in large part because there was no equivalent to the governments-in-exile and popular resistance movements from which they benefited in Europe. Nevertheless, the British Special Operations Executive (SOE), the American Office of Strategic Services (OSS), and Special Operations Australia supported guerrilla operations, for example, by the Malayan People's Anti-Japanese Army.

In Europe, the German conquests of 1939–41 were promptly followed by the establishment of resistance movements, albeit not at once by large-scale resistance. However, the murderous brutality of German policy helped energize resistance, for example, in Serbia in 1941, where the army killed many thousands after rapidly conquering Yugoslavia. As a result, what had been a success became an incubus. Meanwhile, the British, who were gathering governments-in-exile in London, sought to support resistance in occupied Europe by means of the SOE, which was established in July 1940. In August 1941, a British strategic review noted the consequences of British forces being unable to compete with the Germans in continental Europe. The response was to seek strategic advantage from indirect attack in the shape of blockade, bombing, and subversion, each being designed to hit the German economy and German morale.[4]

Two months earlier, when the Germans invaded the Soviet Union in Operation Barbarossa, Stalin ordered guerrilla activity and proclaimed a "patriotic war" against the Germans. Initially, however, there was little real partisan threat to the advancing German forces and, instead, some popular support for the Germans, notably in Lithuania, Latvia, and Ukraine, all of which had been brutally occupied by Soviet forces: from 1940, 1940, and 1919–21, respectively. The Soviets had not prepared for partisan warfare, partly because of confidence in their military and its ability to defend the Soviet Union and partly because of suspicion of the idea of the nation in arms: people's warfare was associated with Stalin's former rival, Leon Trotsky. There was confusion in the Soviet Union in 1941 about how best to organize and control partisan activity, and the surprise nature of the attack accompanied by the rapidity of the German advance anyway made it difficult to organize a response.

Most of the early partisans in the Soviet Union were Communist Party or Communist Youth League members, but many were ineffective. Indeed, the search for supplies played a central role in their activity. Furthermore, many partisans deserted. Some early partisan opposition came from units of the Red Army that had been cut off by the German advance and from units from the NKVD (secret police). However, with time, partisan support became far more widespread, although Stalin distrusted the autonomy they displayed. The German use of indiscriminate brutality reduced the options for the population and encouraged support for the partisans.[5]

The Soviet winter counteroffensive in 1941–42 also proved highly effective in rallying support for resistance, as it showed that German victory was not inevitable, and maybe, indeed, was unlikely. The Germans, who were driven back from near Moscow and suffered heavy losses, responded with increased mass killing. The influences that conditioned German military thinking on antiguerrilla warfare were already brutalizing before the Nazis came to power in 1933, but Nazi ideas greatly intensified these influences. Among the German officers were fanatics who could draw no distinction between partisans and the remainder of the population, as well as moderates and self-styled pragmatists. This diversity, nevertheless, did not lead to any marked lessening of an institutional ruthlessness that was accentuated by Nazi ideology.[6]

Partisan activity contributed to the Germans' sense of the alien character of the occupied territories, a sense that also had a strong ideological element. This was a situation more generally true for counterinsurgency forces, for example, the French in Spain in 1808–14 and the Austrians in Bosnia in 1878, with the religious zeal of their opponents a factor cited by both the French and the Austrians. There was a degree of continuity between the harshness of Austrian counterinsurgency practice in the Balkans and that of the German forces, among whom the Austrians were prominent, during the Second World War. As with the Japanese in China, this alienation linked to partisan activity affected the Germans particularly in eastern Europe because of its vastness, the strength of prior racial indoctrination and attitudes, and the intractable nature of opposition. Consequently, this sense of disorientation and alienation among ordinary soldiers contributed to their implementation of harsh policies and to the brutality and sadism often displayed. The public execution of partisans by the Germans reflected the attempt to terrorize the population.

German methods proved self-defeating. Both the ruthlessness of the occupation policy and the lack of adequate resources for security made it difficult to conduct an effective occupation policy, whether peaceful or warlike, and particularly jeopardized the chances of economic benefit from the conquest while also throwing away the initial willingness of many to collaborate with the Germans.[7] A lack of sufficient manpower for the extensive long-term occupation of areas susceptible to the partisans helped lead to a reliance on high-tempo brutality, deterrent repression by vicious example, which was, to a degree, a correlate of the nature of German war making at the front. Units recruited from local allies, for example, of Lithuanians, helped in antipartisan operations, but the Germans lacked sufficient support from the local population to hold large areas.

There was a marked increase in partisan activity in the occupied Soviet Union from August 1942. Increasingly, partisan groups acted in large units, moving from base areas in order to mount raids. This helped spread the impact of opposition from the forested and swamp areas, such as the Belorussian Pripet Marshes, where it was strong, to others, such as southern Ukraine, where the natural cover and political circumstances were less supportive. Terrain and natural cover also helped account for variations in resistance activity elsewhere. Thus, in France there was less resistance in the flat and well-cultivated Loire Valley than in the mountainous Massif Central. At the same time, challenging any environmental determinism, the variegated nature of ethnic identities, religious affiliation, political commitment, and foreign support all played a role.[8]

The discouraging nature of reprisals was important, especially the shooting of large numbers of civilians when German troops were killed. The Germans were deliberately brutal. Thus, the mortal wounding in Prague on May 27, 1942, by Czech agents trained by the SOE, of Reinhard Heydrich, the senior German official in Bohemia and a key figure in German mass-murder, led first to the execution of two thousand Czechs and then to the wiping out of Lidice, a village, in order to teach the Czechs subservience. All men and dogs were shot, the women were sent to concentration camps, and the children were gassed or selected for Germanization. However, brutality could make resistance appear a matter of survival as well as having the opposite deterrent effect, a point more generally true.

Resistance to the Germans (as to the Japanese) was greatly affected by the detailed configuration of local geography, ethnicity, politics, religion, and society. This configuration was related to the nature of occupation and the complex dynamic of collaboration and opposition. Thus, in western Belarus, there was rivalry between Polish and Soviet partisans. Moreover, political rivalries between Communists and conservative nationalists led to conflict in Albania, Greece, and Yugoslavia.[9] These situations were made more complex by frequently ambivalent relations between sections of the resistance and the occupying power, for example, between the Chetniks (the Serbian, anti-Communist guerrilla movement) in Yugoslavia and the Germans.[10] This factor was accentuated by the reliance of the Germans on local allies and of the Japanese on de facto truces. As occupiers, the Italians and Germans followed different policies.[11] In turn, postwar politics was greatly to affect the presentation of this factor, as cooperation with wartime occupiers became a key charge to throw at opponents.

The better-armed Germans were generally able to defeat partisans in open conflict, as in the spring of 1942 in the Soviet Union, when Stalin insisted that the partisans hold positions in the rear of the German Army Group Center, or when the Germans suppressed major uprisings in Warsaw, Slovakia, and the Vercors plateau in France, all in 1944, in each case inflicting major losses. In addition, the Germans were usually effective in maintaining control of the cities and their supply lines. The Germans proved less successful in successive attacks on the Communist partisans in Bosnia in 1942–44, although the partisans suffered heavy casualties.

Large numbers of troops, however, had to be deployed by the Germans in order to limit resistance operations or to prevent their possible outbreak. As a result, aside from the successful German (and Japanese) suppression of resistance, many areas under partisan control, for example, parts of the Western Balkans, were so, at least in part, because the Germans (and the Japanese) chose not to deploy troops to occupy them. Nevertheless, the resistance still achieved much. Most important was the diversion of large amounts of German and Japanese resources to dealing with the threat, as well as the need to adopt antipartisan policies that affected the efficiency of German and Japanese rule and of economic and transport activities. Considerable damage and disruption were inflicted by guerrilla attacks and sabotage, for example, on the Danish rail system from 1943. Such activity was greatly aided by Allied air support and special operations. Insurgents enjoyed a particular legitimacy when representing exiled governments, although it helped greatly by this stage of the war that they were on the winning side.

Resistance attacks were most useful when coordinated with Allied operations, such as in support of the Soviet offensive in early 1942 and, again on the Eastern Front, in fighting near Kursk in 1943. In 1944, the cutting by French partisans of transport links by which the Germans might move troops complemented the Anglo-American air offensive in preparing for the Normandy landings by isolating German forces in the area and making it difficult to move reinforcements. The Allies also benefited from large quantities of crucial intelligence from the resistance, for example, on defenses, troop movements, bomb damage, and the development of German rocketry.

Resistance, moreover, achieved the vital political goal of weakening collaboration and undermining coexistence. This isolated the German, Japanese, and allied militaries, increasing their sense of vulnerability and the violence they displayed and, as a vital aspect of the struggle for support, made their new orders appear transient and thus not worth supporting.[12] This element has always been key to insurgency activity and is a crucial strategic goal and operational and tactical means. Therefore, this element is a vital one for counterinsurgency struggles.

In turn, the Germans and Japanese proved far less successful in developing resistance movements as the Allies advanced. The speed of the German military collapse in 1945 and the Nazi movement's dependence on Hitler were crucial, but so also was the absence of unoccupied bases from which resistance could be encouraged and supplied. The Nazi Werewolf organization inflicted little damage in 1945–46, principally killing a few German officials who cooperated with the Allies, notably the mayor of Aachen, as well as some Allied officials and troops. The emperor's surrender in Japan ensured that there was no resistance to occupation there, although some Japanese soldiers continued lone battles on islands for decades.

Conversely, during the war, the Allies did not face large-scale resistance within their empires and areas of influence. However, nationalist pressure was particularly a factor in India, where the war witnessed a marked increase in pressure for independence. The British government offered the Hindu-dominated Congress Party a constituent assembly after the war with powers to draft a new constitution for India and Congress being invited to join the central government in the meanwhile. Congress, however, sought a bigger role at once, including in the direction of India's war efforts, which Winston Churchill, the British prime minister and an active prewar opponent of Congress pressure, was unwilling to grant. From April 1942, at a time when Britain's position in Asia was under great challenge from the Japanese advance, Gandhi started to employ the slogan "Quit India" against British rule, and he swiftly pressed for a civil disobedience campaign to thwart the government.

The crisis built up in August 1942. As Congress increased the pressure for the end of British rule, Gandhi and other leaders were arrested. In response, rioting, strikes, and sabotage spread, with many attacks on the railways. These affected the British ability to respond to the threatening Japanese advance in neighboring Myanmar. Under the strain of war, the government relied on force. Most of the police and civil administration remained passive. In contrast, large numbers of troops (of the British-commanded Indian Army), supported by British overflying aircraft, were deployed in an attempt to restore order, and tens of thousands of Congress supporters were arrested, many for the remainder of the war, while the party was banned. The crisis ended swiftly, in part because much of the population was not involved,[13] but Congress became more hostile to the continuation of British rule. However, Congress did not collude with the Japanese. Moreover, those nationalists who did ally with them were a much smaller group: the Japanese-backed Provisional Government of Free India and Indian National Army, formed by the nationalist Subhas Chandra Bose and stimulated markedly by the Japanese advance into Myanmar, had little impact.

The British realized that in case of a further dispute they could not rely wholesale on the police or administrators. The viceroy, Field Marshal Wavell, observed in 1944, "On the whole, India is getting along reasonably well. . . . Once the Japanese war is over, our troubles out here really will begin."[14] The army was loyal. Helped by the plentiful resources available during the second part of the war, the Indian Army was not to become unstable until the onset of postwar demobilization and demoralization in 1945.[15] Prior to that, there were murmurings within the army about a desire for independence once the war was won. In the event, independence came in 1947, after, and while, large-scale communal rioting and slaughter forced the army into a counterinsurgency role.[16]

POSTWAR

As the Germans were driven back and withdrew from their conquests in 1944, conflicts within the resistance became more apparent. This was particularly apparent in Eastern Europe and ensured that there was no clear division between the war and the postwar world. Resistance was mounted to the reimposition and subsequent brutalities of Soviet rule in Ukraine, especially western Ukraine, and the former Baltic republics, above all Lithuania, and to the extension of this rule into Poland. The suppression of this resistance took years, involved large numbers of troops, and entailed much brutality, including much killing and the deportation of large numbers of people, notably from southeastern Poland and western Ukraine. Disoriented by the killing and seizure of activists, opposition in Poland was demoralized and worn down in the late 1940s, although armed resistance lasted into the 1950s.[17] In western Ukraine, where the nationalist insurgency of the Ukrainian Insurgent Army was particularly strong, the records suggest that 110,825 partisans were killed in 1944–46. The insurgency lasted until 1951 and in isolated cases until 1960. The Soviet authorities succeeded in part by deporting about 250,000 people from western Ukraine to Siberia and by infiltrating the opposition. They also benefited from divisions among the opposition.[18] Despite efforts by the United States and Britain, the guerrillas, both there and elsewhere, received little effective support from the West, and this discouraged resistance.

The use of troops to suppress opposition in the Soviet Union and Eastern Europe was part of a continuum in the Communist world under Stalin, dictator from 1924 until 1953, of the brutal control ceaselessly advocated by Lenin. Terror, violence, force, and surveillance were routinely employed to maintain control and to implement policies. The Leninist-Stalinist system worked in large part by creating an all-pervasive sense of surveillance and fear, a sense that drew on the reality of a large and powerful secret police.

Conversely, British troops intervened in Greece in 1944 in order to back the Royalist side in its conflict with ELAS, the left-wing Greek People's Army of Liberation, a conflict from the wartime resistance to the Germans that spilled over into the postwar Greek Civil War. One British soldier recalled the difficulty of operating against resistance groups:

> The enemy was just the same as any other Greeks as far as we knew, they didn't have any uniform as such. . . . It was a situation that was quite completely different to the way we had been used to fighting. . . . As an average infantryman, one of the first questions that you ask is "Which way is the front?" so that you know if the worst comes to the worst which way you can go to get out of the bloody place. In this sort of situation, which is a typical urban "battlefront," it's all around you.[19]

It is pertinent to ask why, if the Germans failed to suppress resistance activity, the Soviets were so much more successful in the late 1940s, while, in addition, the Royalists won the Greek Civil War, defeating the Communist insurgents. In part, German failure reflected the international context in that there was strong foreign aid for the resistance to the Germans. For example, the SOE and its supporting special-duty air squadrons delivered close to a half-million small arms to the French resistance alone, although geographical proximity made this a relatively easy task. In contrast, Western support for the postwar resistance to the Soviets suffered from the extent to which the resistance was operating from badly damaged and disrupted societies and in exhausted terrains.[20] Moreover, the Germans had control for a far briefer period, for example, in 1941–44 in Yugoslavia and Belarus, than the Communists and occupied Greece only from 1941 to 1944.

In Greece, the Communists suffered from a failure to sustain international backing as Tito's rift with Stalin in 1948 closed Yugoslav bases to them. Moreover, the Greek army learned to be effective in counterinsurgency conflict, while it also benefited from a massive effort, a multifaceted counterinsurgency strategy that included social and economic drives, and from Anglo-American support, including aircraft.[21] The Germans, in contrast, had had to devote most of their resources to conflict at the front and only relatively rarely diverted troops from the front to operations against the resistance.

The Greek army benefited from its abandonment in 1948 of a policy of static defense and, instead, its introduction of an offensive policy with a systematic clearance of guerrilla forces out of particular areas. The Greek army was also helped by the extent to which much of the population supported the government as well as by the Communists' adoption of more conventional methods of fighting. This was a political decision, taken in 1947, and rested on the belief that by establishing a Communist government in parts of northern Greece near the neighboring Communist states, Bulgaria, Yugoslavia, and Albania, it would be possible to secure Soviet aid to

counteract that from the United States for the Greek government, for example, American Helldiver aircraft. However, it proved impossible for the
Communists to recruit the manpower anticipated, the Soviets did not provide
the heavy weaponry that was sought, let alone intervene, and the Communists' reliance on position warfare helped lead to their defeat. The Communists were driven back to their strongholds in western Macedonia and were
finally defeated there. Both sides killed prisoners and civilians deemed hostile. David Galula, a French officer who, having fought in Algeria, wrote on
counterinsurgency and is discussed at the close of the chapter, had been an
observer in the Greek Civil War.

In 1945, the fall of Hitler and Mussolini led to a widespread assumption
that Francisco Franco, the Fascist dictator of Spain, could also be overthrown. Based in France, a Communist insurgency began in northern Spain.
It failed, in part due to the brutality of the governmental repression and in
part to the extent to which much of northern Spain was very much an anti-
Communist area. In addition, the insurgents' need for food led them to raid
villages and thus to lose the prospect of local support. With food very much a
key weapon, one that is all too easy for well-fed modern commentators to
ignore, the government took pains to keep the amount of food in the region
limited. The government also benefited from serious divisions within the
opposition between Communists and anarchists and from the French government becoming hostile to the insurgency from the end of 1946, in particular
as it became more suspicious of Communism, both within France and more
generally.

The principal insurgency conflict in the late 1940s also marked a continuation of earlier rivalries, in this case between the Guomindang and the Communists in China. This rivalry had continued during the war with Japan but
was very much subordinated to the latter. The Guomindang was seriously
weakened by the long war with Japan, with key military units destroyed in
1937, the major cities lost, and great damage to the economy and the social
fabric in what became a shattered land. Moreover, there was no recovery in
the latter half of the war. Instead, the Guomindang were particularly hard hit
by large-scale Japanese advances in 1944 and 1945 that overran much of
southern China. During the subsequent civil war, the Communists benefited
from superior strategic conceptions, operational planning and execution,
army morale, political leadership, and the handing over of captured weapons
by the Soviet army when it defeated the Japanese in Manchuria in 1945.
Pursuing a doctrine of people's war, the Chinese Communists were able to
make the transfer from guerrilla warfare to large-scale conventional operations, from denying their opponents control over territory to, instead, seizing
and securing it.

The Communist victory became important to the account not only of
Chinese history but also of insurgency warfare. However, this classic treat-

ment of the war as a Communist victory of "hearts and minds" that indicated the supposedly superior virtues of Communism has been qualified recently by more detailed attention to the course of the conflict. Indeed, until 1948, the Guomindang largely held their own. In turn, in 1948–49, the Communists were able to benefit greatly from defeating their opponents in Manchuria, thus creating a safe base there and using it for operations elsewhere. This helped cause the rapid collapse of the Guomindang in central and southern China from the spring of 1949. The Communists profited from the American unwillingness to provide troops to the Guomindang. Moreover, the Guomindang were unable to translate the strategic advantage offered by a monopoly of airpower into decisive tactical and operational impact. The Communists learned how to reduce the impact of airpower, for example, by moving supplies at night, by switching between rail and road transport, and by developing an antiaircraft capability. Nevertheless, the key element was that the Communists defeated the Guomindang in a series of offensives in 1948–49.[22] Once successful, the Communists enforced their control with the mass murder of those they deemed socially unacceptable.

In part as a result of the cult of Mao and also in order to underline their significance, the Chinese Communists saw their success as a model for activity elsewhere and notably for moving from guerrilla to conventional operations. This indeed eventually proved successful in Vietnam in 1954 and in Cuba in 1958. In Vietnam, Ho Chi Minh, the Communist head of the nationalist Viet Minh, exploited the vacuum of power left by the Japanese surrender in August 1945 and, seizing power, proclaimed the foundation of the Democratic Republic of Vietnam on September 2. Determined, however, to retain their imperial position and thereby great-power status, the French refused to accept the loss of colonial control and sent troops. Negotiations and fighting continued into 1946, when large-scale conflict broke out. Although effective in guerrilla operations, the Viet Minh was unsuccessful in conventional conflict, notably in 1951 and 1952. Mass attacks on French *hérissons*, fortified hedgehog positions, in the open areas of the Red River delta, for example, at Vinh Yen and Mao Khé, failed. The French were able to employ their conventional forces and airpower, including napalm. The French held all the major towns.

Nevertheless, the Communist victory in the Chinese Civil War in 1949 ensured that the Viet Minh had a secure neighboring base as well as arms supplied by the Chinese. Moreover, a brutal process of social mobilization and political indoctrination enforced a degree of cohesion.[23] In addition to this narrative, much depended on the determination of the counterinsurgency force. In 1954, when the forward French base at Dien Bien Phu was overrun, the French government, despite still holding all the major towns, felt exhausted, while the Americans, who were paying much of the financial cost, were not willing to intervene with troops and air attacks.

In the late 1940s, the Dutch faced nationalist opposition in Java and Sumatra, the two key islands in the Netherlands East Indies (modern Indonesia). The Dutch fought back, notably in July–August 1947 and December 1948, with what they called police actions: as they considered the archipelago as theirs, it was an internal issue and not an international one. The Dutch forces achieved some important successes, especially capturing Sukarno, the nationalist leader, in a surprise commando-paratrooper assault on Yokjakarta in 1948. This raid was a political failure because it cost much international goodwill, but it showed what could be done. Indeed, the Dutch military felt they were generally being prevented by their political masters from going "all out" in their counterinsurgency war. [24] This was a common theme in such conflicts. In practice, the Dutch were not able to defeat the Indonesians. After the second "police action," an eight-month guerrilla war then took as many Dutch lives as had been lost in the three preceeding years. Spread thin, although supported by local allies, especially on the outer islands, the Dutch were forced to accept that their sole realistic option was to leave. Talks began in August 1949, and a peace agreement was signed on November 2. Military issues played a role in Dutch withdrawal, but so did Dutch weakness after the Second World War, as well as strong American pressure on behalf of the nationalists and for the Dutch to focus on Europe.

The Americans also pressed Britain to yield to Jewish interests in Palestine in 1945–48. This ensured that Britain, which did not find it easy to operate in the midst of the contrary pressures there, did not hit hard at Jewish insurgent groups, and certainly not in comparison with the stance taken toward the Arab Rising in Palestine in 1937–39. [25] Unable to control the situation, Britain proved keen to bring its rule of Palestine to an end in 1948.

Nor were the Americans willing to support the Batista regime in Cuba against the insurrection led by Fidel Castro, who gained power in the winter of 1958–59. The Batista regime had been unsuccessful in its use of aircraft in the mountainous Sierra Nevada range, where the insurgents presented a far more disparate target than the marines who had unsuccessfully rebelled in the city of Cifuengos in 1957. Castro benefited from the extent to which his insurrection was not yet seen by the American government as Communist.

As in the case of Castro initially, the Americans took a different view to that of the Dutch to the far more favorable policy they adopted toward the French in Southeast Asia. They saw the opponents of the Dutch as nationalists ready to stand up against Communists: the Americans were far more opposed to those they regarded as Communist nationalists. As a result, the Americans supported the Philippines, which had become independent in 1946, against the Communist Hukbalahap insurrection in 1946–54. This was not only a matter of military support. The Americans backed the attempt to alter the social situation in Mindinao, an island that traditionally was a center of insurrection, by moving settlers there from the island of Luzon to create a basis for reliable local support.

In Korea, there was civil war in the late 1940s between Communist nationalists based in the north and non-Communist nationalists in the south before the outbreak of full-scale conflict in the shape of the Korean War in 1950. The Communists put much effort into overthrowing the south. The civil war included the large-scale and unsuccessful Cheju insurgency in South Korea in 1948.

Unlike the Americans in Vietnam and Cuba in the 1950s, the Soviet government in Hungary in 1956 eventually proved willing to launch a full-scale invasion in order to crush popular opposition to Soviet control and Communist orthodoxy, opposition that had led to a change of government and policy that were unwelcome to the Soviets. Hungary had withdrawn from the Soviet-dominated Warsaw Pact. In Budapest, the Soviets used tanks backed by airpower, while the outnumbered resistance relied on gasoline bombs and sniping. Soviet Spetsnaz special forces went door to door and sniffed the hands of the men they detained. If they found traces of gunpowder, they shot the men on the spot. The Soviet Union thus preserved its imperial control of Eastern Europe.

PRESERVING EMPIRE

Western colonial powers made major efforts to maintain control of many of their colonies. Although eventually prepared to yield over Vietnam, the French made a significant effort to retain control of Algeria, while the British did the same in Malaya, Kenya, and Cyprus. The British benefited in each case because the insurrections were weakened by their location in sectional (rather than general) opposition to imperial rule. Thus, in Malaya in 1948–60, opposition was by the Chinese population rather than the Malays; in Kenya in 1952–56, primarily by the Kikuyu, Embu, and Meru tribes; and in Cyprus, by EOKA, a Greek Cypriot paramilitary organization. Moreover, the British developed effective counterinsurgency policies ranging from the use of airpower and a forward offensive policy to the movement of apparently hostile civilians out of areas of operation. There was little evidence of the policy of minimum force that was subsequently to become important in British military doctrine, sometimes being deployed in a somewhat self-satisfied fashion in drawing a contrast with American and French policies.

In Malaya, the British benefited because air superiority provided mobility and stopped foreign insurgents from being airlifted in, while they had a secure regional base in Singapore as well as the backing of Australia and New Zealand. The British navy's first operational helicopter squadron was formed in 1952 in order to help antiguerrilla operations in Malaya. The legacy of relevant recent experience was also significant. Key British commanders and advisers, notably Hugh Stockwell and Robert Thompson, already had experience of counterinsurgency or irregular warfare. A counter-terror strategy in 1948–49[26] was followed by a less rigorous stance in which persuasion played a role. The movement of people into villages was a key policy, while in February 1952 it was determined that Malaya should in time "become a fully self-governing nation."[27] Searching for the outnumbered Communist guerrillas by means of jungle patrols proved frustrating.[28]

The military and political environments varied greatly. Thus, Cyprus provided greater opportunities for the British than Malaya and Kenya, in part because there was far less tree cover, while the area of operations was smaller and aircraft were based more closely. However, lacking adequate intelligence, the British in Cyprus in 1955–59 were unable to separate the Greek Cypriot insurgency movement, EOKA, from the civilian population and to protect the latter from often murderous EOKA intimidation. As a result, EOKA could be checked but could not be destroyed and was not deprived of its means of regeneration.[29]

In Kenya, the British benefited in fighting the Mau Mau uprising from local military and police units as well as British forces, such that a civil war among the Kikuyu and the non-European population was an aspect of the struggle. This element was downplayed after independence. The move from the initial defensive stage, in which the British suffered from not learning the lessons from Malaya, to a recapture of the initiative, in which these lessons were applied, was crucial. This move entailed the development of an integrated system of command and control encompassing army, police, and administration, and the implementation of appropriate military tactics. Moreover, airpower proved significant, notably in 1953–54 in being able to attack the Mau Mau in areas beyond the reach of the army, especially the distant forests around Mount Kenya and in the Aberdare Mountains. Airpower served to demonstrate the strength of the government, while there was broadcasting from the sky and the dropping of large numbers of pamphlets in order to influence opinion. As part of what was seen as a crucial battle for opinion, care was taken to lessen civilian casualties when mounting air attacks. In Kenya, as in Malaya and Cyprus, but not Palestine, British counterinsurgency benefited from a largely supportive or apathetic, or at least not-too-critical, domestic public opinion.[30]

At the same time, the key element of coercion needs to be underlined because of the misleading tendency to underplay this role in British COIN.[31] Collective punishment, large-scale detentions, with a peak in December 1954 of 71,346 detained in Kenya, and the movement of people (i.e., mass eviction) relied ultimately on the availability of overwhelming and coercive force and on the central role of the army, for which minimum force meant minimum necessary force. British policies entailed the mistreatment of civilians, including killings and torture, as well as beatings in order to produce confessions and witness statements. This was largely the policy of subordinates, but senior commanders proved unwilling to control the abuses attendant on the use of force, while also accepting them as a way to end the crisis.[32] Following guilty verdicts, 1,090 Kenyans were hanged. Public executions were employed as exemplary force, as a form of intimidation, and as an aspect of a multifaceted propaganda war.[33] British policy became more lenient from the summer of 1953 with an emphasis on amnesties and a growing willingness to punish brutality or, at least, conspicuous brutality.

Alongside coercion, there was some criticism in Britain of the methods of control, including detention without trial and the movement of people into villages. The use of coercion was in part a response to imperial overreach and notably to the weakness of Britain after the costs of the Second World War and the loss, with Indian independence, of the highly important manpower support of the Indian Army. Force was a response to a sense of weakness and to the reality of a shortage of troops and a lack of local control and intelligence. Force was seen as the way to maintain authority. At the same time, concern about the Cold War and the tendency to see Communist planning behind nationalist pressure, a tendency that was generally misplaced, encouraged this reliance on force, a reliance that extended to a manipulation of judicial systems and regulations. These points are highly relevant given the extent to which British counterinsurgency was subsequently to be held up as a model in the United States and was turned into a doctrine in Britain. The political concessions that were subsequently praised were not the first step and came only after the use of force. Indeed, the British concept of opposition as a threat to a benign bulk of the population ensured that such a use of force was regarded as very necessary.

The British reliance on force and the use of collective punishments appear anachronistic from the perspective of imminent decolonization, but the latter was less apparent in the mid-1950s, let alone the late 1940s, than by the end of the decade. For example, Cyprus appeared to many in a military light, offering a military base in the eastern Mediterranean to compensate for the loss of that in Egypt. Moreover, such a reliance on force was seen elsewhere. In response to Palestinian terrorism and drawing on the earlier British example, notably against the 1937–39 Arab Rising, Israel faced the need to develop counterterrorist thinking and practice. A reprisal policy became a central military and political means for Israel.[34] Some of the Israeli Defense Force had fought in the British army in the Second World War, while some had fought with the Haganah, the Israeli "freedom fighters."

In Algeria in 1954–62, the French ultimately faced a more difficult situation than that which had faced Britain. It was complicated by the significance of nearby Algeria: France's largest colony was treated by the French as part of France itself. The size of the French settler population was also significant: most of them were adamantly opposed to the indigenous nationalists who sought independence. The French government, notably from 1956, sought a middle way, that of military firmness against the nationalists, while also attempting to win the support of the bulk of the indigenous Muslim population by introducing reforms. The context, however, was made more difficult by the political and military determination to avoid a failure comparable to that in Vietnam, by the decision to send large numbers of reservists to Algeria, and by the rise of pan-Arab nationalism, although there was no equivalent to the strategic issue in Vietnam posed by Communist success in neighboring China in 1949.

By the end of the 1950s, the outcome was uncertain. French counterinsurgency policies, including sealing the borders, focusing on the people as the prime sphere for operations, using the army for police tasks, forcibly resettling approximately a quarter of the peasantry into guarded camps, and employing considerable brutality, notably torture, contained the National Liberation Front (FLN). Brutal itself, the FLN, rather than the French, was responsible for the majority of deaths of Algerian Arabs and Berbers. French policies reflected the significance of military considerations in the French colonial presence. Algeria had been conquered in the first place, and the military remained important in the colonial mind-set. Moreover, the use of helicopterborne assault forces took the war to the FLN. The designation of large freefire zones, cleared by forced resettlement, in which French aircraft could bomb and strafe freely, increased the effectiveness of these attacks. Unlike later insurgent groups under air assault, the FLN lacked antiaircraft missiles, while the terrain was far more exposed to air attack than the forested lands of Southeast Asia. However, the indiscriminate character of the French use of strafing and bombing was all too characteristic of a failure to distinguish foes from the bulk of the population and was counterproductive in winning the loyalty of the latter.[35]

The Algerian war was subsequently to play a major role in the development of counterinsurgency theory, doctrine, and practice, not least because of the wider influence of French soldiers and the need in the United States, Latin America, Francophone Africa, and elsewhere for understanding counterinsurgency methods. The brutal repression used by the Argentine military dictatorship in the "Dirty War" of 1976–82 looked back to the French example. There was also a strand of French influence on American doctrine. David Galula went to the United States and wrote *Pacification in Algeria, 1956–1958* for Rand and *Counterinsurgency Warfare* (1964), both originally written in English. Galula argued that population-centric practices were central and pressed the need, accordingly, to focus the army on policing responsibilities, to separate the population from the rebels, and to devise and apply a COIN doctrine.

Nevertheless, the reality was that despite his claims, the presence of many troops, and the use of brutal practices, Galula was not able to end FLN activities in the Djebel Aissa Mimoun area where he operated in 1956–57. "The people," for Galula as for Mao, were the key element, but the means to strategize and instrumentalize this slogan were not adequately expounded. In Iraq in 2007, the American commander, General David Petraeus, referred to Galula, whose books had been reprinted in the United States the previous year, as "the Clausewitz of COIN."[36] In practice, like the pedigree for insurgency thought, this approach to counterinsurgency (COIN) involved a highly partial reading of past texts and episodes.[37] In part, this practice, like that of much discussion of strategy, reflected the tendency to replace experience with knowledge of the "handbooks" type.

Although the most prominent, Galula was not the only French commentator to appear in print and to influence American opinion. Roger Trinquier, another veteran, emphasized the use of counterinsurgency methods that were very different from conventional warfare, ranging from forced population transfer to attacks on terrorist networks. His approach was harsher than that of Galula and did not seek to address popular grievances. Trinquier's major work, *La guerre moderne* (Paris, 1961), was quickly published in London and New York in an English translation. The French experience was also analyzed by non-French commentators, notably by Peter Paret in the United States.[38]

At the end of the 1950s, the concept of success through revolutionary warfare that had appeared so clear after the results of the Chinese Civil War (1946–49) and the Vietnam conflict (1946–54) appeared far more problematic as a result of the British success in Malaya and Kenya and what appeared to be French success in Algeria. In practice, the situation had been varied throughout, not least with the failure in the late 1940s and early 1950s of insurgencies in Greece, the Baltic republics, and the Philippines.

Chapter Eight

The Fall of Empires, 1960–80

Hesitations about the success of insurgency appeared far less to the fore by 1980. The intervening two decades had brought total French failure in Algeria, British in Aden, and American in Vietnam, as well as failures for non-Western forces, notably for the Egyptians in Yemen. Yet some insurgencies had been totally unsuccessful, particularly the Kataganese separatist rebellion in Congo and the Biafran separatist rebellion in Nigeria and, on a far smaller scale, that by opponents of President Castro of Cuba, the attempt by Che Guevara to launch a revolution in Bolivia, and the American-supported Tibetan opposition to Chinese control.

ALGERIA

French tactical and operational successes in Algeria did not bring strategic victory. The reasons were multiple, including the inability to end guerrilla action, but essentially political. The brutal and ruthless nationalist insurgents had destroyed the prospects for a middle way advanced by the French government in 1956 and had terrorized other Muslim political forces. Moreover, French reprisals, for example, at Philippeville in 1955, were a contributing factor to the narrowing space for conciliation. Compromise therefore was no longer an option.

As for the French in Vietnam in 1954, the apparently intractable nature of the struggle in Algeria built up political pressure in France for a solution. The large-scale call-up of reservists to help wage the war made it more politically sensitive. As a result of this call-up, France came to deploy over a half-million troops as well as about two hundred thousand *harkis*, loyal Muslim militia. The French white settler population in Algeria as well as most of the military leadership was determined to retain the colony. In 1958, their mutiny helped bring down the government of France and install a new one under Charles de Gaulle, paving the way for his establishment, with the Fifth Republic, of a more presidential form of government. However, in the face of a lack of victory and despite the hopes of the settlers, de Gaulle proved willing to cut the link with Algeria. In part, this was because he saw France's destiny as European rather than colonial. De Gaulle also believed that France's military options would improve when France acquired nuclear status. Therefore, it would not be necessary to retain Algeria as a source of North African troops, which had been an important support in both world wars. An attempt by rebellious generals to overthrow de Gaulle in 1961 failed, and in 1962, independence was conceded.[1] In turn, Algeria served as a basis of inspiration for insurgencies elsewhere against colonial control. One element in sustaining the revolutionary outcome in Algeria was provided by the departure from the country of about eight hundred thousand Europeans and eighty thousand *harkis*.

END OF EMPIRE

More generally, European governments and forces found it troublesome to hold onto colonies. In part, this was because they could no longer enjoy sufficient tactical and operational advantages and in part because, resting on the defensive, they suffered from the strategic unwillingness to accept that only partial control was possible. These military factors interacted with the breakdown of the ability of imperial powers to ensure the incorporation of native elites and peoples within their empires and a lack of support at home for continued imperial efforts. Loss of political will and the related unwillingness to pay the requisite military price were different from the tactical and operational inability to maintain control, but both played a role. It no longer appeared appropriate to "soldier on" in order to hope that something would turn up, although sometimes, as with the British in the Indonesian Confrontation of 1963–66 and later in Northern Ireland, that strategy worked as a means to contain a problem and then look to a solution.[2]

In 1967, Britain abandoned the colony of Aden in the face of an intractable local insurgency. Nationalist agitation there, which had been increasingly strident from 1956, had turned into revolt in 1963. The British deployed nineteen thousand troops, the bulk of the army then allocated to maintaining control of British colonies, but their position was undermined by the failure to sustain local support. The British-officered Federal Regular Army proved unreliable, and in June 1967, the South Arabian Police and the Aden Armed Police rebelled in the city of Aden. Furthermore, the British were unable to support allied sheikhs in the interior against the guerrilla attacks of the National Liberation Front (NLF). The conflict was an aspect of the Cold War, of the struggle for regional dominance, and also of the related one over Arab nationalism. The Egyptian presence in neighboring Yemen was important to all three, and the insurgency in Aden was linked to this presence.

The airpower, scorched-earth tactics, and resettlement policies used by the British in Malaya in the 1950s were deployed again, not least with punitive tactics against resistance, but the NLF's inroads forced an abandonment of the interior in the early summer of 1967. Once the British were clearly on the way out, they found it hard to obtain accurate intelligence, and this made mounting operations difficult. Reduced to holding onto Aden, where the garrison itself had to be protected, the only initiative left was to abandon the position, which was done in December 1967, bringing to a humiliating end a rule that had begun in 1839.[3] Field Marshal Montgomery observed that when a force was reduced largely to protecting its own position, its presence had become largely redundant.

Its government overthrown in 1974 by discontented army officers, Portugal abandoned its African empire in 1974–75, giving victory to insurgents in Angola, Mozambique, and Guinea-Bissau. Just as ideologies of cultural superiority had not provided victory for the French in Indochina or Algeria, so they could not ensure lasting domestic support for the expensive and lengthy Portuguese war effort, one that involved the use of conscripts. At the same time, this outcome reflected the serious military difficulties the Portuguese had encountered and, therefore, the problems of assessing the key elements in counterinsurgency failure, problems also apparent to those contemporaries involved on the ground.[4] Most notably, the use by the insurgents from 1973 of the Soviet shoulder-launched SAM-7 (designated the SA-7 and first introduced in 1968) changed the situation tactically by reducing the mobility of Portuguese forces as well as powerfully contributing to the sense that they had lost the initiative. Despite the use of obsolete equipment, such as the American B-26, which suffered from wing failure, airpower, indeed, was particularly significant due to the size of the Portuguese colonies and their very limited surface communications. This airpower was used for interdiction, ground support, bombing, reconnaissance, and logistics.[5]

CUBA AND INDONESIA

By the 1960s, the Americans had changed their views both about the acceptability of Castro in Cuba and about the Sukarno regime in Indonesia, the second of which challenged the political order the British had successfully created in Malaysia, a state created from Malaya and from the former British colonies in northern Borneo. This change in American views served as a reminder of the range of factors in play in counterinsurgencies and not least in their international context, a reminder also valid for 1946–60. The newly established Castro regime faced American opposition as it pushed through a socioeconomic revolution, notably the nationalization of assets. International support from the nearby United States appeared a key element. In 1960, anti-Communist exiles in Florida used aircraft to send supplies to opponents of Castro based in the Cuban mountains. However, in April 1961, President John F. Kennedy's failure to provide the necessary air support to a force of 1,300 CIA-trained anti-Communist exiles was blamed for the total defeat of their invasion at the Bay of Pigs. In practice, poor planning and stiff opposition were also highly significant. The air dimension itself indicated the role of a number of factors and contingencies. On April 15, American aircraft, disguised with Cuban markings and piloted by Cuban exiles, bombed Cuban airfields, but this attempt to destroy the Cuban air force failed as the aircraft had already been moved and camouflaged. When the exiles landed on April 17, they met damaging air attacks, while the next day, bombers sent to open the way for the landing of the necessary supplies for the stranded invasion force were mostly shot down. The supplies never arrived, and the force surrendered. Subsequently, the Cuban regime faced guerrilla opposition in the mountains for a number of years, but it was largely overcome by the mid-1960s.

In turn, the Cubans actively sponsored insurrection elsewhere, both in Latin America and in Africa. Che Guevara, a colleague of Castro who had been influenced by Mao in his attempt to develop a strategy for revolutionary war, went to fight in Congo before being killed in Bolivia in 1967. He had sought to organize a peasant insurgency, but it did not gather momentum and was rapidly suppressed with American assistance.[6] In practice, the development of revolutionary activity in Latin America had indigenous and particular roots, as well as being influenced by wider international currents and models.[7] In Congo-Brazzaville, the Cubans trained the MPLA (Popular Movement for the Liberation of Angola) from the mid-1960s before also taking a similar role against the Portuguese in Guinea-Bissau.[8] There was also widespread anxiety, especially but not only in American policymaking centers, that Cuba would encourage revolution elsewhere or act as a model for it.[9] In turn, once their allies had been established in power, the Cubans became key allies in their counterinsurgency struggles, notably in Angola.

In Borneo, an island shared by Indonesia, Malaysia, and pro-British Brunei, British tactical and operational successes in 1963–66 hit the Indonesian infiltration infrastructure. However, these successes did not end the Indonesian determination to continue attacking Malaysia. Moreover, domestic economic and financial problems for the British government, particularly balance-of-payment crises, led to growing concern there that the confrontation with Indonesia could not be sustained whatever American pressure to that end.[10] The Americans increasingly saw this struggle as a broader one to maintain Western interests and allies in Southeast Asia, which became far more significant in their views of the Cold War in the mid-1960s. The struggle with Indonesia ended with the American-backed overthrow of the Sukarno regime by right-wing generals. They unleashed a massacre of Indonesian Communists in order to thwart what they presented as a planned Communist rising. Thus, violent uses of power were a key element in the political crisis in Indonesia in the mid-1960s.

VIETNAM

In Vietnam, the South Vietnamese government and its American backer faced a Communist insurgency by the Viet Cong and invasion by North Vietnamese forces. In the late 1950s, the Diem regime had alienated sympathies by brutality and corruption, and this provided opportunities for the Communists. In 1959, the Hanoi Politburo decided to wage armed struggle in the south, a decision imbued with risk in view of the North Vietnamese leadership's awareness of the American aerial devastation of North Korea during the Korean War. The Communists proved well led and organized, and their political system and culture enabled them to mobilize resources and sustain the struggle. The battlespace was prepared by the North Vietnamese and then escalated into a full-scale, albeit masked, invasion.

In turn, in the early 1960s, American military advisers were rapidly replaced by combat units, and the American military presence rose in an attempt to contain Communism and drawing on a misperception both of American capabilities and of the probable response. Moreover, the American-backed military overthrow of the Diem regime in 1963 destabilized South Vietnam, not least because of the revolving-door governments that followed.

In the event, the North Vietnamese and Viet Cong were not only determined to persist but also proved more willing to suffer losses than the Americans, in part because the American concept of limited war did not mean anything to them. Thus, American operations failed to move from causing considerable casualties, which they did, to achieving strategic effect, a situation compounded by the lack of levers to affect North Vietnamese policy until late in the conflict, when the Americans totally transformed the international situation by means of an alignment with China. In the meantime, peace initiatives failed due to completely incompatible goals, mutual mistrust, and a drive to seek military advantage. In particular, determined not to abandon the Viet Cong, the North Vietnamese were unwilling to promise to cease attacks and stop moving arms south if the Americans agreed on a halt to bombing of the north.[11]

The Vietnam War demonstrated the limitations of airpower when fighting insurgencies, notably its weakness as a tool for interdiction. The Americans, moreover, found that they could neither bomb their way to victory nor control the countryside, and they also did not grasp the extent to which their advantages were nullified by their opponents' refusal to fight on their terms as well as by their own conduct of the conflict. At the tactical and operational levels, the Viet Cong and the North Vietnamese forces made an effective use of Maoist principles and guerrilla doctrines and responded ably to the circumstances of Vietnam, both physical and political. They were able to sustain a long struggle and to retain the initiative even though, by late 1968, both the Viet Cong and the North Vietnamese army had been defeated.

The deployment of large numbers of troops did not bring success to the counterinsurgency side. By the start of 1968, the Americans deployed 486,000 troops, with the South Vietnamese fielding 350,000 regulars and 300,000 militia. Large numbers of casualties had been inflicted on the North Vietnamese and Viet Cong, but in 1967, more significantly, these casualties were more than replaced by new recruitment for the Viet Cong and the dispatch of troops from North Vietnam. Moreover, far from the Americans holding the initiative and moving toward victory, as their lackluster commander, General Westmoreland, claimed, notably in November 1967, it was their opponents who initiated many of the engagements. As so often, the capacity of the counterinsurgency force to project power was not matched by an ability to hold the tactical initiative. As a consequence, the intervening operational level was a key one, and there both sides sought to grasp the initiative and thus the dynamic of the conflict.

It took time for the Americans to learn how to respond, but there was a significant learning process.[12] The Americans developed a more effective counterinsurgency strategy from 1968, in large part because their opponents' conventional-style Tet Offensive was defeated that year, while a new American commander, Creighton Abrams, was appointed. The peak American troops strength, 543,000, was reached in the spring of 1969. Abrams set out to contest the village-level support the Viet Cong enjoyed. Indeed, American and South Vietnamese counterinsurgency policies worked in some parts of Vietnam. Nevertheless, they were generally unsuccessful. On small-scale COIN operations, the Americans were frequently successful because they focused on harnessing local knowledge and skills, learning how the enemy operated, and turning all that to their advantage. On a larger scale, however, there was a more general failure, in part because many American servicemen could not understand local communities nor, indeed, readily identify the enemy, and especially because the army did everything it could to remove the soldier from the battlefield and relied increasingly on technology as well as the application in a military environment of systems analysis, which proved a bogus "military revolution."[13]

Conversely, support for the Viet Cong should not be exaggerated. The pacification program entailed a "battle for hearts and minds" involving

American-backed economic and political reforms, while the Viet Cong also battled to that end. The American reforms were difficult to implement, not only because of Viet Cong opposition and intimidation and the effectiveness of their guerrilla and small-unit operations, but also because the South Vietnamese government was half-hearted, corrupt, and weak. The Americans, who could not work out who supported the Viet Cong, could not find or create a popular alternative to the Viet Cong; as the Americans also brought much devastation and disruption, pacification faced additional problems. Resettlement policies were inherently contradictory to winning "hearts and minds."[14]

In line with Maoist principles and policies, Viet Cong direction and intimidation of the population was designed to serve political as well as military purposes. Non-Communist revolutionaries were executed, while Communists were periodically purged. Civilians judged unacceptable were murdered. The "extermination of traitors campaign" was directed against South Vietnamese leaders, civil servants, and others. There were also many executions during the "Land Reform" program. In the city of Huế, when it was occupied in 1968 at the time of the Tet Offensive, about five thousand civilians were slaughtered. The people slaughtered during Tet were the officialdom, the families of the military leadership, and the intelligentsia. More generally, indoctrination and food rationing were part of the system of Communist control. This policy matched that of North Vietnam's ally, China, which was killing large numbers of citizens in that period during the "Great Proletarian Cultural Revolution" in 1966–68, just as it had been responsible for the deaths of millions during the earlier "Great Leap Forward," in 1958–62. These campaigns represented Mao's destructive attempt to stage the Communist revolution in China as a continuous process of violent, transformative insurgency.

Meanwhile, opposition to the war markedly increased in the United States. The absence of victory, in notable contradiction to claims made before Tet, sapped the American will to continue fighting and, in particular, political support for it, even though the Americans had defeated the Tet Offensive. Moreover, as with Portugal in Africa, conscription played a major role in the growth of disenchantment. Lyndon Johnson, the president from 1963, did not stand for reelection in 1968, while Richard Nixon, who was elected president, promised peace with honor and sought both the "Vietnamization" of the military effort (in other words, a reliance on South Vietnamese forces) and American disengagement.

In the end, the negotiated American withdrawal in 1973 left South Vietnam vulnerable, with North Vietnamese forces in occupation of about a quarter of the country and the remainder threatened with attack. The American government promised continued financial support as well as airpower if the North Vietnamese attacked. Such airpower had played a crucial role in repelling the North Vietnamese in the 1972 Easter Offensive. Due to congressional opposition, however, neither came, and the South Vietnamese army was desperately short of supplies when a major North Vietnamese offensive was launched in 1975. It took three months to conquer the country. Large numbers of South Vietnamese were then imprisoned in brutal circumstances and used for forced labor. This was one of the key ways in which any prospect of opposition, or even debate, was crushed by the new order.[15]

Frequently drawing, as in West Germany, on a latent anti-Americanism, most Western commentators proved eager to accept the views of left-wing writers who argued that people's warfare was invincible. The emphasis was on guerrilla warfare, popular mobilization, and political radicalism and not on conventional operations and professionalism. In 1965, Lin Piao, a leading Communist military figure during the Chinese Civil War and minister of defense from 1959 to 1971, published *Long Live the Victory of People's War*, a proclamation of the invincible nature of the people's war as a means to defeat imperialism and the West. This was an aspect of debate within the Chinese leadership over how best to respond to a possible American invasion if the Americans were victorious in the Vietnam War. No such invasion was intended, but consideration of such moves was significant as it was earlier with regard to Chinese fears of American success over North Korea during the Korean War of 1950–53. This consideration played a part in the long-standing Chinese tension between an emphasis on a popular militia and one on a regular army. The context for the document was severe rivalry in the Chinese Politburo in the buildup to the unleashing of the "Cultural Revolution" in 1966. Lin Piao was engaged in a power struggle with Liu Shao Chi, and perhaps with Chou En Lai, over policy in the wake of the collapse of the "Great Leap Forward" by 1962. The deliberate, polemical outfall from *Long Live the Victory of People's War* was therefore a screen.

The debate between popular militia and regular army went back in Russia to the Civil War and was a struggle that waged off and on until 1940, when the Soviet leadership understood that the purging of the military leadership in 1937 had hit the army hard. Another reason for the shift in policy in China during the mid-1960s, when the old uniforms and old rank devices were discarded, is that, thanks to the Sino-Soviet split that had gathered pace in the early 1960s, the Chinese leadership did not have much to fall back on, inasmuch as its Soviet source of newer weaponry had been cut off, and this doctrine, moreover, may have been intended to scare the Soviets as much as the Americans.

Lin Piao himself used the "Cultural Revolution" to increase his power in the military, remove his opponents, and in 1968 become Mao's designated successor. However, in 1971, after an alleged coup attempt, Lin Piao was killed in an air crash while fleeing to the Soviet Union, on the long-standing pattern of domestic opponents seeking foreign support.

The Chinese emphasis on political motivation and education for the army meant that professionalism and technology were not stressed. This preference for motivation affected the Chinese attack on North Vietnam in 1979, as, indeed, it had earlier operations in Korea in 1950–53. "Human wave" attacks that supposedly demonstrated the political strength of the Chinese in practice failed and suffered heavy casualties, but this failure did not attract the attention devoted to earlier American operations in Vietnam.[16]

American failure in Vietnam created the impression that irrespective of the problems of colonialism, Western militaries could not prevail over non-Western popular warfare. In some respects, this impression prefigured that created by conflict in Iraq and Afghanistan in the 2000s. In practice, an essentially conventional strategy and operational means had been employed by the Communists to bring military victory in China in 1949 and South Vietnam in 1975, but both were part of a political determination for total struggle and absolute control that proved difficult to overcome.

In addition, to write off American failure is to downplay the serious faults not only of the South Vietnamese government but also of the South Vietnamese military, each in a way due to the lack of national identity, a lack that reflected the state's brief history. A politicized South Vietnamese army, with appointment and promotion overly dependent on patronage, and the army also divided over religion, was not the best basis for nimble counterinsurgency warfare or, indeed, for conventional conflict. The North Vietnamese army was better trained. Despite the strength, bravery, and success of some South Vietnamese units, notably in 1972,[17] the army was weak in doctrine, organization, motivation, and practice.[18] These interacted, not least in an inability to take the war to the enemy. Among other serious flaws, the misleading treatment of former Viet Minh supporters as automatic Viet Cong supporters was a classic mistake—namely, that of the misunderstanding of the nationalist dimension and the potential support it offered.

The balance of terror lay with the Viet Cong and North Vietnamese. The South Vietnamese army could not effectively protect its villagers, whose leaders, if identified as government officials, were often assassinated. This factor greatly affected morale within the rank and file in the South Vietnamese army since the common soldiers knew that local Viet Cong intelligence knew of their having been drafted or having enlisted in the army and were fearful of reprisals being taken against their family members.

As far as failure is concerned, it is also appropriate to note the serious defeats suffered by the Viet Cong and North Vietnamese, notably in 1968 and 1972. In the latter case, the North Vietnamese army had shifted to conventional strategy but was beaten back by well-trained South Vietnamese troops and American airpower.

The overthrow of South Vietnam in 1975 was accompanied by that of pro-Western military regimes in Laos and Cambodia. In each case, these were episodes in the Cold War, with foreign intervention on behalf of the local Communist insurgents playing a major role alongside the withdrawal of American assistance to the regimes.

The American army preferred after the war to concentrate on a more conventional and, despite the nuclear arsenals, in practice limited confrontation with the Soviet Union in Europe.[19] Similarly, the British army focused on the possibility of war with the Soviet Union rather than on its intractable struggle with the Provisional IRA in Northern Ireland and, as a result, devoted relatively limited attention to thinking about counterinsurgency, although that remained a task of much of the infantry due to the continued military presence in Northern Ireland.

A RANGE OF CONFLICTS

Far from insurgents necessarily succeeding, the separatist insurgent force failed against the regular military in the Biafran (or Nigerian Civil) War of 1967–70. This large-scale conflict reflected the extent to which Nigeria, which gained independence in 1960, had enjoyed coherence and identity only as a British colony. There was no ethnic, religious, or geographical unity to the state, and the federal system established with independence did not work well. The main ethnic groups were the Fulani and Hausa of the north, who are overwhelmingly Muslim, the Ibo in the east, who are heavily Christian, and the Yaruba in the west, who are both Christian and Muslim. Prior to the separatist rebellion in 1967, there was already a high level of violence in Nigerian politics and society, and this violence lowered the barriers to insurrection. More particularly, the slaughter of large numbers of members of the Ibo tribe, indeed possibly thirty thousand of them, in the massacres that followed a military coup in Nigeria in July 1966 led by northern commanders resulted in a collapse of Ibo support for the idea of a federal and multiracial Nigeria. The new military government, which had overthrown a military regime that had an Ibo head and had been established by another coup in January 1966, was unsympathetic to the Ibo demand for a looser confederation, while the Ibo leadership challenged the legality of the federal government.

Violence within Nigeria became part of a political sequence. In 1967, the Ibo republic of Biafra was proclaimed by Colonel Chukwuemeka Ojukwu, the regional military governor, in the part of southeastern Nigeria where the Ibos lived. In order to suppress it, the federal government launched what it termed a "police operation." The federal forces greatly outnumbered the Biafrans and also benefited from British and Soviet arms supplies. International support was more generally significant. In order to challenge British influence in Nigeria, France sought to support Biafra. Foreign support helped make the sea and air dimension crucial, as, unlike the Viet Minh with China and the Viet Cong with North Vietnam, the Biafrans were swiftly cut off from foreign land links. This situation greatly exacerbated their lack of food and military supplies. The Nigerian navy both imposed a debilitating blockade of the Biafran coast and enabled the army to seize ports and coastal positions, especially Port Harcourt. This success increased the number of fronts on which the Biafrans were under attack. The Nigerians were also far stronger in the air.

As an instance of insurgency and counterinsurgency conflict, the Biafran War marked an important stage. In place of struggles against imperial rule, this was the first major war in sub-Saharan Africa during the twentieth century in which the combatants and commanders were African. The Biafran War also showed the difficulties encountered in facing up to the challenges of insurgency and counterinsurgency warfare. Both sides confronted the commonplace problem of rapidly expanding armies containing untrained men and inexperienced officers. In addition, it proved difficult to apply force effectively. Air attacks were frequently ineffective, and artillery was often poorly aimed. Infantry weaponry proved more important. The federal army had major advantages, not least British-supplied armored personnel carriers to which the Biafrans had little response. Moreover, in operational terms, the federal army was greatly helped in its counterinsurgency task by the fact that this was a war with front lines rather than a guerrilla struggle. Thus, there were clear targets: Biafra, its military, and its population.

However, the role of ethnic and factional considerations greatly weakened the federal army's fighting competence, not least because logistical support in the difficult terrain was not improved by chaotic command and organizational systems that were characterized by serious corruption. In the end, mass starvation proved a key element, with the hard-pressed Biafrans finally surrendering in January 1970: the loss of their air strip at Uli had severed their remaining supply link. The Biafrans were hit hard by the war, while the relatively conciliatory policy of the federal government after the war helped ensure that resistance did not continue.

Also, in Africa, CIA-provided aircraft and mercenaries, as well as the movement of Belgian paratroopers, helped General Mobuto suppress opposition in eastern Congo in 1964–65. Earlier, Katangese separatism in southern Congo had been overcome by United Nations forces. In 1978, in Congo, Belgian and French paratroopers, supported by American and French air transport, helped suppress a Cuban-backed insurgency in the province of Shaba. Thus, insurgencies were part of the Cold War.

In a different context, the white-minority government in Southern Rhodesia (now Zimbabwe) faced a Chinese and Soviet-backed insurgency in the 1960s and 1970s by the Zimbabwe African National Army and the Zimbabwe People's Revolutionary Army. This insurgency became more serious when the end of the Portuguese Empire in 1974–75 ensured that the insurgents were, in addition to their bases in Zambia, easily able to use bases in Angola and Mozambique. In turn, Southern Rhodesia and its ally, South Africa, backed potent insurgent movements against these states: UNITA and RENAMO, respectively.

As before, the international context was crucial in insurgency and counterinsurgency struggles. This was seen at a variety of scales. Under Gamal Abdel Nasser, Egypt intervened from 1962 to 1967 in a civil war in North Yemen on behalf of a radical republican regime that had seized power in a coup in 1962 but that was facing a large-scale tribal insurgency. The regime, as well as Egypt, suffered from the support the insurgents received from neighboring Saudi Arabia, as well as from Britain, which had the neighboring colony of Aden, and from Israel. By 1965, seventy thousand troops, about a third of the Egyptian army, were committed in Yemen in what was an unsuccessful proxy war with Saudi Arabia: a war over leadership of the Arab world and also reflecting very different ideologies. The Egyptians dropped poison gas in Yemen, and there was repeated Egyptian bombing of royalist bases in Saudi Arabia, but neither ended the struggle. The Egyptian army was to some extent demoralized. Rebel forces would behead captured Egyptian soldiers and leave the decapitated remains. In the end, a compromise was negotiated in 1970.[20]

Meanwhile, the attitude of Iran was important in enabling the Kurds to sustain an insurrection against Iraq in 1961–75. In addition, as part of its struggle with much of the Arab world, Israel supported an insurgency in southern Sudan by non-Arabs and non-Muslims who were very much mistreated by the northern-based Arab Muslim regime.

Large-scale Indian intervention in 1971 was instrumental in ensuring that the Bengali independence movement in East Pakistan succeeded. This movement, which developed in response to a rigged election that ignored Bengali demands and the voting results, was facing a very brutal counterinsurgency campaign by the Pakistani army, one that involved the slaughter of many civilians and the rape of many women. The relatively small size of East Pakistan and the dense village clusters hindered the insurgency. The conflict led to a breakdown of civil order, with the killing by both sides accompanied by that arising from other causes, in particular, Bengalis killing other Bengalis for reasons of ethnicity and politics, a pattern also seen in other insurgencies. Indian intervention proved the decisive military factor, not least because, despite American hopes, it was not countered by China. It was safe for the Indian army to attack East Pakistan in October 1971 because, by that time, snow in the Himalayas had blocked the Chinese army. India was aligned with the Soviet Union and Pakistan with the United States.[21] In turn, at a very different scale and in a very different context, the unwillingness of

India to support the Americans in backing Tibetan opposition to Chinese control helped defeat the attempt.[22]

The contexts of counterinsurgency were (and are) frequently highly complex and contentious. For example, the Turkish invasion of Cyprus in 1974 remains a legally unresolved issue. Turkish interest was long-standing, but the precipitant was a coup in Cyprus that launched a civil war among the Greek Cypriots. This coup, by the EOKA-B organization, the self-styled successor to the EOKA organization that had campaigned against the British in the 1950s, was masterminded by the military junta that had itself seized power in Greece in 1967. The coup was intended to overthrow the government of Cyprus and lead to *enosis* (union) with Greece while also driving out or destroying the minority Turkish Cypriot community. A large but disputed number of Turkish Cypriots were killed in the coup. This provided the Turks with an opportunity to invade, an invasion that was accepted by the United States. This was a counterinsurgency with a difference, one in which the attempt by EOKA-B to take over was totally unsuccessful. The island was partitioned, there was no "ethnic cleansing" of the Turkish Cypriots, and the compromised junta in Greece fell.

In Northern Ireland, the British army was handicapped by the extent to which terrorists could take shelter in neighboring Ireland, as well as by the support of the Soviet Union, of Libya, and of American sympathizers for the terrorists, support that provided weaponry and funds. Britain deployed troops from 1969 in order to thwart separatism in Northern Ireland. This deployment was successful at one level, with troops in 1972's Operation Motorman moving into "no-go areas" of Londonderry and Belfast hitherto controlled by the Provisional IRA,[23] a violent, radical Marxist separatist group based in the Catholic community. Having driven the police away, the Provisional IRA saw these areas as a stage in the Maoist theory of revolutionary warfare. The success of Motorman led the IRA instead to follow the course of terrorism rather than that of waging guerrilla warfare. Terrorism, notably through sniping and bombings, proved far more difficult to overcome.

As a result of changing circumstances, the army was principally in place from the mid-1970s to support the police. The Special Branch of the Royal Ulster Constabulary (police) focused on intelligence-led operations, but the army continued to play an important role. This was notably so on the extensive border with the Republic of Ireland. The army made extensive use of helicopters to supply fortified posts (as roads were vulnerable to mines) and employed intelligence gathering in order to strike at terrorists and thwart their operations. There was a limit to what could be achieved. At the same time, the terrorists were unable to overthrow policing or to drive the army out of Northern Ireland.[24] The situation was made more difficult by police and army security tactics that alienated many Catholics, as well as by the rogue behavior seen when some troops shot at demonstrators in 1972.[25] The situa-

tion was also complicated when Protestant "loyalist" movements developed
that, in turn, were committed to sectarian violence.

As the Provisional IRA struck at the Unionist Protestant community as
well as the British military, while the "loyalists" attacked Catholics, the
situation drifted from crisis toward chaos. The attritional character of terrorism and counterterrorist operations was apparent. The police and army had to
maintain a semblance of order sufficient to demonstrate to the Provisional
IRA that they could not win and also to encourage intransigent Catholic and
Protestant politicians eventually to see that there was no alternative to talking
to each other. Northern Ireland placed a major strain on the British army's
manpower and morale. IRA terrorism made it difficult for the army to frater-
nize with the population, while the IRA found shelter in the Republic of
Ireland, and it proved impossible to control the long border. The difficulty of
ending terrorism in the absence of widespread civilian support from part of
the community became readily apparent in Northern Ireland.

British military policy would probably have been different had there been
a conscript army. Conscripts might have been unwilling to serve in Northern
Ireland, and the deployment and tactics employed might have placed a greater emphasis on avoiding casualties. In the event, the infantry, who bore most
of the commitment, proved resilient, training adjusted to the particular challenges of the task, and the army acquired considerable experience in antiter-
rorist policing. Military proficiency was measured in traditional infantry
skills, such as patrolling and the use of cover, while intelligence success was
a key element, and the IRA was penetrated at a high level. There was considerable confusion as to whether this was a counterinsurgency or a law-and-
order situation. Eventually, the latter view prevailed as part of a strategy to
end the crisis by political means.[26] The army and police contained the situation sufficiently to allow negotiations that produced a peace settlement in
1998. In a major success for counterinsurgency, terrorism had clearly failed
by then. The lack of foreign armed intervention on behalf of the IRA, as
opposed to the provision of arms supplies by the Soviet bloc, was a significant factor. So also was Britain not being at war, with the exception of the
short-lived Falklands War in 1981. The British would have found the Northern Ireland crisis far more difficult had it coincided with the Kenya, Malaya,
and Cyprus crises of the 1950s or those in Borneo and Aden in the 1960s.

The international context also played a role in the Sultanate of Oman's
westernmost area, the province of Dhofar, where there was an insurgency
that was supported by the radical Marxist government of neighboring South
Yemen, a country that had close ties to the Soviet Union, which established a
naval base there. With American encouragement, Britain, Iran, and Jordan
provided military help to the government. Success was obtained in the mid-
1970s after a major offensive had severed the supply route to Yemen. The
government benefited from air and sea control. "Hearts and minds" also

played a role: medical teams, livestock, and water-drilling equipment were flown into the mountainous and inaccessible interior.

The balance between the two counterinsurgency elements, force and "hearts and minds," has been a matter of debate, notably how far a "population-centric" approach was followed in Dhofar, an issue that also occurs more generally. The role of the international context was underlined by the extent to which the British withdrawal in 1967 from Aden (which became South Yemen) ensured that the PFLO (Popular Front for the Liberation of Oman) acquired significant support, rather as the opposition to white control in southern Rhodesia (Zimbabwe) greatly benefited from Portuguese withdrawal from neighboring Angola and Mozambique. The insurgents were able to outgun the underresourced army of the Sultanate of Oman and to drive it from most of western Dhofar by late 1969. Harsh government tactics against local people who were distrusted, notably the destruction of crops, houses, and wells and the detention of adult males, did not end the insurgency.

In 1970, Britain supported a palace coup in Oman that led to a new sultan. This was followed by an expansion of the military and by systematic counterinsurgency operations. Initially, success was limited, but from December 1973 to June 1974, Hornbeam, a line of positions providing an anchor for the sultan's forces, was constructed. The civilian population between Hornbeam and the South Yemeni frontier was moved to the east of the line, in other words, leaving an area near the frontier without inhabitants, and in 1975, the PFLO was obliged to engage in battle in order to defend its supply routes and bases and was beaten. This successful Omani infantry operation was supported by air attacks. As with Franco's forces in Spain in the late 1940s and the Communists in Poland in the same period, the Omani government benefited from controlling food supplies. Divisions within the PFLO were also significant, not least because this affected local opinion. The government's "hearts and minds" campaign was secondary and essentially dependent on military success, while the recruitment of local tribes to the sultan's forces was useful in weakening the insurgency but did not provide reliable forces.

The international balance was also important. The support for the sultanate contrasted with the weakening of backing for the PFLO, as China and Egypt sought improved relations with the West in the early 1970s, while Iraq agreed in 1975 to abandon support for the PFLO, and the Soviet Union treated it as a marginal commitment.[27] Having succeeded, the Omani government, with British support, ably grounded the new system, not least by integrating former insurgents into the army. This proved very valuable in maintaining stability and, as a result, the attempt in 1987 by a warlord in eastern Yemen to invade Dhofar was unsuccessful despite an ethnic similarity.

In other circumstances, the Soviet Union could support allies against insurgencies, as when it backed Ethiopia against separatism both in Eritrea, where the insurgency had come close to success in 1978, and in the Ogaden, where it was supported by Somalia. Operating with the assistance of the Cubans there, and in Angola, the Soviets and their African allies acquired much experience in counterinsurgency conflict. The Soviets backed the Marxist regime led by Mengistu Mariam that had seized power in Ethiopia in a 1974 revolution. An earlier attempted revolution in 1960 involving the son of Emperor Haile Selassie had failed, in part because the police and most of the army remained loyal. In contrast, in 1974 the army was discontented by the lack of a pay raise, and a group of radical officers was able to seize control, overthrowing the monarchy and installing the Provisional Military Administrative Council, the Derg. The new regime consolidated its position with a Red Terror in 1977–78 that slaughtered two million people. This was a key aspect of its prophylactic counterinsurgency policy.

CONCLUSIONS

The significance of the Vietnam War, coming alongside a series of counter-insurgency struggles, ensured that counterinsurgency as an issue and a sub-ject became of great significance in this period. This led to publications, notably the Frenchman David Galula's *Counterinsurgency Warfare: Theory and Practice* (1964) and two works by British writers: Robert Thompson's *Defeating Communist Insurgency: Experiences from Malaya and Vietnam* (1966) and, less prominently, Julian Paget's *Counter-insurgency Campaign-ing* (1967). Eventual failure in the Vietnam War also led to an extensive and continuing debate in the United States as to whether a different policy would have led to success. This approach, however, suffers from the output/out-come contrast. More military pressure on North Vietnam, notably in the shape of heavier and less restricted bombing[28] or even a ground offensive in North Vietnam, would not necessarily have led to a settlement on US terms. The military dimension has to be located in a wider strategic understanding, one that is aware of the United States' broader Cold War commitments, notably in Europe, the Mediterranean, and Korea. The Americans all along during the Vietnam War were scared of possible Chinese intervention and had to be cautious. In August 1965, American jets pursued two North Vietna-mese interceptors, which sought sanctuary in Hainan Island. In response to the American jets having intruded into Chinese air space, Chou En Lai de-livered a stiff warning to the Americans, who backed down. The Americans did not wish to see a repetition of the 1950 Chinese intervention in Korea. In the United States, the military and the politicians both underestimated the opposition in Vietnam and misunderstood the nature of the conflict, but in 1968 they drew opposite lessons over escalation or not. Debates on policy in part reflected the use of analogies, including the Greek Civil War.[29]

Alongside debates on the past, there were also, in the case of insurgencies, anticipations of the future. This was especially the case with Lebanon after 1975. It became an instance of the failure of states to retain a monopoly on violence, of the interaction of this factor with sectarian and ethnic rivalries, and of the unpopularity of foreign interventions, both in the domestic politics of the country sending troops and in the country receiving them. The crisis in Lebanon looked toward the fate of other states that were not going to be able to contain insurgencies.

Chapter Nine

The Variety of Goals and Means, 1980s

Insurgencies in the 1980s again encompassed an astonishing variety, both politically and militarily. To indicate this, it is appropriate to focus on major military struggles, notably in Afghanistan and Central America. However, it is also instructive to discuss the fall of the Soviet Empire as an aspect of insurgency conflict, one that began with the Polish crisis in 1981 and continued to the very fall of the Soviet Union in 1991.

AFGHANISTAN

On December 27, 1979, in part to assert control over a neighboring state, Soviet forces intervened in Afghanistan, overthrowing the Marxist government of Hafizollah Amin, a onetime client taking an independent line, and installing their client Babrak Karmal as president. The Soviets undertook the intervention with some reluctance, although it proved relatively easy to seize the cities, in part by the use of airborne troops. Indeed, they were supported by a faction within the warring PDPA (People's Democratic Party of Afghanistan). Moreover, in 1973 and 1978, there had already been coups transferring control, the latter mounted by the PDPA.

However, the weakness and unpopularity of the new government and the resistance it faced led the Soviets into a wider commitment they had not initially intended. A short-term intervention, designed to ensure regime change and in particular to stabilize the situation on the Soviet southern border, became a lengthy campaign. In the late 1970s, the Soviet government had some concern over possible spillover into Tadzhikistan, then part of Soviet Central Asia, which is to the north of Afghanistan. The Soviets were also encouraged to act by concern that the Afghan government might turn to

China, thus extending the threat to Soviet borderlands already posed by China.

For the Soviets, guerrilla resistance in the Afghan countryside by the *mujahideen* proved very different from engaging with the concentrated target of cities. This intractability was a matter of the nature of Afghan society and politics, at once bellicose and fragmented and in part the limitations shown in counterinsurgency warfare in an extremely difficult military environment. Linking the two was the problem of translating operational success into lasting advantage. As would be the case with Western intervention in Afghanistan in the 2000s and 2010s, the Soviets exaggerated the strength and popularity of their local allies and failed to appreciate those of opponents whom they stigmatized as reactionary but who saw themselves as motivated by religious war. The mistaken Soviet beliefs that insurrectionary movements were the characteristic of progressive forces and that conservative systems lacked real popularity, an ideological analysis shared by much of the Left, ensured not only that Soviet attempts at political indoctrination failed, but also that they did not have the necessary military doctrine to confront the Afghan resistance nor an understanding of the relationship between military moves and political outcomes in Afghanistan. The *mujahideen*, who in part represented the hostility of rural society to urban-based reform, were greatly divided by ethnic, religious, and factional factors, but the Soviets proved unable to exploit these divisions to significant political benefit. Moreover, the Soviets' failure to win encouraged the population to doubt the durability of the Afghan government.

The geography of counterinsurgency was also significant. Neither Vietnam, Afghanistan, nor Iraq bordered the United States, and this ensured that its intervention in these cases was a "war of choice." In contrast, Afghanistan bordered the Soviet Union, which helped to increase Soviet concern about developments there and ensured that the Soviet government did not feel that it had an easy exit strategy once the war went badly.

There were also operational and tactical parallels between the Soviets in the 1980s and later Western forces in Afghanistan. The difficulty of distinguishing opponents from the remainder of civil society was a problem, as was the linked ability of the guerrillas to avoid having battle forced on them. Soviet advances tended, therefore, to have only short-term benefit and were followed either by leaving vulnerable outposts or by a return to base that created a sense of futility. There was a lack of enough troops to provide both sufficient security for controlled areas and the ability to launch large-scale campaigns into areas that were not under control, while convoy escort tied down many troops and disease weakened large numbers. In the absence of a COIN doctrine and a linkage of military operations to winning popular support, the Soviet emphasis on conventional doctrine, tactics, and operations matched what was designed for the conduct of war against NATO in Europe.

However, motorized columns were prone to ambushes, although, with time, the Soviets proved better at using air support. For example, in a series of attempts to occupy the Pandsher/Panjshir Valley, the Soviets concentrated air assets, including using helicopter forces, in order to stop the withdrawal of the *mujahideen* and to engage them from unexpected directions. Nevertheless, the *mujahideen* proved able, when necessary, to blend in with the civilian population while also making frequent use of ambushes. The defection of Afghan soldiers helped to replenish *mujahideen* numbers.[1] By early 1985, Soviet forces controlled less territory than they had done in 1980.

Designed to weaken the *mujahideen*, the targeting of noncombatants did not win the Soviets any friends. Driving the population off land that could not be controlled did not increase support and was further compromised by Soviet indiscipline and atrocities. This was an aspect of the lack of a viable Soviet strategy. About five million refugees from a population of fifteen million fled the country. The Soviets sought to build up the Afghan army, but it suffered from ethnic and patronage divisions as well as from the consequences of rapid expansion. From the mid-1980s, more success was obtained by building up militia forces.

Help from the United States, Saudi Arabia, Britain, China, Iran, and Pakistan was useful to the *mujahideen*, and the difficulty of sealing the Afghan frontiers made this assistance more useful. Neighboring Pakistan was heavily involved in the resistance from the outset, and the Soviets failed to cut the supply route. Pakistan also proved a conduit for Saudi support, and the two powers contributed to an accentuation of the Islamicist nature of the resistance as well as to fulfilling Pakistani regional goals, particularly weakening Afghanistan, which was seen as a tool of Indian competition with Pakistan, notably because both powers looked to the Soviet Union. Aside from strengthening religious fundamentalism, the provision of arms created and enhanced the position of warlords, with traditional social patterns, in contrast, breaking down. From 1985, American- and British-supplied ground-to-air missiles proved especially valuable in lessening the effectiveness of Soviet airpower and hitting Soviet morale. The majority of combat missions had been carried out by aircraft flying at low altitudes, especially the Su-25 ground-attack aircraft. That was no longer viable. American Stinger missiles had a maximum ceiling of ten thousand feet and a range of five miles, thus inhibiting close air support.

These remarks, however, mistakenly assume that the Soviets could have succeeded if only the resource equation was different. There is no basis for this conclusion. Instead, a perception of the conflict as absurd and pointless contributed to discontent in the Soviet Union. However, there was nothing in terms of domestic discontent that stood in the way of the Soviet government or general staff implementing their wishes, and certainly nothing remotely comparable to the American protests during the Vietnam War.

The Soviet intervention contributed greatly to instability in the Islamic world as well as to regional tensions and to great-power rivalry. Soviet policy changed after Mikhail Gorbachev became the Soviet leader in March 1985. He regarded the commitment to Afghanistan as detrimental to the Soviet Union's international position. Having warned the Afghan leader, Babrak Karmal, in March 1985 that Soviet forces would not stay forever, Gorbachev decided that autumn that the Afghan regime would have to be able to defend itself by the summer of 1986. Prior to that, Gorbachev supported fresh military activity, including more attacks on *mujahideen* bases in Pakistan, so as to leave as favorable a situation as possible in Afghanistan. In a clear breach from traditional Soviet policies that reflected the desire as well for a political strategy, Karmal was urged in October 1985 to rely on traditional elements, including Islam, in order to strengthen the regime. This focus on national reconciliation affected the morale of the Afghan armed forces, encouraging desertion.

Withdrawal from Afghanistan took longer than anticipated. Implementation, as so often, proved far more difficult than devising policy and strategy. In part, this was because, as with other militaries in their counterinsurgency campaigns, the Soviet army did not wish to appear to have lost the war and, in part, because it proved difficult to arrange an international settlement that would cover the retreat. The risk of spreading disorder, a domino effect in reverse, was seen in April 1987 when a Pakistani-backed *mujahideen* group launched a deadly attack in the Soviet republic of Uzbekistan, which bordered Afghanistan. This attack led to a Soviet threat to attack Pakistan. Such activity encouraged those in the Soviet Union who urged caution before withdrawing from Afghanistan.

Finally, under a UN-brokered Geneva Accords of April 14, 1988, the Soviets withdrew by February 15, 1989, leaving a Communist regime that finally fell in 1992 when the *mujahideen* entered the capital, Kabul. This was a culmination of a struggle in which military operations were most effective if part of a viable political strategy. The *mujahideen* attacked the Afghan garrisons. In 1989, the *mujahideen*, however, exaggerated their potential after the Soviet withdrawal in attacking the city of Jalalabad, a major center. This was a turn to conventional warfare, and it failed badly. As such, it was another instance of what had been seen in Vietnam with the Viet Minh in 1951–52 and the Viet Cong in 1968. In practice, as with many insurgency groups, the *mujahideen* had limited effectiveness as a more conventional and offensive force and were divided.

In contrast, the city of Khost was captured in 1991 because of the *mujahideen*'s ability to exploit the serious divisions in the Afghan government. Herat fell as a consequence of negotiations and Kabul as a result of governmental divisions as well as attritional warfare. A key element was provided by the sudden end of Soviet financial assistance in early 1992, a consequence of the total collapse of the Soviet Union. The end of assistance led to the disintegration of the Afghan army and to the government being unable to maintain its financing of supportive militias. There was no alternative financial base, in part because the country was poor and in part because the *mujahideen* controlled much of it. Thus, politics was a key element of the military struggle, and the latter was in part a matter of affecting the former.

The Soviet failure reinforced the impression created by American failure in Vietnam but placed it in a different political context. The asymmetrical warfare raised continued questions about the nature of military capability and the pursuit of effectiveness in war. The main issue in each case was the inability to develop a homegrown government that the population would support, an inability that owed something to a total misreading of the local political situation but also to a lack of options in the face of the attitudes of local allies.[2] Bordering the Soviet Union and in part sharing the ethnic and religious configuration of its Central Asian republics, Afghanistan was a more challenging defeat for the Soviet Union than South Vietnam had been for the United States. Failure in Afghanistan, moreover, in the sole war it fought after 1945, hit the morale of the Soviet military. This had an impact on the army's uncertain response to the crises caused by the collapse, from 1989, of Soviet and Communist dominance in the Soviet bloc.

The subsequent fate of the *mujahideen* and of Afghanistan raises important issues about the location of insurgencies and counterinsurgency activity and, as a consequence, helps explain the value of the chronological approach, notably when it is broken up into many sections, for running these together can lead to a failure to note changes in location. In particular, whereas the United States was to ally with some former *mujahideen* groups in the 2000s, it was to oppose others as well as to have a more complex relationship with Pakistan.[3] Pakistan itself had seen the success of the *mujahideen* as a way to weaken the Indians in Kashmir, notably after the elections there were allegedly fixed in 1987. The Pakistanis sponsored insurgent groups, a process that became more pronounced in the 1990s. Furthermore, Pakistani troops disguised as irregulars were infiltrated into Kashmir.[4] Some of the *jihadists* in Afghanistan gravitated into al-Qaeda, seeing the Soviet defeat as proving that the United States could, and should, also be defeated.

Jihad took many forms. Thus, in Saudi Arabia, Hezbollah al-Hejaz, an avowedly Khomeinist armed group drawing on the inspiration of the Iranian revolution, attacked the ruling dynasties as illegitimate, as it also did in Bahrain and Kuwait. Saudi security forces had the upper hand in the asymmetrical conflict, and many of the group fled to Iran, while a truce on Saudi terms was established in 1992.

LATIN AMERICA

In Central America, local rivalries interacted with Cold War intervention in a wide-ranging cycle of violence. In this, traditional themes of division were accentuated by new ideological divisions in fast-changing economies open to global pressures.[5] For example, in Nicaragua, where the left-wing Sandinista guerrilla movement gained power from the Somoza dictatorship in 1979, it faced American pressure. This pressure included the mining of its harbors and the secret arming, from 1981, of the Contras, a counterrevolutionary movement based in neighboring Honduras. Although the Contras helped to destabilize Nicaragua, inflicting considerable damage, they could not over-throw the Sandinistas and instead increased their bellicosity. As with the *mujahideen* in Afghanistan, UNITA in Angola, and Solidarity in Poland, the United States supported insurgencies of some type or other in order to weak-en Cold War opponents and to respond to its inability (due to unwillingness) to deploy ground troops.

Conversely, in El Salvador, where civil war broke out in 1981, the Americans backed the government against the Farabundo/Marti National Liberation Front (FMLN). This backing included funds, helicopter gunships, and a major effort to train the army for counterinsurgency.[6] The commitment of numerous American advisers was not followed by ground troops, which enabled the Americans to define the struggle as low-intensity conflict. How-ever, the struggle did not appear in this light to the population as civilians were caught between guerrillas and brutal counterinsurgency action that fre-quently took the form of terror. The American hope that the election of the moderate José Napoleon Duarte as president in 1984 would lead to peace proved abortive. Nevertheless, the FMLN could not incite a popular uprising. The failure of either side to win led eventually, in 1992, to a settlement under which the FMLN translated its activism to civilian politics. The settlement came about due to the December 1991 disintegration of the Soviet Union. Insurgency movements had played a major role in the Cold War, but they had a longer heritage in Latin America, and some were to continue thereafter.[7] Moreover, counterinsurgency strategies and methods developed by the Unit-ed States in Central America were then applied elsewhere.[8]

Not all the conflicts were so closely linked with the Cold War, although they could be interpreted in Cold War terms. In Peru, the key element was a local opposition to the disruptive consequences of economic change, an op-position that drew on long-standing traditions of peasant activism but was also open to Maoist ideas of social revolution and redistribution. The insur-gency by the Sendero Luminoso (Shining Path) movement began in 1980 and became a bitter civil war, one in which the attempt by the military to suppress the insurgency was very much affected by the particular dynamics of individual peasant communities, some of which bitterly resisted the insurgents.[9] The Andean Mountains became the strong point of Shining Path, one where ethnic division came into play. The major Peruvian Indian group, the Quechua, live there. Shining Path initially could agitate successfully among the poorer Indian regions neglected by the capital, Lima, although over time, that strategy started to fail as Shining Path terrorist acts surpassed those of governmental counterinsurgency responses. The capture in 1992 of Shining Path's leader contributed to its decline.

In Argentina, the army set out to destroy what it saw as subversion. In the province of Tucumán, five thousand troops and police were deployed in 1975 to "annihilate subversion," and about 565 people disappeared as the military seized and killed people without trial. That year, the state of siege imposed in Tucumán was extended to the rest of the country. In 1976, right-wing military leaders seized power in the "Process of National Reorganization." Ruling until 1982, they used brutal methods in the "Dirty War" to defeat a left-wing guerrilla movement. The kidnapping, torture, and murder of thousands, many of whom were scarcely, if at all, involved with the guerrillas, was a key feature of the counterinsurgency. Conventional politics and guerrilla opposition alike were repressed.

AFRICA

Separatist insurgencies continued in a number of African states, including Ethiopia and Sudan. These insurgencies overlapped with civil wars that contested control over entire states, as in Angola. Moreover, there was large-scale intervention by other states. In part, this was a matter of the extrapolation and implementation of the Cold War. Alongside the role of non-African states, notably Cuba, the Soviet Union, and the United States, African states also played a role, as with Libya in Chad and South Africa in Angola and Mozambique.[10] In Angola, the battle of Cuito Canavale (1987), purportedly the largest in Africa since El Alamein in 1942, was waged by clients of rival Angolan governments: Cuba and South Africa for the MPLA and UNITA, respectively. Cuban victory was followed in 1988 by a cease-fire and subsequently by the withdrawal of first South African and then Cuban forces.

EUROPE

Poland in the 1970s and 1980s proved a lightning rod for the unpopularity of Communist rule, with the added ingredients of traditional hostility to Russia and a strong national Christian commitment. Large-scale strikes in 1980 were precipitated by an increase in the price of meat, but the establishment of an unofficial trade union, Solidarność (Solidarity), challenged the authority of the government and concerned other Communist regimes. The Soviet defense minister, Dmitriy Ustinov, supported intervention, but his colleagues were reluctant to do so, while the Soviet Union was warned not to by President Reagan. There was also anxiety that the Poles would fight and concern about the effect that an invasion of Poland would have on Soviet troops, especially on the morale of men from neighboring areas, particularly western Ukraine. Yuri Andropov, the KGB head, argued that the Soviet Union had used up its quota of interventions.

Instead, the Polish army, in the person of General Wojciech Jaruzelski, prime minister and first secretary of the Polish Communist Party, acted to impose control. Martial law was declared in December 1981, and special paramilitary forces were used: ZOMO (Zmotoryzowane Odwody Milicji Obywatelskiej, the People's Militia Motorized Units). Solidarity's leaders as well as thousands of others were detained without trial. Scores were killed. There was no violent response.

In 1989, similarly, the army was used by the Communist leadership violently to suppress pressure in China for political liberalization. Thousands were killed when tanks were sent against demonstrators in Beijing. Deng Xiaoping, the Chinese leader, who had played a significant role in the Chinese Civil War and had been active in the slaughter of supposed counterrevolutionaries in the early 1950s, was ready to send in the army against what was inaccurately described as a "counterrevolutionary rebellion."

In contrast, Communist regimes collapsed in Eastern Europe in 1989. Popular demonstrations played a major role, and only in Romania was there an attempt to use force against them. There, in December, a full-scale anti-Communist revolt in Timişoara, a city with a large ethnic Hungarian population, led the government to send in tanks, which fired on the demonstrators, as well as deploy factory workers armed with clubs. However, in the face of a crowd of over one hundred thousand people, the army there changed sides. On December 21 in the capital, Bucharest, a popular demonstration in the face of an address by the dictator Nicolae Ceauşescu began with the crowd booing him, whereupon he left the podium. The demonstration was crushed by the gunfire and armored cars of the Securitate, the Romanian secret police, who also used tanks to smash through hastily erected barricades and to crush demonstrators. Over one thousand people were killed. However, the following day, renewed demonstrations led Ceauşescu to flee. The army eventually acted in support of the public agitation, providing force sufficient to overawe the Securitate and to overthrow the regime. Ceauşescu was detained, tried, and killed by the army.

In East Germany, in contrast, the police used water cannon and batons, while the protestors responded with Molotov cocktails and stones, but no one was killed. The events in Eastern Europe may not appear to deserve consideration as insurgencies with the exception of Romania, where the extensive fighting offers more justification. That approach, however, brings up the question as to whether the defiance and overthrow of government is the key element in an insurgency or the level of violence.

In the Soviet Union, there was no serious attempt to use the military power available to maintain government authority. Already, in 1986–87, the government had refused to employ force to support party leaders in the Baltic republics. When the crisis rose to a height from 1989, counterreform attempts by the Soviet military, as in Georgia in 1989 and Azerbaijan in 1990, were small scale. In January 1991, troops were used in order to stop republics from becoming independent. This led to clashes in Riga and Vilnius, the capitals of Latvia and Lithuania, respectively, in January 1991. Fourteen unarmed people protecting the television tower in Vilnius were killed, and five civilians in the seizure of the Interior Ministry in Riga. These steps did not intimidate the nationalists and, instead, led to the building of barricades in both cities. The government did not persist in its action.

In turn, motivated by loyalty to the party and the state and by concern about their own position, hardline Communists, organized as the State Committee for the State of Emergency in the USSR, or the Gang of Eight, attempted a coup in Moscow on August 19, 1991. This proved an abject failure, with street fighting in which three protesters were killed by the army showing that Soviet citizens were no longer supine. The failure was followed by the dissolution of the old system. The Soviet Union was dissolved that December. In a surprising fashion and with force not to the fore, the dynamic of insurgency and counterinsurgency had had a major consequence.

Chapter Ten

After the Cold War, 1990s

Once the Cold War had ended with the collapse of the Soviet Union, some states found it difficult to retain control in the face of insurrections. This was certainly the case in Yugoslavia, where the Soviet Union was not available to deter Western intervention on behalf of insurgents. Other insurgencies succeeded for reasons unrelated to the end of the Cold War, especially in Rwanda and East Timor. However, certain insurrections failed, as with the Shi'a in southern Iraq in 1991 and with Chechnya, while in some cases, notably southern Sudan, insurgencies of the period continued but the situation was not transformed. At the same time, the counterinsurgency conflicts of the period revealed the limitations of the conventional military, as with Israeli attempts to contain Palestinian discontent.

FORMER YUGOSLAVIA

The disintegration of Yugoslavia into its constituent republics in 1991 was followed by a sustained Serbian attempt to hold as much of the country together as possible. This led to bitter fighting in Croatia and Bosnia from 1991 to 1995 and to conflict in Kosovo from 1996 to 1999. These conflicts saw not only military operations but also large-scale "ethnic cleansing": the expulsion of members of an ethnic group in order to ensure ethnic homogeneity and thus control and to suppress opposition. The precipitant was the declaration of independence by Croatia, one of the republics, in 1991 and a Serbian insurrection in the Krajina and Slavonia regions of Croatia that saw vicious slaughter and the driving out of large numbers of Croats. A short-term settlement in 1992 was followed by a widening of the conflict to include Bosnia, where a Bosnian Serb Army was formed and mounted a vicious insurrection in which large numbers of Muslim and Croat civilians were murdered.

The fighting overlapped with traditional themes of brigandage and more generally with the wealth to be gained from violence and criminality. Thus, the Kosovo Liberation Army (KLA) benefited from the money and other support provided by Albanians abroad, notably in Switzerland and, it is alleged, also profited from the drug trade.[1] The transfer of assets through the forcible seizure of movable and unmovable property in a way that transcended doctrines, ideologies, alibis, fables, and excuses was a common theme in the Balkan upheavals of the 1990s, and not only then and there.[2]

In both Bosnia and Kosovo, Western intervention helped ensure that the Serbs failed to suppress opposition and had to back down. The shooting down of four Serb aircraft over central Bosnia by NATO aircraft enforcing a UN no-fly zone was a key move against the Serbs. In 1995, a settlement was negotiated as the Serbian government abandoned the Bosnian Serbs, in part due to American pressure but also in response to the successes of Croat and Bosnian Muslim forces. In the subsequent Dayton Peace Accords, Bosnia was, in effect, partitioned. In turn, a similar conflict in Kosovo led to the failure of the Serbs, in large part as a result of Western military pressure in 1999, including the bombing of Serbia. This pressure brought to an end a brutal ethnic cleansing that was a key aspect of the Serbian counterinsurgency strategy.

THE CAUCASUS

In a comparable fashion to Yugoslavia, there was conflict within and between several of the former republics of the Soviet Union. The Nagorno-Karabakh dispute, which focused on an Armenian enclave within Turkic-speaking Muslim Azerbaijan, led in 1992–94 to a war that overlapped with an insurgency. Both sides committed atrocities such as burning and crucifying people alive. Armenia was successful, and over one million Azeris became refugees. The Georgian army used force from 1992 to resist separatism by the Muslim province of Abkhazia, but the latter received Russian military assistance and was able to defy the pressure. More than two hundred thousand Georgians (over half the population of Abkhazia) were driven from their homes.[3]

The major insurgency in which a leading state was defied in the 1990s was that in Chechnya. This reflected the collapse of the Soviet Union and in particular the interaction between its weakness and assertive Islam. A crisis of Russian power in the northern Caucasus mountains resolved itself into an independence struggle in Chechnya, a long-standing area of Islamic resistance to Russian power. Declaring independence on November 1, 1991, the

Chechens tried to extend the breakup of the Soviet Union in 1991 to Russia, but the Russian leader, Boris Yeltsin, was unwilling to accept such separatism. Chechnya had always been a part of the Russian Soviet Socialist Federation, and there was never an option for Moscow to allow Chechnya to opt out as the former union republics, such as Estonia and Kazakhstan, could. This political decision, which had clear military consequences, also reflected the fear that such separatism would be contagious and that it would root radical Muslims near southern Russia as well as an awareness that concessions would discredit the new non-Communist political order with Russian nationalists. Initially, Yeltsin backed groups opposed to the Chechnyan government, but in December 1994 the Russian army was committed in a full-scale invasion.

This struggle juxtaposed the Chechnyan familiarity with irregular warfare to the Russian reliance on conventional methods and, notably, on firepower. In that sense, the Russians were like the Americans in the 1990s in that both employed Cold War weaponry and methods for which they had understandably been prepared. However, the American reliance on this approach proved more appropriate in the case of Iraq in 1991 than the Russian one did in Chechnya later in the decade. In large part, that reflected the extent to which the Iraqis provided a concentrated target while the conflict only lasted so long. In contrast, Chechnya provided a more diffuse opponent. It proved possible for the Russians to focus in 1994–95 and 1999–2000 on the Chechen capital, Grozny, but once that had been taken in an offensive very much emphasizing firepower, notably intensive artillery barrages and bombing, there was not any clear target: guerrilla resistance continued. As in Afghanistan in the 1980s, army morale became an issue.[4]

In the end, a form of compromise settlement was reached in 1996, one that showed that the Russians had less control in this marginal region than the regime of Saddam Hussein did in southern Iraq after suppressing a rising by Shi'a in 1991 in the wake of defeat in the First Gulf War. However, when, in the context of an increasingly unstable Chechnya, Chechens mounted attacks farther into Russia, the response was forceful and brutal, especially with a major invasion launched in late 1999. Control was imposed, but guerrilla resistance continued. Within Chechnya, the Russians increasingly relied on and supported local allies.

In assessing the military aspects of the situation, it is necessary to note not only the lack of an appropriate Russian doctrine and training but also the large Chechen numbers and the extent to which the Chechens, while poorly disciplined, were well armed (if short of ammunition) and determined. Many, indeed, had also been trained through conscription in the Russian army. The rebels, moreover, were able to receive support from across the region's borders. Opposition was firmest in the mountainous south. The extent to which news could be managed in Russia helped ensure that the apparently intract-

able nature of the situation received insufficient attention other than in terms
of a dangerous terrorist movement.[5]

IRAQ AND SOMALIA

The suppression of the 1991 Shi'a rising in Iraq reflected the role of international intervention. The Americans were not willing to intervene, even to the
extent of employing airpower in order to prevent the regime's use of helicopter gunships. The regime of Saddam Hussein employed great cruelty. The
1991 uprising led to the regime's agents pouring petrol down the throats of
rebels and setting them alight. In Baghdad, the "Special Treatment Department" cut up the living with chainsaws and squeezed their heads with metal
vises. In contrast, the deployment of American and British aircraft to police a
"no-fly zone" in northern Iraq as well as British marines on the ground
provided a crucial margin of protection to the Kurds and therefore gave their
long-standing insurgency against Iraqi control a measure of security.

The significance of airpower made the international context of particular
risings of great note. At the same time, that factor did not necessarily determine outcomes. Thus, in October 1993, in Mogadishu, the capital of Somalia, American action did not suppress warlord opposition. Whether the latter,
however, should be seen as an insurgency is less clear. The clan warlords
were in control because the Somali government had been overthrown in
1991, but their opposition to the United States was not thereby an insurgency. The United Nations forces, which the American contingent was part of,
having arrived in 1992 to bring humanitarian relief and resolve immediate
security problems, had been given in May 1993 the task of disarming the
factions and controlling all heavy weapons. At any rate, the conflict with the
United States abruptly demonstrated the extent to which a higher-technology
military was not necessarily able to prevail, in particular, in urban terrain and
against an opponent that was well integrated into local society.

This lesson greatly affected military opinion and notably in the United
States. Indeed, the difficulties the Americans faced in Mogadishu encouraged
a focus on airpower rather than on troops on the ground, a focus that was
very much to be seen with American policy in the Balkans later in the
decade. The American withdrawal in 1994 also impressed US opponents,
especially Saddam Hussein, who apparently seems to have assumed that any
American invasion of Iraq could be blunted by being drawn into city fighting. Moreover, the fact of American withdrawal from Somalia impressed
other opponents, in particular al-Qaeda and its Afghan allies.

In arriving at these conclusions, observers made the classic mistake, seen
so frequently in assessing insurgency and counterinsurgency warfare, of
drawing conclusions across the entire range of warfare and, in particular, in

assuming that one case proves another. Instead, as the course of both types of warfare repeatedly indicated, specifics were of key importance.

RWANDA

In Rwanda, the ethnic violence was genocidal, with an extremist group of Hutus that took over and then controlled the government slaughtering probably over a million Tutsi and moderate Hutus in a butchery launched in April 1994. This was carried out in order to prevent Hutu-Tutsi power sharing. If such a power sharing was seen as a challenge, then the slaughter was a brutal, preventive counterinsurgency. Nothing effective was done by the United Nations, United States, or other foreign powers to stop the slaughter. Indeed, France provided the killers with direct assistance. The regime was then overthrown in July 1994 by the ably commanded and well-disciplined Tutsi Rwanda Patriotic Front. In November 1996, it went on to attack Hutu extremists that had taken refuge in nearby parts of Congo and then, in May 1997, to overthrow the government there.

ANGOLA

The struggle between the government and the UNITA opposition movement was stilled with a cease-fire in 1988, after which the South Africans first withdrew and then the Cubans. However, having rejected the results of the 1992 election, UNITA resumed its conflict with the government, which was now weakened by the withdrawal of the Cuban and Soviet assistance that had greatly helped in 1975–91. Nevertheless, defeated by the scale of such a large country, neither side was able to win. The operational effectiveness of the government's conventional forces declined in the wet season, a season which favored UNITA guerrilla tactics. Both sides attacked the supply systems of the other but did not deliver fatal blows. Negotiations in 1994 led to a de facto partition of Angola between zones of control that lasted until 1997, when the government, bolstered by its oil wealth, attacked. UNITA was hit by the loss of its supply route through Congo and due to divisions. UNITA did badly, but a final settlement was achieved only after Jonas Savimbi was killed in fighting in 2002.

THE BALANCE OF ATTENTION

The potential strength of insurgencies was increasingly measured by Western commentators in terms of confrontation with airpower, and this emphasis on airpower encouraged an assessment of counterinsurgency options, notably in the United States, in terms of a supposed "revolution in military affairs"

(RMA) in which such power was emphasized. At the same time, the notion of a "war between civilizations," one advanced in 1993 by the American political scientist Samuel Huntington,[6] presented a more fundamental cultural and social rejection of the dominance of technologically advanced powers. The following decade was to demonstrate and amplify this contrast between perceptions based on an RMA and those focused on a "war between civilizations."

However, to stop at that point risks putting the clash between Western powers, notably the United States, and non-Western opponents too much to the fore. Instead, it is necessary to underline the extent to which the range and potency of insurgencies in the 1990s reflected a host of conflicts. Some attracted particular Western attention, notably the *intifada* (shaking off) in Palestine against Israeli control in 1987–94 and, anew, in 2000–2005, and, at a different scale, the terrorist campaign of the Provisional IRA in Northern Ireland. Others did not attract comparable attention. Nevertheless, there were significant insurgencies, notably in Zaire/Congo, Sri Lanka, and Algeria. Moreover, there were other insurgencies that were large scale even if they were not comparably important for the individual state.

This was the case for the Naxalite insurgency, a Maoist movement in east-central India that was important to regional politics and society but not at the national level, although in the 2000s, it became more potent.[7] Moreover, there were differences between Sudan, Sri Lanka, Myanmar, and Zaire (Congo), where insurgent groups controlled territory, and India, where in Kashmir, a region with a substantial Islamic population, it was more a case of terrorism. Sikh separatism had been a significant problem in India in the early 1980s. Nevertheless, by 1997, the Sikh insurgency in the Punjab had come to an end, in part because of the more cautious stance of the central government in the handling of Punjabi politics but also thanks to the strength and methods of Indian counterinsurgency. The ratio of troops was greater than with the Americans in Iraq in the 2000s, in part because the cost of using paramilitaries in India was far lower. In addition, the Punjab police recruited local auxiliaries. The Indian military was in part organized from independence in order to ensure that it did not mount coups. However, in terms of a wider military system, including the large number of paramilitaries, India proved effective at counterinsurgency operations.[8]

The net impression in the 1990s was of the limitations of counterinsurgency. Yet again, the range of insurgencies emerged clearly. These were significant as the end of the Cold War in 1989–91 helped usher in another stage of anti-imperial wars. This could be seen in the challenges to the Serbian and Russian imperialisms that underlay Yugoslavia and Russia, respectively.

In Afghanistan, the Soviets had put Mohammad Najibullah in power in 1987 as a more conciliatory replacement to Babrak Kemal and as part of the

Soviet search for a new solution to the Afghan problem. The fall of the Soviet Union greatly weakened his regime as it meant that there was no more money to pay the army. In April 1992, Najibullah was overthrown when the *mujahideen* entered Kabul. However, regional tensions escalated, notably between the non-Pushtun northerners and the Pushtuns of the south. The latter were more ready to adopt radical Islamic policies, particularly those of the Pakistani-backed Taliban movement which, in 1996, overran much of the country, benefiting from the weakness and divisions of the warlords. The Taliban were able to present themselves as a Pashtun national movement offering Islamic justice.[9] In 1996, they seized Kabul and captured Najibullah, who was hoisted upon a lamppost, whereupon his genitalia were either blow-torched away or cut off.

Anti-imperial conflict was also the case with insurgencies, notably with the challenges to Ethiopian rule over Eritrea, separatist activity in Sudan, and Israeli control over the West Bank of the Jordan and the Gaza Strip.[10] In Eritrea, the end of the Cold War hit Ethiopian control, and the Eritrean People's Liberation Front was able to capture the capital, Asmara. This was an instance of the degree to which the new wars of decolonization entailed challenges to the territorial configuration inherited from the political trans-formations of 1918–75, including the end of empires. Their fall had not ended imperial boundaries, many of which had subsequently been main-tained as the frontiers of independent states. Again, foreign intervention played a key role in these new wars. Thus, the dispatch of foreign forces, notably from Rwanda and Uganda into Congo/Zaire in the late 1990s, helped ensure that the warfare there became the bloodiest since the Second World War.

In contrast, foreign pressure, notably from Australia and the United Na-tions, led to the end of the violent Indonesian counterinsurgency struggle in East Timor. Waged since 1975, this struggle had seen large-scale violence, the destruction of crops, and the internment of much of the population in disease-ridden camps. Armed resistance in East Timor had had little success against a powerful military determined to maintain control. The role of the military in running Indonesia from 1966 to 1998 ensured that this approach was maintained, and East Timor won independence only after this role ceased.[11]

The nature of foreign intervention varied greatly. It could be the product of particular branches of the state or extend to the entire state mechanism. The former was readily apparent with Pakistani support for insurgencies in Afghanistan and India, not least with army and intelligence agency (ISI) backing for an Islamic separatist insurgency in Kashmir. Alongside the po-tential for conventional war (and occasional artillery barrages), there was also a Pakistani-backed insurgency.

Thailand suffered from Malaya's support for ethnic southern province Malays, who had begun an insurgency in 1980. The insurgency ended in 1997 in large part because the Thai government persuaded Malaya to end support, just as in 1979 it had persuaded China to stop its support for the Communist insurgency that had begun in 1965. At the same time, the robust Thai response was also significant: alongside social policies came military operations in a political context where the army was strongly entrenched. [12]

Foreign intervention could also lead to a settlement, as with the long-standing tension between the Issas and the minority Afars in what had become French Somaliland and, from 1997, Djibouti. This tension was accentuated when postindependence attempts to form a balanced government failed. Instead, in 1981, Djibouti became a one-party state under the Issa leader, Hassan Gouled Aptidon. In 1991, an Afar rebellion there began. However, the government benefited greatly from the active support of the former colonial power, France, and many of the rebels accepted a power-sharing agreement in 1994. Those who held out finally signed a peace treaty in 2000.

Postimperial rebellions saw a repetition of themes from anti-imperial rebellions but in a very different context. Most obviously, Algeria returned to civil conflict in 1992. The FLN, which had opposed French rule in 1954–62, was, by the 1990s, perceived as corrupt and Westernized. It had proved unable to meet expectations, was unwilling to respond to the popular will, and was affected by a rise in Islamicism. In 1992, the State Council proclaimed a state of emergency in order to block the rise of the fundamentalist Islamic Salvation Front (FIS), which had gained 25 percent of the popular vote in parliamentary elections in December 1991. Religious fanaticism was the driver in the Algerian civil war, in which over 150,000 people were killed. Islamic terrorists used many of the tactics employed by the FLN against the French in the late 1950s and early 1960s. In response, the government, in turn, adopted the earlier techniques of the French, including helicopter-borne pursuit groups, large-scale sweep-and-search operations, and the use of terror as a reprisal. Success was only partial but was much greater than in the case of France in 1954–62. This contrast reflected the major difference in political context rather than military means, notably the fact that the terrorists in the 1990s and 2000s were not up against a distant power. The same element was apparent in Ireland in the ability of the new Irish government to defeat the antitreaty forces in 1922–23, whereas the British had failed to overcome the IRA in 1919–21.

The Western power (albeit a Western power in the Middle East) most involved in handling counterinsurgency was Israel. The Israeli response to the *intifada* that began in 1987 involved tactical virtuosity but a strategic disappointment borne of an intractable situation as well as a preference for the use of force. This preference reflected the strong links between the Israeli military and the political establishment. The *intifada* underlined the weakness of imposed political settlements where the bulk of the population felt alienated and exposed the limitations of regular troops in the face of popular resistance. Violence fed violence on both sides. The Israeli military encountered problems in dealing with what was to them a novel form of warfare, one far less welcome than conventional conflict with regular Arab armies. [13]

The response to changing international circumstances, notably American dominance and Soviet collapse, was less positive for Israel than that in Northern Ireland. There, the Provisional IRA found that its terrorism had broken neither the British will to remain in Northern Ireland nor that of the majority of the people of Northern Ireland to remain British. This led to a settlement of differences with the Good Friday Agreement of 1998. Given the difficulties of its task, the British army, with the exception of the brutal and badly mishandled response to a nationalist demonstration in Londonderry on Bloody Sunday, maintained a high level of professionalism. That conduct did not protect them from criticism from many who appeared less willing to condemn the deliberate terrorist policy of the murder of civilians employed by the Provisional IRA. By the 1990s, the Provisional IRA was running low on supporters willing to lose their lives, while large social welfare payments, funded from the British Exchequer, helped lessen support of the nationalist cause. [14]

THINKING ABOUT COUNTERINSURGENCY

Alongside the focus on the RMA, the end of the Cold War encouraged interest in discussing counterinsurgency, although not on the scale that was to be seen in the 2000s. This interest could be seen in particular in Britain and in American discussion of recent British military history. A key work, Thomas Mockaitis's *British Counterinsurgency, 1919–1960* (1990) discerned what was presented as a British practice of minimum force, which was presented as an alternative to American conduct. This interest was taken further by the appearance in 1996 of an American edition of Charles Callwell's *Small Wars: Their Principles and Practice* (1896). The British *Army Field Manual* offered institutional form with the claim in 1995 that the army had, from its experience of over a century, developed a doctrine for countering insurgency. In practice, one reason for British low-intensity responses has been a lack of resources and manpower. At any rate, this interest in the 1990s looked toward the flowering of COIN doctrine in the 2000s. There was no comparable development in the doctrine of insurgency other than on the part of Islamic movements arguing that opponents benefiting from advanced weaponry could be defeated, in part because their willpower was lower.

Chapter Eleven

Interventionism and Its Failings, 2000s

Although developments in other states, such as Sri Lanka, were of great significance, the perception of insurgency in the 2000s was dominated by the cases of Afghanistan and Iraq. In each case, American interventions, while rapidly successful, were followed by a large-scale and sustained insurgency that proved difficult to suppress. These insurgencies encouraged a debate about the need to reconceptualize war. Linked to this came a discussion of a need for new advances in doctrine and training. Thus, to an extent that represented a major change in policy from the 1980s, counterinsurgency was pushed to the fore, at least for the United States and Britain, each of which at times served as foils for praise and blame within and by the other.[1] Counterinsurgency was reestablished as a key method of American war fighting, with the lessons of Vietnam relearned.[2] A new dynamic was certainly created by the Western military presence in Afghanistan and Iraq and the great difficulty in moving from input to outcome in the shape of a pro-Western settlement.

These struggles proved a key subject for this decade. At the same time, other insurgencies need to be discussed, not least for the purpose of comparison. These included other Islamic insurgencies, notably in Aceh (in Sumatra) and Somalia. At the same time, there were other insurgencies that cannot be discussed in these terms. These would include those in Congo/Zaire and Sudan. The comparison with American efforts invites attention as to whether their resource and technological advantages are seen as a key factor determining the outcome or as an element that is overrated.

There were successes in limiting insurgencies, for example, in Aceh, Sumatra, in 2005, as well as in Colombia in the mid-2000s. In the latter, a state with a long history of instability faced acute challenges from large paramilitary groups, both left wing and right wing, and also confronted a lack of control over large parts of the country as well as difficult relations with neighbors, especially Venezuela. The great value of the drug trade funded the paramilitaries. Concern about having a "failed state" on the southern shore of the Caribbean, combined with the opportunities of a relatively benign international situation, led the Americans, from Plan Colombia in 1999, to provide large-scale security assistance, notably with helicopters and training. Both enabled the army to take conflict to the guerrillas, but so also did a president of Colombia, Álvaro Uribe (r. 2002–10), who pressed it hard to act. Uribe, moreover, negotiated hard to divide the paramilitaries, such that he derived help from some against the left-wing FARC guerrilla movement.[3] The contrasting degree of success in counterinsurgency underlined the centrality of the political dimension, and thus the importance of aligning military with political strategies.

In some countries, most notably Afghanistan, counterinsurgency faced the problems of the rise of warlordism in the context of "failed states" or could not adequately co-opt it. So also with the extent to which power more generally operated in "failed states." In the cases of Liberia in 1989–2003 and Sierra Leone in 1991–2002, the political objectives of insurgents beyond the capture of power were hazy. As a result, there was extensive discussion of the motivation of the insurgents and their extraordinarily cruel tactics. The questions of rationality in goals and means were debated. There is certainly a need to distinguish between leaders and fighters, for example, with the Revolutionary United Front (RUF) in Sierra Leone. That fighting provided a role, power, enjoyment, and compensation for apparent humiliation appears crucial, given that ethnic and religious differences were not to the fore. Indeed, the RUF was composed of fighters from differing ethnic and religious groups. The RUF internal propaganda presented the cities, notably the capital, Freetown, which was attacked in 1999, as "rotten," and thus conveyed a rejection of order and organization. "Civil wars" in Liberia and Sierra Leone benefited from the large-scale availability of small arms and were financed primarily by criminal operations and forced extortions. There were no clear-cut chains of command nor uniforms distinguishing "troops" from other fighters.

The politics could be one in which individuals moved between being warlords, rebels, generals in government forces, and presidents. In turn, the army and police became an integral and violent part of the political system, one in which elements rebelled and others fought them, with insurgency and counterinsurgency scarcely readily defined in this context. An eventual aspect in the suppression of disorder was the creation of new forces able and willing to take a different approach.[4]

Resource and technological issues were involved in these conflicts as they were when more major powers acted. Thus, in Sudan, where the dictatorial military-based government of Omar Hassan al-Beshir faced separatism in the south and west, it benefited from its control over the central point of the capital, Khartoum, from the funds gained from oil, which enabled it to buy Chinese and Russian arms, and from its use of airpower and artillery. At the same time, other means were also employed. In response to the rebellion by the Sudan People's Liberation Army based in Darfur in the west, a rebellion dating to the 1970s but breaking out with greater intensity in 2003, the government used its regular forces to ally with a militia, the Janjaweed, in order to slaughter native tribes. Environmental change, notably in the form of desertification, was a vital factor in the rise of the Janjaweed. Alongside large-scale slaughter, notably of men and boys, and the systematic rape and mutilation of women, natives were driven away, their cattle and therefore livelihood seized, the wells poisoned with corpses, and dams, pumps, and buildings destroyed. This was a scorched-earth policy designed to deny the rebels shelter. As in southern Sudan, the government was assisted by serious divisions among the opposition, with ethnic and political tensions related to factionalism.

By 2009, fighting had eased in Darfur, and in 2011, a peace agreement was drawn up. However, several of the rebel factions did not accept it, and fighting swiftly revived. The violence became more anarchic, with groups on each "side" fighting each other, notably over resources, especially water and cattle. The Sudanese government was greatly helped by the funds gained from oil, which enabled large-scale expenditure on the army and on arms, including MiG-29s from Russia. The Sudanese military employed the same techniques elsewhere, for example, in the province of Southern Kordofan in the early 2010s.

The extent to which the military played a central role in the government and/or political process could make it difficult to distinguish insurgencies from what were in that context the ordinary processes of opposition and contesting power. For example, in Uzbekistan, where the authoritarian regime of Islam Karimov claimed that opposition was led by Muslim terrorists, opposition was in practice broader based. The nature of both this opposition and the response underlined the difficulties of distinguishing them from politics, as in 2005, when troops fired on a crowd in the city of Andijan demonstrating against the poor economic situation. More generally, it is typical of questionable authorities to label opposition as terrorism. This process reduces the value of the term and people's understanding of it, which are already serious issues.

The frequent use of force by military and military-based regimes ensured that the suppression of opposition overlapped with counterinsurgency intentions and methods. Thus, in Zimbabwe, the military-dominated Joint Operations Command that became more powerful in 2008 orchestrated the use of force in order to maintain Robert Mugabe in power against popular pressure and democratic methods. The army, whose members and former members had gained assets and government posts, was linked to violent gangs in brutalizing opponents, many of whom fled abroad. Such flight was at once a means of ending opposition and a way in which it was sustained as an international presence. Across the world, although refugees sought peacefully to rebuild their lives, others provided a basis for insurrectionary activity.

In a pattern similar to that in Zimbabwe, Laurent Gbagbo, the president of Ivory Coast, defeated in the 2010 election, used force in 2010–11 in an eventually unsuccessful attempt to ignore this defeat. The army in Guinea, having seized power in a coup in 2008, suppressed pro-democracy demonstrators in 2009, killing and raping many.

In Nepal, the weakness of civilian institutions made it easier for an insurgency to take root and for the military to assume a leading role in governing Nepal. The forcefulness, often brutality, of the military response was important to the counterinsurgency struggle against the Janayuddha (People's War) launched by the People's Liberation Army of Nepal, a Maoist movement, in 1996. The insurgents had many women and children among their forces but were outnumbered by the army and police. However, helped by the mountainous and forested terrain, by Chinese assistance from across the Tibetan border, and by their own brutality, the guerrillas were able to avoid defeat and to continue attacking, which ensured that they remained a factor in politics. Moreover, the Maoists benefited from their ability to use personal power networks and the numerous ethnic cleavages at the local level in Nepal, notably among low-caste groups and others who felt excluded from power.[5] The war was responsible for more than thirteen thousand deaths and over two hundred thousand displaced by the time a peace agreement was signed in 2006.

IRAQ

The insurgency in Iraq that followed the American overthrow of the Saddam regime in 2003 attracted much more attention than those in Africa and Nepal. The difficulty in securing domestic support in Iraq had been underrated in a serious failure of prewar American planning. Aside from a serious failure of political understanding, the military operationalization of the American approach meant that the focus was on the force required to defeat the Iraqis and not on that necessary to contain the subsequent situation. Fewer troops were sent than the army chief of staff had recommended, and this made it impossible to secure the infrastructure. There was little support for the American choice as leader, Ahmed Chalabi. Due to overconfidence, a failure to consider contingencies, and an army doctrine focused on conventional operations, there was also totally inadequate preparation for postwar disorder and division. The limitations of Iraq's civilian infrastructure were not understood.

Moreover, the disbandment of the Iraqi army in May 2003 rallied support for insurrection as well as helping ensure that arms were extensively distributed. This was a major American mistake, as was the attempt at "de-Ba'athification," the removal of all elements close to the regime, a process that, in the event, led to large-scale unemployment.

This failure is worth slowing down in order to isolate several of the key elements and events. However, at the same time, the stress on American failure is mistaken if it leads to a reluctance to note the autonomy of other agents, notably groups in Iraqi society, as well as Iran, which provided support for Shi'a militia in Iraq. Indeed, as with the discussion of the Vietnam War, there can be a mistaken tendency to focus largely on the counterinsurgency forces as if they had the capacity to direct and even control events.

The immediate failure of planning for the transition to a favorable Iraqi regime was compounded by the extent to which the Office of Humanitarian and Reconstruction Assistance under Jay Garner, a retired general, lacked adequate support, notably manpower, funds, and backing. Garner was rapidly dismissed and replaced by Paul Bremer, who directed the Coalition Provisional Authority. He disbanded the Iraqi army (despite it being a separate force to Saddam's favored Revolutionary Guards), dismissed Ba'athists, and deliberately set out to break with the pattern of Iraqi tribalism by not heeding the traditional leaders. This policy very much conformed with that of the Soviets in Afghanistan in the 1980s, and for similar reasons and with similar consequences. There was a drive for modernization in which tribalism, like sectarian and ethnic difference, were seen as dated and a challenge to any chance for progress. The result was to inject an additional element of volatility and fear into a society already transformed by American conquest and the overthrow of Saddam. Those who did not welcome change and those who saw it as an opportunity sought to affect the process by turning to force and violence.

In large part, the Americans suffered from a failure to appreciate the nature of Iraqi society, notably the strength of sectarianism in society. Moreover, under Saddam, there had been a politicization of government, a destruction of Iraqi intermediate institutions, and a hollowing out of civil society. These processes ensured that American occupation lacked institutional and social anchors and levers of cooperation and had no real understanding of the situation. The overthrow of Saddam exacerbated the divisions between and within the Sunni and Shi'a communities, and the Americans found themselves under wide-ranging and divergent attack from 2004, as their attempt at nation building cut across the realignment of political and economic interests and power that followed Saddam's fall. This problem helped compromise American attempts to create competent and reliable Iraqi police and military forces.[6]

The insurgency fulfilled some of Saddam's prewar plans. He had established safe houses and hidden weapons and funds to oppose an occupying force, and these proved an element in the subsequent crisis, with supporters of the regime and demobilized troops both providing manpower. There was violent opposition to the new American-imposed government from the outset. In turn, for the Americans, the failure to command the expected response helped cause disorientation. With a preference for a short war followed by turning control over to newly trained Iraqi security forces, the American lack of a coherent strategy to defeat the insurgency became readily apparent, as did the problems of intelligence failure. The "boots on the ground" strategy provided targets for the insurgents and the opportunity to undermine American resolve. In turn, there was no unity among the insurgents and no organization that could be readily suppressed.

Clashes led to civilian casualties and hostility, which lessened the social space within which American forces could safely operate and encouraged a defensiveness and alienation on the part of these forces, one that led to an emphasis on "kinetic" operations. The public defiance of American power escalated with the burned bodies of ambushed contracted guards employed by an American private security company, Blackwater, left hanging from a bridge in Fallujah on March 31, 2004. Far from being in the margins of occupied Iraq, this was a city close to Baghdad. It also became a center for al-Qaeda in Iraq and thus a clear sign of the American failure there. This encouraged the Americans to capture the city, which they did in November 2004 in difficult urban fighting. Such fighting became important in a larger process of regaining impetus and using it with greater skill, a process that involved military and political learning but that also faced serious challenge from the resilience of insurgent forces.[7]

Against considerable political and military opposition, President George W. Bush decided to respond to the crisis in 2007 by sending thirty thousand additional combat troops in what in effect was a counteroffensive. Designed to provide the opportunity to create an effective relationship between the Iraqi public and government and to limit the range of violence within society, this "surge" enabled the Americans to regain the initiative. That worked only because the availability of more force was linked to an appropriate forward stance, especially platoon combat outposts among the people, as well as to an adroit political strategy in which the Americans sponsored the formation of neighborhood militias committed to stability while also negotiating with former insurgent groups. The "surge" thus combined with a "tribal awakening" that led to the raising of self-defense militias against al-Qaeda control.

This was an aspect, as part of a rediscovery of counterinsurgency ideas,[8] of a more perceptive response to Iraq's sectarian divides, particularly by creating a shared political and military constituency with the Sunnis (earlier, the basis of Saddam's position) while, at the same time, reducing dependence on the Shi'as and giving them more reason to compromise. The Shi'a population was detached from the Shi'a militia and encouraged, instead, to look to the government. Such an account, however, gives an unwonted degree of agency to the Americans, because in large part they benefited, as they had earlier suffered, from divisions among the Iraqis and the manner in which these developed. In particular, in early 2006, in the western part of Anbar Province, the Sunni Abu Mahal tribe revolted against the brutal and doctrinaire dominance of al-Qaeda in Iraq. Their success led other tribes to follow, creating a possibility for American-backed civil pro-Iraqi government forces, one that was to be followed in other areas such as Fallujah. Differentiating among opponents worked because it was information driven. The situation became more stable. This instance indicated the centrality of intelligence in COIN operations, notably patiently building up the picture of who the opposition is and how they are operating. The former is frequently unclear. Initially in Iraq, the American forces had not known whom they were fighting.

The rediscovery of counterinsurgency ideas was part of a political and military battle over responsibility for the failure to stabilize Iraq. Initially, the focus of blame was on hidden supporters of Saddam and on Iran encouraging opposition, but with time, Allied failures in planning and implementation, as well as the range, complexity, and severity of the insurgency, were all understood, and an explicit engagement with counterinsurgency doctrine developed.

In turn, this development entailed a reassessment of the American military role in the Vietnam War, most notably with the argument that after the defeat of the Tet Offensive in 1968, the Americans were winning the war, only for this to be thrown away as a result of political failure at home. This argument appeared to be vindicated by the success of the "surge" and led to the advance of particular individuals and groups in the promotions and patronage of military politics, notably General David Petraeus, commander of the multinational forces in Iraq. He played a prominent role in analyzing the problems facing the American army in Iraq and then in advancing the case for developing and implementing a new doctrine, training, and practice, as well as the relevant equipment.[9] Similarly, there were consequences for appointments and courses in military history, with an interest in COIN courses becoming prominent.

Bedeviled by poor leadership as well as by the undoubted lack of resources, including manpower, that they found it convenient to blame, the British army did badly in its sphere of operations. It lost control of its area of operations and was unable to expel the Shi'a Mahdi army from Basra in 2007–8, which left the Iraqis and Americans obliged to regain control there.[10] The British failure in Iraq matched another serious failure in Helmand Province in Afghanistan, where, from 2006, the British forces were stretched too thin when they moved into a series of isolated outposts.[11] In part, this reflected not simply "overstretch" but the unaccustomed role of a commitment to an ambitious nation building, a political strategy that was not really coupled to the localized, military one.[12]

The Iraqi situation underlined broader questions about the reliance on COIN, for aside from the practicality of counterinsurgency operations in particular contexts, it might well be unusual in the future to be able to achieve and afford such a focus in commitments. The costs of the commitment raised the overlapping questions of the strategic value of the commitment, the operational effectiveness of COIN, and whether a long-term "militarization" of a political situation was desirable even if victory, however defined, could be attained. In short, did recent discussion of the best doctrine for COIN miss the point, as the cost was too high, or was this only the case in terms of the particular circumstances and specifications of the Iraq crisis?

AFGHANISTAN

The situation in Afghanistan proved even more difficult than that in Iraq. Overthrown in 2001 by American-backed action, with local allies supported by airpower, special forces, and money, the Taliban regained momentum from 2005. The Taliban had been strong but also vulnerable in 2001. During the civil war of the late 1990s, they had relied on forcible conscription, which was highly unpopular. There were approximately sixty thousand Taliban fighters in 2000–2001, and they were very well organized, but they proved very exposed to American airpower. The Taliban proved less so when they came back from 2005 on, and they were more intermingled with the population, in part because, at least in Helmand Province, they relied mostly on voluntary recruitment. Aside from a degree of popularity, the Taliban enhanced its influence over the population through violence and thus lessened the options for the government and its foreign supporters. In addition, Taliban forces were ably led, well trained, and organized. The American "surge" in Afghanistan in 2009–10 helped stabilize the military situation, notably in the provinces of Helmand and Kandahar, but proved less successful than its Iraqi counterpart. This was a reflection not only of very different military and political factors and operational and cultural environments, but also of the near relationship of success and failure.

In a classic instance of the misleading reference to history, it proved all too easy to mention Afghanistan's long history of resisting central control and foreign invasion. The country certainly has a low density of population, a variegated ethnic and religious pattern, a mountainous terrain that has acted against the idea of national identity, and a tradition of local political activism, all of which ensured that much of the narrative and analysis of insurrectionary and counterinsurgency warfare was local and regional rather than national.[13] Nonetheless, there had been a degree of national cohesion from the late nineteenth century, and the Americans were successful in 2001.

It is more pertinent to focus on the particular factors in the 2000s and 2010s because they help explain why the traditional practices of compromise did not work. The Americans, who had adopted contradictory military and political approaches in 2001, lacked a viable strategy, not least because the opportunity for incorporating the Taliban into the political system was not taken. The Bush administration had simply wanted the Taliban regime overthrown and the al-Qaeda terrorists (a different movement and force) wiped out but had been determined to limit the commitment of troops and to avoid nation building. The focus was to be Iraq, and scant effort was devoted to stabilizing Afghanistan. As a consequence, the Americans were delighted to hand the task over to NATO, which, however, was not up to it.[14] American policymaking suffered from a serious failure to understand the local political situation, not least the nuances of the patronage system, the character and dynamics of tribal and ethnic relationships, and the dislike of outside interference.[15]

So also with the British, who were deployed in Helmand as part of the NATO-ISAF (International Security Assistance Force) from 2006. A poorly conceived policy, a mistaken strategy, a lack of necessary resources, and a problematic command-and-control system were matched by a lack of situational awareness, with the British rapidly involved in local power struggles. The dismissal of the corrupt and unpopular governor, Sher Mohammad Akhundzada, who held the position because he was a warlord, led his militia to switch to the Taliban. The Taliban were beaten by the British in 2006–7, but this did not end a struggle that proved intractable. So also in Kandahar, where the Canadians defeated an attempt to seize the city in 2006, only for attacks in the city and region to continue.[16]

The unpopularity of the corrupt and ineffective government of Hamid Karzai, president from 2004 to 2014 (although not of Karzai personally), including the highly fraudulent election of 2009, ensured that there was a very weak basis for the efforts of the Afghan military and police to maintain order and for the nation and institution building pursued by Western powers.[17] These goals and policies did not match the situation on the ground, not least in the inability to provide security and in attempts to reduce a dependence on narcotic production in Afghanistan. As a result, the Allies failed to formulate viable strategies, military, political, or diplomatic, or to pursue practical implementation. In particular, there was a failure to provide a strategy that would bring over regional powers, notably Pakistan. Within Afghanistan, governmental corruption assisted the puritanical reform demands and attitudes associated with the Taliban, attitudes derived from Wahhabi ideologies in Saudi Arabia.[18] Moreover, the Karzai government's attempts to monopolize power ensured an undermining or bypassing of warlords opposed to the Taliban, and this increased instability, as did the very power of the warlords.[19] Built up under Karzai, the Afghan army suffered from poor recruitment, low morale, high rates of desertion, corruption, patronage, and ethnic rivalries. Repeatedly, the army's effectiveness has been limited.

The key opposition to the Afghan government in the 2000s and 2010s came not from warlords but from the Taliban. Despite their incompetence in government in the late 1990s, their determination, resilience, brutality, grounding in local society, and ability to draw support from bases in Pakistan were all significant. The Taliban also benefited from the serious weaknesses of Allied military leadership, not least a mistaking of assertion and confidence for ability and perception and of tactical successes for strategic achievement. These weaknesses were particularly seen at the senior level. In addition, the "surge" in Afghanistan under President Obama, announced in December 2009, involved thirty-two thousand men, far fewer troops than the number requested and described as the minimal necessary by the generals, although generals tend to ask for too much. Under Obama, American force levels rose from around thirty thousand men to ninety-eight thousand. The problem was his simultaneous announcement that the "surge" was limited in time and thus implicitly also in scope of mission. He put an eighteen-month deadline on the "surge" forces before the drawdown would start. There could be no sustainable success on this timescale.

In addition, the Allies responded differently in accordance with their national doctrines and practices.[20] They also faced difficulties in explaining their efforts to their publics and notably in reconciling transnational defense policies focused on NATO and the United States with national defense rhetorics.[21] The Taliban fought on long enough to ensure war-weariness among the powers providing troops for the International Security Assistance Force (ISAF). Ultimately, the inability to end the struggle made it appear a failure. Projecting power for many years had been very expensive and had not fulfilled expectations, although ironically the skill of the ISAF operations increased with time, at least in terms of situational awareness.[22] However, the problems posed by the support of the Taliban from Afghanistan's neighbor Pakistan were never overcome despite American efforts. Both the Pakistani army and the intelligence service support Islamist radicals, including allowing the Taliban to base themselves in Pakistan. As they were safe there, the NATO forces in Afghanistan suffered from not being able to hit their opponent's center of gravity, mirroring the problem posed for the Americans in the Vietnam War by focusing on the Viet Cong and not the North Vietnamese.[23] The Taliban also benefited greatly from its links with drug production and trafficking. Indeed, the ability of the Taliban, like other insurgent groups, to draw on different constituencies, and thus support systems, makes it very resistant.[24]

COIN operations in Iraq and Afghanistan indicated the value of air supremacy in providing a relative freedom of movement as well as offensive air support, each aspects of a more general asymmetric advantage that helped counter the advantages the insurgents enjoyed. The presence, firepower, support, intelligence, and command and control of counterinsurgency forces all depended, both immediately and ultimately, heavily on airpower. The strategic airlift offered through moving forces to theater was matched by its operational and tactical counterparts. Situational understanding and network-enabled capabilities were especially reliant on airpower. Air mobility was particularly significant due to booby traps, mines, and ambushes of American and NATO forces. Helicopters provided mobility, logistics, and firepower. Given the freedom to fly largely unhindered across the whole battlespace, helicopters and aircraft permitted the protection of beleaguered garrisons and patrols as well as opportunities for air attack. Air reconnaissance, using sophisticated visual and radar sensors, provided the detail of vehicle and personnel movement to permit such attacks to be executed with minimal collateral damage.

At the same time, the effectiveness and numbers of unmanned air vehicles (UAVs) increased, and they began to be equipped with air-to-ground munitions. Their long endurance and low detectability progressively offered commanders an effective alternative to the fast jet. In the 1990s, the Clinton administration had frequently resorted to cruise missile attacks in preference to the use of manned aircraft. In part, this was because the use of unmanned vehicles was seen as a low-risk option without the political and psychological impact of the possible capture of downed pilots. Subsequently, UAVs or drones developed, initially for intelligence, surveillance, and reconnaissance and subsequently for carrying weapons. UAVs have become increasingly important in making pinpointed attacks on specific targets as well as for surveillance. The relative low cost of UAVs compared to manned aircraft makes them cost effective, although the cost of the missiles is the same irrespective of the platform from which they are fired.

Even with the sophistication of the sensors and the capabilities of the aircraft and UAVs, there were difficulties with the use of airpower. With only limited numbers of aircraft, with rules of engagement constraining targeting, and with the limitations imposed by poor weather, it proved difficult to be decisive. Insurgents contested the Allied use of airpower, not by having an air force, but by sporadic antiaircraft fire from small arms, by mortar and infantry attacks on airfields, by operating among civilians and from civilian dwellings, and by propaganda about civilian casualties. With the extreme sensitivity to collateral damage, the integration of intelligence and the surveillance picture to identify legitimate targets from among civilian personnel and traffic proved difficult. The advisability of bombing in counterinsurgency operations was questioned, given the frequent difficulty of identifying targets and the problems posed by a hostile response to bombing in a context within which local support was sought. Thus, in Afghanistan, air strikes compromised such support and also had an adverse impact elsewhere, notably in Pakistan.

So also with the situation on the ground. Counterinsurgency practice found it difficult to match the doctrine of winning the support of the civilian population. In part this was because of the risk imposed as a result. In particular, it proved difficult to overcome the Taliban's ability to make ground operations unpredictable and dangerous and to undermine the government's ability to support local allies. A journalist with an American marine unit that faced an ambush in 2009 noted that "firepower can become meaningless when the enemy makes skillful preparation on the ground and has no scruples about cloaking itself with the lives of the local population."[25] The latter practice was an example of "playing by different rules" and thereby gaining a brutal advantage as well as a balance to any technological asymmetric disadvantage.

For both ground forces and supporting airpower, tactical and operational limitations, including logistics and the security of bases, were matched by strategic counterparts, notably the difficulties of obtaining an end to insurrection. This issue continued a key element in the equations of force. More specifically, insurgents contested counterinsurgency operations and their impact, not least by the use of propaganda about casualties. Moreover, the insurgents often lacked a fixed leadership, a clear governmental structure, and an infrastructure to provide targets for these operations.

Failure to defeat the Taliban led to a rethinking of Iraq-based lessons about counterinsurgency, including the arming of local tribal forces.[26] In particular, there was a querying of the value of "hearts and minds" as opposed to an emphasis on force or "kinetic" operations focused on opposing troops. This led also to a rethinking of earlier episodes such as the Vietnam War. The effectiveness of COIN was presented as a "myth" deployed to suggest the possibility of "better wars" and of transforming foreign societies. It was argued that it was an "illusion" to believe that Muslim hearts and minds could be won at gunpoint.[27]

Rather than focusing on Western flaws, it is worth noting the problems Pakistan faced in counterinsurgency in the Federally Administered Tribal Areas (FATA), especially from 2007. This was the case both with military operations and with attempts to ensure a measure of peace by means of "peace deals." The latter became more difficult because of the overlapping nature of the struggle in Afghanistan as well as the rise of Islamic fundamentalism and the links with wider regional and global pressure. The Pakistani Taliban became increasingly active. Similarly, the Pakistanis found it very difficult to contain large-scale violent opposition in Baluchistan[28] and found it convenient to claim that this opposition was armed by India.[29]

SRI LANKA

A very different impression was created in March–May 2009 by the Sri Lankan military's crushing of the insurgency by the Liberation Tigers of Tamil Eelam. At the same time, the insurgency had been difficult to crush, and that conflict, which had lasted from 1983 until 2002 and then from 2006 until 2009, resulted in at least sixty thousand casualties, including approximately eighteen thousand combatants killed on each side, with over two million refugees in addition. The war drew heavily on Tamil separatism, which was opposed by most of the Sinhalese majority. For long the Tigers relied on guerrilla operations in the Tamil heartland and terrorist strikes elsewhere. The instructive contrast, however, between insurgent failure in Sri Lanka and success in Afghanistan indicates the role of particular factors. The Tigers suffered from a shift to conventional warfare and also lost support among the Tamil population as a result of the continuation of the war and their own brutal techniques. The Sri Lankan military, however, did not provide a "hearts and minds" policy. The insurgency was crushed with heavy civilian casualties and no discrimination between noncombatants and armed rebels. The Tigers had also suffered from seriously alienating the Indian government.

DISCUSSION AND DOCTRINE

The 2000s saw much more discussion of COIN than in the 1980s or 1990s. John Nagl's *Learning to Eat Soup with a Knife: Counterinsurgency Lessons from Malaya and Vietnam* (2002) came to be very influential as the Americans debated how best to respond to the chaos in Iraq after its conquest in 2003.[30] The British experience was important to Nagl and to Montgomery McFate's emphasis on acquiring "cultural knowledge" of enemies.[31] American officers operating in Fallujah in 2007 read Thompson, Galula, and T. E. Lawrence.[32] Kitson found himself of considerable interest to American audiences.[33]

Although the situation subsequently changed greatly, circumstances in Iraq initially appeared to support the British example. In the south, where the British were based, they adopted a light touch and, until 2006, this was held to be more successful than the American zone, where there was more emphasis on firepower, which was held to encourage resistance.[34] This light touch was related to the idea that, as the 2008 Canadian Forces doctrine asserted, "the primary strategic centre of gravity is the civilian populace." Assuming an active minority for the insurgent cause and an active minority against it, this meant the need to influence the neutral or passive majority. Linked to this, the destruction of the insurgents was regarded as of limited value without addressing fundamental grievances so as to influence the neutral population.[35]

The American discussion ranged widely.[36] There was an extensive consideration of the Vietnam War. In particular, the ambitious Civil Operations and Revolutionary Development Support (CORDS) program adopted there as pacification and nation building, a transition from the earlier Office of Civil Operations, was held up for praise and emulation, notably by *Counterinsurgency*, Field Manual (FM) 3-24, which was published in December 2006. It is notable as a sign of interest that a study of CORDS[37] was awarded, by the American Commission on Military History, the 2015 Brigadier General James L. Collins Prize in Military History for the best book written in English on American military history. The manual itself was published as a book by the University of Chicago Press in 2007 and sold well, and it was also used by many armies across the world. An emphasis on the limitations of insurgencies, unless helped by the serious weaknesses of the counterinsurgency struggle, attracted attention.[38] The achievements of the American "surge" in Iraq also received much discussion,[39] not least because it contributed to the idea of "fully resourced counter-insurgency."[40]

However, the vigor of insurgencies, and notably if opposed by democracies, attracted more attention.[41] So also with the argument that local allies unable to make necessary reforms were a crucial limitation to counterinsurgency effectiveness in both Vietnam and Iraq.[42] The difficulties armies faced in learning lessons and accepting the difficulties and disciplines of counterinsurgency warfare were important themes,[43] but at the organizational level, it was clear that heavy ground forces had to be adapted while it was also necessary to have a heavy force capability for deterrence purposes.[44] The former goals risked losing skills, as when American artillery units were employed as infantry. This helped make the reluctance in the Department of Defense and American army[45] (let alone navy and air force) to accept the focus on counterinsurgency understandable. Moreover, there was a cyclical pattern in counterinsurgency doctrine, with an emphasis either on "hearts and minds" or on open military force. Short time horizons and a consequent move by strategists from one approach to another was a major problem.

CONCLUSIONS

In Iraq, Afghanistan, and other states, there were echoes of earlier forms of politics and warfare, echoes that represented major problems for those intervening in order to ensure and maintain the peace and to (re)build states. It is unclear in practice how far the insurgents in Iraq or the Taliban in Afghanistan had a clear or strong sense of the broader pattern of military change. However, they were able to locate their own activities in an experience that provided not only motivation but also an ability to respond to challenges. Considered in another light, these insurgents found that their ideas and practices brought less success than they had anticipated. Indeed, this failure, seen also with that of the Andizhan insurgency in Uzbekistan in 2005 and those in the Caucasus, Algeria, and Sri Lanka, contributed to a general inability to warmaking in 2001–8 to achieve desired results. This suggests that criticism of counterinsurgency warfare and, notably, but not only, of this warfare as conducted by Western powers should be set in a wider context of failure that includes examples of insurgency warfare.

The case of Iraq and Afghanistan also raised questions about the ability of military planners to think strategically concerning the nature of domestic support for long-term military commitments. The discussion of public will is highly relevant and helps ensure that, while it is for the politicians to gauge whether a proposed course of action will carry sustained domestic support, generals also need to be aware of the issues. This situation reflects a major change. Imperialism no longer enjoys public support, while militarist values are publicly displayed in relatively fewer societies than in the past. Indeed, there has been a revolution in attitudes to the military representing a profound change in the context of conflict, notably so in the West, especially Europe and Canada.[46] The importance of political will in this context and its consequences for policy were, and are, readily apparent and take precedence over the added counterinsurgency capability provided by computers, GPSs, and other systems and tools.

As a result, there were questions about the ability to intervene in (and thus generally conquer) and rebuild nations, a process that generally takes many years, without endangering domestic support and coalition cohesion, let alone harming, or at least affecting, wider strategic interests. This issue of ability led to unwelcome questions about capacity and doctrine as well as to the issue of the integration of the political and military. Far from this being simply a question of the integration of political goals with military means, the goals and the means related both to the political and to the military.

Chapter Twelve

A World without Shape? The Present

Insurrections in Syria, Iraq, and Ukraine have dominated the discussion of the situation in the 2010s. However, as before, that does not exhaust the subject. Instead, the range of insurrections included previous areas, notably Somalia and Sudan, as well as areas that had not been prominent in this category, such as Mali and Nigeria. Islamic transnationalism acted as an effective ideology and practice of insurrection.[1]

AFGHANISTAN

Although overshadowed by a spate of struggles elsewhere in the world, conflict with the Taliban continued, albeit with a continuing mismatch of goals and resources, as well as with poor coordination on the counterinsurgent side and a lack of political support, both within the region and in the home countries of those intervening.[2] The Afghan National Army (ANA) had been built up behind the cover of foreign military resistance, and its role and that of the Taliban became more significant as NATO contingents withdrew or became smaller or less active, a process largely complete by 2015. Despite large-scale investment, notably by the United States as it sought to pursue "transition" toward a greater Afghan role, the ANA found it difficult to provide internal security. In part, the ANA's combat effectiveness and morale were at issue, and justifiably so. ANA weakness included a lack of airpower, on which Western forces and methods were totally reliant. The Western powers withdrew their airpower with their ground forces. However, more seriously, the Afghan forte is guerrilla fighting, not fighting in regular armies. That, along with terrain and local, clan, and familial ties have made it harder for Kabul to construct meaningful national armies, be they under Soviet or post-Soviet leadership.

There was also concern about Taliban resilience. The areas of Afghanistan in which the Taliban operated and operated frequently increased. While attacks on Afghan army and police rose, so also did the assassination of officials. The numerous and well-supplied Taliban also proved well able to benefit from the decline in NATO activity as well as from regional power politics. For example, in 2014, British and American forces withdrew from Helmand Province. The following year, the Taliban overran the district center of Musa Qala, a town Anglo-American and Afghan troops had captured from them in 2007. Kunduz, a provincial capital, was captured for three days in 2015 in a major failure for the ANA, while Taliban forces also advanced on Lashkar Gah, the capital of Helmand. Such attack created fear and threatened the stability of the government. While President Karzai was increasingly critical of ISAF, the ANA favored different attitudes to COIN than those of Western forces. The possibility of achieving stalemate was unclear, but even more, the transience of order in the circumstances of Afghanistan in the 2010s appeared apparent. The problems posed by the tribal values and psychology of a clan system have been greatly exacerbated by the impact of religious fundamentalism and conflict. Resistance to a foreign presence extends to hostility toward what is seen as its puppet government.

IRAQ AND SYRIA

Counterinsurgency doctrine came to the fore anew in the West as the difficulty of confronting ISIS (Islamic State of Iraq and Syria) became readily apparent in 2014–15. In practice, the key issue was not the strength or weakness of the United States with regard to its opponent but, rather, the extent to which ISIS was able to benefit from the divided sectarianism and baleful political legacies of Iraq and Syria. The two combined in Iraq in the chaos that followed the American invasion of 2003, particularly the failure to bring Sunni Iraqis and former Ba'athists into the political system established in the legacy of the invasion, and, notably, the spoils system it represented. This opportunity was taken by the leader of al-Qaeda in Iraq, a Jordanian-born jihadist, Abu Musab al-Zarqawi, who had considerable success in establishing influence in western Iraq and who is treated as the founder of ISIS. Killed by an American air strike in 2006, he was replaced by Abu Omar al-Baghdadi, a former officer in Saddam Hussein's General Security Directorate who adopted the tribal lineage and nomenclature of the Prophet and proclaimed himself caliph of an Islamic State of Iraq. His violence and overthrow of local leaders led, in the Anbar Awakening, to Sunni cooperation with the American surge. After he blew himself up to avoid capture in 2010, Abu Omar al-Baghdadi was replaced, as would-be caliph, by Abu Bakr al-Qurashi al-Husseini al-Baghdadi. He intervened in the civil war in Syria, thus claiming to advance the Islamic State of Iraq and Syria.

In part on the pattern of Lebanon from the 1970s, the crisis in Syria from 2011 saw conflict between the Assad regime and its rebel opponents as well as fighting between the latter, notably between ISIS and less radical rebels. However, in Syria, unlike Lebanon, there was a central government deploying a lot of force, albeit with far less success than it had done in 1979–82 when the Muslim Brotherhood in Syria was largely destroyed, notably with the seizure of the city of Hama in 1982 and the killing of maybe twenty thousand civilians there.

President Assad (the son of the president in power in 1979–82) deployed approximately three hundred thousand active military personnel in 2012, with his counterinsurgency operations using the weapons and methods of conventional warfare, as the Russians had done in Chechnya. The army made destructive use of artillery, shelling rebel-held areas, and killing and maiming large numbers of civilians. Aircraft, rockets, and tanks were also employed in urban fighting. The bombing of rebel-held areas, such as the cities of Aleppo and Homs, was highly indiscriminate. Barrel bombs, oil drums packed with explosives and shrapnel and dropped on residential areas from aircraft and helicopters, for example, on Douma near Damascus in 2015, proved particularly deadly but were probably counterproductive. Seeking to make life in rebel-held areas unbearable was taken further by blockades that prevented food supplies and by cutting off gas and water. At the same time, concern about its own military casualties ensured that the regime was reluctant to order attacks by ground forces unless near strategic routes.

The regime increasingly lost control of the domestic situation and found it difficult to control territory other than where its forces operated or where it had ethnic and sectarian backing. This led the army to give out rifles to Alawites, members of the same Muslim sect as Assad, who also received backing from Russia, Iran, and Iran's protégé, the Hezbollah ("party of Allah") movement in Lebanon, although coalition warfare, as usual, posed major problems. The belief that a military solution was possible was exemplified by the supply of weaponry and advisers. Thus, by the winter of 2013–14, the Russians were operating reconnaissance drones able to provide the Syrian army with accurate information on their opponents to help targeting. In 2015, there were reports of Russians first operating the latest Russian armored car, the BTR-82A, which includes sophisticated stabilization night vision and satellite navigation systems, and also delivering and piloting MiG-31M aircraft, and then a public commitment of airpower, including helicopter gunships, bombing, and the use of cruise missiles fired from warships in the Caspian Sea. This use of airpower led to the American-backed Syrian rebels pressing for antiaircraft missiles. They had already profited from the supply of American TOWs—tube-launched, optically tracked, wire-guided missiles—in order to destroy government tanks. The United States also supplied ammunition.

The war caused terrible disruption. By mid-2015, out of a prewar population of about twenty-two million, over two hundred thousand had died, about four million had fled abroad, and about eight million were refugees within Syria.

The war in Syria threatened to lead to border conflict with neighboring Turkey, which backed some of the insurgents, and notably after Syria shot down a Turkish reconnaissance plane in 2012. There was talk then of a safe zone for insurgents within Syria as well as of a no-fly zone in Syria designed to limit government air attacks. However, aside from the political commitment, the maintenance of such zones would have required a formidable effort by the Turkish air force. It would have been necessary to suppress Syrian air defenses, a major task, as well as to overcome Syrian airpower. Russian intervention in 2015 made such a zone impossible.

National and local conflicts converged with regional rivalries and international tensions, creating a dangerously unstable situation. In neighboring Iraq, the dislike and mistreatment of the Shi'a-dominated government for the Sunni minority ensured that the army was unable to resist ISIS when it advanced on Mosul in June 2014, benefiting from the experience of former Ba'athist officers and from the fanaticism of about twenty thousand (in 2014) foreign volunteers from a range of countries. The Sunni militias that could have aided resistance to ISIS were provided with no money by the Iraqi government.[3] In Mosul, ISIS seized money and masses of materiel, and its transition from an insurgency to a de facto state gathered pace. ISIS's violent prospectus had been outlined in "The Management of Savagery," an Arabic document added to a jihadist Internet forum in 2004. This called for the establishment of a sectarian caliphate that was to achieve its goals in part by the very public demonstration of violence and by the related use of terror. In these methods, ISIS drew on *jihadi* traditions but also the Ba'athist use of terror as a means of governance.[4] ISIS also proved proficient in exploiting the social media in order to communicate, influence, and recruit.

The crises in Iraq and Syria demonstrated the vitality and significance of insurgencies. In 2014–15, air attacks by a potent alliance of powers, including the United States, Britain, Canada, Denmark, France, Jordan, the Netherlands, Abu Dhabi, and Saudi Arabia, played a role in helping to limit ISIS advances, although the reliance on airpower posed major problems, as did the weaknesses inherent to coalition warfare. Moreover, COIN, both as doctrine and as pragmatism, both military and political, proved of limited relevance as ISIS moved straight into holding ground and open war. ISIS pressed on to capture the city of Ramadi, the capital of Anbar Province and a site of bitter struggle during the American occupation.

The crises in Iraq and Syria spread into Turkey, as Kurds blamed the government for failing to protect them from ISIS attacks. In 2015, the situation deteriorated with Turkish air attacks on Kurdish bases in northern Iraq, while in southeast Turkey, where many of Turkey's fifteen million Kurds live, the government responded with large-scale arrests, the declaration of "special security zones," and the killing of Kurdish activists. In turn, Kurdish militants sought to limit the mobility of the security forces by mining roads, digging ditches, and erecting barricades. The ready availability of weapons meant that the militants were armed with rocket-propelled grenades as well as automatic guns. By January 2016, the violence in southeast Turkey had displaced two hundred thousand people.

The complex international dimension was much to the fore in these interacting crises. Thus, Saudi Arabia and Qatar helped the rebels (but not, apparently, ISIS) against the Assad regime, while in 2015 there were tensions between Iran and Russia over their influence with the latter, which led to the unfounded suggestion that Russia might abandon Assad. The crisis in all three states was part of broader struggles for influence between Iran and Saudi Arabia (both states with disturbing religio-political agendas) and between Russia and the United States. American concern to get Turkish support against ISIS ensured that America did not back the Kurds.

As yet, the crisis does not centrally involve Israel. However, the general volatility contributed first to a struggle between Israel and Hamas in 2014 as Israel sought to end rocket attacks from Gaza, in effect a state-to-state conflict, and then to the upsurge in tension and violence on the West Bank in 2015, violence that led to talk of a new *intifada*. Far from this being a struggle solely between Palestinians and the Israeli security forces, there were major divisions among the former, while the Israelis also had to confront the violent anti-Palestinian actions of some of the Jewish settlers on the West Bank. Among both Palestinian extremists and their settler counterparts, there was a tendency to strike against civilians as they were not only more vulnerable but also central to the politics of intimidation.

UKRAINE

COIN proved of limited value when confronted with the success of separatist pro-Russian insurgents in eastern Ukraine in 2014–15. They benefited greatly from Russian assistance, which made it impossible for Ukraine to bring its conventional superiority to bear successfully. Russian missiles shot down Ukrainian aircraft transporting troops to beleaguered positions in eastern Ukraine, while Russia used drones to guide separatist artillery fire in eastern Ukraine. In addition, fearing a growing Ukrainian capability, Russian and separatist forces fired on all unknown drones, including those operated by the

OSCE monitoring the cease-fire. There were also suggestions of Russian ambitions farther west, including alleged plans in 2015 to spark rebellion and, in concert with Russian special forces, declare an independent "Bessarabian People's Republic," based in the city of Odessa.[5] By 2015, a stalemate had ensued with the "Donetsk People's Republic" (DPR) in control of part of eastern Ukraine. This stalemate was a significant outcome as it meant that Ukraine was neutered as a military power, while Russia had demonstrated that it could be a threat to the stability of other neighboring states. The hybrid nature of Russian war making, its ability to combine conventional with irregular forces and operations, which had proved particularly successful in Crimea in March 2014, remained a threat. From the Russian perspective, the overthrow of the democratically elected pro-Russian Viktor Yanukovych in February 2014 as a result of popular pressure constituted an illegal insurgency directed against Russia and sponsored by the United States and Germany. In 2015, there were reports that the DPR was seeking to develop a radioactive dirty bomb with the help of Russian nuclear scientists but also a sense that Russia was seeking to control the crisis in order to focus on Syria.

AFRICA

Conflict also developed in Libya in 2011. The rebellion by Islamist militia in the city of Benghazi in February, a traditional center of opposition to control from the capital, Tripoli, gathered momentum because Abdel Fatah Younis, the interior minister, who was sent to suppress it, instead decided to try to lead it, a key aspect of the divisions within the regime that helped weaken it. The insurgents made plentiful use of unarmored vehicles, both to transport themselves and to mount weapons, especially antiaircraft guns. By aiding speedy advances and retreats, these vehicles provided a mobility that helped explain rapid changes of fortune in the campaigning. The heavier, conventional units of the Libyan army were more deadly, but they were countered and then seriously damaged by NATO air attack. After the successful establishment of the no-fly zone and the halting of the advance, it became clear that a stalemate existed on the ground, with the rebels unable to make progress against the might of Gaddafi's army. The concern then was that Gaddafi would grow stronger while the rebels weakened, and so, under pressure from France and Britain, the target selection widened to target Gaddafi's army directly and thereby to facilitate regime change. The provision of NATO advisers and arms helped the insurgents to victory that year. In a final *coup de grace*, NATO air reconnaissance detected Gaddafi's attempted escape and halted it, giving the militia time to hunt him down.

In contrast, in 2013, NATO forces intervened in neighboring Mali to support the government, which had been threatened since 2012 by Islamist

Tuareg insurgents. They were rapidly pushed back into the Sahara Desert by Malian and allied West African forces backed by the French. As an instance of the more general extent to which struggles in one state could lead to conflict elsewhere, the insurgency in Mali owed something to the return home of men who had served Gaddafi, as well as to long-established separatist tendencies in northern Mali. At the same time, the increase in insurgent activity threatened the earlier success of counterinsurgency policies in Algeria.

The difficulties of dealing with *jihadist* insurrections were clearly seen in the struggles against Boko Haram in Nigeria and al-Shabaab in Somalia, both countries affected by desertification and population growth. The Nigerian army found it impossible to suppress the movement that instead spread into neighboring countries, notably Chad and Cameroon. There was a lack of air support for the army, both with the air attacks on Boko Haram by Nigeria, Chad, and Niger and with regard to Western support. For example, Britain deployed for long periods just a single Tornado aircraft to northern Nigeria to carry out reconnaissance across the area thought to be occupied by Boko Haram. Although the movement was driven back in 2015, it retained a deadly capacity. Boko Haram, which looked for inspiration to Iran, al-Qaeda, and the Taliban, provides a key instance of the extent to which Islamism is proving effective as an ideology of protest and radicalization. No other ideology is proving as effective in the Islamic world. In turn, these Islamic protest movements feed off opposition to brutal suppression. In 2015, Boko Haram increasingly used suicide bombers.[6]

In Somalia, the interventions of Ethiopia and later of AMISOM (the African Union Mission in Somalia) were successful in hitting al-Shabaab, as in 2006–9 and 2011–12, but found it impossible to end the serious threat the movement posed, let alone to end the conflict. The Ethiopians in particular, Christians with whom the Somalis have had centuries of strife, proved an unpopular presence. Attempts to build up Somali security forces against al-Shabaab have largely failed.

LATIN AMERICA

The nature of insurgency continued to vary greatly. In some countries, notably Mexico, the major problem was posed by violent drug-trafficking gangs such as the Sinaloa and Zeta Cartels. American drug demand has come close to destroying Mexico. Infiltration of the Mexican government by cartel-friendly interests has compromised its effectiveness in handling a large number of domestic concerns and has lowered the morale of the Mexican people. The scale of the problem was indicated by the possibly one hundred thousand dead in 2006–14 in the wars between drug gangs and between them and the police. In 2013, the army, navy, and federal police took over the port of Lázaro Cárdenas, the second biggest in Mexico, in order to challenge the power of one of the gangs, the Knights Templars, but the federal forces were not able to dictate the agenda nor control the dynamics of the situation. By 2015, the Zeta Cartel dominated much of Mexico, and the Sinaloa Cartel had been beaten back into the northwestern and coastal areas of the western mainland. In Latin America, there were also long-standing guerrilla forces, notably FARC in Colombia. In 2015, peace talks were again under way in the last case.

EAST AND SOUTH ASIA

Insurgency continued to play a role in a number of South and East Asian states. It was especially important, albeit preponderantly regional, in Myanmar, Thailand, India, Pakistan, and the Philippines, and far less important but also regional in China. At the same time, another source of insurrectionary pressure was provided by the military. This was seen in particular in Pakistan and Thailand. Thus, in Thailand, there were successful coups in 1932, 1951, 1957, 1976, 1977, 1991, and 2014 and attempted coups in 1949, 1951, 1981, and 1985. These were not separate to other aspects of the political process. Thus, in 2014, the army seized power after the constitutional court ordered the prime minister out of power. This was related to the tension between conservative protestors, strong in the capital, Bangkok, and the poorer, rural population of the north and northeast. Thus, the army acted after the demonstrating "Yellow Shorts" had failed to overthrow the prime minister. Her supporters, the "Red Shirts," were then intimidated by the military. Radio programs supporting the "Red Shirts" have been stopped, and the "twelve core values" enunciated by the coup leader are recited every day by schoolchildren in order to inculcate obedience. At the same time, Thailand continues to be challenged by its inability to engage politically with the separatist Muslim insurgency in the south. Instead, there is a reliance on force, including the use of torture, with a range of interests, from the professional army to volunteers hired on short contracts, benefiting from the continuation of the war.[7]

In India, the Naxalite insurrection continued, while violence elsewhere in India threatened to lead to protracted problems. Thus, in Gujarat Province in 2015, mobs of upper-caste Patels demanding government benefits, notably reserved jobs and college places, attacked police, and in response, the police and paramilitary opened fire. Described as an "uprising" as well as a riot, the crowds were numbered in the hundreds of thousands. The crisis saw both traditional counterinsurgency methods, notably a curfew and sending in five thousand paramilitaries as well as the army, and more novel ones, particularly the blocking of mobile phone communications in order to stop the coordination of rioting.[8] The Indian security services use considerable brutality in repressing Muslim separatist pressure in Kashmir, pressure that is attributed to a Pakistani influence that is in fact only partly responsible. In 2010, for example, protesting youth were killed and imprisoned. India suffers from a lack of cohesion in counterinsurgency operations, with a range of competing agencies generally failing to get to grips with the problem and being far too dependent on the army.[9]

In neighboring Myanmar, long-standing regional-ethnic separatist movements that had started with the Karens in 1949 continued despite periodic peace talks, notably a cease-fire in 2015 with eight of these ethnic armies. The cease-fire was rejected by seven others, and the government accused neighboring China of interfering with the talks in order to wreck any deal.

INTERNAL ORDER

The use in many countries of the military as the internal arm of the state helped ensure that there was a military dimension to policing. This was seen not only in the "Third World" but also, for example, in Europe. Thus, terrorist attacks in Paris in early 2015 ensured that the largest single deployment of French troops that year was in French cities. In part, that reflected the rising threat posed by terrorists, in terms of not only the frequency of attacks but also their sophistication. Thus, in 2015, the French army made contingency plans to win back control of hostile neighborhoods, a reflection in part of the readiness with which automatic rifles and antitank missiles were obtainable in France and that, as a result, the police were outgunned: "There are a lot of alienated fourth-generation immigrant kids in the suburbs and the prospect of radicalisation is increasingly likely. The idea that attacks like the one on the train are carried out by individuals on their own is not credible. We're dealing with highly-organised networks of militant Islamists embarked on a campaign of violence and determined to intensify it."[10]

This use of troops underlines the extent to which, across the world, the significance of the military in part rests on it being a body of trained and disciplined men (and, increasingly, women) accustomed to taking orders and available to fulfill governmental instructions. Moreover, these forces are increasingly prepared for COIN, as in the United States, where the Humvee was replaced by the better-protected and more mobile Joint Light Tactical Vehicle. However, as before, costs are a limiting factor in maintaining COIN arsenals and training that may well not be used or be relevant to new operations, for example, with the use by Britain of Land Rovers designed for Northern Ireland in Afghanistan, where they proved too vulnerable.

In France, the emphasis now is on the army, not on the police, as had been the case with the attempt to control dissent during the Algerian War. At the same time, in many countries, this very presence of the military can become a key element in politics and can encourage a reaction, violent or otherwise, that is seen as an insurrection. The definitions of both insurgencies and counterinsurgencies remain contested, and these contests are frequently highly politicized. In particular, there is significant controversy over how best to treat terrorism. In many respects, it is a form of insurgency. There are clear differences between terrorism with a national focus and that which is more clearly transnational. Pakistani-based Lashkar-e-Toiba attacks on India are a clear example, with terrorist assaults, such as those at Delhi (2000 and 2001) and Mumbai (2008), linked to the struggle to drive the Indians from Kashmir. [11]

CONCLUSIONS

The situation in the mid-2010s provides an opportunity to reconsider some of the political, military, and academic discussion of the 2000s, notably so because of the continuation of crisis in Iraq and Afghanistan, albeit with a very different context in the former case. In 2008, *Operations*, the American army's Field Manual 3-0, was released. It took forward the perspective of Robert Gates, who had become secretary of defense in 2006, succeeding Donald Rumsfeld. Gates argued, notably at the 2007 conference of the Association of the United States Army, that the army had failed, with dire consequences, to focus sufficiently on unconventional warfare after the Vietnam War. As a result, 3-0 made postconflict stability operations equal with established conventional priorities, a decision that led to criticism from those concerned to maintain conventional capability. [12] More specifically, it was argued that a belief in COIN served to support an American interventionism that underplayed the difficulties of transforming foreign societies and, more specifically, of winning Muslim hearts and minds at gunpoint and creating viable nation-states on the Western model. [13]

There are signs that doctrinal, training, and procurements changes in the 2000s did indeed increase the tactical and operational effectiveness of American, British, and other forces in counterinsurgency conflict in the 2010s, notably so in Afghanistan. However, in terms of strategic success, the situation was far less positive. Moreover, the consequences of the costs of commitments [14] were not only financial but also serious in terms of domestic and international politics. These costs rose due to the revival of great-power rivalry from the 2000s and the crisis in the world economy and fiscal system from the late 2000s.

The model of failure has led to different lessons to those offered in the aftermath of the successful Iraq "surge." Now, failure in Iraq appears a prelude to that in Afghanistan. Moreover, there is skepticism about the long-term viability of agencies that might work in the short term, such as the "Afghan Local Police," agencies that were established on the basis of the success of such units in Iraq in the late 2000s. As in Iraq, it is also clear that counterinsurgency does not determine, still less dictate, the pattern of local developments but instead becomes an aspect of them, one that provides opportunities for power brokers as another product of government activity and sphere for negotiation and conflict. Counterinsurgency activity compounds enmity and accentuates mistrust, providing a new dynamic that both the brokers and the COIN forces have to engage with. Working with, not against, the brokers and bringing them over is a key goal and means,[15] but one that depends on a degree of deterrent presence that, at least in Afghanistan and Iraq, can no longer be sustained.

Chapter Thirteen

Speculations about the Future

The likely military and political contexts of future insurgencies and counter-insurgencies are by their nature unclear. In large part, the likely answer reflects not just a reading of the present situation but also, more profoundly, assumptions concerning how societies operate and will operate. Most obviously, competition for resources thus appears a more valid explanation for Western commentators concerned to adopt a materialist explanation, one related to sociological, anthropological, and psychological considerations. This competition will be related to population trends and changing assumptions about the distribution of goods.

Conversely, ideological factors, notably those linked to religion or nationalism or to a mixture of both may seem more reasonable to commentators in particular cultural spheres or assessing such spheres.[1] These spheres are not identical to geographical regions but have a connection with them. For example, nationalism appears more pertinent than religion if considering the situation in East Asia, notably the antagonism between China and Japan. Conversely, the role of religious animosity in ethnic strife is apparent in Thailand, Myanmar, Sri Lanka, and western China. Religious animosity is also strong in the Sahel belt of Africa, where Islam has long been characterized by violent expansionism, not least the exploitation and racism linked to the large-scale enslavement of non-Muslims, as in Sudan and Mauritania. *Jihadis* have long existed in the area of northern Nigeria, where the Boko Haram insurgency became very powerful in the 2010s, and were especially important there in the early nineteenth century. Indeed, the concept of a cyclical pattern to insurgencies appears especially pertinent in these areas.[2] Such a pattern raises the need to distinguish between structural causes and precipitants when discussing insurgencies, and it also raises issues for the analysis of counterinsurgencies.

Religious animosity is also a key element in Southwest and South Asia. It readily links to other factors and helps encourage a sense of clear divisions between sides. This sense is important to crossing the "killing ground" both to the identification and killing of others—insurgency by massacre—and to insurgency against the state. At the same time, religious strife and ethnicity are manipulated by political leaders, in Africa and elsewhere. The conflicts in the former Yugoslavia in the 1990s amply demonstrated this.[3] Universal military service can be a problem as it provides a pool of military-trained civilians as well as local weapons depots whose contents could be pilfered.

Insurgencies will continue to reflect a sense of difference within states, and that sense will go on arising from the range of identities and interests that can be seen and presented in terms of hostility. From a materialist perspective, related issues will affect the significance of "belief-based groups,"[4] and the most likely precipitant of animosity will be the consequences of the unprecedented population increase taking place across much of the world. This increase will create "pinch points" in terms of resources, notably land, water, food, fuel, and government jobs. This pressure exists irrespective of the contentious questions of the extent, speed, causes, and consequences of climate change. In particular, whatever the situation with these criteria, the more urgent pressure stems from the massive rise in the global population, a rise that has not been countered by increases in disease nor, so far, by Malthusian factors focused on famine. The world's population reached one billion in about 1804, two in 1927, three in 1960, four in 1974, five in 1987, six in 1999, and seven in 2012, and it is currently regarded as likely to rise to at least nine and probably well over ten by 2100. This situation has major implications, not least when combined with gender imbalances leading to a relative shortage of young women. Earlier optimism that rising prosperity will lead to a decline in fertility has been called into question.[5] In particular, there is a huge potential for conflict over water, both within and between states. Water is a grave problem in a large number of states, including, most acutely, Yemen, where the government was overthrown in an insurgency in 2015. These and other pressures will interact with a perception of challenge from others within the community. An international dimension is readily present, not least due to large-scale migration.[6]

The "pinch points" will be particularly acute in cities. The percentage of the world's rising population who live in cities will continue to increase. Although individual predictions vary, the trend is clear. The United Nations suggests that, while more than half of the world's population of seven billion lived in cities in 2012, by 2030 the number will be more than five billion. There are also projections that three quarters of the global population by 2050 will be living in cities, with most of the increase occurring in Asia and Africa. Indeed, in 2015, about 56 percent of the thousand largest urban areas were in Asia, as well as the eight most populous urban agglomerations. Cities therefore serve to highlight the issue of managing unprecedented growth, not least because of concerns about the social and political consequences of unsuccessful expansion. It is scarcely surprising that dystopias are now very much seen in terms of urban chaos and an unmanaged cityscape—a theme that links imaginative works, such as the vision of Gotham City (New York) in the *Batman* films and of the city in *Blade Runner* (1982), to more grounded studies. Indeed, it is in urban locations that change affects human drama with the most intensity and pungency.

The net effect will be a geography of insurgency in which urban areas are its key locations,[7] as in the Kurdish part of Turkey in the winter of 2015–16. Thus, in Pakistan it will be Karachi, not the mountainous fringe in Waziristan, that is the central area of risk, in Brazil Sao Paolo, not Amazonia, in India the big cities, not Orissa, and in China the same, and not ethnic areas, notably Xinkiang and Tibet. The focus will be on urban activism and warfare and on the related problems of counterinsurgency. This is notable in the United States, where police forces have become militarized, with all sorts of body armor, armored vests, helmets, army rifles, armored vehicles, and special optical equipment (including night-fighting sights). Police trade shows display this equipment lavishly, and federal subventions exist to help purchase it.

Among the dynamic elements in the future on the global scale will be the relationship between insurgencies and criminal networks, each of whom benefit from the other. In addition, the pressures arising from resource issues will interact with those from groups rejecting the very logic and processes of the global economy and its consequences. These groups are able to encourage and benefit from social unrest.[8]

Tension and violence do not necessarily lead to insurgent activity, let alone a full-blown insurgency. Many states with a high population growth rate, for example, Senegal and Zambia, do not suffer from civil war or from proactive factors of control designed to prevent the possibility of insurgency, in other words, the deterrent aspects of counterinsurgency. However, it is likely that violence between groups within a state will frequently involve a defiance of the authority of the latter and thus constitute an insurgency. This is particularly so as most states seek to monopolize violence. In opposition to this attempt, the cheapness and ready availability of lethal weapons is a key element. The relationship seen from 1990 to 2007—of about 220,000 people killed in interstate wars, compared to over 3.6 million dying as a result of conflict within states—is likely to continue. It certainly has in the period 2008 to 2015. In considering this and other issues, there are problems with definitions and measurements. For example, how far should the violence in Iraq from 2004 onward be classified as an aspect of the 2003 war? How many people in Congo or Sudan would have died of disease and malnutrition whether or not there had been war? Nevertheless, the trend in casualties between different types of war is apparently clear.

To add to the complexity, there is the question whether insurgencies, with their emphasis on force, will necessarily be violent, an approach that in an extreme form leads to the index entry in a recent major American work: "insurgency. *See* terrorism."[9] In an important study of the American civil rights movement, Mark Grimsley argues that it was an insurgency, claiming, in doing so, that the lens of the Maoist doctrine of revolutionary war and its resulting emphasis on violence was unhelpful. Instead, the struggles for control of the population and of the grand narrative of the issue are presented by Grimsley as crucial to what he describes as a complex, divided, and often sophisticated insurgency.[10] What this argument means for the future is unclear, but it underlines the need for caution in adopting particular paradigms and analyses.

A focus on insurgency and counterinsurgency warfare can lead to a lack of attention to the prospect that future warfare may involve confrontation or conflict between regular forces. Indeed, most military investment is for just such a capability, and notably so in East and Southeast Asia. Moreover, much discussion and planning is for this type of conflict, particularly between the United States and China. The variety of modern challenges and warfare and the range of future prospects underline the extent to which the nature of developments is unclear. It was striking how rapidly new states created armies, for example, in the former Yugoslavia in the 1990s, and this was an aspect of the rapid changes produced by the unraveling of the Cold War order and the reduction of its militaries.[11]

Whatever their frequency, the technological basis is not static for insurgencies or counterinsurgency. Thus, in Afghanistan, the antiaircraft missiles and rocket-propelled grenades that proved effective against Soviet forces in the 1980s were succeeded in the 2000s by improvised explosive devices (IEDs) or roadside bombs. In response, new combat vehicles, such as the American Mine Resistant Ambush Protected vehicle, were built with *V*-shaped hulls specifically designed to project outward the kinetic energy of an exploding bomb. The Americans also came to use more body armor. However, the insurgents in Afghanistan responded with more powerful bombs. This process was one encouraged by the ready diffusion of new techniques from conventional warfare, by the arms trade, and by the money available to support insurgencies, in part due to the overlap with criminal activity, including extortion and drug-smuggling. From a different perspective, such activity reflects a grab for sovereignty, especially in terms of tax-raising powers and control over trade.

Technological possibilities are fast changing, as with ISIS in Iraq in 2015 seeking to interfere with the GPSs of the opposing coalition. A worrying change for the future is the proliferation, certainly in the West, of increasingly sophisticated short-range reconnaissance (toy) drones available relatively cheaply on the open market. Their potential, operating in large numbers at up to a few thousand feet and within a radius of a few miles, has yet to be fully exploited by malcontents, terrorists, or full-fledged insurgent movements.

With insurgency and counterinsurgency warfare, technology is a variable rather than a cause. It is dramatic in its impact, notably as in the terrorist attacks on the United States in 2001, for an age in which visual images of destruction are particularly potent, not least on the imagination, and thereby in part also represent a form of "soft power." However, the technological dimension is less crucial than the drives to rebel and control and the drive toward violence that help explain the strategic dimension. Here, rather than assuming that the prime discontinuity is between present and future, with the need, therefore, to explain changes into the future, it is more pertinent to consider change and continuity in terms of a chronological and conceptual range in which both present and future are incorporated.

An important point of departure is that of the situation of strong states, in the sense of states able to suppress violent opposition and the extent to which their position has changed across time. In the past, empires (strong states) played a major role in repressing or limiting local tribal conflicts, regional opposition, and piracy. Turning to the future, it is unclear whether larger powers will tolerate chaos if they have the will and means to stop it by imposing their power, including in effect their imperial power, the emphasis in part being on "if." General Stanley McChrystal, the American former head of the NATO forces in Afghanistan, observed in 2014, "As time passes, political will becomes your biggest, most important resource."[12] The era of European powers (excluding Russia) has passed, while, in large part in reaction against the commitments in Iraq and Afghanistan, American experiments in imperial governance are in momentary eclipse. However, this situation does not mean that the idea of empire is being abandoned. While the West lacks the will, Russia has it, while China's involvement in foreign states has become more marked, notably in Africa.

Aside from power projection abroad, there is the question of whether large states have the will and the means to repress domestic opposition and, if so, how far the nature of effectiveness and the parameters of control have changed. The ability of large numbers of asylum seekers to enter Europe in the mid-2010s and to ignore governmental attempts at control indicated the potential weakness of the state faced by the breakdown of its warning processes. Indeed, that was a point that emerged most clearly in the politics of the 2010s. Insurgency movements did not necessarily achieve their goals, but the weaknesses of government emerged frequently, whether in the overthrow of the Mubarak regime in Egypt during the "Arab Spring" in 2011 or in the inability of Ukraine to prevent or overawe Russian-backed separatists in Crimea and eastern Ukraine in 2014–16.

A major contrast, hitherto, is posed by China. There is persistent internal discontent, particularly from Muslim separatists in Xinkiang and also in Tibet, and also frequent riots against actions seen as corrupt, especially clearing peasants from the land in order to make way for development. Nevertheless, this action has not cohered into any significant movement, despite widespread social disruption as a consequence of a high level of economic change as well as limited social welfare. The situation in China invites attention to the role of ideology, the monopolization of political and governmental power, and a strong system of surveillance in being able to prevent potential insurrectionary movements. Moreover, riots and other disturbances can be seen as an integral, albeit disruptive, part of the political system rather than as a cause or means of its overthrow. The same point can be made in other countries and, yet again, direct attention to the context and politics of situation rather than to the forms of action. The extent to which China will operate more generally as a model is unclear. It is likely to have limited relevance as a model for Europe, but far more so for non-Western societies. The closest term to COIN is "internal war," which exemplifies the Chinese approach to COIN. In the Chinese experience, COIN is largely seen as an internal problem, one distinct from the Western model of expeditionary wars and interventions.

In considering both the present and the future, an intellectual problem is posed by the lack of agreement over the nature of developments in the past, a lack that helps explain the significance of historical studies of the subject. In particular, what is meant by "premodern" revolt is contentious, and this point affects the consideration of the changes in, and from, the French Revolution of 1789. The growing gap between rulers and ruled and the enhanced imbalance in power emerges as a key element in the past, but so also do social changes below the elite level.[13] The extent to which these can be read into the future is unclear and, notably, the degree to which the relationship between government and others is crucial or, rather, tensions within the latter. Ethnicity comes into the issue of rifts within the bulk of the population, as with the Tamil role in Sri Lanka.[14]

As another point looking to the future, the extent to which the "laws of war," or whatever is meant by war's norms, and indeed the regulation of civil-military relations can keep pace with changes in the use of force and the need to use force is unclear.[15] This point is related not only to the extent of hybrid warfare and of "grey" operations that blend both regular and irregular warfare but also to the treatment of insurgencies and of counterinsurgent action as well as their definition.

Chapter Fourteen

Conclusions

I congratulate you on the interesting news from Naples. It secures the efforts of
Spain and Portugal, and must cheer the mind of every man of Philanthropy
with the prospect it holds up of the extension of representative government to
the whole continent of Europe except Russia which too in the end will become
capable of it. In what a glorious station does it place us at the head of the world
in a revolution from the despotism under which they have been held through
all times, or a maniac licentiousness, to a state of well regulated liberty of
which we have furnished the example.

—Thomas Jefferson, 1821[1]

A focus on insurgency conflict means a concentration on civil warfare as a
key element in warfare and politics rather than a concern primarily with wars
between states. That approach to insurgency conflict, however, makes the
boundary of the state the central element in defining insurgencies, which is
an approach that may well be misleading. There is an argument, instead, that
insurgencies can in practice be broader ranging and/or arise in accordance
with an agenda that does not correspond to state authority and boundaries.
Concepts of broader-ranging insurgencies, and ones with just such a conception, include religious revivals, class conflict, decolonization, and revolutionary movements. Each, indeed, can aspire to a great scale, but frequently they
take on weight in accordance with more particular local configurations and
conjunctures. This was true, for example, of the religious warfare of the
sixteenth and seventeenth centuries and the Cold War of the twentieth. It was
also the case with insurgencies against colonial rule and, more recently, of
aspects of Sunni-Shi'a rivalry, Islamic fundamentalism, al-Qaeda, and the
"war on terror."[2] So also with counterinsurgency warfare, not only thanks to
alliances but also because of the question at present of how long states will
remain states or, at least, truly independent. Thus, interstate cooperation,

alliances, unions, and international bodies run alongside cross-border insurgencies.

It is readily possible, therefore, to turn to an account of the subject that involves a consideration of individual conflicts followed by an attempt to develop a typology of insurgency and counterinsurgency warfare. Such an approach is valuable, and more so if not accompanied by "how-best-to" commentary. The latter approach unfortunately suffers from ahistoricism in that circumstances are generally highly specific and there are also major changes in context. As key instances of the latter point, the means of interventionism alter. So also does the way in which causing civilian casualties is widely viewed. The focus on circumstances also explains why insurgent groups change in structure and method. Alongside factors for cohesion, notably the interaction of leadership, vanguard groups, and ideology, there are others for fragmentation. These include elements inherent to the particular group, the consequences of alliances (both local and international), and the impact of counterinsurgency operations. [3]

It is necessary also to address the issue of the broader context and notably in terms of the very idea of rejecting authority and contesting power. This idea, however, is not a constant but instead a variable one. It is an idea that is affected by local circumstances, which helps explain motivation and other aspects of the context of conflicts. Yet, at the same time, links and parallels between insurgencies and, in addition, between counterinsurgency struggles, whether these links are planned, unintended, or by inspiration, are all of significance. Moreover, this element has attracted greater attention in recent decades.

So also with a related change. The central narrative of military doctrine and military history that has been dominant for so long has focused on "high-tempo" symmetrical warfare ending in victory and defeat. Alongside the continued threat in military history, doctrine, and preparedness of such conflict, emerges, however, those of "little wars" and also of insurgencies, counterinsurgencies, and civil control. As the Dutch Revolt against Philip II and the American, French, Russian, and Chinese Revolutions all demonstrated, these conflicts could be of great significance for the history of individual states, as also for that of the world as a whole, and it is understandable that they have, both individually and collectively, been given a major analytical as well as narrative significance.

Nevertheless, these struggles did not set the paradigm for all insurgencies. In particular, the assumption that "people's warfare" is bound to prevail is of limited validity. Examples of post-1945 insurrections failing include those in Greece, the Philippines, Malaya, Kenya, Bolivia, Nicaragua, El Salvador, Colombia, Sri Lanka, and Algeria (in the 1990s). Moreover, many insurgencies were often not won or lost but instead ended in stalemate, although the reality and understanding of what that entailed were far from fixed. The assessment was very much part of the politics of the situation.

The course of both insurgency and counterinsurgency war reflect, along-side failures to do so, a capacity to learn from examples. This has classically attracted attention as legacies of insurgency warfare have been traced, for example, by Thomas Jefferson, as quoted at the start of the chapter, from the American Revolution, or from the IRA in Ireland in 1919–21 to later oppo-nents of British imperialism, or from the French to the Russian Revolution, from Mao Zedong to the Viet Minh and then to anti-imperial struggles, or from the Muslim Brotherhood to the "Arab Spring." Inspiration, example, and direct support have all proved very significant. C. L. R. James's book on the Haitian Revolution, *The Black Jacobins: Toussaint L'Ouverture and the San Domingo Revolution* (1938), was deliberately written in order to provide inspiration for a new generation of revolutionaries in Africa and the Ameri-cas. Concepts, ideas, and dictums were, and are, borrowed and reworked, with Mao, for example, influencing al-Qaeda doctrine.[4] Dzhokhar Dudayev, who led the Chechnyan opposition to Russia in the 1990s until his death in 1996, had been impressed, while serving with the Soviet air force in Afghan-istan in the 1980s, by the nationalism and guerrilla tactics of the Afghans.

There was a tendency not to devote the same attention to counterinsur-gency warfare. In part, that tendency reflects the extent to which such war-fare is usually carried out by national armies that prefer to look to their own traditions rather than those of other powers. There have been exceptions, for example, the American scrutiny during the Vietnam War of the British expe-rience in Malaya the previous decade. More commonly, however, it is valu-able to have continual experience within a national tradition, as the British did in counterinsurgency warfare after 1945, although of late, the ability of the British to plan and conduct such warfare successfully has been queried. In part, this reflects the examples of unsuccessful British counterinsurgency operations in Iraq and Afghanistan and, in part, a reassessment of the military course and political context of conflicts between 1945 and 2000, notably, but not only, those involving Britain.

As is so often the case in insurgency and counterinsurgency warfare, the process of learning is not new and can be seen in very different political and technological contexts. For example, in the Java War of 1825–30, the Dutch were initially thwarted by the mobility and the guerrilla tactics of their native opponents. In response, they developed a network of fortified bases from which they sent out mobile columns that policed the local population, pre-vented the consolidation of rebel positions, and attacked the rebels. Short of troops, the Dutch benefited from local allies. In a very different context, the French, having initially faced serious difficulties, adopted similar methods in Algeria in the 1840s, again with success. Such processes of learning during an individual conflict could characterize both sides in the insurgency/

counterinsurgency relationship, as in that between the Viet Minh and French in Vietnam in 1946–54. Moreover, there was a need to respond to initiatives and improvements on the part of opponents. This action-reaction sequence was important and sits beside the tendency to focus on the history and influence of particular legacies, both for insurgency and for counterinsurgency warfare.

At the same time, this account of learning and responding suggests a rational process of maximizing effectiveness rather than that of creating a politicized analysis of war. The latter, however, is particularly apparent with this type of warfare and can be seen with both military and political commentators.[5] This is especially, but not only, the case when the conflict in question is within the state rather than in overseas territories or otherwise abroad. It is understandable that a politicized analysis is developed for what is often very much politics by another means, indeed sometimes by a well-established one. However, this analysis is usually a central part of the very politics of the situation and needs to be considered in this light. So also does the degree to which the military itself is commonly a political sphere, agency, and means, whatever its ethos, whether apolitical or not.

The key politicized analysis is that which focused on insurgency warfare, and notably as refreshed and reconceptualized by and on behalf of Mao Zedong. His emphasis on guerrilla warfare took further the hostility to any focus on technology seen in early Communist ideas and their linked stress on the value of the revolutionary mass. This approach remained central to Chinese Communist military thought until the 1990s, even though under Mao, there was in practice a commitment to new weaponry, certainly in the form of jet aircraft and atomic warheads. Mao's ideas did not bring victory over the American-led United Nations forces in the Korean War (1950–53), but an emphasis on will, mass, and the negating of the technological advantages of the other side all proved significant across the world in the repeated anti-Western insurgency struggles that began in the late 1940s.

Although success or failure for insurgencies proved far more complex, in their causes and contexts, both militarily and politically, than suggested by Mao's dictums, the problems, tactical, operational, and strategic, of counterinsurgency warfare were also prominent.[6] The continuing significance of insurgency and counterinsurgency warfare, both in themselves and due to their wider ramifications, ensure that they require study, and without political blinkers, national prejudices, or conceptual and historiographical confusion.

Notes

PREFACE

1. David Fitzgerald, *Learning to Forget: US Army Counterinsurgency Doctrine and Practice from Vietnam to Iraq* (Stanford, Calif.: Stanford University Press, 2013).

2. Ian Beckett, *Modern Insurgencies and Counter-Insurgencies: Guerrillas and Their Opponents since 1750* (New York: Routledge, 2001), vii.

3. J. B. Sykes, ed., *The Concise Oxford Dictionary*, 6th ed. (Oxford: Oxford University Press, 1976), s.v. "insurgency."

1. INTRODUCTION

1. John Nagl, *Knife Fights: A Memoir of Modern War in Theory and Practice* (New York: Penguin, 2014); David French, *The British Way in Counter-Insurgency, 1945-1967* (Oxford: Oxford University Press, 2011).

2. Rupert Smith, *The Utility of Force: The Art of War in the Modern World* (London: Allen Lane, 2005), 19–20.

3. Samuel P. Huntington, "The Clash of Civilisations?," *Foreign Affairs* 72 (1993): 21–49.

4. Lorraine White, "Strategic Geography and the Spanish Habsburg Monarchy's Failure to Recover Portugal, 1640–1668," *Journal of Military History* 71 (2007): 399.

5. Michel van Groesen, ed., *The Legacy of Dutch Brazil* (New York: Cambridge University Press, 2014); Hendrik Kray, "Arming Slaves in Brazil from the Seventeenth Century to the Nineteenth Century," in *Arming Slaves: From Classical Times to the Modern Age*, ed. Christopher Brown and Philip Morgan (New Haven, Conn.: Yale University Press, 2006), 146–79; A. J. R. Russell-Wood, *Slavery and Freedom in Colonial Brazil* (London: Oneworld, 2002).

6. Jerome Greene, *American Carnage: Wounded Knee, 1890* (Norman: University of Oklahoma Press, 2014).

7. Christopher Clapham, ed., *African Guerrillas* (Bloomington: Indiana University Press, 1998).

8. Michael Broers, *Napoleon's Other War: Bandits, Rebels and Their Pursuers in the Age of Revolutions* (Witney, U.K.: Peter Lang, 2010). Among the many pieces dealing with issues of definition, General Sir Michael Rose, "Meaning of War," in *What Is War? An Investigation in the Wake of 9/11*, ed. Mary Ellen O'Connell (Leiden: Brill, 2012), 167–76 and Beatrice

Heuser, "Introduction: Exploring the Jungle of Terminology," *Small Wars and Insurgencies* 25 (2014): 741–53.

9. Susan Mattern, "Counterinsurgency and the Enemies of Rome," in *Makers of Ancient Strategy: From the Persian Wars to the Fall of Rome*, ed. Victor D. Hanson (Princeton, N.J.: Princeton University Press, 2010), 178.

10. Philip Blood, *Hitler's Bandit Hunters: The SS and the Nazi Occupation of Europe* (Dulles, Va.: Potomac, 2006).

11. For the Ottoman Empire, *International Journal of Turkish Studies* 8, nos. 1 and 2 (2002).

12. George Lepre, *Fragging: Why U.S. Soldiers Assaulted Their Officers in Vietnam* (Lubbock: Texas Tech University Press, 2011).

13. David Starkey, ed., *Pirates and Privateers: New Perspectives on the War on Trade in the Eighteenth and Nineteenth Centuries* (Exeter, U.K.: University of Exeter Press, 1997); Tonio Andrade, "The Company's Chinese Pirates: How the Dutch East India Company Tried to Lead a Coalition of Pirates to War against China, 1621–1662," *Journal of World History* 15 (2004): 415–44; Martin Murphy, *Small Boats, Weak States, Dirty Money: Piracy and Maritime Terrorism in the Modern World* (London: Hurst, 2009).

14. Thomas Schelling, *Choice and Consequence* (Cambridge, Mass.: Harvard University Press, 1984); Edward Luttwak, *The Virtual American Empire: War, Faith, and Power* (New Brunswick, N.J.: Transaction, 2009); Ioan Grillo, *Gangster Warlords: Drug Dollars, Killing Fields, and the New Politics of Latin America* (London: Bloomsbury, 2016).

15. Hilary Beckles and K. Watson, "Social Protest and Labor Bargaining: The Changing Nature of Slaves' Responses to Plantation Life in Eighteenth-Century Barbados," *Slavery and Abolition* 8 (1987): 272–93, esp. 275; Hilton Root, *Peasants and King in Burgundy: Agrarian Foundations of French Absolutism* (Berkeley: University of California Press, 1987); William H. te Brake, *Shaping History: Ordinary People in European Politics, 1500–1700* (Berkeley: University of California Press, 1998).

16. George Satterfield, *Princes, Posts and Partisans: The Army of Louis XIV and Partisan Warfare in the Netherlands, 1673–1678* (Leiden: Brill, 2003).

17. Rod Thornton, *Asymmetric Warfare: Threat and Response in the 21st Century* (Cambridge: Polity, 2007).

18. Mary Ellen O'Connell, ed., *What Is War? An Investigation in the Wake of 9/11* (Leiden: Martinus Nijhoff, 2012).

19. Maule to Andrew Fletcher, March 4, 1746, Edinburgh, National Library of Scotland, MS 16630, fol. 66.

20. Jeremy Black, *Culloden and the '45* (Stroud, U.K.: Alan Sutton, 1990), 178.

2. INSURGENCY TO 1500

1. Norman Housley, "Ideology, Careerism and Civic Consciousness: The Crusade against Basel, 1482–1485," *English Historical Review* 130 (2015): 1396–97.

2. Stephen Dyson, "Native Revolts in the Roman Empire," *Historia* 20 (1971): 239–74; Martin Goodman, *The Ruling Class of Judaea: The Origins of the Jewish Revolt against Rome, A.D. 66–70* (Cambridge: Cambridge University Press, 1987).

3. Keith Bradley, *Slavery and Rebellion in the Roman World, 140 BC–70 BC* (Bloomington: Indiana University Press, 1989); Brent Shaw, *Spartacus and the Slave Wars* (Boston: Bedford, 2001); Theresa Urbainczyk, *Slave Revolts in Antiquity* (Stocksfield, U.K.: Acumen, 2008); Barry Strauss, "Slave Wars of Greece and Rome," in *Makers of Ancient Strategy*, ed. Victor D. Hanson (Princeton, N.J.: Princeton University Press, 2010), 185–205.

4. Michael Penman, *Robert the Bruce: King of the Scots* (New Haven, Conn.: Yale University Press, 2014).

5. Spencer Dimmock, *The Origin of Capitalism in England, 1400–1600* (Leiden: Brill, 2014).

6. Armen Ayvasyan, *The Armenian Military in the Byzantine Empire: Conflict and Alliance under Justinian and Maurice* (Glendale, Calif.: Editions Sigest, 2012).

7. Edward Dreyer, *Early Ming China: A Political History, 1355–1435* (Palo Alto, Calif.: Stanford University Press, 1982).

8. Owen Latimore, "Social History of Mongol Nomadism," in *Historians of China and Japan*, ed. William G. Beasley and Edwin G. Pulleyblank (London: Oxford University Press, 1961), 328–43; Gérard Chaliand, *Nomadic Empires: From Mongolia to the Danube* (Piscataway, N.B.: Transaction, 2004).

9. Hans van de Ven, "Introduction," in *Warfare in Chinese History*, ed. Hans van de Ven (Leiden: Brill, 2000): 9–10.

10. Jaroslaw Pelenski, *Russia and Kazan: Conquest and Imperial Ideology, 1438–1560s* (The Hague: Brill, 1974).

3. CONTESTING RELIGION AND POWER, 1500–1700

1. For India, Johannes C. Heesterman, "Warrior, Peasant and Brahmin," *Modern Asian Studies* 29 (1995): 637–54.

2. Kenneth Swope, *The Military Collapse of China's Ming Dynasty, 1618–44* (New York: Routledge, 2014).

3. The society was established by Pope Paul III in 1540.

4. A. C. Hess, "The Moriscos: An Ottoman Fifth Column in Sixteenth-Century Spain," *American Historical Review* 74 (1968): 1–25; Marya Green-Mercado, "The Mahdi in Valencia: Messianism, Apocalypticism and Morisco Rebellions in Late Sixteenth-Century Spain," *Medieval Encounters* 19 (2013): 193–220.

5. Charles Tilly, *Coercion, Capital and European States, AD 990–1990* (Oxford: Oxford University Press, 1990).

6. Paul Avrich, *Russian Rebels, 1600–1800* (New York, Schocken, 1972).

7. Michael Khdarkovsky, "The Stepan Razin Uprising: Was It a 'Peasant War'?," *Jahrbücher für Geschichte osteuropas* 42 (1994): 1–19.

8. Chester S. L. Dunning, *Russia's First Civil War and the Founding of the Romanov Dynasty* (University Park: University of Pennsylvania Press, 2001).

9. A. V. Berkis, *The Reign of Duke James in Courland, 1638–1682* (Lincoln: University of Nebraska Press, 1960), 140–41.

10. Guy Rowlands, "Louis XIV, Vittorio Amedeo II and French Military Failure in Italy, 1689–96," *English Historical Review* 115 (2000): 543.

11. Tim Harris, *Rebellion: Britain's First Stuart Kings* (Oxford: Oxford University Press, 2014).

12. Roger Manning, "Styles of Command in Seventeenth-Century English Armies," *Journal of Military History* 71 (2007): 671–99.

13. Ian Gentles, *The New Model Army in England, Ireland and Scotland, 1645–1653* (Oxford: Oxford University Press, 1992).

14. Henry Reece, *The Army in Cromwellian England 1649–1660* (Oxford: Oxford University Press, 2013).

15. Noel Malcolm, *Agents of Empire: Knights, Corsairs, Jesuits and Spies in the Sixteenth-Century Mediterranean World* (London: Allen Lane, 2015), 428.

16. Jack Goldstone, *Revolution and Rebellion in the Early Modern World* (Berkeley: University of California Press, 1991).

17. Karen Barkey, *Bandits and Bureaucrats: The Ottoman Route to State Centralization* (Ithaca, N.Y.: Cornell University Press, 1994).

18. Bampfylde to John, 4th Duke of Bedford, the overall commander of the Devon militia, August 10, 1759, Exeter, Devon Record Office, L1258, M/Militia/3.

19. Valerie Kivelson, *Desperate Magic: The Moral Economy of Witchcraft in Seventeenth-Century Russia* (Ithaca, N.Y.: Cornell University Press, 2013).

4. ENTERING THE MODERN?
THE EIGHTEENTH CENTURY

1. Brett Walker, *The Conquest of Ainu Lands: Ecology and Culture in Japanese Expansion, 1590–1800* (Berkeley: University of California Press, 2001).

2. John Whitney Hall, ed., *Early Modern Japan*, vol. 4 of *The Cambridge History of Japan*, ed. John Whitney Hall, Marius B. Jansen, Madoka Kanai, and Denis Twitchett (Cambridge: Cambridge University Press, 1991): 459, 465–67, 483, 573.

3. Luciano Petech, *China and Tibet in the Early Eighteenth Century* (Leiden: Brill, 1972), 116–44.

4. Joanna Waley-Cohen, *The Culture of War in China: Empire and the Military under the Qing [Manchu] Dynasty* (London: I.B. Tauris, 2006), 57–61.

5. Robert Entemann, "Andreas Ly on the First Jinchuan War in Western Sichuan, 1747–1749," *Sino-Western Cultural Relations Journal* 19 (1997): 6–21, quote from 7–8.

6. Dan Martin, "Bonpo Canons and Jesuit Cannons: On Sectarian Factors Involved in the Ch'ien-lung Emperor's Second Gold Stream Expedition of 1771 to 1776, Based Primarily on Some Tibetan Sources," *Tibet Journal* 15, no. 2 (Summer 1990): 3–28; Yingcong Dai, "*Yingyun Shengxi*: Military Entrepreneurship in the High Qing Period, 1700–1800," *Late Imperial China* 26 (2005): 50–51; Ulrich Theobald, *War Finance and Logistics in Late Imperial China: A Study of the Second Jinchuan Campaign, 1771–1776* (Leiden: Brill, 2013).

7. Susan Naquin, *Shantung Rebellion: The Wang Lun Uprising of 1774* (New Haven, Conn.: Yale University Press, 1981).

8. Daniel McMahon, "New Order on the Hunan Miao Frontier, 1796–1812," *Journal of Colonialism and Colonial History* 9 (2008): 1–26; and Daniel McMahon, "Geomancy and Walled Fortifications in Late Eighteenth Century China," *Journal of Military History* 76 (2012): 373–93.

9. Philip Kuhn, *Rebellion and Its Enemies in Late Imperial China: Militarization and Social Structure, 1796–1864* (Cambridge, Mass.: Harvard University Press, 1970).

10. Lindsay memorandum, August 31, 1791, vol. 58, p. 19, Bland Burges Deposit, Bodleian Library, Oxford.

11. Karen Barkey, *Bandits and Bureaucrats: The Ottoman Route to State Centralization* (Ithaca, N.Y.: Cornell University Press, 1994); and Karen Barkey, *Empire of Difference: The Ottomans in Comparative Perspective* (Cambridge, Mass.: Harvard University Press, 2008).

12. John T. Alexander, *Emperor of the Cossacks: Pugachev and the Cossack Jacqueries of 1773–75* (Lawrence, Kans.: Coronado Press, 1974).

13. W. Gregory Monahan, *Let God Arise: The War and Rebellion of the Camisards* (Oxford: Oxford University Press, 2014).

14. Zenon Kohut, *Making Ukraine: Studies on Political Culture, Historical Narrative, and Identity* (Toronto: CIUS Press, 2010).

15. Orest Sultelny, *The Mazepists: Ukrainian Separatism in the Early Eighteenth Century* (Boulder, Colo.: Eastern European Monographs, 1981).

16. Orest Subtelny, *Domination of Eastern Europe: Native Nobilities and Foreign Absolutism, 1500–1715* (Stroud, U.K.: Alan Sutton, 1986); Linda Frey and Marsha Frey, *Societies in Upheaval: Insurrections in France, Hungary, and Spain in the Early Eighteenth Century* (Westport, Conn.: Greenwood, 1987).

17. John Grenier, *The Far Reaches of Empire: War in Nova Scotia, 1710–1760* (Norman: University of Oklahoma Press, 2008).

18. Mark Santiago, *The Jar of Severed Hands: The Spanish Deportation of Apache Prisoners of War, 1770–1810* (Norman: University of Oklahoma Press, 2011).

19. Murdo MacLeod, *Spanish Central America: A SocioEconomic History, 1520–1720*, 2nd ed. (Austin: University of Texas Press, 2008), 345–61.

20. James Byrd, *Sacred Scripture, Sacred War: The Bible and the American Revolution* (New York: Oxford University Press, 2013).

21. Jeffrey Dorwart, *Invasion and Insurrection: Security, Defense, and War in the Delaware Valley 1621–1815* (Cranbury, N.J.: Associated University Presses, 2008).

22. Kevin Weddle, "'A Change of Both Men and Measures': British Reassessment of Military Strategy after Saratoga, 1777–1778," *Journal of Military History* 77 (2013): 837–65.

23. Tim Breen, *American Insurgents, American Patriots: The Revolution of the People* (New York: Hill and Wang, 2010).

24. Wayne Bodle, "The Ghost of Clow: Loyalist Insurgency in the Delmarva Peninsula," in *The Other Loyalists: Ordinary People, Royalism, and the Revolution in the Middle Colonies, 1763–1787*, ed. Joseph Tiedemann, Eugene Fingerhut, and Robert Venables (Albany: State University of New York Press, 2009), 27–28.

25. Greene to Morgan, 7, December 16, 1778, National Archives, Papers of the Continental Congress, vol. 172, Washington, D.C.; T. B. Myers, ed., *Cowpens Papers* (Charleston, S.C.: News and Courier Book Press, 1881), 9–10.

26. Scott D. Aiken, *The Swamp Fox: Lessons in Leadership from the Partisan Campaigns of Francis Marion* (Annapolis, Md.: Naval Institute Press, 2012).

27. John Hall, "An Irregular Reconsideration of George Washington and the American Military Tradition," *Journal of Military History* 78 (2014): 901–93.

28. Gordon M. Sayre, ed., *The Memoir of Lieutenant Dumont* (Chapel Hill: University of North Carolina Press, 2012), 250.

29. Claire Robertson, "Racism, the Military, and Abolitionism in the Late Eighteenth- and Early Nineteenth-Century Caribbean," *Journal of Military History* 77 (2013): 433–461, esp. 446, 458.

30. Philippe Girard, *The Slaves Who Defeated Napoleon: Toussaint Louverture and the Haitian War of Independence, 1801–1804* (Tuscaloosa: University of Alabama Press, 2011).

31. Leonard Richards, *Shays's Rebellion: The American Revolution's Final Battle* (Philadelphia: University of Pennsylvania Press, 2002); Sean Condon, *Shays's Rebellion: Authority and Distress in Post-Revolutionary America* (Baltimore, Md.: Johns Hopkins University Press, 2015); Thomas Slaughter, *The Whiskey Rebellion: Frontier Epilogue to the American Revolution* (New York: Oxford University Press, 1986); Terry Bouton, *Taming Democracy: "The People," the Founders and the Troubled Ending of the American Revolution* (Oxford: Oxford University Press, 2007).

32. Samuel Scott, *The Response of the Royal Army to the French Revolution: The Role and Development of the Line Army, 1787–1793* (Oxford: Oxford University Press, 1978).

33. Timothy D. Watt, "Taxation Riots and the Culture of Popular Protest in Ireland, 1714–1740," *English Historical Review* 130 (2015): 1447.

34. J. S. Donnelly, "The Whiteboy Movement, 1761–5," *Irish Historical Studies* 21 (1978): 20–54.

35. Jon Tetsuro Sumida, *Decoding Clausewitz: A New Approach to "On War"* (Lawrence: University Press of Kansas, 2008), 92.

36. Michael Broers, *Napoleon's Other War: Bandits, Rebels and Their Pursuers in the Age of Revolutions* (Witney, U.K.: Peter Lang, 2010).

5. INSURGENCIES IN AN AGE OF IMPERIALISM: THE NINETEENTH CENTURY

1. Rush to James Madison, former American president, August 30, 1820, Pennsylvania Historical Society, Am 13520, Philadelphia.

2. Kwang-Ching Liu, "The Ch'ing Restoration," in *Late Ch'ing, 1800–1911, Part 1*, vol. 10 of *The Cambridge History of China*, ed. Denis Twitchett and John Fairbank (Cambridge: Cambridge University Press, 1978), 406–34, 477–92.

3. Hala Fattah and Candan Badem, "The Sultan and the Rebel: Sa'dun Al-Mansur's Revolt in the Muntafiq, c. 1891–1911," *International Journal of Middle East Studies* 45 (2013): 677–93.

4. Ussama Makdisi, *The Culture of Sectarianism: Community, History and Violence in Nineteenth-Century Ottoman Lebanon* (Berkeley: University of California Press, 2000).

5. Christon Archer, "Insurrection-Reaction-Revolution-Fragmentation: Reconstructing the Choreography of Meltdown in New Spain during the Independence Era," *Mexican Studies* 10 (1994): 63–98.

6. Michael Ducey, "Village, Nation, and Constitution: Insurgent Politics in Papantla, Veracruz, 1810–1821," *Hispanic American Historical Review* 79 (1999): 471–76.

7. Criston Archer, "The Army of New Spain and the Wars of Independence, 1790–1821," *Hispanic American Historical Review* 61 (1981): 710.

8. John H. Elliott, *Empires of the Atlantic World: Britain and Spain in America, 1492–1830* (New Haven, Conn.: Yale University Press, 2006), 388–89.

9. Henry H. Hammill, "Royalist Counterinsurgency in the Mexican War for Independence: The Lessons of 1811," *Hispanic American Historical Review* 53 (1973): 470–81; Timothy Henderson, *The Mexican Wars of Independence* (New York: Hill and Wang, 2009).

10. M. Coreia de Andrade, "The Social and Ethnic Significance of the War of the Cabanos," in *Protest and Resistance in Angola and Brazil*, ed. Ronald H. Chilcote (Berkeley: University of California Press, 1972), esp. 98–103.

11. Wolfgang Gabbert, "Of Friends and Foes: The Caste War and Ethnicity in Yucatan," *Journal of Latin American Anthropology* 9 (2004): esp. 102–4.

12. John Lawrence Tone, *War and Genocide in Cuba, 1895–1898* (Chapel Hill: University of North Carolina Press, 2006).

13. John Lynch, "Bolívar and the Caudillos," *Hispanic American Historical Review* 63 (1983): 45; Criston Archer, "Banditry and Revolution in New Spain, 1790–1821," *Bibliotheca Americana* 1 (1980): 88.

14. Scarlett to British Foreign Secretary, Earl Russell, February 27, 1865, NA. FO. 50/385 fol. 113.

15. Jack A. Dabbs, *The French Army in Mexico, 1861–1867: A Study in Military Government* (The Hague: Mouton, 1963).

16. David Bigler and Will Bagley, *The Mormon Rebellion: America's First Civil War 1857–1858* (Norman: University of Oklahoma Press, 2011).

17. Joachim Remak, *A Very Civil War: The Swiss Sonderbund War of 1847* (Boulder, Colo.: Westview, 1993).

18. John Matsui, "War in Earnest: The Army of Virginia and the Radicalization of the Union War Effort, 1862," *Civil War History* 58 (2012): 180–223.

19. Jason Phillips, *Diehard Rebels: The Confederate Culture of Invincibility* (Athens: University of Georgia Press, 2007).

20. Regarding Columbia County, Pennsylvania, in 1864, see Richard Sauers and Peter Tomasak, *The Fishing Creek Confederacy: A Story of Civil War Draft Resistance* (Columbia: University of Missouri Press, 2013).

21. Stephen Davis, *What the Yankees Did to Us: Sherman's Bombardment and Wreckage of Atlanta* (Macon, Ga.: Mercer University Press, 2012); Matthew Carr, *Sherman's Ghosts: Soldiers, Civilians, and the American Way of War* (New York: New Press, 2014).

22. James McPherson, "No Peace without Victory, 1861–1865," *American Historical Review* (2004): 10.

23. Michael Fellman, *Inside War: The Guerrilla Conflict in Missouri during the American Civil War* (Oxford: Oxford University Press, 1989); Daniel E. Sutherland, *A Savage Conflict: The Decisive Role of Guerrillas in America's Civil War* (Chapel Hill: University of North Carolina Press, 2009).

24. Robert R. Mackey, *The Uncivil War: Irregular Warfare in the Upper South, 1861–1865* (Norman: University of Oklahoma Press, 2004); Clay Mountcastle, *Punitive War: Confederate Guerrillas and Union Reprisals* (Lawrence: University Press of Kansas, 2009); Joseph Beilein Jr., "The Guerrilla Shirt: A Labor of Love and the Style of Rebellion in Civil War Missouri," *Civil War History* 58 (2012): 151–79; Joseph Beilein Jr. and Matthew Hulbert, eds., *The Civil War Guerrilla: Unfolding the Black Flag in History, Memory, and Myth* (Lexington: University Press of Kentucky, 2015).

25. John Witt, *Lincoln's Code: The Laws of War in American History* (New York: Free Press, 2012), but see comments in Fred L. Borch, "Lieber's Code: A Landmark in the Law of War but Not Lincoln's Code," *Journal of Military History* 77 (2013): 671–74.

26. Joseph Danielson, *War's Desolating Scourge: The Union's Occupation of North Alabama* (Lawrence: University Press of Kansas, 2012).

27. David Pickering and Judy Falls, *Brush Men and Vigilantes: Civil War Dissent in Texas* (College Station: Texas A&M University Press, 2000).

28. Mark Grimsley, "Wars for the American South: The First and Second Reconstructions Considered as Insurgencies," *Civil War History* 58 (2012): 6–36.

29. Clayton Newell and Charles Shrader, "The U.S. Army's Transition to Peace, 1865–66," *Journal of Military History* 77 (2013): 875.

30. Robert Bruce, *1877: Year of Violence* (Chicago, Ill.: Quadrangle, 1970).

31. Milton Finley, *The Most Monstrous of Wars: The Napoleonic Guerrilla War in Southern Italy, 1806–1811* (Columbia: University of South Carolina Press, 1994).

32. John Morgan, "War Feeding War? The Impact of Logistics on the Napoleonic Occupation of Catalonia," *Journal of Military History* 73 (2009): 83–116.

33. Charles Esdaile, *Outpost of Empire: The Napoleonic Occupation of Andalucia, 1810–1812* (Norman: University of Oklahoma Press, 2012).

34. Richard Stites, *The Four Horsemen Riding to Liberty in Post-Napoleonic Europe* (Oxford: Oxford University Press, 2014).

35. David Laven, *Venice and Venetia under the Habsburgs 1815–1835* (Oxford: Oxford University Press, 2002).

36. Jonathan House, *Controlling Paris: Armed Forces and Counter-Revolution, 1789–1848* (New York: New York University Press, 2014).

37. Edyta Bojanowska, "Empire by Consent: Strakhov, Dostoevskii, and the Polish Uprising of 1863," *Slavic Review* 71 (2012): 1–24.

38. László Bencze, *The Occupation of Bosnia and Herzegovina in 1878* (New York: Columbia University Press, 2005).

39. Roger Price, "The French Army and the Revolution of 1830," *European Studies Review* 3 (1973): 243–67.

40. Carolyn P. Boyle, *Praetorian Politics in Liberal Spain* (Chapel Hill: University of North Carolina Press, 1979).

41. Elliot, later 1st Earl of Minto, to George Tierney, June 30, 1807, BL. Add. 58945 fol. 222.

42. Martijn Kitzen, "Between Treaty and Treason: Dutch Collaboration with Warlord Teuku Uma during the Aceh War, a Case Study on the Collaboration with Indigenous Powerholders in Colonial Warfare," *Small Wars and Insurgencies* 23 (2012): 93–116.

43. Daniel Whittingham, "'Savage Warfare': C. E. Callwell, the Roots of Counter-insurgency, and the Nineteenth Century Context," *Small Wars and Insurgencies* 23 (2012): 595.

44. Pearson to his parents, July 19, August 1, 1857, BL. India Office papers, MSS. Eur. C 231, pp. 51, 56.

45. Lister to Secretary to the Governor of Bengal, February 2, 1850, BL. Add. 49016 fol. 88.

46. Raymond Dumett, "A West African 'Fashoda': Expanding Trade, Colonial Rivalries and Insurrection in the Côte d'Ivoire/Gold Coast Borderlands: The Assikasso Crisis of 1897–98," *Journal of Imperial and Commonwealth History* 41 (2013): 710–43.

47. Pekka Hämäläinen, *The Comanche Empire* (New Haven, Conn.: Yale University Press, 2008).

48. Deborah and Jon Lawrence, *Violent Encounters: Interviews on Western Massacres* (Norman: University of Oklahoma Press, 2011).

49. William Kiser, *Dragoons in Apacheland: Conquest and Resistance in Southern New Mexico, 1846–1861* (Norman: University of Oklahoma Press, 2013).

50. Robert Utley, *Geronimo* (New Haven, Conn.: Yale University Press, 2012).

51. Lyndall Ryan, "Untangling Aboriginal Resistance and the Settler Punitive Expedition: The Hawkesbury River Frontier in New South Wales, 1794–1810," *Journal of Genocide Research* 15 (2013): 219–32.

52. Emory Upton, *The Military Policy of the United States* (Washington, D.C.: GPO, 1940), xiii.

6. THE IDEOLOGY OF PEOPLE'S WAR REFRACTED, 1900–1940

1. Geoffrey Best, *Humanity in Warfare: The Modern History of the International Law of Armed Conflicts* (London: Weidenfeld and Nicolson, 1990).

2. See, for example, René Pélissier, *Les guerres grises: Résistances et révoltes en Angola, 1845–1941* (Orgeval: Éditions Pélissier, 1978); René Pélissier, *La colonie du Minortaure: Nationalismes et révoltes en Angola, 1926–1961* (Orgeval: Éditions Pélissier, 1978); René Pélissier, *Naissance du Mozambique: Résistances et révoltes anticoloniales, 1854–1928* (Orgeval: Éditions Pélissier, 1984).

3. Brian Linn, *The U.S. Army and Counterinsurgency in the Philippine War, 1899–1902* (Chapel Hill: University of North Carolina Press, 1989); Brian Linn, *The Philippine War, 1899–1902* (Lawrence: University of Kansas Press, 2000); Robert D. Ramsey III, *Savage Wars of Peace: Case Studies of Pacification in the Philippines, 1900–1902* (Fort Leavenworth, Kans.: Createspace, 2007); James Arnold, *The Moro War: How America Battled a Muslim Insurgency in the Philippine Jungle, 1902–1913* (New York: Bloomsbury, 2011).

4. Matthew Smallman-Raynor and Andrew Cliff, "The Epidemiological Legacy of War: The Philippine-American War and the Diffusion of Cholera in Batangas and La Laguna, South-West Luzón, 1902–1904," *War in History* 7 (2000): 60.

5. Leticia A. Pérez, "Politics, Peasants, and People of Color: The 1912 'Race War' in Cuba Reconsidered," *Hispanic American Historical Review* 66 (1986): esp. 536–37.

6. Isabel Hull, *Absolute Destruction: Military Culture and the Practices of War in Imperial Germany* (Ithaca, N.Y.: Cornell University Press, 2005).

7. Dominik Geppert, William Mulligan, and Alexander Rose, eds., *The Wars before the Great War: Conflict and International Politics before the Outbreak of the First World War* (Cambridge: Cambridge University Press, 2015).

8. BL, Add. 50300, fol. 176.

9. Alan J. Ward, *The Easter Rising: Revolution and Irish Nationalism*, 2nd ed. (Hoboken, N.J.: Wiley-Blackwell, 2003).

10. David Woolman, *Rebels in the Rif: Abd el Krim and the Rif Rebellion* (Stanford, Calif.: Stanford University Press, 1968).

11. General Staff, "The Situation in Turkey, 15th March, 1920," NA. CAB. 24/101, fol. 313.

12. David M. Leeson, *The Black and Tans: British Police and Auxiliaries in the Irish War of Independence, 1920–1921* (Oxford: Oxford University Press, 2011).

13. William Kautt, *Ambushes and Armour: The Irish Rebellion 1919–1921* (Dublin: Irish Academic Press, 2010); William Sheehan, *A Hard Local War: The British Army and the Guerrilla War in Cork 1919–21* (Barnsley, U.K.: Pen and Sword, 2011), esp. 169–76.

14. Chetwode to General Archibald Montgomery-Massingberd, July 1, 1921, London, King's College, Liddell Hart Library, Montgomery-Massingberd papers 8/22.

15. General Staff, "British Military Liabilities," June 9, 1920, NA. CAB. 24/107, fol. 256.

16. Séan McConville, *Irish Political Prisoners, 1920–1962: Pilgrimages of Desolation* (London: Routledge, 2014).

17. *Report of the Committee Appointed by the Government of India to Investigate the Disturbances in the Punjab, etc* (London: HMSO, 1920), 112; Nick Lloyd, *The Amritsar Massacre* (London: I.B. Tauris, 2011).

18. D. George Boyce, "From Assaye to the *Assaye*: Reflections on British Government, Force, and Moral Authority in India," *Journal of Military History* 63 (1999): 643–68.

19. Peter Lieb, "Suppressing Insurgencies in Comparison: The Germans in the Ukraine, 1918, and the British in Mesopotamia, 1920," *Small Wars and Insurgencies* 23 (2012): 627–47.

20. Martin Thomas, *Empires of Intelligence: Security Services and Colonial Disorder after 1914* (Berkeley: University of California Press, 2008).

21. Nigel Collett, *The Butcher of Amritsar: General Reginald Dyer* (London: Hambledon Continuum, 2005), 251–67.

22. Cesare G. Segrè, *Fourth Shore: The Italian Colonization of Libya* (Chicago, Ill.: University of Chicago Press, 1974).

23. James Lunt, *The Arab Legion* (London: Constable, 1999); Matthew Hughes, "British Private Armies in the Middle East? The Arab Legion and the Trans-Jordan Frontier Force, 1920–56," *RUSI Journal* 153, no. 2 (April 2008): 70–75.

24. Chiefs of Staff, "Appreciation of the Situation in the Event of War against Germany," September 14, 1938, NA. CAB. 24/278, p. 346.

25. Matthew Kelly, "The Revolt of 1936: A Revision," *Journal of Palestine Studies* 44, no. 2 (2015): 28, 42.

26. Andrew M. Roe, *Waging War in Waziristan: The British Struggle in the Land of Bin Laden, 1849–1947* (Lawrence: University Press of Kansas, 2010); Bruce Collins, "Defining Victory in Victorian Warfare, 1860–1882," *Journal of Military History* 77 (2013): 928.

27. Ernest P. Young, *The Presidency of Yuan Shih-k'ai: Liberalism and Dictatorship in Early Republican China* (Ann Arbor: University of Michigan Press, 1977).

28. William Wei, *Counterrevolution in China: The Nationalists in Jiangxi during the Soviet Period* (Ann Arbor: University of Michigan Press, 1985).

29. Mao Zedong, *On Guerrilla Warfare*, trans. S. B. Griffith (Urbana: University of Illinois Press, 2000), 41–42, 80.

30. Mao, *On Guerrilla Warfare*, 46.

31. Mao, *On Guerrilla Warfare*, 47.

32. Edward O'Dowd, "Ho Chi Minh and the Origins of the Vietnamese Doctrine of Guerrilla Tactics," *Small Wars and Insurgencies* 24 (2013): 561–87.

33. Emile Simpson, *War from the Ground Up: Twenty-First Century Combat as Politics* (London: Hurst, 2012).

34. Keith Bickel, *Mars Learning: The Marine Corps Development of Small Wars Doctrine, 1915–1940* (Boulder, Colo.: Westview, 2001).

35. Thomas Rath, *Myths of Demilitarization in Postrevolutionary Mexico, 1920–1960* (Chapel Hill: University of North Carolina Press, 2013).

36. Matthew Butler, *Popular Piety and Political Identity in Mexico's Cristero Rebellion: Michoacán, 1927–1929* (Oxford: Oxford University Press, 2004).

37. Erik Ching, *Authoritarian El Salvador: Politics and the Origins of the Military Regimes, 1880–1940* (Notre Dame, Ind.: University of Notre Dame Press, 2014).

38. Herbert Klein, "David Toro and the Establishment of 'Military Socialism' in Bolivia," *Hispanic American Historical Review* 45 (1965): 29, n11.

39. Klein, "David Toro and the Establishment of 'Military Socialism' in Bolivia," 25–52.

40. General Staff, "The Military Situation in Russia," July 22, 1919, NA. CAB. 24/84 fols. 282–84.

41. Mark Von Hagen, *Soldiers in the Proletarian Dictatorship: The Red Army and the Soviet Socialist State, 1917–1930* (Ithaca, N.Y.: Cornell University Press, 1990).

42. General Staff, "Military Situation," NA. CAB. 24/84, fol. 284.

43. Orlando Figes, *A People's Tragedy: The Russian Revolution 1891–1924* (London: Penguin, 1996), 768.

44. Peter Holquist, "Violent Russia, Deadly Marxism? Russia in the Epoch of Violence, 1905–21," in *The Twentieth-Century Russia Reader*, ed. Alastair Kocho-Williams (Abingdon, U.K.: Routledge, 2011), 114–15.

45. Marie Broxup, "The Last *Chazawat*: The 1920–1921 Uprising," and Abdurakhman Avtorkhanov, "The Chechens and Ingush during the Soviet Period," in *North Caucasus Barrier: The Russian Advance towards the Muslim World*, ed. M. Broxup (London: Hurst, 1992), 112–45, 157–61, 183.

46. Adeeb Khalid, "The Soviet Union as an Imperial Formation: A View from Central Asia," in *Imperial Formations*, ed. Ann Stoler, Carole McGranahan, and Peter Perdue (Santa Fe, N. Mex.: SAR, 2007), 121–22.

47. Bernd Fischer, *King Zog and the Struggle for Stability in Albania* (New York: East European Monographs, 1984).

48. José E. Álvarez, "The Spanish Foreign Legion during the Asturian Uprising of October 1934," *War in History* 18 (2011): 200–224.

49. Report by Thompson, October 13, 1937, circulated next day by Foreign Secretary to Cabinet colleagues, NA. CAB. 24/271, fol. 303.

50. NA. WO. 105/1580, pp. 2–7.

51. Leon B. Poullada, *Reform and Rebellion in Afghanistan, 1919–1929* (Ithaca, N.Y.: Cornell University Press, 1973).

52. Stephanie Cronin, *Tribal Politics in Iran: Rural Conflict and the New State, 1921–1941* (London: Routledge, 2006).

7. INSURRECTIONS AT A HEIGHT, 1940–60

1. "The Present Sino-Japanese Military Situation," report by Chiefs of Staff, December 9, 1939, NA. CAB. 66/4/2, pp. 16–19.

2. "Sino-Japanese Military Situation," 19, 23.

3. Dagfinn Gatu, *Village China at War: The Impact of Resistance to Japan, 1937–1945* (Vancouver: University of British Columbia Press, 2007).

4. British strategic review for regional commanders, August 16, 1941, Canberra, Australian War Memorial, archive, 3 DRL/6643, 1/27.

5. Kenneth Slepyan, *Stalin's Guerrillas: Soviet Partisans in World War II* (Lawrence: University Press of Kansas, 2006).

6. Ben Shepherd, *War in the Wild East: The German Army and Soviet Partisans* (Cambridge, Mass.: Harvard University Press, 2004); Truman Anderson, "Incident at Baranivka: German Reprisals and the Soviet Partisan Movement in Ukraine, October–December 1941," *Journal of Modern History* 71 (1999): 589–623.

7. Jonathan Steinberg, "The Third Reich Reflected: German Civil Administration in the Occupied Soviet Union, 1941–44," *English Historical Review* 110 (1995): 620–51.

8. David Stafford, *Mission Accomplished: SOE and Italy 1943–1945* (London: Bodley Head, 2011).

9. Bernd Fischer, "Resistance in Albania during the Second World War: Partisans, Nationalists and the SOE," *East European Diplomacy* 25 (1991): 21–47.

10. Melissa K. Bokovoy, *Peasants and Communists: Politics and Ideology in the Yugoslav Countryside, 1941–1953* (Pittsburgh, Penn.: University of Pittsburgh Press, 1998); Philip B. Minehan, *Civil War and World War in Europe: Spain, Yugoslavia, and Greece, 1936–1946* (New York: Palgrave Macmillan, 2006).

11. Gregor Kranjc, *To Walk with the Devil: Slovene Collaboration and Axis Occupation, 1941–1945* (Toronto: University of Toronto Press, 2013).

12. Marko Hoare, *The Bosnian Muslims and the Second World War* (Oxford: Oxford University Press, 2013).

13. Andrew Buchanan, "The War Crisis and the Decolonization of India, December 1941–September 1942: A Political and Military Dilemma," *Global War Studies* 8 (2012): 5–31.

14. Wavell to Field Marshal Brooke, July 4, 1944, King's College, London, Liddell Hart Library, Alanbrooke papers, 6/4/12.

15. Kaushik Roy, "Military Loyalty in the Colonial Context: A Case Study of the Indian Army during World War II," *Journal of Military History* 73 (2009): 528–29.

16. Daniel Marston, *The Indian Army and the End of the Raj* (Cambridge: Cambridge University Press, 2014).

17. Anita Prazmowska, *Civil War in Poland, 1942–1948* (Basingstoke, U.K.: Palgrave, 2010).

18. William Risch, *The Ukrainian West: Culture and the Fate of Empire in Soviet Lviv* (Cambridge, Mass.: Harvard University Press, 2011).

19. Peter Hart, *The Heat of Battle: The 16th Battalion Durham Light Infantry; The Italian Campaign, 1943–1945* (Barnsley, U.K.: Pen and Sword, 1999): 201–2; Yannis Skalidakis, "From Resistance to Counterstate: The Making of Revolutionary Power in the Liberated Zones of Occupied Greece, 1943–1944," *Journal of Modern Greek Studies* 33 (2015): 155–84.

20. Alex Statiev, *The Soviet Counterinsurgency in the Western Borderlands* (Cambridge: Cambridge University Press, 2010).

21. Christine Goulter, "The Greek Civil War: A National Army's Counterinsurgency Triumph," *Journal of Military History* 78 (2014): 1017–55.

22. Harold Tanner, *Where Chiang Kai-shek Lost China: The Liao-Shen Campaign, 1948* (Bloomington: Indiana University Press, 2015).

23. Christopher Goscha, "A 'Total War' of Decolonization? Social Mobilization and State-building in Communist Vietnam, 1949–54," *War and Society* 31 (2012): 136–62.

24. Otto G. Ward, *De Militare Luchtvaart van Het KNIL in de Na-oorlogses Jaren 1945–1950* (Houten, Netherlands: Van Holkema and Warendorf, 1988), English summary, 372–73.

25. David Cesarini, "The War on Terror That Failed: British Counter-insurgency in Palestine 1945–1947 and the 'Farran Affair,'" *Small Wars and Insurgencies* 23 (2012): 648–70; Bruce Hoffman, "The Palestine Police Force and the Challenges of Gathering Counterterrorism Intelligence, 1939–1947," *Small Wars and Insurgencies* 24 (2013): 609–47; Goodman Giora, "'Troops Were Then Forced to Fire': British Army Crowd Control in Palestine, November 1945," *Small Wars and Insurgencies* 26 (2015): 271–91.

26. Huw Bennett, "'A Very Salutary Effect': The Counter-terror Strategy in the Early Malayan Emergency, June 1948 to December 1949," *Journal of Strategic Studies* 32 (2009): 415–44.

27. Karl Hack, "The Malayan Emergency as Counter-insurgency Paradigm," *Journal of Strategic Studies* 32 (2009): 383–414.

28. Peter Dennis and Jeffrey Grey, *Emergency and Confrontation: Australian Military Operations in Malaya and Borneo 1950–1966* (St. Leonards, Australia: Allen and Unwin, 1996).

29. David French, *Fighting EOKA: The British Counter-insurgency Campaign on Cyprus, 1955–1959* (Oxford: Oxford University Press, 2015), 303.

30. Susan Carruthers, *Winning Hearts and Minds: British Governments, the Media and Colonial Counter-insurgency, 1944–1960* (Leicester, U.K.: Leicester University Press, 1995).

31. Alex Marshall, "Imperial Nostalgia, the Liberal Lie, and the Perils of Postmodern Counter-insurgency," *Small Wars and Insurgencies* 21 (2010): 233–58; Benjamin Grob-Fitzgibbon, *Imperial Endgame: Britain's Dirty Wars and the End of Empire* (Basingstoke, U.K.: Palgrave, 2011); Christopher Hale, *Massacre in Malaya: Exposing Britain's My Lai* (Stroud, U.K.: History Press, 2013); Douglas Porch, *Counterinsurgency: Exposing the Myths of the New Way of War* (Cambridge: Cambridge University Press, 2013).

32. David French, *The British Way in Counter-insurgency, 1945–1967* (Oxford: Oxford University Press, 2011); David French, "Nasty Not Nice: British Counter-insurgency Doctrine and Practice, 1945–1967," *Small Wars and Insurgencies* 23 (2012): 744–61; Huw Bennett, *Fighting the Mau Mau: The British Army and Counterinsurgency in the Kenya Emergency* (Cambridge: Cambridge University Press, 2013). For a less critical view, Andrew Layton, "The Jewel in the Crown—The British Empire's Unknown and Unintended Legacy: Counter-insurgency Tactics," *British Army Review* (summer 2010): 30–36.

33. Myles Osborne, "'The Rooting Out of Mau Mau from the Minds of the Kikuyu Is a Formidable Task': Propaganda and the Mau Mau War," *Journal of African History* 56 (2015): 77–97.

34. Ze'ev Droy, *Israel's Reprisal Policy 1953–56: The Dynamics of Military Retaliation* (London: Frank Cass, 2005).

35. Martin Evans, *Algeria: France's Undeclared War* (Oxford: Oxford University Press, 2012).

36. Grégor Mathias, *Galula in Algeria: Counterinsurgency Practice versus Theory* (Santa Barbara, Calif.: Praeger, 2011); A. A. Cohen, *Galula: The Life and Writings of the French Officer Who Defined the Art of Counterinsurgency* (Santa Barbara, Calif.: Praeger, 2012).

37. Jacques Frémeaux, "The French Experience in Algeria: Doctrine, Violence and Lessons Learnt," *Civil Wars* 14 (2012): 49–62; Jonathan Hill, "Remembering the War of Liberation: Legitimacy and Conflict in Contemporary Algeria," *Small Wars and Insurgencies* 23 (2012): 4–31.

38. Roger Trinquier, *Modern Warfare: A French View of Counterinsurgency* (London: Pall Mall, 1964; New York: Praeger, 1964); Peter Paret, *French Revolutionary Warfare from Indochina to Algeria: The Analysis of a Political and Military Doctrine* (New York: Praeger, 1964);

Christopher Cradock and M. L. R. Smith, "'No Fixed Values': A Reinterpretation of the Influence of the Theory of *Guerre Révolutionnaire* and the Battle of Algiers, 1956–1957," *Journal of Cold War Studies* 9, no. 4 (2007): 68–105; Etienne de Durand, "France," in *Understanding Counterinsurgency: Doctrine, Operations, and Challenges*, ed. Thomas Rid and Thomas Kearney (New York: Routledge, 2010), 11–27.

8. THE FALL OF EMPIRES, 1960–80

1. Martin Evans, *Algeria: France's Undeclared War* (Oxford: Oxford University Press, 2012).

2. Christopher Tuck, *Confrontation, Strategy and War Termination: Britain's Conflict with Indonesia* (Farnham, U.K.: Ashgate, 2013).

3. Jonathan Walker, *Aden Insurgency: The Savage War in South Arabia 1962–67* (Staplehurst, U.K.: Spellmount, 2005).

4. Norrie MacQueen, *The Decolonization of Portuguese Africa: Metropolitan Revolution and the Dissolution of Empire* (Harlow, U.K.: Longman, 1997); Bruno Reis and Pedro Oliveira, "Cutting Heads or Winning Hearts: Late Colonial Portuguese Counterinsurgency and the Wiriyamu Massacre of 1972," *Civil Wars* 14 (2012): 80–103.

5. John Cann, *Counterinsurgency in Africa: The Portuguese Way of War, 1961–1974* (Westport, Conn.: Greenwood, 1997); John Cann, *Flight Plan Africa: Portuguese Airpower in Counterinsurgency, 1961–1974* (Solihull, U.K.: Helion, 2015).

6. Paul Dosal, *Comandante Che: Guerrilla Soldier, Commander, and Strategist, 1956–1967* (University Park: Pennsylvania State University Press, 2003); Che Guevara, *Guerrilla Warfare*, 3rd ed., ed. Brian Loveman and Thomas Davies (Lincoln: University of Nebraska Press, 1985).

7. Alberto Álvarez and Eudald Orero, "The Genesis and Internal Dynamics of El Salvador's People's Revolutionary Army, 1970–1976," *Journal of Latin American Studies* 46 (2014): 663–89.

8. Piero Gleijeses, *Conflicting Missions: Havana, Washington, and South Africa, 1959–1976* (Chapel Hill: University of North Carolina Press, 2002); Piero Gleijeses, *Visions of Freedom: Havana, Washington, Pretoria, and the Struggle for Southern Africa, 1976–1991* (Chapel Hill: University of North Carolina Press, 2013).

9. Ian Speller, "An African Cuba? Britain and the Zanzibar Revolution, 1964," *Journal of Imperial and Commonwealth History* 35 (2007): 283–302.

10. Christopher Tuck, "'Cut the Bonds Which Bind Our Hands': Deniable Operations during the Confrontation with Indonesia, 1963–1966," *Journal of Military History* 77 (2013): 599–623.

11. Lloyd Gardner, *Pay Any Price: Lyndon Johnson and the Wars for Vietnam* (Chicago, Ill.: Ivan Dee, 1995); David Kaiser, *American Tragedy: Kennedy, Johnson, and the Origins of the Vietnam War* (Cambridge, Mass.: Belknap, 2000).

12. David Toczek, *The Battle of Ap Bac Vietnam: They Did Everything but Learn from It* (Annapolis, Md.: Naval Institute Press, 2001); Gregory Daddis, "Eating Soup with a Spoon: The U.S. Army as a 'Learning Organization' in the Vietnam War," *Journal of Military History* 77 (2013): 229–54.

13. Richard A. Gabriel and Paul L. Savage, *Crisis in Command: Mismanagement in the Army* (New York: Hill and Wang, 1978).

14. Gregory Daddis, "Out of Balance: Evaluating American Strategy in Vietnam, 1968–72," *War and Society* 32 (2013): 252–70.

15. George Veith, *Black April: The Fall of South Vietnam 1973–1975* (New York: Encounter, 2012); Nguyen Cong Luan, *Nationalist in the Vietnam War: Memoirs of a Victim Turned Soldier* (Bloomington: Indiana University Press, 2012).

16. Edward O'Dowd, *Chinese Military Strategy in the Third Indochina War: The Last Maoist War* (London: Routledge, 2007).

17. Thomas McKenna, *Kontum: The Battle to Save South Vietnam* (Lexington: University Press of Kentucky, 2011).

18. This theme was also found in fiction: John Keene, *Pettibone's Law* (New York: Simon & Schuster, 1991).

19. David Fitzgerald, *Learning to Forget: US Army Counterinsurgency Doctrine and Practice from Vietnam to Iraq* (Stanford, Calif.: Stanford Security Studies, 2013). On deficiencies, John Tierney, *Chasing Ghosts: Unconventional Warfare in American History* (Washington, D.C.: Potomac, 2006).

20. Spencer Mawby, "The Clandestine Defence of Empire: British Special Operations in Yemen, 1951–64," *Intelligence and National Security* 17 (2002): 105–30; Asher Orkaby, "The Yemeni Civil War: The Final British-Egyptian Imperial Battleground," *Middle Eastern Studies* 51 (2015): 195–207.

21. Sarmila Bose, *Dead Reckoning: Memories of the 1971 Bangladesh War* (New York: Columbia University Press, 2011).

22. Kenneth Conboy and James Morrison, *The CIA's Secret War in Tibet* (Lawrence: University Press of Kansas, 2002).

23. Andrew Sanders, "Operation Motorman (1972) and the Search for a Coherent British Counterinsurgency Strategy in Northern Ireland," *Small Wars and Insurgencies* 24 (2013): 465–92. I have benefited from the opportunity to discuss the situation with General Sir Frank Kitson.

24. Desmond Hamill, *Pig in the Middle: The Army in Northern Ireland, 1969–1984* (London: Methuen, 1984); Chris Ryder, *The RUC: A Force under Fire* (London: Methuen, 1989).

25. Thomas Hennessey, *The Evolution of the Troubles, 1970–72* (Dublin: Irish Academic Press, 2007); Douglas Murray, *Bloody Sunday: Truth, Lies, and the Saville Inquiry* (London: Biteback, 2012).

26. Charles Townshend, *Britain's Civil Wars: Counterinsurgency in the Twentieth Century* (London: Faber and Faber, 1986); Thomas Leahy, "The Influence of Informers and Agents on Provisional Irish Republican Army Military Strategy and British Counter-Insurgency Strategy, 1976–94," *20th Century British History* 26 (2015): 122–46.

27. Marc DeVore, "A More Complex and Conventional Victory: Revisiting the Dhofar Counterinsurgency," *Small Wars and Insurgencies* 23 (2012): 144–73; Geraint Hughes, "Demythologising Dhofar: British Policy, Military Strategy, and Counter-Insurgency in Oman, 1963–1976," *Journal of Military History* 79 (2015): 423–56.

28. John Carland, "Rostow's War: Vietnam, 1961–1969," *Journal of Military History* 73 (2009): 617–18.

29. Yuen Foong Khong, *Analogies at War: Korea, Munich, Dien Bien Phu, and the Vietnam Decisions of 1965* (Princeton, N.J.: Princeton University Press, 1992).

9. THE VARIETY OF GOALS AND MEANS, 1980S

1. J. Bruce Amstutz, *Afghanistan: The First Five Years of Soviet Occupation* (Washington, D.C.: National Defense University Press, 1986), 88.

2. Antonio Giustozzi, *War, Politics and Society in Afghanistan, 1978–1992* (Washington, D.C.: Georgetown University Press, 1999); William Maley, *The Afghanistan Wars* (Basingstoke, U.K.: Palgrave, 2002); Rodric Braithwaite, *Afgantsy: The Russians in Afghanistan 1979–89* (London: Profile, 2012).

3. Steve Coll, *Ghost Wars: The Secret History of the CIA, Afghanistan and Bin Laden: From the Soviet Invasion to September 10, 2001* (London: Penguin, 2004).

4. Peter Lavoy, *Asymmetric Warfare in South Asia: The Causes and Consequences of the Kargil Conflict* (Cambridge: Cambridge University Press, 2009).

5. Hal Brands, *Latin America's Cold War* (Cambridge, Mass.: Harvard University Press, 2010).

6. Robert Ramsey, *Advising Indigenous Forces: American Advisors in Korea, Vietnam, and El Salvador* (Fort Leavenworth, Kans.: Combat Studies Institute Press, 2006).

7. Timothy Wickham-Crowley, "Two 'Waves' of Guerrilla-Movement Organizing in Latin America, 1956–1990," *Comparative Studies in Society and History* 56 (2014): 215–42.

8. Todd Greentree, *Crossroads of Intervention: Insurgency and Counterinsurgency Lessons from Central America* (Westport, Conn.: Praeger, 2008).

9. Miguel La Serna, *Corner of the Living: Ayacucho on the Eve of the Shining Path Insurgency* (Chapel Hill: University of North Carolina Press, 2012).

10. Terry Mays, *Africa's First Peacekeeping Operation: The OAU in Chad, 1981–1982* (Westport, Conn.: Praeger, 2002).

10. AFTER THE COLD WAR, 1990S

1. Henry Papasotiriou, "The Kosovo War: Kosovar Insurrection, Serbian Retribution, and NATO Intervention," *Journal of Strategic Studies* 25 (2002): 39–62; Henry H. Perritt Jr., *Kosovo Liberation Army: The Inside Story of an Insurgency* (Urbana: University of Illinois Press, 2008); James Pettifer, *The Kosovo Liberation Army: Underground War to Balkan Insurgency, 1948–2001* (London: Hurst, 2012).

2. Pauline Kola, *The Myth of Greater Albania* (New York: New York University Press, 2003); Sabrina P. Ramet, Albert Simkus, and Ola Listhaug, eds., *Civic and Uncivic Values in Kosovo: History, Politics, and Value Transformation* (Budapest: Central European University Press, 2015).

3. Edgar O'Ballance, *Wars in the Caucasus, 1990–1995* (Basingstoke, U.K.: Palgrave, 1996).

4. Pjer Simunovic, "The Russian Military in Chechnya—A Case Study of Morale in War," *Journal of Slavic Military Studies* 11 (1998): 63–95.

5. James Hughes, *Chechnya: From Nationalism to Jihad* (Philadelphia: University of Pennsylvania Press, 2007); James Hughes, "The Chechnya Conflict: Freedom Fighters or Terrorists?," *Demokratizatsiya: The Journal of Post-Soviet Democratization* 15 (2007): 293–311; Robert Schaefer, *The Insurgency in Chechnya and the North Caucasus: From Gazavat to Jihad* (Santa Barbara, Calif.: Praeger, 2011).

6. Samuel P. Huntington, "The Clash of Civilizations?" *Foreign Affairs* 72 (1993): 21–49.

7. Peter Mahadevan, "The Maoist Insurgency in India: Between Crime and Revolution," *Small Wars and Insurgencies* 23 (2012): 203–20; Srobana Bhattacharya, "Changing Civilian Support for the Maoist Conflict in India," *Small Wars and Insurgencies* 24 (2013): 813–34.

8. Steven Wilkinson, *Army and Nation: The Military and Indian Democracy since Independence* (Cambridge, Mass.: Harvard University Press, 2015).

9. James Fergusson, *Taliban: The True Story of the World's Most Feared Guerrilla Fighters* (New York: Bantam, 2010).

10. Niccolò Petrelli, "Deterring Insurgents: Culture, Adaptation and the Evolution of Israeli Counterinsurgency, 1987–2005," *Journal of Strategic Studies* 36 (2013): 666–91.

11. Clinton Fernandes, *The Independence of East Timor: Multi-dimensional Perspectives—Occupation, Resistance, and International Political Activism* (Eastbourne, U.K.: Sussex Academic Press, 2011); Awet Weldemichael, *Third World Colonialism and Strategies of Liberation: Eritrea and East Timor Compared* (Cambridge: Cambridge University Press, 2012).

12. Jeff Moore, *The Thai Way of Counterinsurgency* (Arlington, Va.: Muir Analytics, 2014).

13. Sergio Catignani, "The Strategic Impasse in Low-Intensity Conflicts: The Gap Between Israeli Counter-insurgency Strategy and Tactics during the Al-Aqsa Intifada," *Journal of Strategic Studies* 28, no. 1 (2005): 57–75; Sergio Catignani, *Israel Counter-insurgency and the Intifadas: Dilemmas of a Conventional Army* (London: Routledge, 2009); Sergio Catignani, "The Israel Defense Forces and the *Al-Aqsa Intifada*: When Tactical Virtuosity Meets Strategic Disappointment," in *Counterinsurgency in Modern Warfare*, ed. Daniel Marston and Carter Malkasian (Oxford: Osprey, 2010), 233–50; Sergio Catignani, "Israeli Counterinsurgency: The Never-Ending 'Whack-a-Mole,'" in *The Routledge Handbook of Insurgency and Counterinsurgency*, ed. Paul B. Rich and Isabelle Duvesteyn (Abingdon, U.K.: Routledge, 2012), 263–75; Efraim Inbar and Eitan Shamir, "Mowing the Grass: Israel's Strategy for Protracted Intractable

Conflict," *Journal of Strategic Studies* 37 (2014): 65–90; Zeev Maoz, *Defending the Holy Land: A Critical Analysis of Israel's Security and Foreign Policy* (Ann Arbor: University of Michigan Press, 2006).

14. Richard English, *Armed Struggle: The History of the IRA* (Basingstoke, U.K.: Macmillan, 2003).

11. INTERVENTIONISM AND ITS FAILINGS, 2000S

1. See the articles in *RUSI Journal* 154, no. 3 (June 2009): 4–34.

2. John Nagl, *Knife Fights: A Memoir of Modern War in Theory and Practice* (New York: Penguin, 2014).

3. Robert Ramsey, *From El Billar to Operations Fenix and Jaque: The Colombian Security Force Experience, 1998–2008* (Fort Leavenworth, Kans.: Combat Studies Institute Press, 2009).

4. Paul Jackson and Peter Albrecht, *Reconstructing Security after Conflict: Security Sector Reform in Sierra Leone* (London: Palgrave Macmillan, 2011); Peter Albrecht and Cathy Haenlein, "Sierra Leone's Post-conflict Peacekeepers," *RUSI Journal* 160, no. 1 (February/March 2015): 28; Kieran Mitton, *Rebels in a Rotten State: Understanding Atrocity in Sierra Leone* (London: Hurst, 2015).

5. Oliver Housden, "Nepal's Elusive Peace," *RUSI Journal* 155, no. 2 (April/May 2010): 70.

6. Thomas Mahnken and Thomas Kearney, *War in Iraq: Planning and Execution* (London: Routledge, 2007); Dale Herspring, *Rumsfeld's Wars: The Arrogance of Power* (Lawrence: University Press of Kansas, 2008); James Kiras, "Modern Irregular Warfare: Afghanistan and Iraq," in *The Practice of Strategy*, ed. John Andreas Olsen and Colin S. Gray (Oxford: Oxford University Press, 2011), 277.

7. Terene McNamee, ed., *War without Consequences: Iraq's Insurgency and the Spectre of Strategic Defeat* (London: RUSI Books, 2008); Richard H. Shulz, *The Marines Take Anbar: The Four-Year Fight against Al Qaeda* (Annapolis, Md.: Naval Institute Press, 2013).

8. David Petraeus, "Learning Counterinsurgency: Observations from Soldiering in Iraq," in "Counterinsurgency Reader," special issue, *Military Review* (October 2006): 45–55.

9. For a more critical view, Lawrence Korb, Brian Katulis, Sean Duggan, and Peter Juul, *How Does This End? Strategic Failures Overshadow Tactical Gains in Iraq* (Washington, D.C.: Center for American Progress, 2008).

10. Warren Chin, "Why Did It All Go Wrong? Reassessing British Counterinsurgency in Iraq," *Strategic Studies Quarterly* (Winter 2008): 119–35.

11. Christopher Elliott, *High Command: British Military Leadership in the Iraq and Afghanistan Wars* (London: Hurst, 2015); Jonathan Bailey, Richard Iron, and Hew Strachan, eds., *British Generals in Blair's Wars* (Farnham, U.K.: Ashgate, 2013).

12. David Jones and M. L. R. Smith, "Myth and the Small War Tradition: Reassessing the Discourse of British Counter-insurgency," *Small Wars and Insurgencies* 24 (2013): 456.

13. Robert Kemp, "Counterinsurgency in Nangarhar Province, Eastern Afghanistan, 2004–2008," *Military Review* 40 (Nov.–Dec. 2010): 34–42.

14. Tim Bird and Alex Marshall, *Afghanistan: How the West Lost Its Way* (New Haven, Conn.: Yale University Press, 2011).

15. Carter Malkasian, *War Comes to Garmser: Thirty Years of Conflict on the Afghan Frontier* (London: Hurst, 2013); Lucy Edwards, "How the 'Entry' Defines the 'Exit': Contradictions between the Political and Military Strategies Adopted in 2001 and How They Have Deleteriously Affected the Longer-Term Possibilities for Stabilisation in Afghanistan," *Conflict, Security and Development* 14 (2014): 593–619.

16. Michael Clarke and Valentina Soria, "Charging up the Valley: British Decisions in Afghanistan," *RUSI Journal* 156, no. 4 (Aug./Sept. 2011); Frank Ledwidge, *Losing Small Wars: British Military Failure in Iraq and Afghanistan* (New Haven, Conn.: Yale University Press, 2011); Ed Butler, "Setting Ourselves Up for a Fall in Afghanistan: Where Does Account-

ability Lie for Decision-Making in Helmand in 2005–06," *RUSI Journal* 160, no. 1 (February/March 2015): 46–57.

17. Seth Jones, *Counterinsurgency in Afghanistan*, vol. 4 of *Rand Counterinsurgency Study* (Santa Monica, Calif.: Rand, 2008).

18. Shivan Mahendrarajah, "Saudi Arabia, Wahhabism, and the Taliban of Afghanistan: 'Puritanical Reform' as a 'Revolutionary War' Program," *Small Wars and Insurgencies* 26 (2015): 383–407.

19. Antonio Giustozzi, *Empires of Mud: Wars and Warlords in Afghanistan* (London: Hurst, 2009).

20. Jerry Meyerle, Megan Katt, and Jim Gavrilis, *Counterinsurgency on the Ground in Afghanistan: How Different Units Adapted to Local Conditions* (Washington, D.C.: CNA, 2010); Theo Farrell, Frans Osinga, and James Russell, eds., *Military Adaptation in Afghanistan* (Stanford, Calif.: Stanford University Press, 2013).

21. Thomas W. Cawkwell, *UK Communication Strategies for Afghanistan, 2001–2014* (Farnham, U.K.: Ashgate, 2015), 137.

22. Jack Fairweather, *The Good War: The Battle for Afghanistan 2006–14* (London: Jonathan Cape, 2014).

23. C. Christine Fair, *Fighting to the End: The Pakistan Army's Way of War* (Oxford: Oxford University Press, 2014).

24. Sean Maloney, "On a Pale Horse? Conceptualizing Narcotics Production in Southern Afghanistan and Its Relationship to the Narcoterror Nexus," *Small Wars and Insurgencies* 20 (2009): 210–12.

25. Tom Coghlan, "The World Went Silent . . . Being Blown Up Was Too Quick to Be Frightening," *Times* (London), August 1, 2009, 6.

26. Stephanie Cronin, "Building and Rebuilding Afghanistan's Army: An Historical Perspective," *Journal of Military History* 75 (2011): 84.

27. Gian Gentile, *Wrong Turn: America's Deadly Embrace of Counterinsurgency* (New York: New Press, 2013), esp. 136–40; Gian Gentile, "A Requiem for American Counterinsurgency," *Orbis* 57 (2013): 549–58; Douglas Porch, "The Dangerous Myth and Dubious Promise of COIN," *Small Wars and Insurgencies* 22 (2011): 239–57.

28. Brian Cloughley, *Wars, Coups and Terror: Pakistan's Army in Years of Turmoil* (New York: Skyhorse, 2008).

29. Rudra Chaudhuri, "The Proxy Calculus: Kabul, not Kashmir, Holds the Key to the Indo-Pakistani Relationship," *RUSI Journal* 155, no. 6 (2010): 56–57.

30. David Petraeus, "Learning Counterinsurgency: Observations from Soldiering in Iraq," *Military Review* (Jan.–Feb. 2006): 2–11; Thomas Ricks, *The Gamble: General David Petraeus and the American Military Adventure in Iraq, 2006–2008* (London: Allen Lane, 2009).

31. Montgomery McFate, "The Military Utility of Understanding Adversary Culture," *Joint Forces Quarterly* 38 (3rd quarter 2005): 42–48.

32. Daniel Green and William Mullen, *Fallujah Redux: The Anbar Awakening and the Struggle with Al-Qaeda* (Annapolis, Md.: Naval Institute Press, 2014).

33. General Sir Frank Kitson, interview by the author, January 10, 2016.

34. Nigel Aylwin-Foster, "Changing the Army for Counterinsurgency Operations," *Military Review* (Nov.–Dec. 2005): 2–15.

35. Marc Verret, "Comparing Contemporary Counterinsurgency Doctrines and Theories," *Baltic Security and Defence Review* 15 (2013): 95–122.

36. David Kilcullen, "Countering Global Insurgency: A Strategy for the War on Terrorism," *Journal for Strategic Studies* 28 (2005); David Kilcullen, "Counterinsurgency Redux," *Survival* 48 (2006); David Kilcullen, *The Accidental Guerrilla: Fighting Small Wars in the Midst of a Big One* (London: Hurst, 2009); John Lynn, "Patterns of Insurgency and Counterinsurgency," *Military Review* 4 (July–Aug. 2005).

37. Frank Leith Jones, *Blowtorch: Robert Komer, Vietnam, and American Cold War Strategy* (Annapolis, Md.: Naval Institute Press, 2013).

38. Anthony Joes, *Victorious Insurgencies: Four Rebellions That Shaped Our World* (Lexington: University Press of Kentucky, 2010); Thomas Marks, "Thailand: Anatomy of a Counterinsurgency Victory," *Military Review* 87 (2007): 35–51.

39. Bing West, *The Strongest Tribe: War, Politics, and the Endgame in Iraq* (New York: Random House, 2008). See also, for work published in this period, Niel Smith, "Retaking Sa'ad: Successful Counter-insurgency in Tal Afar," *Armor and Cavalry Journal* 1 (2008): 28–37.

40. Hew Strachan, *The Direction of War: Contemporary Strategy in Historical Perspective* (Cambridge: Cambridge University Press, 2013), 224.

41. Jeffrey Record, *Beating Goliath: Why Insurgencies Win* (Dulles, Va: Potomac, 2007).

42. Matthew Flynn, *Contesting History: The Bush Counterinsurgency Legacy in Iraq* (Santa Barbara, Calif.: Praeger, 2010).

43. Daniel Marston and Carter Malkasian, eds., *Counterinsurgency in Modern Warfare* (Oxford: Oxford University Press, 2008).

44. Billy T. Brooks and Steven R. Rader, "To the British Army," *RUSI Journal* 155, no. 5 (Oct.–Nov. 2010): 54.

45. For a more critical tone, Brian Linn, *The Echo of Battle—The Army's Way of War* (Cambridge, Mass.: Harvard University Press, 2007); David Ucko, *The New Counterinsurgency Era: Transforming the U.S. Military for Modern Wars* (Washington, D.C.: Georgetown University Press, 2009).

46. Jeremy Black, *Why Wars Happen* (London: Reaktion, 1998), 216–32.

12. A WORLD WITHOUT SHAPE? THE PRESENT

1. Stig Jarle Hansen, *Al-Shabaab in Somalia: The History and Ideology of a Militant Islamic Group; 2005–2012* (Oxford: Oxford University Press, 2013).

2. For a different response, Peter Jakobsen and Jens Ringsmose, "In Denmark, Afghanistan Is Worth Dying For: How Public Support for the War Was Maintained in the Face of Mounting Casualties and Elusive Success," *Cooperation and Conflict* 50 (2015): 211–27.

3. Andrew Hosken, *Empire of Fear: Inside the Islamic State* (London: Oneworld, 2015).

4. Michael Weiss and Hassan Hassan, *ISIS: Inside the Army of Terror* (New York: Regan Arts, 2015); Jessica Stern and J. M. Berger, *ISIS: The State of Terror* (London: William Collins, 2015).

5. "Kremlin Trying to Start New Revolt in Ukraine, Police Warn," *Times* (London), May 2, 2015, 42.

6. Iro Aghedo and Oarhe Osumah, "Insurgency in Nigeria: A Comparative Study of Niger Delta and Boko Haram Uprisings," *Journal of Asian and African Studies* 50 (2015): 208–22; Andrew Walker, *"Eat the Heart of the Infidel": The Harrowing of Nigeria and the Rise of Boko Haram* (London: Hurst, 2016).

7. Dominic McCargo, *Tearing Apart the Land: Islam and Legitimacy in Southern Thailand* (Ithaca, N.Y.: Cornell University Press, 2008).

8. Victor Mallet, "Indian Troops Deployed as Six Die in Upper-Caste Riot," *Financial Times*, August 27, 2015, 6.

9. Amit Mukherjee, "Facing Future Challenges: Defence Reform in India," *RUSI Journal* 156, no. 5 (Oct./Nov. 2011): 35.

10. Unnamed security source, cited in Henry Samuel and David Chazan, "Airlines Are Told to Expect 'French 9/11' as Hollande Warns of More Islamist Violence," *Daily Telegraph*, August 27, 2015, 13.

11. Adam Dolnik, "Fighting to the Death: Mumbai and the Future *Fidayeen* Threat," *RUSI Journal* 155, no. 2 (April/May 2010): 60–68.

12. Gian Gentile, *Wrong Turn: America's Deadly Embrace of Counterinsurgency* (New York: New Press, 2013).

13. Gentile, *Wrong Turn*, 136–40.

14. Joseph Stiglitz and Linda Bilmes, *The Three Trillion Dollar War: The True Cost of the Iraq Conflict* (London: Allen Lane, 2008).

15. Anthony King, "The Power of Politics: Hamkari and the Future of the Afghan War," *RUSI Journal* 155, no. 6 (Dec. 2010): 68–74.

13. SPECULATIONS ABOUT THE FUTURE

1. Mohammed Hafex, *Why Muslims Rebel: Repression and Resistance in the Islamic World* (Boulder, Colo.: Lynne Rienner, 2003).

2. Virginia Comolli, *Boko Haram: Nigeria's Islamist Insurgency* (London: Hurst, 2015).

3. Paul Williams, *War and Conflict in Africa* (Cambridge: Polity, 2011).

4. Development, Concepts and Doctrine Centre (DCDC) of the British Ministry of Defence, *Global Strategic Trends: Out to 2040*, 4th ed. (Shrivenham, U.K.: DCDC, 2010), 133.

5. Shirael Turjapurkar, "Babies Make a Comeback," *Nature* 460 (2009): 693.

6. Eric Jardine, "Population-Centric Counter-insurgency and the Movement of Peoples," *Small Wars and Insurgencies* 23 (2012): 264–94.

7. David Kilcullen, *Out of the Mountains: The Coming Age of the Urban Guerrilla* (New York: Oxford University Press, 2013).

8. Charles Lindholm and José Pedro Zúquete, *The Struggle for the World: Liberation Movements for the 21st Century* (Palo Alto, Calif.: Stanford University Press, 2010).

9. Wayne Lee, *Waging War: Conflict, Culture, and Innovation in World History* (New York: Oxford University Press, 2015), 532.

10. Mark Grimsley, "Why the Civil Rights Movement Was an Insurgency," HistoryNet, last modified February 24, 2010, http://www.historynet.com/why-the-civil-rights-movement-was-an-insurgency.htm.

11. Rajan Menon and Eugene Comer, *Conflict in Ukraine: The Unwinding of the Post-Cold War Order* (Cambridge, Mass.: MIT Press, 2015).

12. Stan McChrystal, "Operational Leadership," *RUSI Journal* 159, no. 2 (Apr./May 2014): 41.

13. Samuel Cohn, "Authority and Popular Resistance," in *Cultures and Power*, vol. 2 of *The Oxford Handbook of Early Modern European History, 1350–1750*, ed. Hamish Scott (Oxford: Oxford University Press, 2015): 432–34.

14. Ahmed Hashim, *When Counterinsurgency Wins: Sri Lanka's Defeat of the Tamil Tigers* (Philadelphia: University of Pennsylvania Press, 2013).

15. Jan Angstrom, "The Changing Norms of Civil and Military and Civil-Military Relations Theory," *Small Wars and Insurgencies* 24 (2013): 224–36.

14. CONCLUSIONS

1. Jefferson to David Hoscick, May 11, 1821, New York, New York Historical Society, Gilder Lehrman Collection, GLC 00262.

2. Lawrence Wright, *The Looming Tower: Al-Qaeda and the Road to 9/11* (London: Allen Lane, 2006).

3. Paul Staniland, *Networks of Rebellion: Explaining Insurgent Cohesion and Collapse* (Ithaca, N.Y.: Cornell University Press, 2014).

4. B. Heuser, "Lessons Learnt? Cultural Transfer and Revolutionary Wars, 1775–1831," *Small Wars and Insurgencies* 25 (2014): 858–76; Norman Cigar, ed., *Al-Qa'ida's Doctrine for Insurgency* (Washington, D.C.: Potomac, 2008).

5. Jonathan Gumz, "Reframing the Historical Problematic of Insurgency: How the Professional Military Literature Created a New History and Missed the Past," *Journal of Strategic Studies* 32 (2009): 553–88; Karl Hack, "Everyone Lived in Fear: Malaya and the British War in Counter-insurgency," *Small Wars and Insurgencies* 23 (2010): 671–99.

6. Douglas Porch, *Counterinsurgency: Exposing the Myths of the New Way of War* (Cambridge: Cambridge University Press, 2013).

Selected Further Reading

Avrich, Paul, *Russian Rebels, 1600–1800* (New York, 1972).

Beckett, Ian, *Modern Insurgencies and Counter-Insurgencies: Guerrillas and Their Opponents since 1750* (New York, 2001).

Beilein, Joseph, and Matthew Hulbert, eds., *The Civil War Guerrilla: Unfolding the Black Flag in History, Memory, and Myth* (Lexington, Ky., 2015).

Bigler, David, and Will Bagley, *The Mormon Rebellion: America's First Civil War 1857–1858* (Norman, Okla., 2011).

Breen, Tim, *American Insurgents, American Patriots: The Revolution of the People* (New York, 2010).

Broers, Michael, *Napoleon's Other War: Bandits, Rebels and Their Pursuers in the Age of Revolutions* (Witney, U.K., 2010).

Clapham, Christopher, ed., *African Guerrillas* (Bloomington, Ind., 1998).

Condon, Sean, *Shays's Rebellion: Authority and Distress in Post-Revolutionary America* (Baltimore, Md., 2015).

Dunning, Chester, *Russia's First Civil War and the Founding of the Romanov Dynasty* (University Park, Pa., 2001).

Evans, Martin, *Algeria: France's Undeclared War* (Oxford, 2012).

Fitzgerald, David, *Learning to Forget: US Army Counterinsurgency Doctrine and Practice from Vietnam to Iraq* (Stanford, Calif., 2013).

French, David, *The British Way in Counter-Insurgency* (Oxford, 2011).

———, *Fighting EOKA: The British Counter-Insurgency Campaign on Cyprus, 1955–1959* (Oxford, 2015).

Girard, Philippe, *The Slaves Who Defeated Napoleon: Toussaint Louverture and the Haitian War of Independence, 1801–1804* (Tuscaloosa, Ala., 2011).

Gladstone, Jack, *Revolution and Rebellion in the Early Modern World* (Berkeley, Calif., 1991).

Grillo, Ioan, *Gangster Warlords* (London, 2016).

Gustozza, Antonio, *Empires of Mud: Wars and Warlords in Afghanistan* (London, 2009).

Henderson, Timothy, *The Mexican Wars of Independence* (New York, 2009).

House, Jonathan, *Controlling Paris: Armed Forces and Counter-Revolution, 1789–1848* (New York, 2014).

Hull, Isabel, *Absolute Destruction: Military Culture and the Practices of War in Imperial Germany* (Ithaca, N.Y., 2005).

Kilcullen, David, *Out of the Mountains: The Coming Age of the Urban Guerrilla* (New York, 2013).

Linn, Brian, *The Philippine War, 1899–1902* (Lawrence, Kans., 2000).

Mao Zedong, *On Guerrilla Warfare* (Urbana, Ill., 2000).

Moore, Jeff, *The Thai Way of Counterinsurgency* (Arlington, Va., 2014).
Murphy, Martin, *Small Boats, Weak States, Dirty Money: Piracy and Maritime Terrorism in the Modern World* (London, 2009).
Nagl, John, *Knife Fights: A Memoir of Modern War in Theory and Practice* (New York, 2014).
Porch, Douglas, *Counterinsurgency: Exposing the Myths of the New Way of War* (Cambridge, 2013).
Smith, Rupert, *The Utility of Force: The Art of War in the Modern World* (London, 2005).
Swope, Kenneth, *The Military Collapse of China's Ming Dynasty, 1618–44* (New York, 2014).
Thornton, Rod, *Asymmetric Warfare—Threat and Response in the 21st Century* (Cambridge, 2007).
Tone, J. L., *War and Genocide in Cuba, 1895–1898* (Chapel Hill, N.C., 2006).

Index